Coffee and Conflict in Colombia, 1886-1910

To the memory of Julio Bohórquez
and to Joel and Andrea

Coffee and Conflict in Colombia, 1886-1910

Charles W. Bergquist

Duke University Press
Durham, N. C.   1978

L.C.C. card no. 78-59581
I.S.B.N. 0-8223-0418-x
Printed in the United
States of America

Contents

List of figures, maps, and tables

Figures

Maps

Tables

Preface

This is a study of the political implications of the rise of the coffee export economy in Colombia during the period 1886-1910. It explores in a detailed way the local impact in Colombia of the powerful economic, political, and cultural currents generated by the economic development of the nations of the North Atlantic basin. The study offers an explanation of Colombian politics and an interpretation of a crucial transitional period in Colombian history based on a premise foreign to the bulk of the literature on nineteenth-century Spanish American politics. It argues that investigation of basic economic trends and analysis of elite ideological and economic interests provide the most fruitful point of departure for an understanding of Colombian political history at the turn of the century.

The study is divided into an introduction and three main parts. The Introduction discusses different explanations of Colombian politics and advances an interpretation of nineteenth-century political insta-bility that is applied in detail in the following chapters. The main divisions of the study correspond to three distinct phases in the economic and political life of the nation during the period under in-vestigation. Part One deals with the period 1886-1898 and traces the origins of Colombia's greatest nineteenth-century civil war (the War of the Thousand Days, 1899-1902) through an analysis of the political ramifications of the coffee boom which developed after 1886. Part Two covers the period of the war and relates both the outbreak of the fighting, and the nature and long duration of the war, to the political and social tensions engendered by depression in the coffee economy after 1898. Part Three deals with the postwar era (1904-1910), a period marked by limited, then rapid revival and expansion of the coffee economy and recounts the steps by which coffee interests spawned in the 1890's and defeated during the war managed to win the peace and consolidate a new order of political stability and export-oriented economic development in Colombia by 1910. The first and last chap-ters of the study, which deal respectively with the last half of the nineteenth century and the first half of the twentieth, should be viewed as interpretive essays. Based primarily on secondary sources, these two chapters attempt to draw out the interpretive threads gener-ated by the detailed analysis which forms the core of the book.

Although the study is primarily concerned with the interaction of

economic and political affairs, I have tried not to ignore the social
dimensions of either. Special attention is focused on the sociology of
political factions, and, as the argument proceeds, some consideration
of the nature of land tenure patterns and labor systems, the influence
of the Church on Colombian life, and the social aspects of political
violence are integrated into the analysis. Most of the material illustrative of the way economic and political affairs affected the lives of
common people is drawn from research focused on the politically
important and in many ways representative department of Cundinamarca.

Knowledge of the history of Colombia in the century following 1850
is still at a rudimentary stage, and, thanks in part to the critics who
have so generously commented on successive drafts of the manuscript, I am well aware of the many gaps and weaknesses of this study.
While the interpretation advanced in the first and last chapters suffers
most from the underdeveloped state of the field, the analysis presented in the core of the book also needs to be complemented by
regional studies and more attention to the grass-roots dimensions of
the economic, social, and political forces analyzed in the book. At the
very least, I hope this study will help to stimulate that research.

Acknowledgments

My first contact with Colombia came in 1963-1965 when I served as a Peace Corps volunteer in western Cundinamarca. In July, 1970, I returned to Colombia to begin fifteen months of research made possible through a grant from the Foreign Area Fellowship Program. Funding for a year of dissertation write-up time was provided by the same program, a Wetter Fellowship from the Department of History at Stanford University, and the Committee on International Studies at Stanford. Since completion of the dissertation I have returned twice to Colombia for additional research thanks to grants from the National Endowment for the Humanities, the American Philosophical Society, and the Duke University Research Council.

Many Colombians aided me in my research. I wish to thank especially Fray Alberto Lee López, archivist at the Colombian Academy of History, who helped orient and enrich my search for primary documents. At the National Library and Archive the entire staff proved friendly and helpful, but Sra. Blanca de Armenta's charm made my early work in the Sala de Investigadores especially enjoyable. Special thanks go also to Dr. Jaime Duarte French, who, as Director of the Biblioteca Luis Angel Arango, extended me every aid to research in that modern, pleasant library rich in materials on twentieth-century Colombia; to the officials at the Archive of the Ministry of Defense who assisted me in the use of the 170 volumes of telegrams relating to the war housed in that repository; and to the congenial and efficient staff of the notary public at Fusagasugá, Cundinamarca, who made work in that warm coffee-country town a pleasure.

The example of a new and dynamic generation of Colombian historians has greatly influenced this work. In their quest for solutions to the problems of the present, these young historians are overcoming the formidable material obstacles to serious historical research in an underdeveloped country and transforming the quality of Colombian historiography. I have benefited particularly from discussions with Hector Melo, Marco Palacios, and Hermes Tovar.

In the United States, I would like to thank John Johnson, whose great humanity, dedication to scholarship, and support over the years created the environment which made this study possible. David Bushnell provided encouragement and many constructive suggestions at a critical stage in the work, as did John TePaske, my colleague at

Duke. Frank Safford, a friendly but severe and demanding critic, gave generously of his time and understanding of nineteenth-century Colombian history and helped me to clarify many points in my argument. William McGreevey also read the manuscript and offered helpful suggestions. Dot Sapp, whose efficiency and graciousness are legendary at Duke, typed the final draft of the manuscript.

To all these institutions, committees, functionaries, and scholars I wish to express my appreciation for their interest and support. Naturally, all statements and conclusions presented are my own and do not necessarily reflect the views of any of the sponsors or critics of the study.

Finally, thanks go to my wife, Magola, who has taught me much about Colombia that is difficult to glean from books and old papers, and who contributed to the completion of this study in many indirect but profound ways.

The book is dedicated to the memory of my wife's father, Julio Bohórquez, and to our children, Joel and Andrea. Their grandfather was three years old when the War of the Thousand Days began, and throughout his life, as a small coffee grower in Cundinamarca, he grappled individually and creatively, if ultimately unsuccessfully, with many of the same historical forces I have attempted to analyze in this history. As our understanding of these historical forces increases, so also will the ability of my own generation to work collectively to build a freer, more egalitarian social order in the world for our children.

Coffee and Conflict in Colombia, 1886-1910

Chapter I

Introduction: The Political Economy of Nineteenth-Century Colombia

In the closed, stratified Colombian society of the last century, economic resources were monopolized by a small upper class interested in preserving its position and generally unable or unwilling to generate new wealth. The lack of new economic opportunities in a stagnant domestic economy made politics an inordinately important avenue for social mobility. Politics and government provided suitable employment in a culture that encouraged training in the traditional professions and reserved highest prestige for accomplishments in the classical skills of rhetoric and polemics. Government offered opportunities for travel and occasion for enrichment through favors and contracts. Control of government was a prize coveted by new, energetic, ambitious men who sought to improve their social position. Groups of men from all classes of society, bound together by traditional patron-client relationships, disputed for control of government with practically every means at their disposal. Once control was achieved, it was guarded with religious exclusivism.

Nineteenth-century Colombian politicians and political commentators recognized and deplored this violent competition for public posts and the perquisites of office and often correlated it with the political instability characteristic of the nineteenth century. One observer, Juan Francisco Ortiz, believed that competition for the limited number of public positions contributed in large part to the political disorders of the post-Independence period, and as early as 1833 future Liberal[1] politicians Lorenzo María Lleras and Florentino González were denouncing *"empleo-manía"* in the press.[2] At different times during his long, influential career in Colombian politics, Rafael Núñez linked the lack of economic opportunities outside government to political violence. Nearing the end of his first presidential term,

1. Throughout this study capitalization will be used to designate the Colombian Liberal and Conservative parties, their members, and their programs. The parties were formed by the mid-nineteenth century and have dominated Colombian politics to the present day. When referring to parties outside Colombia or when a more general meaning of the term is implied, the lower case form will be employed.
2. Robert Henry Davis, "Acosta, Caro, and Lleras. Three Essayists and Their Views of New Granada's National Problems, 1832-1853" (Ph.D. Diss., Vanderbilt University, 1969), p. 19.

Núñez used harsh language to denounce the "uncompromising materialism" that threatened to make politics a "vile business of plunder," nothing more than "naked commercial speculation." As soon as a new chief executive takes office, Núñez exclaimed, he is besieged by an "army of office seekers" and, unable to satisfy them all with public posts and favors, he must watch them swell the ranks of a new and formidable political opposition.[3]

The contemporary who most carefully described the link between a stagnant domestic economy and political turmoil was José María Quijano Wallis, prominent Liberal merchant and politician during the second half of the nineteenth century. Looking back on eighty years of Colombian history from Independence until the end of the War of the Thousand Days, a period marked by seven major civil wars and more than a score of smaller outbreaks of political violence, Quijano Wallis wrote in his memoirs:

> The lack of development of our national wealth and the consequent impoverishment of our people, has led the military *caudillos*, most of the time, to seek their livelihood and personal aggrandizement in the hazards of civil war, or in the intrigue and accommodations of politics. Thus, one can say that in Colombia, the first, if not the only industries of national, popular character, have been civil war and politics.[4]

Accusations that political dissidents, in spite of their elaborate ideological, economic, and administrative reform programs, were really motivated only by their desire for public posts were commonplace in the nineteenth century. Revealingly, one of the most perceptive political commentators of the last third of the nineteenth century did not expressly deny that charge leveled at his party of dissident Conservatives by the Liberal press in 1899. Instead he pleaded that political debate, for the honor of the country, take a higher ground. In the incisive, candid style typical of his writings, Carlos Martínez Silva argued that to believe that the distinguished Conservative dissidents were motivated only by the search for personal improvement would lead to the conclusion that in Colombia all notion of honor and dignity was lost. Use of that line of argument was dangerous, for the weapon cut both ways. Proof could be found in the attitude of the same Liberal press which bitterly censured Liberals who had accepted posts with the present government, accusing them of abandoning their Liberal ideas and principles.

3. Rafael Núñez, *La reforma política* (2nd ed., Bogotá, 1886), pp. 106-107. See also the extract from his report as minister of finance in 1856, p. 51.

4. José María Quijano Wallis, *Memorias* (Rome, 1919), pp. 524-25. Another statement of the same idea appears on p. 231.

Is there any assurance that if the offers were to multiply, the so-called abdications would not also increase? And if that were so, could not one also come to the conclusion that the Liberals, who complain so of the injustices and iniquities of the government in power, are likewise motivated by an appetite for temporalities.[5]

Many twentieth-century Colombian scholars and politicians, influenced by Colombia's mid-twentieth century experience with political violence,[6] have continued the school of thought sketched by Quijano Wallis, stressing the quest for public posts and the perquisites of office as the motor of Colombian political instability. Historian Fernando Guillén Martínez is the most convincing exponent of this interpretation of Colombian national character and history. Guillén argues that the Colombian political parties formed out of the desire to compete for control of the "primary employer, the government."

> Under the appearance of "profound" ideological differences, those parties grouped people of every social condition and of every professional, political and regional interest into rival hordes. What really united them was not their "statements of principle," but rather the sensation that that amalgam—in each "Party"—strengthened its members in order to dispute with their rivals that inextinguishable treasure that was and continued to be the Government.[7]

While Guillén emphasized the elements of national character involved in the desire to seize and monopolize government, Camilo Torres analyzed the same quest for political spoils from a sociological point of view. In Colombia, he argued, upper-class monopoly of economic and cultural resources had choked off all avenues for social mobility except politics, which was dominated by the two traditional elite-led vertical parties.[8] In this manner Camilo Torres explained the

5. Carlos Martínez Silva, "Revista política, mayo, 1899" in Luis Martínez Delgado, ed., *Revistas políticas publicadas en el Repertorio Colombiano* (Bogotá, 1934), II, 451-52.

6. Called *la violencia*, civil strife broke out in Colombia in 1946 and reached major proportions during the decade 1948 to 1958. Although superficially distinct from the nineteenth-century civil wars fought between elite-led armies, the *violencia* offers striking parallels to nineteenth-century political violence in general and specifically to the War of the Thousand Days. The most intensively studied period of Colombian political strife, the *violencia* has generated a respectable literature in both Spanish and English. See Russell W. Ramsey, "Critical Bibliography on La Violencia in Colombia," *Latin American Research Review*, 8:1 (Spring, 1973), 3-44.

7. Fernando Guillén Martínez, *Raíz y futuro de la revolución* (Bogotá, 1963), p. 134.

8. A similar argument, although not tailored specifically to Colombian realty, was advanced by United States political scientist Merle Kling in his article, "Toward a Theory of Power and Political Instability in Latin America," *Western Political Quar-*

traditional goals expressed by partisans during periods of political violence in spite of the fact that large numbers of the economically and socially dispossessed classes were armed and participating in politics.[9]

That present-day Colombian elite politicians implicitly have shared the view of their nineteenth-century counterparts that competition for government jobs is the root cause of political strife is obvious from the nature of the plan they devised to end the political strife in 1957. Called the *Frente Nacional*, that plan provided for the alternation of the Liberal and Conservative parties in the control of the presidency and equal division of all government posts at all levels between the two traditional parties.

Competition for the spoils of government, then, is an interpretation advanced by important nineteenth- as well as twentieth-century observers and participants as the best explanation for Colombian political violence. Especially when couched in the setting of a closed, stratified society of limited economic opportunities, it is a thesis appealing in its simplicity and powerful in its interpretive force. Its major weakness lies in its inability to explain adequately long periods of relative political peace and stability, such as the period 1902 to 1946. Proponents of the competition for spoils thesis also depend on normative cultural explanations of upper-class divisions into opposing parties and factions by stressing the alleged pernicious influence of supposedly Latin defects inherited from the Spaniards. Similarly, they view the elaborate, profoundly different ideologies and programs that articulate upper-class differences as nothing but smokescreens that hide the personal appetite of politicians for public posts and the honors, distinctions, and titles which accompany them.

Quijano Wallis, for example, found the roots of the profound division among Colombians and the "hatred between the parties" in the

> atavistic sentiment, bequeathed by the Spanish colonizers, who like all Latins, have preoccupied themselves a great deal with principles and theories and political interests, and very little with the real economic concerns and with material progress, which distinguishes the nations of the races which populate the countries of the North in Europe and America.[10]

---

terly, 9:7 (March, 1956), 21-35. Kling postulated that the roots of Latin American political instability could be traced to the importance of control of government in a society in which resources were poorly distributed and mobility severely limited.

9. Camilo Torres Restrepo, "La violencia y los cambios socioculturales en las areas rurales colombianas" in *Memoria del Primer Congreso Nacional de Sociología, 8, 9 y 10 de Marzo de 1963* (Bogotá, 1963), pp. 95-152.

10. Quijano Wallis, *Memorias*, p. 523.

Guillén Martínez's more extreme argument builds an elaborate case for the Spanish origins of the "psychological disease" of the Colombian body politic—the insatiable thirst for the perquisites of public office. Guillén denounces the "farce" of Colombian politics in which the real motives of members of political groups are disguised in ideological garb. Although he admits at one point the sincerity of many partisans who believe they fight for principles, he admonishes them for their incapacity to discern their unconscious drives.[11]

Close analysis of nineteenth-century Colombian history reveals, however, that the root structure of Colombian political violence was far more complex than the advocates of the quest-for-spoils thesis indicate. Divisions within the upper class and the systematic philosophical and programmatic positions that define them are not merely political manifestations of cultural traits; they reflect diverging economic interests within the upper class as the nineteenth century wore on. Simple competition for control of government was complicated and overlaid by the periodic appearance of new economic opportunities as Colombians responded to the demands for tropical agricultural exports by the industrializing nations of the North Atlantic basin. Colombia experienced these export booms beginning in the 1840's with tobacco, later with cinchona bark and to a lesser degree with indigo, and finally, near the end of the century, with coffee. During the nineteenth century, however, Colombians found that after an initial boom period, when prices were high, they could not compete with other tropical areas once world supply had met demand and prices fell.

Participation in export agriculture drew groups of Colombians more fully into the economic, political, and intellectual currents of the developing West. Direct links with the liberal "leading nations" nurtured a group of upper-class Colombians engaged in exporting primary goods and importing foreign manufactures. These men came to share the values and aspirations of the liberal world view dominant in the industrializing West. The success of export agriculture led to the rise and dominance of the Liberal party in Colombia after 1850. The hegemony of liberal thought and politics characterized the history of the nation during the next quarter century. After 1875, however, ex-

---

11. Guillén, *Raíz y futuro*, pp. 134 and 183-84. Much of United States political scientist James L. Payne's provocative *Patterns of Conflict in Colombia* (New Haven, 1968), is a "scientific" extension of Guillén's thesis. Payne argues that Colombian culture breeds politicians motivated by a personal quest for status, virtually exclusive of programmatic, economic or ideological motivations. For a critical review of recent literature on clientelist politics see Robert R. Kaufman, "The Patron-Client Concept in Macro-Politics: Prospects and Problems," *Comparative Studies in Society and History*, 16:3 (June, 1974), 285-308.

port agriculture entered a period of rapid decline, and by the early 1880's the industry was in crisis. In 1885 Liberals lost control of politics to Conservatives, the liberal world view was repudiated, and a conservative political and economic philosophy consistent with Colombia's reversion to a relatively closed agrarian economy became dominant in Colombia.

The success and failure of export agriculture in nineteenth-century Colombia modified and complicated the "politics of scarcity" generally associated with a stagnant, closed domestic economy with limited social mobility. Increased economic power led to growing real political power for certain groups and demands for government policies favorable to their interests and consonant with their values and aspirations. Furthermore, because government derived its main income from custom duties, periods of export boom meant increased government revenues and allowed governments to meet their obligations, expand their activities, and invest, if necessary, in the coercive apparatus needed to preserve their control. Conversely, a decline in the value of the export earnings of an economic sector decreased its relative political weight, called into question its economic and political philosophy, stimulated the demands of other sectors, placed government in severe financial straits, and forced political groups in power to retrench and become more blatantly coercive.

Colombia's two traditional political parties crystallized in the 1840's and reflected in many respects the dual nature of the Colombian economy. Although systematic work on the early sociology of the parties remains to be done, it is clear that the programs and policies of the Liberal party more closely reflected the interests of exporters of agricultural products and importers of foreign goods. Liberals, for reasons which undoubtedly have to do with their ideological predisposition and economic and social interests inherited from the colonial period, appear to have participated much more fully in the opportunities afforded by export agriculture, although, again, confirmation of this generalization awaits detailed investigation. These Liberals not only produced for export, but became export-import merchants who thrived with the increase in foreign trade fostered by the export economy.[12]

The rise of the Liberal party in the late 1840's, its long period of

12. It is important to point out that many of the characteristics and values attributed to members of the Liberal party in this and the following paragraphs would also apply to a fraction of the Conservative party, especially Conservatives from the region of Antioquia, where the export mineral and agricultural economy was relatively well developed in the nineteenth century. These economically liberal Conservatives did not share the mainstream Liberals' view of the Church as a primary obstacle to economic and political progress, however.

hegemony in Colombian politics, and its decline and loss of power to the Conservatives after 1880 closely parallel the growth and decline of export agriculture, particularly tobacco, during the same period. Beginning with tentative reforms and meeting stiff resistance in the 1850's, Liberals ultimately succeeded, after the decisive civil war of 1860-1862, in writing their organic Liberal world view into the Constitution of 1863. The hegemony of the Liberals' philosophy and their control of government were not challenged until the last half of the 1870's, when their ideas and policies were subjected to telling criticism and their control of politics confronted serious and ultimately successful challenge. Earnings from tobacco exports fluctuated between 100,000 and 200,000 pesos annually in the mid-1840's. Beginning in the late 1840's, they expanded rapidly to more than five million pesos annually in most years between 1850 and 1875.[13] Tobacco exports began their "definitive decline" after 1876 as importers began to favor the higher, more uniform quality of tobaccos from other tropical regions, and by the mid-1880's tobacco exports had declined to less than half a million pesos.[14]

Other export products rose to ephemeral importance during the period of nineteenth-century Liberal hegemony. The most important of these was quinine, extracted from the forests of Colombia in the form of cinchona bark. Export earnings assumed importance in the 1850's, averaging about half a million pesos annually during that decade, declined somewhat in the 1860's, and then rose to a peak of over five million pesos in the year 1880-81.[15] But the boom in quinine exports came to an abrupt end after that year; the world price of quinine sulphate fell from thirteen shillings an ounce in 1879 to three shillings sixpence in 1883 as high quality cultivated quinine from British and Dutch plantations in the East Indies flooded the market. By 1885 foreign exchange earnings from quinine had declined to virtually nothing.[16]

13. William Paul McGreevey, *An Economic History of Colombia, 1845-1930* (Cambridge, Eng., 1971), p. 98. For treatment of the tobacco economy, see John P. Harrison, "The Evolution of the Colombian Tobacco Trade to 1875," *Hispanic American Historical Review*, 32:2 (May, 1952), 163-74; Luis Eduardo Nieto Arteta, *Economía y cultura en la historia de Colombia* (Bogotá, 1942); Luis F. Sierra, *El tabaco en la economía colombiana del siglo XIX* (Bogotá, 1971). Harrison estimates that tobacco accounted for between 70 and 90 percent of Colombia's exports during the period 1852-1875. For a lower estimate, see Miguel Urrutia and Mario Arrubla, eds., *Compendio de estadísticas históricas de Colombia* (Bogotá, 1970), pp. 207-8.

14. The phrase is Nieto Arteta's, *Economía y cultura*, p. 284. No data are available for the period 1881-1888; Nieto Arteta lists just over one million pesos for the year 1880-1881 and not quite 700,000 pesos for 1888 after exports began to rise again. *Economía y cultura*, p. 283.

15. *Ibid.*, pp. 300-1.

16. Carlos Calderón, *La cuestión monetaria en Colombia* (Madrid, 1905), p. 8. Minor

The success of export agriculture achieved under Liberal aegis strengthened the Liberal party physically and ideologically. At first glance the political impact of the tobacco industry, backbone of the export economy during the third quarter of the nineteenth century, appears to have been slight. Comprising only a tiny fraction of total agricultural production,[17] tobacco was exported and marketed by an oligopoly tied to European commercial houses. The political significance of the tobacco industry stemmed from the fact that it began to produce large amounts of foreign exchange for the first time since Independence and spawned a powerful class of merchants engaged in importing European goods. As these goods moved through the custom houses, they provided government revenues on an unprecedented scale.[18] In the late 1840's and early 1850's, under the aegis of the Liberal party, import-export interests acquired preponderant political power, and the initial success of their laissez-faire economic reforms won approval or acquiescence from upper-class leaders identified with both political parties.[19] But if many Conservatives acquiesced in or supported the passage of narrow economic reforms confined to questions of tariff policy or tobacco monopoly, they opposed Liberal attempts to deal with larger, more fundamental issues of political economy, such as the role of the State and the Church in Colombian

export items included indigo which peaked at 182,000 pesos in the year 1870-1871 and declined to negligible amounts by the late 1870's, and cotton, which enjoyed a brief boom as a result of civil war in the United States, rising to a high of over half a million pesos in the year 1866-1867 and declining thereafter. Nieto Arteta, *Economía y cultura*, pp. 306-9.

17. McGreevey estimates only 11,000 hectares devoted to production of export products of all kinds in 1857 while 332,000 hectares provided for the domestic market. *An Economic History*, p. 122.

18. Imports rose from a low of about 1.5 million current U. S. dollars in 1847 to a high of 39 million in 1873, according to McGreevey's estimates. Twelve years later, in 1885, as the crisis of Liberalism in Colombia reached its climax, imports fell to a low of 16.1 million. McGreevey, *An Economic History*, p. 99. The trend is represented graphically in Figure 4, p. 102. These estimates, like the ones on land usage cited above, are based on suspect procedures and have been subjected to detailed criticism by Alberto Umaña, "Problemas estadísticos en el análisis del período liberal, 1845-1885," a paper presented at the Seminario sobre Historia Económica de Colombia, Bogotá, July, 1975. They are used here, not to convey absolute values, but to illustrate trends referred to in the text.

19. Luis Ospina Vásquez, *Industria y protección en Colombia, 1810-1930* (Medellín, 1955), p. 247, affirms the dominion of laissez-faire economic thought during the period and notes that Conservatives ignored strictly economic issues in their criticism of Liberal policies. Frank R. Safford likewise notes a consensus of elites on economic issues during the period. See his "Commerce and Enterprise in Central Colombia, 1821-1870" (Ph.D. diss., Columbia University, 1965), pp. 9, 209, 248. The concept of ideological hegemony, developed by the Italian Marxist Antonio Gramsci, seems particularly applicable here. As long as the export economy flourished, Liberal ideology succeeded in convincing, neutralizing, or forcing onto the defensive, many whose interests were not directly benefited (and may have been hurt) by Liberal policies.

society. Imbibing an integral world view which had become dominant in the industrializing nations of the West, Liberals ultimately sought to write into law a philosophy of man and society fundamentally at odds with the structure of the society they lived in—a society their Conservative opponents cherished and fought to maintain.

Surveying their society at mid-century, Colombian Liberals were appalled by the restraints on individual freedom and initiative inherited from the colonial period. The conservative reaction following the civil war of 1839-1841 had eliminated many of the tentative liberal reforms achieved during the government of Francisco de Paula Santander. These included moderate reduction in import and export taxes, measures designed to limit the accumulation of property in mortmain by the Church, and efforts to reduce the role of the Church in education.[20] The conservative Constitution of 1843 provided for centralized government under a strong executive and subsequent policy favored the Church and sought to arrest the spread of liberal ideology. Under the direction of future Conservative president Mariano Ospina Rodríguez, the educational system was reorganized. Liberal texts like those of Jeremy Bentham were banned from the classroom and new courses designed to foster Catholic and conservative thought were instituted.[21]

Liberalism began to revive during the administration of the nominal conservative Tomás Cipriano de Mosquera. Mosquera's government fostered developments in rail and river transportation and reforms in the measurement and monetary systems. In 1847 a new tariff cut duties by 25 percent.[22] The rapid growth of tobacco production led to the passage of a bill which abolished the state tobacco monopoly inherited from the Spanish and permitted free cultivation of the crop. The bill went into effect on January 1, 1850, and symbolized the advent of a new era dominated by liberal thought and policies.[23]

Liberals won control of the national executive with the election of José Hilario López in 1849 and immediately began to implement their many-faceted reform program for Colombian society. They abolished slavery, accelerated the division of Indian lands, expanded civil liberties and instituted unlimited freedom of the press, abolished the death penalty for political crimes, decentralized tax revenues and administration, gave local governments more control over the Church,

20. David Bushnell provides an excellent account of this early experiment with liberalism in *The Santander Regime in Gran Colombia* (Newark, Delaware, 1954).

21. Delpar, "The Liberal Party," pp. 31-32.

22. David Bushnell, "Two Stages in Colombian Tariff Policy: The Radical Era and the Return to Protection (1861-1885)," *Inter-American Economic Affairs*, 9:4 (Spring, 1956), 4.

23. Harrison, "Evolution," pp. 163-64.

and abolished special ecclesiastical courts. Liberals gave these reforms constitutional expression in the Charter of 1853. In addition, the Constitution of 1853 broadened the suffrage by abolishing property and literacy requirements, instituted direct, secret elections, and provided for the election of many previously appointed government officials.[24]

Reaction to the Liberal reforms led to division within the Liberal party, political turmoil, and an attempt to reverse some of the Liberal measures under the moderate Conservative regimes of the late 1850's. Liberals regained control of government during the civil war of 1860-1862 and decreed a set of radical measures aimed at curtailing the political, social, and economic power of the Catholic Church, which had allied itself with the Conservative opponents of the Liberal reforms. Mosquera, now a full-fledged Liberal, decreed that clergymen were required to seek authorization from civil officials in order to exercise their functions. The Jesuits, who had returned under the previous Conservative administration of Mariano Ospina, were once again expelled. Finally, Mosquera struck directly at the heart of the Church's temporal power; on September 9, 1861, he decreed the disamortization of Church property.[25] Church property was to be sold at public auction and proceeds were to be applied to payment of the nation's internal debt.

Victorious in the civil war, Liberals moved to consolidate their power and write their recent reforms into the basic law of the land. The constitution written at Rionegro, Antioquia, and promulgated in 1863 ratified Mosquera's anti-Church measures, provided an extremely decentralized political organization for the country, amplified individual rights to include unrestricted freedom of expression and the right to possess and to traffic in arms, abolished the death penalty, and limited incarceration to ten years.[26] In 1863 the Liberals also instituted a massive reduction in tariff rates under a new system of duties by weight. The downward trend in tariff duties continued throughout the decade.[27] The delegates at Rionegro contemplated moving the capital of the republic away from the isolated, overwhelmingly conservative highlands of Cundinamarca to Panama, where government would be subject to the "salutary" influences of

24. William Marion Gibson, *The Constitutions of Colombia* (Durham, N. C., 1948), pp. 194-214.

25. The decree actually adjudicated to the nation all property of any kind belonging to civil and ecclesiastical corporations, excepting that property actually used by the corporation in performing its functions, but the primary target was the Catholic Church, the value of whose holdings has been estimated at between 15 and 24 million pesos. McGreevey, *An Economic History*, pp. 72-73.

26. Gibson, *Constitutions*, pp. 236-96.

27. Bushnell, "Two Stages," p. 5.

Europe and the United States, but security considerations caused them to reconsider.[28]

This review of their reforms makes it clear that Colombian Liberals shared a world view fundamentally different from that of their Conservative opponents. Linked through their ideological and economic interests to the industrializing nations of the North Atlantic basin, Colombian Liberals found their inspiration in England, France, and the United States; there they traveled, bought their books on political and economic philosophy, studied, and observed first hand the success of liberal economic and political organization.[29] Colombian Liberals, like their counterparts in other areas of the West, viewed society as the sum of individual, rational, juridically equal men. They believed that individual men, left alone to pursue their intellectual and material interests, would contribute to the progress of civilization and the well-being of society in general. Man, they affirmed, was basically good and perfectable; he was corrupted by evil institutions.

Theoretically, many of the Liberal reforms sought to free capital and labor frozen in the institutions and corporations inherited from the colonial period. Freedom for slaves and the extension of ordinary rights to Indians served humanitarian purposes and accomplished juridical equality, but also augmented the pool of free labor in the society. Although many domestic artisan industries were hard hit by the influx of cheap foreign manufactures, displaced artisans were freed to move about and fill the labor requirements of agricultural industries in which Colombia had a comparative advantage. Land frozen in Indian communities and Church hands would enter the free market and become available for productive use. Abolition of monopolies would encourage private initiative. Government activities, reduced to the essential protection of property and the facilitation of commerce, would be decentralized and made sensitive to local demands.

In reality, the Liberal reforms often had unfortunate effects quite different from those enthusiastically envisioned by their authors,[30] but

28. Helen V. Delpar, "The Liberal Party of Colombia, 1863-1903" (PhD Diss., Columbia University, 1967), pp. 137-38.

29. In his important book, *The Ideal of the Practical* (Austin, 1976), Frank Safford has shown that many Colombian Conservatives also traveled abroad in pursuit of technical education. But, as his book makes abundantly clear, nineteenth-century Conservative efforts to achieve economic and technical progress were framed within a philosophy alien to liberal political economy. For a discussion of these issues, see Charles W. Bergquist, "On Paradigms and the Pursuit of the Practical," *Latin American Research Review*, 13:2 (Feb., 1978), 247-51.

30. For an introduction to this theme, see J. León Helguera, "The Problem of Liberalism Versus Conservatism in Colombia: 1849-85" in Fredrick B. Pike, *Latin American History: Select Problems* (New York, 1969), pp. 223-58.

14

it was not until the crisis of export agriculture in the late 1870's and 1880's that the impact of the reforms was subjected to critical analysis. At that time a small group of influential Liberals under the leadership of Rafael Núñez joined with intelligent Conservative leaders in a broad attack on the politics of Liberalism, dominant since the 1850's. The bipartisan critics scrutinized the laissez-faire economic policies and discovered that they had undermined artisan industry, inhibited the establishment of new domestic industry, encouraged the consumption of foreign goods, and, when exports were down, drained the country of specie. Doctrinaire attacks on the Church in a country where all but a handful of Liberal reformers were firm believers with strong emotional ties to the Church were not only destructive of political stability, the critics argued, but foolish, alienating the mass of Colombians from the Liberal elite and forcing Liberal leaders to abandon their democratic principles. Moreover, governments with limited resources needed the Church as an essential partner in meeting the necessity for social welfare and educational institutions. Finally, in a country wracked by civil strife since Independence, the Church was an important source of cohesion, a pillar of the social order. Strong centralized government was necessary to promote economic development and to prevent civil strife in a country broken by geography and lacking adequate communication systems.[31]

Old line Liberals, dubbed the "Radical Olympus" by their critics for their doctrinaire aloofness to Colombian reality, did in fact modify some of their policies in response to changing conditions and the strength of their opposition. Radical Liberals countenanced state promotion of transportation developments.[32] The decline in exports and imports put severe strain on the public treasury, forcing Liberals to increase tariff rates during the 1870's and to suspend interest payments on the foreign debt by 1880.[33] After successfully impeding

31. Núñez's own *Reforma política,* cited earlier, is one source for dissident Liberal criticism of the policies practiced under the period of Liberal hegemony; another is [Enrique Cortés,] *La lección del pasado: ensayo sobre la verdadera misión del partido liberal* (Bogotá, 1877). An extremely useful introduction to the intellectual crisis of Liberalism can be found in Jaime Jaramillo Uribe, *El pensamiento colombiano en el siglo XIX* (Bogotá, 1964). See especially his chapter on the thought of Conservative leader Miguel Antonio Caro, pp. 314-56.

32. In fact, much of the Radical Liberals' political opposition in the early 1870's stemmed from charges that the Northern Railroad, a project championed by the Radical Liberal elite, favored the regional interests of Santander at the expense of the rest of the nation. See Helen V. Delpar, "Aspects of Liberal Factionalism in Colombia, 1875-1885," *Hispanic American Historical Review,* 51:2 (May, 1971), 258-60.

33. Bushnell, "Two Stages," p. 8. The suspension of interest payments was particularly embarrassing after the praise heaped on Colombia by foreign bondholders following the successful renegotiation of the foreign debt in 1875. Quijano Wallis, *Memorias,* pp. 287-88.

Núñez's election to the presidency in 1875, the Radical Liberals compromised with the Independent Liberals led by Núñez in their support of Julián Trujillo, who began to implement the Independent Liberal policy of rapprochement with the Church and the Conservative party upon his election to the presidency in 1878.[34] Núñez became president in 1880 and that same year the Independent Liberals established a protective tariff and a National Bank to stimulate economic growth.[35] Radical Liberal opposition to these measures was strong, but the Radicals' greatest fear was that Núñez, abandoned by most of the Liberal party, would turn to the Conservatives for support. The Conservative party endorsed Núñez for the presidency in 1884 and rescued his government when the Radical Liberals revolted in 1885. Victorious in the war, the Independent Liberals and their Conservative allies organized themselves into a new party, the Nationalists, under the direction of Núñez and turned to consolidating their control. The period of Nationalist hegemony, called the Regeneration in Colombian history, began with the writing of a constitution that the Nationalists considered appropriate to Colombian realities.[36]

Núñez admonished the Council of Delegates charged with writing a new charter not to copy foreign models but to write a constitution which would be "the simple and natural codification of the thoughts and desires of the nation."[37] Núñez emphasized his belief that the individual's sphere of activity should be limited by the rights of others and society in general. The educational system should be based on Christianity so that the religiousness of the people could be enlisted in support of the social order. Republics, because of their very nature, Núñez went on, needed to be organized along authoritarian lines. The constitution should provide government with the power necessary to instill respect for authority and to maintain political stability.[38]

The document that emerged in 1886, largely written by the Conservative intellectual Miguel Antonio Caro, conformed to Núñez's precepts and reflected a political philosophy in stark contrast to the one

34. Delpar has argued that the basis of the Liberal split in that year was personal and regional, not ideological. But the crisis in export agriculture became apparent only after that year and during the next few years the small group of Liberals under Núñez broadened their attack, as Delpar's own data show, to include the economic, administrative and Church policies of the Radical Liberals. See Delpar, "Aspects," pp. 250-74.

35. Indalecio Liévano Aguirre, *Rafael Núñez* (Lima [1944?]), pp. 170-82; Delpar, "Aspects," p. 295. Liévano Aguirre's study has strongly influenced the interpretation of Núñez advanced in this and subsequent paragraphs.

36. The term Regeneration harks back to Núñez's call for "fundamental administrative regeneration" in his speech as President of the Senate at the inauguration of President Trujillo in 1878.

37. Quoted in Delpar, "The Liberal Party," p. 295.

38. *Ibid.*, pp. 294-95.

codified in the Liberal Constitution of 1863. The Constitution of 1886 created a unitary, highly centralized political organization with power concentrated in the hands of the president, who could assume extraordinary powers in case of disruption of public order. Public authorities were required to protect the Church, which was recognized as an essential element of the social order. Although the Church and State were to be formally separate and freedom of religion was granted, the Constitution recognized Catholicism as the religion of the nation and declared that education was to be organized in accordance with the Catholic religion. The government was authorized to enter into formal negotiations with the Vatican to normalize Colombian relations with the Church. The press was made responsible under law for injuries to personal honor and for disturbance of the social order and public peace. A transitory clause that became especially odious to political dissidents in subsequent years authorized the government to regulate the press and punish abuses until Congress enacted a press law. The right to possess and traffic in arms was abolished. Suffrage in national elections was limited by literacy and property requirements, and many previously direct elections were made indirect.[39]

The Conservatives in control of government in Colombia after 1886 shared with Liberals a commitment to republican political institutions, but based their economic, social, and political policies on a conception of man and society fundamentally at odds with the Liberal world view. Lacking strong ties with the liberal community of the West, these Conservatives found their intellectual nourishment in Catholic and Spanish thought. Nationalist Conservatives viewed society as a hierarchy of men with different capabilities and functions. Strong institutions such as the family, the Church, and the State were needed to control men susceptible to evil passions and anti-social behavior unless instilled with a moral code capable of uniting men on a spiritual level. Economic policy, under the direction of the State, should promote the general welfare not the selfish interests of individuals. Attempts to weaken the Church not only attacked an effective political ally, but threatened the source of the social and spiritual cement of a hierarchical society. Satisfied with their position in life and aloof from foreign critics, Nationalist Conservatives felt no shame over the "backwardness" of the country. Unlike their Liberal opponents they found virtue in its Spanish heritage, its Catholic purity, and the intellectual and literary achievements of its elite.

While the rise of liberal thought and the dominance of the Liberal party reflected the growth and success of export agriculture in the

39. Gibson, *Constitutions*, pp. 299-349.

third quarter of the nineteenth century in Colombia, the decline of export agriculture and the crisis of liberalism in the years following 1875 witnessed a resurgence of conservative forces in a society still overwhelmingly characterized by traditional agriculture for domestic consumption. The Constitution of 1886 signaled the victory of conservative thought and the consolidation of a new regime headed by Conservatives. The Independent Liberal politicians who had accompanied Núñez, deprived of a power base among rank and file Liberals, were largely displaced by old-line Conservatives in the control of the new Nationalist party. The Liberal party, its doctrines and policies discredited, its material strength shattered by military defeat, its members denied access to political power and conventional civil liberties, lapsed into a period of resignation and political disorganization. The architects of the Regeneration, confident in the validity of their political philosophy and certain of the viability of their newly created institutions, predicted a new era of political stability and material progress. Few Colombians, even among the opposition, could have predicted the dramatic resurgence of liberalism during the next few years that would seriously undermine the conservative philosophical foundations of the new regime, and ultimately mount a military challenge to the government of unprecedented scope and tenacity.

Part One

The Origins of the War

Chapter II

A Decade of Regeneration, 1886-1896

Ironically, the consolidation of the Regeneration in 1886 coincided with the beginning of a new export cycle as Colombians responded to the spectacular rise in world coffee prices which occurred in the late 1880's and early 1890's. Coffee had been cultivated in Colombia on a small scale since the start of the nineteenth century. Although world production and consumption of coffee more than doubled between 1820 and 1855, Colombian expansion did not begin until the 1860's, when improved river transportation and a rise in prices stimulated production.[1] In the early 1870's Colombian coffee exports exceeded 100,000 bags of sixty kilos each annually, reaching a peak in 1874 when 172,420 bags were exported. Coffee exports declined after that year and, although complete statistical evidence is lacking, probably leveled off at less than 100,000 bags annually for most years until the late 1880's (see Figure 2:1). The decline in production reflected falling world coffee prices after 1875. The average price of Colombian coffee on the New York market fell from 20.5 cents per pound in 1875 to 10.1 cents per pound in 1884.[2] Because coffee trees produce their first crop only four or five years after planting, price generally exerts little immediate effect on coffee production.[3] Consequently, when coffee prices rose precipitously after 1887, there was considerable lag until production figures demonstrated the massive increase in coffee cultivation that occurred in Colombia in the late 1880's and early 1890's. The average price of Colombian coffee on the New York mar-

1. For an interesting, anecdotal account of the growth of coffee consumption in Europe during the eighteenth and nineteenth centuries and different versions of the manner in which coffee arrived in Central and South America and spread to Colombia, see J. A. Osorio Lizarazo, *Biografía del café* (Bogotá, 1945). An excellent study of the Colombian coffee industry, cited extensively in this and subsequent chapters, is Robert Carlyle Beyer, "The Colombian Coffee Industry: Origins and Major Trends, 1740-1940" (Ph.D. diss., University of Minnesota, 1947).

2. The crash in coffee prices contributed to the crisis of export agriculture discussed in Chapter I and probably influenced the outbreak of the civil war of 1885. That war was triggered by a local conflict in the state of Santander, at that time the primary coffee-producing region of Colombia.

3. Price fluctuation can exercise some rapid effect on production through increased or decreased care of trees and in handling, storage, and transport of the bean. Beyer, "Coffee Industry," p. 59. Of course, a major decline in coffee prices can make harvesting uneconomical in high-cost production areas and result in an immediate drop in export statistics.

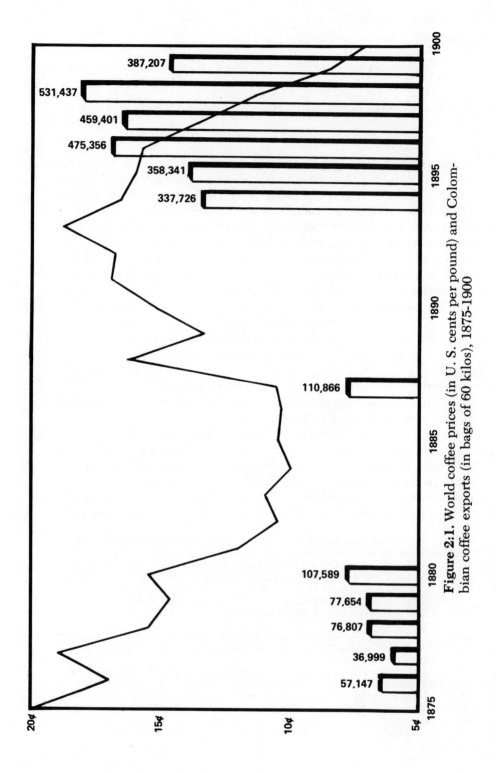

Figure 2:1. World coffee prices (in U. S. cents per pound) and Colombian coffee exports (in bags of 60 kilos), 1875-1900

ket rose from 10.6 cents a pound in 1887 to a peak of 18.8 cents a pound in 1893. Coffee exports tripled during the same period, rising from 110, 866 bags in 1887 to 337,726 bags in 1894. By 1898, when all of the trees planted up to 1893 had come into production, exports stood at 531,437 bags. During the mid-1890's coffee accounted for well over half of the value of Colombia's total exports, and for the peak years 1895 and 1896 coffee made up about 70 per cent of the value of total exports.[4]

Although much of Colombia's mountainous surface would eventually prove to be uniquely suited to the cultivation of coffee, the early period of coffee expansion was largely confined to the northern section of the eastern cordillera of the Colombian Andes in what was then called the State of Santander.[5] The most serious student of the Colombian coffee industry has estimated coffee production (including domestic consumption) in Santander in 1874 at about 100,000 bags, or almost 90 percent of total Colombian production.[6] In 1888 a British consular official estimated Santander's share of the nation's coffee production at about 55 percent, with the department of Cundinamarca, situated in the southern portion of the eastern cordillera, contributing about half of the remaining 45 percent.[7] The decline in Santander's position resulted from the high cost and complications of international transport and the relatively poor quality of the coffee from Santander. Since coffee growers in most of Santander were deprived of a viable outlet to the Magdalena River, they were forced to ship most of their coffee out via Venezuelan rivers to Lake Maracaibo, where it was finally loaded aboard ocean-going vessels for transport abroad.[8] Venezuelan transit fees, storage costs, and delays seriously

4. Beyer, "Coffee Industry," Appendix Table II, p. 361, gives coffee as a percentage of total exports using a three-year running average. Diego Monsalve, *Colombia cafetera* (Barcelona, 1927) graphs data for individual years, p. 630. Monsalve's book is full of useful information, although sources of data are not cited. Statistics on coffee production and prices conform generally to subsequent estimates made by the Federación Nacional de Cafeteros and used extensively by Beyer.

5. Comprising what is now the departments of Norte de Santander and Santander, the Sovereign State of Santander, so called under the Constitution of 1863, became the Department of Santander with the adoption of the Constitution of 1886. The accompanying map shows the boundaries of the departments as established in 1886. No changes were made until after the War of the Thousand Days.

6. Beyer, "Coffee Industry," Appendix Table XI, p. 388.

7. Great Britain, Foreign Office, "Report on the Agricultural Condition of Colombia," *Diplomatic and Consular Reports on Trade and Finance*, Annual Series, No. 446 (London, 1888), p. 10.

8. By 1888 Santander enjoyed the services of a fifty-five kilometer railroad connecting Cúcuta to Puerto Villamizar on the Zulia River, but the railroad only exacerbated commercial relations with the Venezuelans who had built a coffee railroad of their own and sought to divert traffic to it by means of customs duties. Archivo del Congreso, Senado, 1898, vol. IV, Proyectos Pendientes, "Memorandum: Cúcuta y su situación comercial en relación con Venezuela. Proyecto de Ferrocarril a Tamalameque," legajo 8, ff. 183-89.

Colombia: major towns, mountains, and rivers

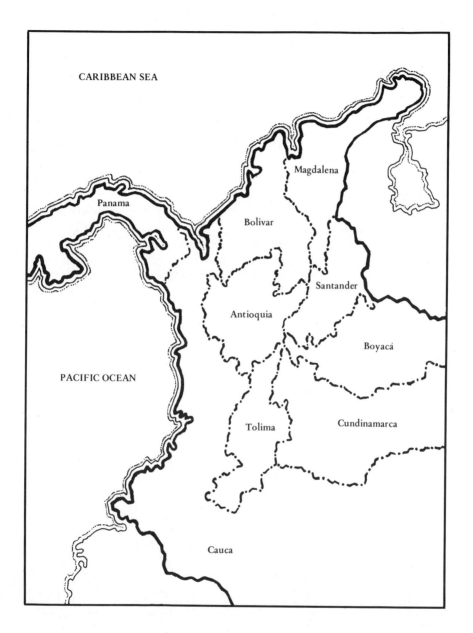

Departments of Colombia, 1886-1904

reduced the profit margin on Santander coffees, which sometimes sold for as little as half the price per pound of the prime coffees from Cundinamarca.[9]

Much of the expansion in coffee production in the late 1880's and early 1890's took place in the department of Cundinamarca, and in the departments of Antioquia and northern Tolima located in the central cordillera.[10] Transport of coffee to the sea, although difficult in Cundinamarca and Antioquia, was cheaper than in Santander. Both regions had outlets on the Magdalena, and though much coffee reached the river by mule, by the 1890's both Cundinamarca and Antioquia had partially built railroads that cut transportation costs.[11]

Coffee cultivation expanded primarily into the undeveloped lands on the mountainsides between the tropical river valleys and the temperate highlands. Some of this land was part of the public domain and could be adjudicated in exchange for certificates of public credit issued by previous governments as compensation for damages incurred or bonuses for services rendered. Public domain land was also available to squatters who put the land under cultivation. During the 1890's thousands of acres of public lands in coffee zones were adjudicated in these ways, although most of the land was distributed in large tracts to a relatively small number of men. Smaller farmers complained that the public lands policy favored the wealthy who attained possession of available lands in a developing area and restricted the growth of smallholders.[12] During the 1890's cases of conflict between settlers who claimed to be squatting on public land and landowners who asserted previous title to the same land were almost always de-

9. In February, 1882, coffee from the Cundinamarcan municipality of Sasaima was selling abroad at twenty cents a pound while coffee from Cúcuta in Santander was going for ten cents a pound. Beyer, "Coffee Industry," p. 117. Other sources indicate coffees from Santander sold for about 20 to 25 percent less than coffees from Cundinamarca. See the quotations published in *La Opinión* (Bogotá), July 11, 1901, or in Great Britain, Foreign Office, "Report on the Present State of the Coffee Trade in Colombia," *Diplomatic and Consular Reports*, Misc. Series, No. 598 (London, 1903), p. 4.

10. Expansion in these last two areas, particularly in southern Antioquia, presaged the shift in the axis of Colombian coffee production to the central cordillera in the first years of the twentieth century, a subject discussed in Chapters IX and X.

11. By the late 1890's the Antioquia railway stretched sixty-six kilometers from Puerto Berrío on the Magdalena River and was carrying over 50,000 bags of coffee annually. Theodore H. Hoffman, "A History of Railway Concessions and Railway Development Policy in Colombia to 1943" (Ph.D. diss., American University, 1947), p. 118; Monsalve, *Colombia cafetera*, p. 283. By 1885 the projected Bogotá-Girardot railroad which, when completed, would wind through the southwestern coffee zone of Cundinamarca, was in operation from Portillo to Girardot on the Magdalena, a distance of thirty-two kilometers. Work reached a point forty-nine kilometers from Girardot by the end of the century. Alfredo Ortega Díaz, *Ferrocarriles colombianos* (Bogotá, 1920), p. 394.

12. Pedro Henao G. to Rafael Uribe Uribe, Calarcá [now in the department of Quindío], August 29, 1896, August 30, 1898, September, 1898, and October [?], 1898, Personal Papers of Rafael Uribe Uribe, Box 5, Academia Colombiana de Historia (hereafter

cided in favor of the latter.[13] Other coffee growers purchased land on the previously marginal hillsides at low prices.[14]

The coffee trade was dominated by large commission houses located primarily in New York and London. While most of these were foreign, some of them were controlled by Colombian capitalists.[15] Large coffee producers shipped directly abroad to the commission houses and were often in debt to them for advances. Smaller growers sold to general stores whose owners either were agents of the foreign-based commercial houses or dealers who financed their purchases by sixty and ninety day drafts on the commission houses. These general stores were at once exporters and importers, wholesale distributors and retailers.[16] In addition, the merchants who ran the stores were often coffee growers as well.

Coffee production depended on a variety of labor systems. Large growers required a seasonal labor force often acquired in Cundinamarca through the system of *enganchamiento,* literally, "hooking." Monetary inducements (which could be accompanied with coercion) were offered workers to encourage them to travel from the cold populous highlands to the warm country during the coffee harvest or

cited as Uribe, ACH). Uribe Uribe proposed a bill to the congress on October 29, 1898, which would have limited to 3,000 hectares (7,413 acres) the amount of public lands adjudicated at any one time. The bill, which was passed in first debate and submitted to a committee for study, would have also required grantees of public lands to cultivate a certain portion of the land (ranging from 40 percent for smaller grants to 15 percent for the largest) within eight years. Uribe, Box 13. ACH.

13. See the following issues of the *Diario Oficial*: 9,127 (April 7, 1893); 9,463 (May 7, 1894); 9,705 (February 22, 1895), 10,020 (May 8, 1896); 10,305 (April 6, 1897); 10,325 (April 29, 1897); 10,566 (February 4, 1898). An especially instructive example of this kind of land dispute was the controversy between the family of Liberal merchant and coffee grower Sixto Durán and small farmers in the area called "Hoyagrande" in the municipalities of Gachalá and Junín, Cundinamarca. A detailed account is given in the *Gaceta de Cundinamarca* 702 (September 30, 1895), 748 (May 12, 1896), and 853 (August 10, 1897).

14. Uribe Uribe gave what is probably a maximum price of sixty pesos per *fanegada* (approximately one and a half acres) in an estimate of the capital investment required to found a coffee estate in the late 1890's. Uribe, Box 17, ACH.

15. The most famous of these was the commercial house founded by Enrique Cortés in London. Specializing in the importation of tropical raw materials, especially coffee, hides, and forest products, and the exportation of manufactured goods, by the end of the century Cortés ran one of the largest commercial houses dealing with Colombia and did an extensive business with other Latin American nations. A Liberal, Cortés' life followed a pattern similar to many other influential men in his party. Widely traveled and partially educated abroad, Cortés was closely identified with the export-import trade throughout his life. During the period of Liberal hegemony he served for several years as secretary of the Colombian legation in Washington. After the War of the Thousand Days, Cortés occupied several high positions in the government of Rafael Reyes. See Ricardo Santa María Ordóñez, "Don Enrique Cortés," *El Tiempo,* Suplemento Literario, March 14, 1943.

16. Phanor James Eder, *Colombia*, 5th ed. (London, 1921), pp. 124-26. For examples

to open up new lands to coffee production.[17] In order to secure a pemanent labor force on their farms larger coffee growers granted workers plots of land and, depending upon their needs and local conditions, collected payment in the form of labor, or in cash or labor.[18] Finally, some coffee was produced with family labor on small farms.

Small coffee farms appear to have been much more common at this time in Antioquia, Santander, and Tolima than in Cundinamarca. In the Antioquia region, large-scale, capital-intensive coffee cultivation was the exception, whereas in Cundinamarca in the 1890's it seems to have been the rule.[19] The contrast in the mode of coffee production between the two departments is suggested by two manuals on coffee cultivation published in the 1880's. The first manual was written by Mariano Ospina Rodríguez, an antioqueño Conservative and a former president of the nation. Its title accurately describes its contents and intended audience: *Coffee Cultivation: Elemental Notions Within the Grasp of All Workers.* The other manual, written by Nicolás Sáenz Pinzón, a Liberal who had founded a great, mechanized plantation in Viotá, Cundinamarca, was filled with botanical names and included instructions for soil analysis and construction of temperature charts. Sáenz's book was aimed at the well-educated, large-scale coffee farmers of Cundinamarca.[20]

---

of the terms of contracts between Colombian coffee exporters and foreign commission houses, see José María Cortés [Agent of Enrique Cortés & Cía] to Sixto Durán, Bogotá, April 25, 1898, Durán Family Papers, Academia Colombiana de Historia (hereafter cited as Durán, ACH); contract between Tovar Hermanos and Schwann and Cía dated October 8, 1901, Documentos relacionados con la Guerra de los Mil Días, Archivo del Ministerio de Defensa, vol. 05783 (hereafter cited as AMD); and contract between Rafael Uribe Uribe and Arbuthnot Latham and Co. of London dated Medellín, June 10, 1897, Uribe, Box 17, ACH. For the terms of a partnership formed in the Cundinamarcan municipio of Viotá to produce, transport, and export coffee and engage "en la compra y venta de mercancías extranjeras y en negocios de comisiones," see Notaría de Fusagasugá, 1903, Tomo 2, escritura no. 614.

17. In one part of Cundinamarca in 1894 laborers got forty centavos a day, a small sum for travel expenses, and a bonus of six pesos if they satisfactorily completed their service. Antonio Suárez M. to Rafael Uribe Uribe, Ubaté [Cundinamarca], November 8, 1894. Uribe, Box 6, ACH. See also Vicente Prieto to Rafael Uribe Uribe, Hacienda de Tudela [Paime?, Cundinamarca], November 26, 1895. Uribe, Box 12, ACH.

18. Contract between Ezequiel Quijano, representative of Sixto Durán, and Coronado Acosta, data "Hoyagrande," June 30, 1891. Durán ACH.

19. Rafael Uribe Uribe, *Discursos parlamentarios* (Bogotá, 1897), p. 228. On Antioquia see James J. Parsons, *Antioqueño Colonization in Western Colombia* (Berkeley, 1949), especially p. 140. A detailed description of coffee production on a Cundinamarcan coffee hacienda can be found in José Manuel Marroquín's costumbrista novel *Entre primos* (Bogotá, 1897), pp. 350-53. Malcom Deas, "Una finca cundinamarquesa entre 1870 y 1910," (mimeograph, Universidad Nacional de Colombia, Centro de Investigaciones para el Desarrollo, 1974) is a valuable study based on the hacienda records of a Liberal's coffee farm located in Sasaima, Cundinamarca.

20. Ospina's manual was published in Medellín in 1880; Sáenz's *Memoria sobre el cultivo del cafeto* in Bogotá in 1888.

Establishment of large-scale coffee haciendas involved a sizable initial investment and no return until the trees began producing. Much of the investment went to cover the heavy labor costs involved in clearing the virgin forest and cultivating the coffee trees for the first four years. In order to meet the problem of labor costs, capital-short landowners devised ingenious labor arrangements that allowed them to establish coffee plantations under circumstances extremely advantageous to themselves. An example of such an arrangement was a five-year contract signed by Sixto Durán, an important Liberal coffee grower and merchant, with one Martín Romero, who took a piece of Durán's land in eastern Cundinamarca and was to plant coffee trees. According to the terms of the contract, Romero would be reimbursed at the rate of 40 pesos per 1,000 trees at the end of the contract, but in the meantime he had to deposit the sum of 320 pesos with Durán, the interest from which would pay for the rent of the land for the five years. Presumably, Romero could also use the land for his own purposes, perhaps by planting food crops between the young coffee trees.[21] This kind of arrangement superbly met the landholders' needs for capital and labor. Possessing only the land, and at no expense to himself, the landholder took over the coffee trees just as they began to produce and he was consequently in a position to reimburse his help.

An example of a more complex contract, somewhat more favorable to the landless partner, was the agreement signed in 1895 between Pedro Betancour and Ramón Zácipa to begin coffee cultivation on a piece of land owned by Betancour in Melgar, Tolima, an area contiguous with the coffee-growing zone of southwestern Cundinamarca. Zácipa was to plant and cultivate coffee on Betancour's land at his own expense for a period of ten years. At the end of the ten years the area planted in coffee would be divided equally between the two men. For the next two years Betancour could not charge Zácipa any rent, but at the end of the two years, the ownership of both the land and all the coffee trees would revert to Betancour. For the duration of the twelve-year agreement, all produce from the area cultivated would be divided equally between the two men and the cost of harvesting the coffee would likewise be shared equally.[22] By the terms of this contract, the landless partner could enjoy the profits produced by half the coffee trees planted for several years before relinquishing ownership.

While the terms of these contracts, particularly the first (which required the landless partner to deposit a sum of money in addition to furnishing his labor), may be exceptional, evidence from notary ar-

21. Contract signed between Sixto Durán and Martín Romero, Junín, Cundinamarca, January 27, 1890. Durán, ACH.
22. Notaría de Fusagasugá, 1895, Tomo 1, escritura no. 269.

chives in southwestern Cundinamarca reveals the widespread nature of similar arrangements through which landowners with limited amounts of liquid capital were able to appropriate most of the profits of coffee cultivation during the 1890's. Landowners would assign a portion of uncultivated forest land within their estate to a tenant and his family with the understanding that the tenant "at his own expense" would clear the land and plant and cultivate coffee "providing proper shade trees" until the coffee trees began to produce. At that point the landowners could purchase the coffee trees and all other improvements made on the land. "Improvements" often included the tenant's split bamboo or wattle and daub house as well as a variety of foodcrops including plantains (commonly used as shade for the coffee trees), yucca, arracacha, corn, and sometimes sugar cane.

Landowners in southwestern Cundinamarca also bought coffee trees planted by landless families in unadjudicated public domain lands. Such purchases were regulated by law and under the terms of such agreements the squatter forfeited all legal claim to the land, leaving the buyer free to seek future adjudication of the public land as a cultivator. The adjudication of public land was a slow, complex, and relatively costly process. The fact that squatters were usually illiterate and adjudication involved the payment of legal and survey costs greatly limited the possibility (at least in Cundinamarca in the 1890's) of landless farmers acquiring title to public lands.[23]

From the notary files it is difficult to establish the rate at which producing coffee trees were purchased. Most sales contracts did not specify the number of trees involved or, when they did, lumped other important items with the coffee trees sold. Even when an approximate rate of purchase can be established, a series of factors, such as the condition of the trees, the accessibility of the site, and the extent of other improvements on the land combined to make the rate vary considerably from place to place. Moreover, inflation and fluctuation of coffee prices during the decade undoubtedly influenced the rate of purchase. Nevertheless, some notion of the range of prices paid for producing trees can be deduced from Table 2:1. It is important to

23. Loss of the right of future claim to the land is sometimes stipulated in the document of purchase. For example, Notaría de Fusagasugá, 1899, Tomo 1, escritura no. 14. For legislation dealing with the adjudication of public lands, see Vicente Olarte Camacho, *Guía para denunciar y pedir en adjudicación tierras baldías por cualquier título* (Bogotá, 1895); J. Roberto Gastelbondo, *El procedimiento para denunciar minas y terrenos baldíos y compilación de leyes, decretos y relaciones de los mismos ramos* (Bogotá, 1893); and especially Julián Restrepo H., *El tratado noveno de la codificación cundinamarquesa* (Bogotá, 1900), pp. 803-850. See also Lopera Berrío Cruz, *Colombia agraria* (Manizales, 1920), pp. 61-69.

Table 2:1. Sample purchases of producing coffee trees, southwestern Cundinamarca, 1893-1898

	Seller	Buyer	Location of sale	Year of sale	No. of doc.	No. of trees	Computed price per tree	Comments
1.	Emperatriz Romero and Basilio Melo	Lucio Capete	Nilo	1893	Tomo 1 No. 345	700	30 centavos	includes 1892 harvest as well
2.	José Hernández	Lucio Capete	Nilo	1893	Tomo 1 No. 345	350	26 centavos	includes 1892 harvest as well
3.	Pedro Bautista Guevara	Cirilo Almanza	Melgar*	1895	Tomo 1 No. 5	2000	25 centavos	includes plantains, yucca, corn, wooden sugar press and straw hut
4.	Natalia Cadena de Díaz	Cirilo Almanza	Melgar*	1895	Tomo 1 No. 5	500	20 centavos	includes plantains
5.	Juan Garzón	Manuel Aya	Escuela de Tibacuy	1895	Tomo 1 No. 324	2000	28 centavos	includes sugar cane, plantains, small pasture
6.	Vicente Liévano	Antonio Lamella G.	Nilo	1895	Tomo 2 No. 677	3000	20 centavos	includes 500 plantain plants
7.	José Melo	Antonio Suárez	Nilo	1895	Tomo 1 No. 209	5000	50 centavos	includes sugar cane, plantains and house
8.	Teófilo Quintero	Baltazar Liévano	Tibacuy	1895	Tomo 2 No. 387	600 (approx)	33 centavos	——
9.	José María Sastre	Enrique Bueno Patiño	Nilo	1895	Tomo 1 No. 133	1700	30 centavos	rate specified
10.	María Casallas	Francisco Guevara	Escuela de Tibacuy	1896	Tomo 3 No. 579	500 (approx)	32 centavos	includes a little house
11.	Javier García	Lisandro Caicedo	Escuela de Tibacuy	1896	Tomo 3 No. 695	1800	21 centavos	includes shade from guamo trees and plantains
12.	Demetrio Rojas	Abdón Caicedo	Escuela de Tibacuy	1897	Tomo 1 No. 148	4000 (approx)	30 centavos	includes mud house and small coffee grove
13.	Luis Garzón	Estate of Manuel María Aya	Escuela de Tibacuy	1898	Tomo 3 No. 699	2681	25 centavos	rate specified
14.	Manuel Torres	Francisco Rodrí-guez Rozo	Nilo	1898	Tomo 3 No. 592	3500 (approx)	43 centavos	includes claim on last three harvests

*Although it lies just outside Cundinamarca in the department of Tolima, Melgar is part of the coffee zone which stretches through southwestern Cuncinamarca.

Source: Notary Archive, Fusagasugá, Cundinamarca.

stress that the examples given are for sales by tenants in lands owned by the buyer.[24]

As a glance at the "comments" column of Table 2:1 indicates, only two of the sample contracts (numbers 9 and 13) specified the rate of purchase. In the other contracts the rate had to be calculated and the result is somewhat obscured due to the extraneous conditions and minor additional purchases noted. Still, these other contracts confirm the general range of the rate of purchase, and it is reasonable to assume that that rate was about 25 to 30 centavos per tree.

Given the high price of coffee on the world market in the mid-1890's these arrangements were extremely advantageous to landowners. Coffees from Cundinamarca sold abroad at about 16 cents (U. S. gold) per pound in the mid 1890's and total production and transportation costs were estimated at about 8 cents (U. S. gold) per pound.[25] That left a profit margin of about 8 cents (U. S. gold), or, at the mid 1890's exchange rate (see Table 2:2) of approximately 160, a profit of about 13 centavos per pound.[26] Contemporary estimates of yield per coffee tree range from one to as high as four pounds dried coffee per year, depending on the age and condition of the trees and the fertility of the soil.[27] Thus, depending on conditions, in one to three years landowners could expect to reimburse themselves for the purchase of the maturing coffee trees, trees which could be expected to produce well for twenty years or more.

Coffee lands were also developed by companies formed by wealthy men of influence, often export-import merchants, who pooled resources to develop the production of tropical agricultural products. One such group was the Compañía Agrícola e Industrial de Rionegro

24. Sales of coffee trees at a much lower price, apparently made to other landless cultivators, were also quite common. For example, Notaría de Fusagasugá, 1895, Tomo 1, escritura nos. 391, 392, and 393.

25. In 1893 a Colombian journal, the *Estadística Mercantil,* put coffee production costs at 4.5 cents per pound while transportation from Bogotá to New York was estimated at 2.9 cents per pound. Quoted in Bureau of the American Republics, "Coffee in Colombia," *Bulletin,* No. 1 (1893), pp. 25-26. A decade later a British consular official estimated production costs at 4 cents per pound and transportation to New York, including seller's commission and other fees, at another 4 cents per pound. Great Britain, Foreign Office, "Present State of the Coffee Trade in Colombia" (London, 1903), p. 6.

26. Note that for purposes of the calculations made here, the level of return should be even higher since a large portion of the estimated production costs given in the previous footnote was destined to pay the initial labor costs of establishing a coffee plantation.

27. In 1888 a British consular official estimated yield at one and one-half pounds per tree, noting that the unit yield was higher in Colombia than in other coffee exporting nations. Great Britain, Foreign Office, "Report on the Agricultural Condition of Colombia," p. 10. An estimate of two and one-half to four pounds per tree was made by a United States observer in 1893. Bureau of the American Republics, "Coffee in Colombia," p. 25. In 1897 Uribe Uribe calculated production on a hypothetical coffee farm of 100,000 trees at a little over one pound per tree. Uribe, Box 17, ACH.

Table 2:2. Average monthly exchange rate of Colombian pesos, 1886-1899

Year	Jan	Feb	Mar	Apr	May	Jun	Jul	Aug	Sep	Oct	Nov	Dec
1886	37	40	44	40	38	36	41	40	42	40	40	40
1887	63	68	69	69	73	76	79	81	84	91	83	82
1888	94	91	93	111	140	100	95	100	111	103	99	102
1889	96	90	91	96	97	95	92	96	95	97	92	95
1890	93	97	98	97	100	97	94	93	95	92	87	90
1891	92	87	86	75	82	84	87	88	90	98	88	90
1892	86	88	88	95	93	99	93	98	101	100	99	101
1893	106	107	116	112	116	124	128	135	159	153	138	144
1894	153	159	173	183	186	176	168	170	178	166	159	158
1895	160	167	185	189	176	173	166	158	157	148	166	139
1896	142	142	142	146	139	138	134	140	140	140	141	138
1897	136	140	141	145	142	143	145	149	153	161	175	152
1898	172	163	166	180	184	185	190	204	214	209	212	217
1899	235	237	241	243	260	293	334	412	388	402	457	550

Source: Adapted from Guillermo Torres García, *Historia de la moneda en Colombia* (Bogotá, 1945), p. 276.

Note: To find the equivalency of the Colombian paper peso in U. S. gold currency, simply divide the number given into 100. Thus the value of the paper peso when the exchange rate reached 250 was 100/250 or .40, i.e., U. S. $0.40 gold.

founded in 1889 by thirteen prominent Bogotá capitalists, most of them Liberal merchants, to exploit 42,000 *fanegadas* (approximately 63,000 acres) in the valley of the Rionegro River near La Paz in western Cundinamarca.[28] Capitalized at 240,000 pesos, the company soon began serious development of the area, bringing in machinery, founding a company store, and paying out 600 to 800 pesos a month in wages. Two years after beginning activities, however, the company dissolved, victim, according to one sympathetic Liberal observer, of government persecution. It is true that small cultivators had been encouraged in the belief that they were legitimately squatting on public lands, not private lands belonging to the company, by government resolutions in 1891 and 1892 that declared the lands part of the public domain.[29] Once that belief spread among the cultivators, "not a single peon could be depended on; tenants, local authorities in La Paz, and other interested parties declared themselves owners and lords and masters of everything."[30] By the time the company dissolved, over 200,000 coffee trees, 15,000 cacao trees, and substantial amounts of other food crops and pasture grasses had been planted on the lands claimed by the company. After dissolving the company, most of its partners became victims of individual persecution and ultimately most abandoned the land.[31] Later in the decade the courts revoked the decision declaring the lands part of the public domain and many of the original partners were able to regain the lands they had previously claimed.[32]

The Liberal merchant and agriculturalist Sixto Durán was partner in a similar company founded to develop coffee lands near San Agustín in the south of Tolima. Like the Rionegro company, the Tolima company planned to engage not only in coffee cultivation, but production of sugar cane and rum and the raising of livestock. The Tolima company also ran into serious labor problems that one of Durán's partners, Leonidas Lara, attributed to the evil influence exerted by Church and government officials on the Indians, especially the "tenants of landlords of certain political inclinations."[33]

The coffee boom brought signs of great material prosperity to Bogotá. In sharp contrast with the modest, almost frugal life styles of

28. Medardo Rivas, *Los trabajadores de tierra caliente* (Bogotá, 1946), p. 313. The first edition of this book was published in Bogotá in 1899.
29. See the resolutions of the minister of hacienda dated September 14, 1891, and May 20, 1892, in the *Diario Oficial*, 8, 562.
30. Rivas, *Trabajadores*, pp. 314-15.
31. *Ibid.*, p. 316.
32. *Diario Oficial*, 9,299 (October 27, 1893), 9,524 (July 17, 1894), 9,525 (July 18, 1894), and 9,526 (July 19, 1894).
33. Leonidas Lara to Sixto Durán, Juntas [Tolima?], June 1, 1896. Durán, ACH.

upper-class *bogotanos* during the decades following Independence, the surge in international trade in the late 1880's and early 1890's reinforced upper-class luxury consumption habits awakened during the Independence era and stimulated during the export booms of the 1850's, 1860's and 1870's.[34] A "practical guide" to Bogotá described a city of filthy streets and dusty plazas whose common people lived in terribly overcrowded, unhygienic housing devoid of water and sewage facilities. Inside the homes of the wealthy, however, the city presented another face.

[T]he luxury, elegance, and comfort in which the wealthy families live is surprising: such that it seems that we are not in Colombia when we enter the magnificent palaces [which are] artistically decorated and adorned, furnished in the best taste, [and] carpeted and hung with tapestries. . . .[35]

The social consequences of the new wealth generated by the coffee boom in the 1890's greatly impressed Julio H. Palacio, a perceptive young man from the Caribbean coast attending school in Bogotá.[36] Palacio described shops stocked with imported luxury items for men and clothing tailored by the "best tailors of Paris and London", private parties, receptions, and dances every bit as magnificent and refined as similar events in the "great capitals of Europe and America"; and expensive public spectacles put on by European performers crowded with spectators, as in the case of an opera company which performed for seven full months in Bogotá in 1891.[37] Another observer decried the amount of gold spent in recruiting the European actors and singers, transporting them to Colombia, and paying them inflated salaries. Those who attended performances at the elegant Teatro Colón in

34. For consumption patterns in the years following Independence and the increasing consumption of imported luxury goods after 1850, see Safford, "Commerce," pp. 20-21, 44-48, 346.

35. Manuel José Patiño, *Guía práctica de la capital; directorio especial del comercio* (Bogotá, 1902), pp. 39, 41. A revealing portrait of late nineteenth-century Bogotá, as well as of the character of one of Colombia's best poets, is provided by Carlos Garcia Prada in his introduction to *José Asunción Silva, Prosas y versos* (Madrid, 1960), pp. 7-42.

36. A native of Barranquilla, Palacio was the son of Francisco J. Palacio, an important Nationalist and former Independent Liberal. His memoirs contain a wealth of information on late nineteenth- and early twentieth-century Colombian life. Palacio maintained close personal ties with such central Colombian political figures as Rafael Núñez, Miguel Antonio Caro, and Rafael Reyes. Unfortunately, only a single volume, constituting the small portion of his memoirs covering the period to 1894, has been published in book form under the title of *Historia de mi vida* (Bogotá, 1942). Palacio's complete memoirs were serialized in the literary supplement to Sunday editions of *El Tiempo* between February 2, 1941, and August 22, 1948. Cited as "Historia de mi vida," subsequent references will be to these *El Tiempo* articles.

37. Palacio, "Historia de mi vida," *El Tiempo*, May 11, 1941, July 12, 1941, and March 9, 1941.

Bogotá, he went on, attired themselves in the finest jewelry and clothes. After the event theater goers indulged in the most exquisite suppers.[38]

All this began to change after 1896. As world supply began to meet the demand for coffee, chiefly as a result of massive increases in Brazilian exports, coffee prices began to fall precipitously. Prices of Colombian coffees on the New York market fell from 15.7 cents a pound in 1896 to 8.5 cents a pound in 1899, the year the War of the Thousand Days broke out (see Figure 2:1). Although the volume of exports remained high during this period, exchange earnings from coffee fell dramatically due to the lower unit price. The fall in prices was particularly devastating in Santander, where profit margins were lower, but the crash created serious problems for growers all over the country, for other sectors of the country's economy, and for the government itself, which was greatly dependent on customs revenues to meet its obligations.

It is against the background of the expanding coffee industry, 1886-1896, and subsequent crisis in the industry, 1896-1899, that the political history of the Regeneration is best understood. The growing ideological and physical strength of the Liberal party during the period, the widening gulf between the governing Nationalists and a dissident wing of the Conservative party that came to be called Historical Conservatives, the explosiveness of the repressive Nationalist policies of political exclusivism, the centrality of the debate over Regeneration fiscal policies, and the complex causes of the War of the Thousand Days itself, can be adequately explained only in the light of the political impact of the phenomenal growth and subsequent decline of the coffee industry during fifteen years of Regeneration governments.

Two themes dominated Regeneration politics from 1885 until the outbreak of the War of the Thousand Days. Politically, the major issue separating the governing Nationalists from their critics was the question of civil rights and political representation for the opposition, composed first of the Liberal party and subsequently of an important faction of dissident Conservatives as well. Economically, the great issue was the system of nonredeemable paper money set up by Núñez in 1885 and expanded and doggedly defended by Miguel Antonio Caro as head of the government from 1892 to 1898. These two great

---

38. Miguel Samper, "Retrospecto" in José María Samper Brush and Luis Samper Sordo, eds., *Escritos político-económicos de Miguel Samper*, 2 vols. (Bogotá, 1925), I, 147-50. Although Samper disapproved of the conspicuous consumption he observed in the Bogotá of the 1890's, he attributed it to the evil influence of paper money and an expanded, corrupt bureaucracy, not to the effects of the coffee boom.

questions were interrelated. Freedom to organize and criticize the government through the press and the opportunity to win fair elections meant increased ability to attack and undermine the fiscal foundations of Regeneration governments. On the other hand, the power to print money constituted a new and significant government resource. Used with moderation, paper money strengthened government and freed it from overdependence on customs revenues and foreign and domestic loans. A degree of independence from these traditional sources of government income was particularly appropriate for the Nationalist Regeneration governments, which, unlike the Radical Liberal governments preceding them, did not find support in the powerful class of export-import merchants and bankers. In fact, as will be shown, the regime of paper money hurt export-import merchants and holders of liquid capital, and it was they, through the old Radical Liberal spokesmen for the Liberal party, and a newly formed dissident wing of the Conservative party, who became the outspoken critics and opponents of the Regeneration during the first years of its existence.

Illustrative of the philosophy of early Regeneration governments and their efforts to curtail political opposition through regulation of the press was President Núñez's decree of February 17, 1888. That decree divided press offenses into crimes against private persons, to be regulated by the courts, and crimes against society, under the jurisdiction of the executive. Crimes against society included publications that encouraged disobedience of the law, impaired the respect and dignity of civil and ecclesiastical authorities, attacked the Church, incited one social class against another, or impugned the monetary system. Sanctions ranged from light to extreme: from prohibitions on announcements of publications and the selling of publications in the streets, to permanent suspension of publication. Under the decree, several Liberal papers were suspended, their directors exiled.[39]

The most powerful tool devised by the Regeneration to suppress criticism of its policies and repress possible subversive activity, however, was the grant of extraordinary powers to the president by the National Legislative Council in May, 1888. Called the Law of the Horses,[40] Law 61 of May 23, 1888 authorized the president to "administratively prevent and repress transgressions against the State affecting the public order." According to the gravity of the offense, the president, with approval of his cabinet, was empowered to punish

39. Antonio Cacua Prada, comp., *Legislación sobre prensa en Colombia* (Bogotá, 1966), pp. 74-85; Delpar, "The Liberal Party," pp. 302-3.

40. The curious name derived from the notice of armed uprising against the government which precipitated the decree. The notice cited the slaughter of several horses in Cauca as evidence of an armed revolt.

violators with imprisonment, deportation, or deprivation of political rights. In addition, the president might remove military personnel whose loyalty to the government was suspect, and inspect scientific and educational institutions with power to suspend any activity considered revolutionary or subversive.[41]

Purely political reasons account for some of the Nationalists' desire to assure their exclusive control of Colombian politics after twenty-five years of exclusion from government by Liberals.[42] Deprived of the spoils of government during the lean years of Liberal hegemony, many of the Conservatives backing Núñez must have felt they were entitled to take any steps necessary to secure their continued exclusive enjoyment of the honors and perquisites of public office. Moreover, many leading Nationalists sincerely believed theirs was a sacred mission to rescue Colombia from the dangers and ignominy of the "quarter-century of anarchy" to which Colombia had fallen prey under the license of civil liberties and weak central government provided by the Constitution of 1863.[43]

The intolerance of Regeneration governments towards their critics also reflected a recognition of the potential strength of the opposition to their unorthodox fiscal policies. Through the Radical faction of the Liberal party, merchants and bankers had unsuccessfully opposed Núñez's tariff reforms and his establishment of a National Bank with the exclusive power to emit circulating bank notes.[44] When the bank was launched in 1881, private capitalists refused to buy up the shares offered to the public.[45] During the war of 1885, the government

41. Cacua Prada, *Legislación*, pp. 75-76; Delpar, "The Liberal Party," pp. 303-4.

42. The political exclusiveness of Liberal governments was extreme. Liberals dominated public posts, controlled and voted the army, and practiced fraud and political intimidation to minimize the electoral power of their Conservative opponents. Nevertheless, the higher number of public offices under the extremely federalist Constitution of 1863 and the relative weakness of the national government allowed Conservatives at different times to participate in government. Delpar, "The Liberal Party," pp. 36-37, 176-78, 187-92, 197. An exceptional case was the state government of Antioquia, which was controlled by Conservatives by virtue of a special modus vivendi with the national government worked out in 1864. Later the government of Tolima also came under Conservative control.

43. Miguel Antonio Caro, "Mensaje al Congreso Nacional, julio 20 de 1896" in Victor E. Caro and Antonio Gómez Restrepo, eds., *Obras completas de Don Miguel Antonio Caro*, 8 vols. (Bogotá, 1918-45), VI, 190.

44. For a detailed exposition of their opposition, see "La protección" and "Banco Nacional" published in the Liberal press by Miguel Samper in 1880 and collected in José María Samper Brush and Luis Samper Sordo, eds., *Escritos político-económicos de Miguel Samper* (Bogotá, 1925-27), I, 195-291 and III, 11-91.

45. In the orthodox Liberal view, banking, like any other private enterprise, should be immune from government interference. Liberals argued that the National Bank constituted a government monopoly, an odious infringement of the freedom of enterprise so vital to a healthy economy.

stopped specie redemption of National Bank notes, and in the months that followed proceeded to establish paper money as legal tender.[46] Stipulation of any currency other than National Bank paper in legal contracts was declared illegal and private banks were required to call in their currencies. Especially as new emissions led to the steady depreciation of the national paper currency (see Table 2:2), bankers and merchants found their interests in jeopardy. Bankers were legally required to accept depreciating national currency for debts previously contracted in gold and were prohibited from stipulating more stable currencies (such as pounds or dollars) in legal contracts.[47] Merchants or anyone else who loaned money within the nation operated under the same handicap. Import merchants were especially alarmed because inflation acted as kind of blanket tariff against imported goods and favored consumption of domestic products.[48]

The dramatic rise in Colombian foreign exchange earnings after 1886 revitalized the export-import trade, which had been moribund in the early 1880's.[49] The effect was to strengthen export-import groups and restore their faith in Liberal laissez-faire economic doctrine.[50]

One of the most influential exponents of Liberal economic orthodoxy, and the most dogged of the liberal critics of Regeneration finance, was Miguel Samper. Samper's career was archetypical of the Liberal exporters and importers who led the opposition to the Regeneration governments.[51] Born of relatively modest but respectable parentage in Guaduas, Cundinamarca, in 1825, Samper was trained as a lawyer but devoted his life to agriculture and commerce. At an early

46. The best single source for the details of Regeneration monetary policy in Guillermo Torres García, *Historia de la moneda en Colombia* (Bogotá, 1945), pp. 200-280.

47. This was the reason given by Quijano Wallis for the liquidation of his Banco Hipotecario soon after the triumph of the Regeneration. Other factors were also at work. During the War of 1885, Núñez forced the Banco Hipotecario to loan his hard-pressed government 30,000 pesos gold. When Quijano Wallis refused, police occupied his bank, finally forcing the board of directors to agree to the loan, but only after the resignation of Quijano Wallis. Quijano Wallis, *Memorias*, pp. 452-54, 490-91.

48. For a provocative study of these issues and the economic impact of Regeneration fiscal policy in general, see the recent study by the Colombian economist Darío Bustamante, "Efectos económicos del papel moneda durante la Regeneración" (mimeograph, Universidad Nacional de Colombia, Centro de Investigaciones para el Desarrollo, 1970).

49. According to McGreevey's estimates (which, given their great disparity with official figures and the risk of his methodology, must be used cautiously), the value of all Colombian exports rose from a low of 10.2 million current U. S. dollars in 1885 to a peak of 23 million in 1891. Meanwhile, imports rose from a low of 16.1 million in 1885 to peaks of over 25 million in 1887, 1888, and 1890. McGreevey, *An Economic History*, Table 12, p. 99 and Table 27, p. 210.

50. At the same time increased customs revenues strengthened the Regeneration governments, and Conservative economists, Miguel Antonio Caro among them, often attributed the economic prosperity to Regeneration fiscal policies.

51. The life patterns of Liberal leaders Aquileo Parra, Santiago Pérez, and Salvador

age he managed sugar cane production for export on his uncle's lands in Guaduas and Chaguaní in western Cundinamarca. Upon the death of his uncle, Samper moved to the Magdalena river port of Honda and established an important commercial house. In the same year he married María Teresa Brush, daughter of an Englishman who had settled in Colombia. With the boom in tobacco in the 1850's, Samper joined his brothers in opening up lands to tobacco production in the upper Magdalena valley. He played an important role in the tariff reform under President Mosquera and served as minister of finance in the cabinets of Liberal presidents Santos Gutiérrez and Francisco Javier Zaldúa. During the 1860's and 1870's he spent considerable time in Europe, attending to business interests and educating himself and his children.[52] From the dawn of the Regeneration until his death in 1899, Miguel Samper carried on a reasoned but implacable campaign against the economic policies of the new order based on orthodox laissez-faire and free trade arguments.

Miguel Samper felt that his belief that Núñez's inaugural speech of April 8, 1880, contained the "virus of state socialism" was confirmed by subsequent events. Regeneration economic and fiscal policies had led to increasing government control of the economy, a fatal tendency whose disastrous implications were evident in the results of the protective tariff, the National Bank, and the regime of paper money. Writing in 1892, Samper noted that protectionism had created artificial and inefficient industries to manufacture matches, cigarettes, candles, paper and cotton cloth.[53] The National Bank had become a creature of government and had failed to redeem paper money as originally stipulated.

Samper's greatest energies and sharpest criticisms were directed

---

Camacho Roldán were remarkably similar to that of Samper. All had relatively modest provincial beginnings, acquired a liberal education, became involved in the export-import trade, and maintained close ties with (and traveled in) the countries of the North Atlantic. Parra, Pérez, and Camacho Roldán served as chief executive during the period of Liberal hegemony; Samper became the Liberal candidate for president in 1897. With the advent of the Regeneration, these men constituted the core of Liberal leadership and opposition to the new regime. Parra's life to 1875 is covered in his *Memorias* (Bogotá, 1912). On Pérez, see Antonio José Rivadeneira Vargas, *Don Santiago Pérez: Biografía de un carácter* (Bogotá, 1966) and Eduardo Rodríguez Piñeres, et al., *Don Santiago Pérez y su tiempo* (Bogotá, 1952). Camacho Roldán's *Memorias* (Bogotá, 1923) provides little information on his personal life. Some data on all these men can be found in Joaquín Ospina, comp., *Diccionario biográfico y bibliográfico de Colombia*, 3 vols. (Bogotá, 1927-1939).

52. The foregoing is a composite of biographical information from Salvador Camacho Roldán, "Miguel Samper" and Carlos Martínez Silva, "El gran ciudadano" found in Samper Brush and Samper Sordo, *Escritos*, I, xix-xxxii and xxxv-lxxxix, respectively. See also Samper's own description of his family's economic interests and activities in III, 93-96.

53. Miguel Samper, "La crisis monetaria" in Samper Brush and Samper Sordo, *Escritos*, III, 180, 182-85.

against the regime of nonredeemable paper money. According to his orthodox view, paper money was intrinsically worthless and therefore violated the cardinal principle of all media of exchange. Moreover paper money constituted a forced loan extracted from individuals in an arbitrary, tyrannical manner by government. Unredeemable paper had caused much capital to flee the country, destroyed the habit of saving, and forced capital into unproductive investment. The result was a shortage of capital to develop agriculture and industry.[54]

Liberals were not the only early critics of Regeneration finance. Carlos Martínez Silva, who was later to become one of the leading opponents of Regeneration fiscal policies, used laissez-faire arguments to combat the idea of a National Bank in 1880. By 1891 a faction of dissident Conservatives, centered in Antioquia and led by Marceliano Vélez, bolted the Nationalist party and nominated Vélez for president on its own separate ticket. Vélez was a determined critic of the system of paper money[55] and regional and economic concerns played an important role in the campaign.

By the early 1890's Antioquia was an important and growing coffee producing area and was also the primary producer of gold, Colombia's other major export item. *Antioqueño* gold had been an important export commodity since the colonial period and in the nineteenth century constituted the only stable and consistent Colombian foreign exchange earner, averaging about two and one-half million pesos annually during most of the century.[56] By the mid-nineteenth century gold production had converted Medellín into Bogotá's banker.[57] Although Antioquia, a predominantly Conservative area, had not controlled the executive since the short-lived administration of Mariano Ospina (1857-1860), during most of the period of Liberal hegemony it had been allowed to manage its own affairs by the national Liberal governments.

Dissatisfaction with the Regeneration among *antioqueño* Conservatives became obvious in 1890 when they opposed the re-election of Carlos Holguín as presidential designate.[58] Then in 1891 a group of

54. Miguel Samper, "Nuestra circulación monetaria," in Samper Brush and Samper Sordo, *Escritos*, III, 101, 110, 148, 116, 114-15, 108.

55. Marceliano Vélez to Jorge Holguín, October 12, 1889, Archivo Histórico Luis Martínez Delgado, Academia Colombiana de Historia. This letter is one of hundreds transcribed by Luis Martínez Delgado. The typewritten transcriptions are bound by years and arranged chronologically within each volume. The collection is henceforth cited as MDT, ACH.

56. McGreevey, *An Economic History*, Table 7, pp. 46, 309.

57. Safford, "Commerce," p. 392.

58. Soon after signing the Law of the Horses, Núñez retired to his home in Cartagena, relinquishing power on August 7, 1888, to his designate, Carlos Holguín, who governed the country during the next two years and was reelected for another two years by congress in 1890.

antioqueño Conservative politicians, joined by Conservatives from other sections of the country, most notably Carlos Martínez Silva of Santander, proposed Antioquia's favorite son, Marceliano Vélez, for vice-president on the Núñez ticket. Doctrinaire Nationalists responded with an alternate ticket: Núñez for president and the *bogotano* Miguel Antonio Caro, author of the Constitution of 1886, for vice-president. Núñez vacillated in his choice of the vice-president, who would in fact exercise power given Núñez's reluctance to serve; but when Vélez publicly criticized the political and fiscal policies of past Regeneration governments, Núñez opted for Caro. Vélez's supporters then decided to run him on a seperate Conservative ticket for president, nominating José Joaquín Ortiz for vice-president.

Liberal leaders supported the candidacy of Vélez, heartened by his moderate position on civil liberties and his criticism of Regeneration finance that paralleled their own. In many areas, however, Liberal rank and file disobeyed instructions from their leaders and continued to abstain from the polls as they had done in previous Regeneration elections.[59] As a result the Nationalist ticket of Núñez and Caro swept into office with an overwhelming majority.

The election of 1891 marked a turning point in Regeneration politics. The split that developed in that year between the governing Nationalists and the dissident Conservatives widened in subsequent years to a point of total estrangement. Many contemporaries and subsequent observers have attributed the split between the two Conservative factions to the personality of Miguel Antonio Caro. Caro's inflexible, authoritarian political style did alienate some Conservatives and did contribute to the polarization of the two Conservative factions, but the split also reflected underlying ideological and economic interests. Núñez's choice of Caro over Vélez for vice-president on the Nationalist ticket was a logical consequence of Caro's fidelity to the principles and policies of the Regeneration.

An understanding of Caro's personality and political style is vital to an appreciation of the course of Colombian political history in the 1890's. Unlike Núñez, who revealed his consummate political sense in his confession that he always found the current and swam with it, Caro became more dogmatic and inflexible as the tide turned against the philosophical bases and practical policies of the Regeneration. As export agriculture revived in Colombia, and brought with it a resurgence of liberal political and economic thought and an increase in the real power of groups connected with the export-import trade, Miguel Antonio Caro only intensified his Conservative philosophical

59. Delpar, "The Liberal Party," p. 313; Rafael Uribe Uribe to Marceliano Vélez, Medellín, January 4, 1892, Uribe, Box 9, ACH.

stance and extended his statist economic policies. While Núñez defended the political and economic policies of the Regeneration primarily on the grounds that they were appropriate to Colombian reality, Caro defended the Regeneration as an absolute good.

In contrast with Núñez's philosophical eclecticism and political flexibility (his critics would say opportunism), Miguel Antonio Caro's life and thought reveal a remarkable consistency, an organic unity. Translator of Virgil, apologist for the Spanish legacy in America, renowned philologist and literary critic, militant Catholic polemicist, and Conservative political and economic philosopher, Caro approached every problem deductively, reasoning from a set of basic Catholic, conservative values: order, hierarchy, cultural unity.[60] Born in 1843 into a family of the highest social status,[61] and orphaned at the age of ten, Caro received his formal education at the Colegio de San Bartolomé in Bogotá, at that time a Jesuit institution. Unlike Núñez, who spent several years as Colombian consul in Liverpool and who traveled in Europe and the United States, Caro never left the highlands surrounding Bogotá. Núñez himself, always a perceptive judge of men, is reported to have described Caro's strengths and weaknesses in late 1893:

> There is not a man in Colombia of more abundant or profound learning than Mr. Caro, nor one endowed with more virtue. . . . Nevertheless, when it comes to government and politics he has a fault which is regrettable: he lacks worldliness; do you know what I mean? I know that he has never gone out in the street and with his own hands bought, or bargained for, a pair of shoes or a hat. He entrusts a person from his family to buy them, he pays for them, and that ends his business.[62]

In his inaugural speech of August 7, 1892, Caro expressed his deep commitment to the political ideals of the Regeneration and issued a clear warning to those who would violate the norms of the new order.[63] A month later he sent an extensive message to congress in which he vigorously defended Regeneration economic policy and ad-

60. Aspects of Caro's works have appeared at different times in many separate publications. The official edition of his complete works is Victor E. Caro and Antonio Gómez Restrepo, eds., *Obras completas de Don Miguel Antonio Caro*, 8 vols. (Bogotá, 1918-1945).

61. Guillermo Torres García, *Miguel Antonio Caro, su personalidad política* (Madrid, 1956), pp. 21-25. For the purposes of this study, Torres García's excellent biography, which emphasizes the political side of the career of the great Colombian humanist, proved especially useful.

62. Palacio, *Historia*, pp. 302-3.

63. Miguel Antonio Caro, "Alocución a los colombianos, 7 de agosto de 1892" in Caro, ed., *Obras completas*, VI, 55.

vanced his controversial views on the monetary system. In six years of operation, he argued, the regime of paper money had stimulated impressive economic growth in manufactures, mining, and agriculture. Exports and imports had risen, government revenues had increased, and commerce found itself in "the most advantageous situation." Caro then moved on to a theoretical defense of an elastic monetary system to meet the needs of an expanding economy. He refuted the Liberal thesis calling for free stipulation of other currencies in contracts. Such a measure would introduce anarchy into the nation's monetary system, and constitute de facto circumvention of the paper money regime established by law. Moreover, argued Caro, "free stipulation" favored a privileged few, such as import merchants: it was "Liberty extended to some at the expense of the rights of the greatest number." Free stipulation granted those who found themselves in privileged commercial positions the power, with the blessing of the state, "to impose onerous conditions on their debtors." Caro believed that behind the demand for free stipulation lay the desire to dismantle the entire regime of paper money that the Regeneration had constructed. Opponents of paper money proceeded from the false assumption that money must have intrinsic worth. That was an anachronistic, limiting belief.[64]

As Caro set forth his political and economic views, Liberals, possessed of a new optimism, were reorganizing their party for the reconquest of power. The first steps toward reorganization had been taken in 1891 under the initiative of Aquileo Parra, the merchant-politician from Santander who had defeated Núñez's presidential bid in 1875. In September, 1892, Liberal delegates from different parts of the country met in Bogotá and named Santiago Pérez director of the party and instructed him to found a paper supported by party funds to articulate Liberal grievances and foster Liberal organization to regain political power through peaceful means.[65]

Santiago Pérez, a stellar figure in the Radical Olympus, had served as president of Colombia and minister to Washington during the apogee of the Liberal hegemony. At the beginning of the Liberal revolt against Núñez in 1885 he moved his family to New York. There, along with his son, Santiago Pérez Triana, he founded a commercial house engaged in importing coffee and quinine. After an initial period of success, Pérez-Triana y Cía. encountered serious financial difficulties that ultimately forced it to dissolve. Santiago Pérez returned to Bogotá and taught school until he was called to head the Liberal party

64. Miguel Antonio Caro, "Mensaje al congreso nacional sobre regulación del sistema monetario, 13 de septiembre de 1892," in Caro, ed., *Obras completas*, VI, 70, 72-73, 74.
65. Delpar, "The Liberal Party," pp. 308, 319.

in 1892. In early 1893 he founded *El Relator* and began an intelligent, militant press campaign against the Regeneration.[66]

Pérez attacked every aspect of the Regeneration, but concentrated on its curtailment of civil liberties, its destruction of an independent judiciary, and most of all its fiscal policies. *El Relator* called for the restoration of property rights

> at present annulled by the fiscal monopolies, by the use of paper money as legal tender, by the prohibition on the stipulation of currency [in contracts], by the impediment placed on the use and extension of private credit, by the repudiation, in practice, of the foreign debt, and by the failure to carry out the terms of the law pertaining to the internal debt. . . .[67]

In May, 1893, Pérez published a ten-point program calling for freedom of the press, effective suffrage, abolition of the National Bank, an end to further emissions of paper money, and amortization of all paper money in circulation. He also denounced the government's reliance on fiscal monopolies and called for decentralization of government revenues to spur regional development. His proposals were applauded by other leaders, including long-time champions of liberal economic orthodoxy Salvador Camacho Roldán and Miguel Samper. The proposals also picked up impressive public support from dissident Conservatives. A manifesto published by Marceliano Vélez in June closely approximated the Liberal program.[68]

Pérez's press attacks and the bipartisan enthusiasm generated by his ten-point program alarmed Caro's government, and when a group of Liberal extremists were discovered in plans to revolt against the government, Caro used the opportunity to crush the Liberal opposition. Caro suspended *El Relator* and two other Liberal papers, confiscated Liberal party funds totaling more than 13,000 pesos, and exiled Pérez along with the Liberals involved in the plot.[69]

Although Liberal political organization was temporarily smashed by Caro's crackdown in August, 1893, Conservative opposition to Caro's policies continued to gain momentum. Through his influential newspaper, *El Correo Nacional,* Carlos Martínez Silva began to criticize the political and fiscal policies of Caro's government. Martínez Silva, who was to become one of the most influential leaders of the dissident

66. Rivadeneira, *Santiago Pérez,* pp. 130-34. A slightly different version of those events is given in Sergio Elías Ortiz, *Santiago Pérez Triana* (Bogotá, 1971).
67. Rivadeneira, *Santiago Pérez,* p. 159.
68. Delpar, "The Liberal Party," pp. 320-21.
69. *Ibid.,* 321-33.

Conservatives, had initially supported the Regeneration.[70] In 1889 he served as minister of the treasury and later that same year he represented Colombia at the Pan American Conference in Washington, D. C. By the early 1890's, however, his opposition to Regeneration economic and political policies was well defined. He supported the candidacy of Marceliano Vélez in 1891, and from 1894 until his death in 1903 he espoused a blend of liberal economic and political views and conservative social philosophy which had much in common with Liberal moderates like Miguel Samper. When he began to criticize Caro's fiscal policies, pro-government forces hit him in a particularly sensitive spot, accusing him of illegally authorizing secret emissions of paper money during his tenure as minister of the treasury in 1889.[71] As congress convened on July 20, 1894, the controversy over Martínez Silva's alleged "secret emissions" was just one aspect of the intense struggle between Caro's government and its critics which would dominate the stormy session.

As was his custom, Caro initiated the session with an impassioned, powerful defense of his political and fiscal policies in a long, closely reasoned message. Caro argued that the repressive measures taken against the Liberal party the year before were justified since the Liberal plot had been a "social threat without precedent" made more serious by the complicity of liberals in neighboring republics. The president needed the extraordinary powers provided by the constitution to insure public order. Although revolutionists had had little success to date, "it would be insanity ... to open the cage of the wild beasts. . . ." Stressing the power of journalists, he conceded that the special faculties granted the executive to regulate the press in the Constitution of 1886 (transitory article K) could be supplanted by a press law written by congress, as long as it conformed to the spirit of the Constitution.

Caro devoted his greatest attention, almost three-fourths of his speech, to a consideration of Regeneration finance. Making some concessions to the growing strength of his critics, who by then included a significant portion of the Conservative party, Caro modified some of

70. Martínez Silva was the son of a Santander liberal of distinguished ancestry and landed wealth who gravitated toward the Conservative party after 1850. The best single source on his life is Luis Martínez Delgado, *A propósito de Carlos Martínez Silva* (Bogotá, 1926).

71. An investigation was conducted by the congress of 1894 which found Martínez Silva guilty. Martínez Silva argued that he had acted in good faith, planning to retire part of the public debt with the secret emissions, but was removed from office before he could complete the operations. Otero Múñoz and Martínez Delgado, eds., *Obras completas del doctor Carlos Martínez Silva* (Bogotá, 1938), IX, 17-141, contains the commission's findings and Martínez Silva's defense. A brief, objective account of the issues involved is provided in Torres García, *Historia*, pp. 253-62.

his previous positions, especially with regard to paper money and the National Bank. Speaking first of the budget, Caro noted the long history of deficits, which dated from the period of Liberal hegemony. He argued against the previous Regeneration practice of balancing budgets with emissions of paper money. Emissions should be reserved, he contended, for financing "extraordinary and productive undertakings." The need for additional national revenues should be met with transfers of departmental revenues to the national government. On the question of new taxes, Caro argued that they should be uniform across the nation and should fall "on real wealth or on industries that stimulate vices" and as little as possible on "resources necessary for work or for subsistence." Although it was not clear what Caro meant by "real wealth," in a subsequent part of his speech he argued that since the depreciation of national paper money had the effect of establishing a bounty on exports, justice dictated an export tax on these favored products. On the issue of a property tax Caro equivocated, noting only that it was an imperfectly organized tax in some departments and rejected by others.

Turning his attention to the issue of the National Bank, Caro argued that the fate of the Bank was not necessarily tied to the regime of paper money. The Bank could be abolished, although he favored its continued existence and emphasized the historic importance of its establishment in Colombia when "dissociative ideas, individualistic liberalism" had grown such deep roots in Colombia that the power to issue money was considered an individual right, not a privilege of the state. Finally, Caro noted that paper money could be redeemed only through increased government revenues, and he disapproved of attempts to buy up the public debt outright or through the practice of secret emissions.[72]

The split in the Nationalist party widened during the next few months, exacerbated by stormy congressional sessions and polemics in the press. Critics attacked many aspects of Caro's government, but debate centered on the monetary system and the fiscal monopolies that Caro had established the year before. The congressional committee formed to investigate the secret emissions found that emissions had exceeded by over nine million pesos the limit of twelve million set by congress in 1887 and religiously upheld by Núñez. Congress proceeded to abolish the National Bank, replacing it with a section of the ministry of the treasury charged with the eventual amortization of paper money. Finally, new emissions, barring external or internal war,

72. Miguel Antonio Caro, "Mensaje dirigido al congreso nacional en la apertura de las sesiones ordinarias de 1894, 20 de julio de 1894," in Caro, ed., *Obras*, VI, 109, 110, 119, 122, 139.

were absolutely prohibited.[73] The debate over the fiscal monopolies was equally explosive. In 1893 Caro's government had established a government monopoly on the manufacture and sale of tobacco, although tobacco production and export remained free. As an additional fiscal resource in some departments, monopolies on the production and sale of aguardiente were also instituted with the approval and encouragement of the Caro government. Opposition to the fiscal monopolies among Liberals and dissident Conservatives was heated, and Núñez himself opposed the tobacco monopoly publicly several times in *El Porvenir* of Cartagena.[74] So threatening did the situation become that Núñez, fearing the destruction of the Nationalist party and the Regeneration itself, resolved to journey to Bogotá. On September 10, 1894, in the midst of his political preoccupations and travel preparations, Rafael Núñez suffered a severe stroke. Eight days later, the remarkable man who had guided the transformation of Colombian institutions known as the Regeneration was dead.

The vacuum created by the death of Núñez and the hostility between the two factions of Conservatives strengthened groups within the Liberal party favoring armed struggle as the only avenue to political power. The bulk of the party probably favored civil war as early as 1892, although in that year they had been outmaneuvered by the peace faction with the selection of Santiago Pérez as director of the party.[75] But with the exile of Pérez, and the destruction of the national Liberal party structure by Caro in mid-1893, the war faction, really a loosely knit coalition of regional leaders, began preparations for revolt.

Primary organizers of the revolt were the wealthy Cundinamarcan coffee grower, Eustacio de la Torre Narváez, and a law professor and newspaper editor from Santander, Juan Félix de León.[76] According to their plan, defecting military units in Bogotá would arm the Liberal rank and file in the city while a small band of Liberals would take the presidential palace and imprison Vice-president Caro. The revolt would be seconded by *pronunciamientos* in several departments. Just as had happened in mid-1893, Caro's government learned of the Lib-

73. Jorge Franco Holguín, *Evolución de las instituciones financieras en Colombia* (México, 1966), pp. 31-32.

74. Palacio, *Historia,* pp. 319-25.

75. Rodriguez Piñeres, *Diez años de política liberal, 1892-1902* (Bogotá, 1945), pp. 8-11.

76. De la Torre, one of the wealthiest men in the Liberal party, owned large coffee haciendas in Viotá, Cundinamarca. Luis de Greiff, *Semblanzas y comentarios* (Bogotá, 1942), p. 16. From the scant biographical information available in Ospina, comp., *Diccionario,* II, 497-98, it is clear that de León had strong ties with Santander. For a time he edited the Cúcuta paper *La Empresa* and during the period of Liberal hegemony he occupied high-level bureaucratic posts in the department.

eral plan in advance and moved swiftly to defuse the revolt. As Liberal preparations neared completion, Caro's police arrested a number of armed conspirators in Bogotá and imprisoned de la Torre and other leaders. Nevertheless, Liberals from Bogotá and western Cundinamarca went ahead with the revolt, issuing their *pronunciamiento* on January 23, 1895, in Facatativá, an important town situated on the Honda road at the western rim of the Sabana de Bogotá. The revolt, led in Cundinamarca by Siervo Sarmiento, Rafael Uribe Uribe, and Nemesio Camacho, was seconded in Santander by José María Ruiz, in Boyacá by Pedro María Pinzón, and in Tolima by Rafael Camacho.[77]

The campaign was short. Within two months, government armies led by Rafael Reyes, Manuel Casabianca, Próspero Pinzón, and others defeated the Liberal forces and re-established order. Caro's preventive measures, excellent choice of military commanders, and ability to emit money to finance the war accounted for the effectiveness of the government response. At the same time the Liberal effort was hindered by division within its own ranks. Leading Liberal political leaders like Aquileo Parra remained largely outside the planning of the revolt, and some of the party's most prestigious military as well as civilian leaders opposed it.[78] Moreover, despite the hopes and predictions of many Liberals, the dissident Conservatives did not support them in the field. Conservative dissidents did, however, seek to form an alliance with a group of Liberal leaders who had opposed the revolt. During the early days of the fighting this bipartisan group made an unsuccessful attempt to end the war through a negotiated settlement based on constitutional and policy reforms. This historical antecedent to similar attempts by the same groups to prevent and later settle the War of the Thousand Days through negotiated reforms failed due to the relative lack of influence of these upper-class groups on the rank and file of their respective parties.[79]

The growth of the coffee industry after 1886 revived groups tied to the export-import economy, strengthening the Liberal party materi-

77. Rodríguez Piñeres, *Diez años*, pp. 25-27; Palacio, "Historia," *El Tiempo*, October 13, 1941.

78. Military men against the revolt included Sergio Camargo and ultimately Santos Acosta, although Acosta had originally supported the movement. Rodríguez Piñeres, *Diez años*, pp. 25-26.

79. The dissident Conservatives included Carlos Martínez Silva and his brother Luis, Jorge Roa, Francisco A. Gutiérrez, Jaime Córdoba, and Marcelino Posada. The Liberal peace faction was composed of Parra, Diego Mendoza, José Camacho Carrizosa, Carlos Arturo Torres, and Laureano García Ortiz. Luis Martínez Delgado, *A propósito*, pp. 252-55, gives an account of this frustrated alliance and attributes its failure to the difficulty of coming to a satisfactory agreement over the Church issue. Chapters IV and V analyze the ineffectiveness of these same groups in preventing and ending the War of the Thousand Days.

ally and philosophically and encouraging Conservatives with economic and ideological ties abroad to abandon the Nationalist fold. At the same time, however, the coffee boom fortified the Regeneration itself. Nationalist governments claimed credit for the economic upsurge, met their commitments, and enjoyed the increased customs revenues that enabled them to support a numerous bureaucracy and equip a large standing army.[80] Although plagued by internal dissent during the first decade of its existence, the Regeneration was never seriously challenged. Even the Revolution of 1895 was easily handled by the strong government headed by Miguel Antonio Caro. Beginning in 1896, however, the tide turned against the Regeneration. Coffee prices began to fall in that year and two years later the drop had seriously affected Colombia's foreign exchange earnings and government customs revenues. Groups tied to the export economy blamed the government for the economic slump and pursued every peaceful means at their disposal to change Regeneration fiscal and political policies.

80. Between 1888 and 1894 the army numbered some six thousand men. By 1896, according to official statistics, ten thousand men were under arms, the maximum number permitted by law. Some observers placed the real figure much higher. The legal limit was officially maintained until 1899 when the government's economy drive reduced the army by a thousand men.

Chapter III

The Failure of Reform, 1896-1898

The political history of the period 1896-1898 is the story of the promise and ultimate failure of the efforts of dissident Conservatives and leaders of the Liberal party to reform the Regeneration through legislative and electoral means. The failure of reform must be understood not only in political terms but in the context of the magnitude of the ideological and economic differences separating the bipartisan reformers from the governing Nationalists. Review of the reformers' efforts to rescind the coffee export tax imposed by Caro during the 1895 revolt, win the presidential election of 1897, and push their reformist program through the congress in 1898 reveals that by the end of the century these upper-class factions were deeply divided along an axis of ties, or lack of them, to the evolving capitalist system of the North Atlantic. Import-export interests, voicing their demands through the Liberal and Historical Conservative parties, found their inspiration in North Atlantic political liberalism and laissez-faire economics. Involved in international trade and domestic finance they sought a return to the gold standard, lower tariffs, abolition of government monopolies and export taxes, and proper attention to the foreign debt. Such measures, they argued, would attract the foreign and domestic capital necessary to expand the economy and build vital railroads to link the Colombian hinterland with the world of commerce.

Nationalists, on the other hand, were not tied to the export-import economy and based their policies on principles derived from conservative Spanish and Catholic thought. Nationalists represented bureaucratic, ecclesiastical, and apparently (although the evidence is largely circumstantial) traditional agricultural interests who benefited from the statist economic policies and centralist, pro-Catholic political policies of the Regeneration governments. Traditional agricultural interests were not threatened and may have been aided by the regime of paper money.[1] Export taxes, fiscal monopolies, and increased tariff

1. A slowly depreciating paper currency would have posed no threat to the interests of traditional agriculturalists who produced for the domestic market and whose capital was largely invested in real estate. The opportunity to pay off debts in depreciated currency would have meant great relief to debtors whose earnings from agriculture did not accrue in the form of gold-based currencies.

rates produced much-needed government revenue in ways consistent with conservative economic philosophy and fiscal practice but did not directly threaten the interests of bureaucrats and traditional agriculturalists. Nationalist railroad policy (which achieved its limited success with domestic, not foreign entrepreneurs) failed to link the interior with the sea, but resulted in effective service for that stronghold of traditional agriculture and Nationalist political support, the Sabana de Bogotá.[2]

Divided from their Historical Conservative and Liberal critics by fundamental political, ideological, and economic interests, Nationalists steadfastly refused to compromise their political and economic policies. But as the coffee crisis deepened, government fiscal resources dwindled, and Nationalist philosophy and programs came under telling attack. Threatened ideologically and weakened physically, Nationalists found it harder to control the political situation. Although they managed to maintain their hold on government until the end of the century, they were forced to resort to increasingly arbitrary and desperate maneuvers. By the end of 1898 the Regeneration stood at the brink of political and fiscal disaster while the nation faced an appalling economic crisis.

In the struggle between the Regeneration and its critics during the last years of the century, the coffee export tax decreed by Caro during the Revolution of 1895 assumed primary importance. The tax was of real and symbolic concern to both the government and its critics: to Liberals and free traders, the tax represented a flagrant violation of laissez-faire economic principles; to Caro's Nationalist government, it represented legitimate government intervention in the economy in order to tax a privileged minority for the good of the society as a whole. The fall in world coffee prices after 1896 contributed to the sense of urgency with which both sides pursued the defense of their interests. The coffee price decline made elimination of the export tax vital to the interests of growers and exporters concerned over profits and Colombia's ability to compete in the world market. At the same time, reduced customs revenues triggered by the drop in trade caused the Nationalist government to search for new sources of revenue while decidedly opposing any plan to eliminate established sources of income. The coffee export tax was hotly debated in the congress of 1896 and continued to occupy a prominent place in the debate between the Regeneration and its critics until 1898. Given its impor-

2. By the end of the century, primarily as a result of construction accomplished by Colombian capitalists during the Regeneration, railroads fanned out from Bogotá to the rim of the Sabana in three directions: to Soacha, some 18 kilometers to the south; to Facatativá, about 40 kilometers to the west; and to Zipaquirá, some 48 kilometers to the north. See the map of Cundinamarca, Chapter VII.

tance to both sides, the debate over the tax provides extraordinary insight into the composition, goals, and attitudes of the two political forces confronting each other during the last years of the Regeneration.

Champion of the coffee interests in the congressional debates of 1896 was Rafael Uribe Uribe, the sole Liberal representative in the congress. Founder of an extensive coffee farm in Antioquia, administrator of vast coffee estates in Cundinamarca, lobbyist for coffee interests in 1894, Uribe Uribe was the first to perceive and articulate the impending crisis in the coffee industry and to use the issue of the coffee export tax to mount a telling campaign against the personages and policies of the Regeneration.[3]

It was not hard for Uribe Uribe to identify the unpopular export tax with the personality of Miguel Antonio Caro and the philosophy and policies of the Nationalist government. Caro had never been friendly to the coffee industry, an attitude revealed in a minor but significant incident that took place soon after his inauguration in 1892. In a gesture widely applauded in the press as indicative of a personal concern for the common people, Caro granted an interview to a young bootblack who complained of the fate of many of his companions who had been forcibly recruited to work on the coffee plantations of Cundinamarca. Caro investigated the charge and reportedly issued orders to put an end to the practice.[4] He had also called for a tax on "favored exports" in his speech to the opening session of congress in 1894, and pro-Caro forces introduced such a bill later in the session. The export tax had passed in first debate when coffee interests submitted the memorial drafted by Uribe Uribe protesting the measure.[5] The forces opposing the tax were successful in tabling the bill in that session, but during the Revolution of 1895 Caro seized the opportunity afforded him by his exercise of extraordinary powers to establish the export tax by decree. Decree No. 75 of March 22, 1895, established a tax on cleaned coffee for export of 1.60 pesos per 50 kilograms, and on uncleaned coffee (beans still covered by their parchment-like shell) of 1.20 pesos per 50 kilograms. In a blow to importers, the decree also raised tariffs by 15 per cent.[6]

Uribe Uribe's speeches in congress in 1896 were designed to refute

3. Uribe Uribe's connections with the coffee industry and other aspects of his career are described in detail in Chapter IV. On the day the legislative session of 1896 opened, Uribe Uribe wrote to a group of men with special interests in the coffee industry proposing to make a tour of the coffee-producing regions of Latin America in search of solutions to the two major problems plaguing the industry, labor and prices. Rafael Uribe Uribe to Eustacio de la Torre Nz., *et al.*, Bogotá, July 20, 1896. Uribe, Box 6, ACH.

4. Palacio, *Historia*, p. 108.

5. Rafael Uribe Uribe, *Discursos parlamentarios* (Bogotá, 1897), pp. 235-41.

6. Beyer, "Coffee Industry," p. 126.

the Caro administration's justification of the export tax. That justification was advanced by Caro's minister of finance, Ruperto Ferreira, and his minister of foreign relations, Jorge Holguín. Ferreira argued that the tax was equitable since coffee growing was extremely profitable. Uribe Uribe responded that to tax an industry because it was successful was unjust and regressive. Government should not punish with taxation those men whose vision, entrepreneurship, and courage had "rescued the country from ruin by furnishing it with its only valuable export product." At any rate, Uribe Uribe contended, the debate concerning the fairness of the tax was overshadowed by a much more vital issue. According to his analysis, trends at work within the world coffee economy would soon jeopardize the very existence of the coffee industry in Colombia. Uribe Uribe outlined the sharp rise in world demand and prices after 1885 that triggered the massive expansion of coffee production in tropical areas throughout the world. By 1894, he argued, world supply had begun to meet demand, but production continued to rise as coffee trees planted in previous years came into production. As a result world supply was outpacing demand and Uribe Uribe predicted the imminent fall of world prices to levels low enough to destroy the most inefficient producers.

Jorge Holguín's more sophisticated argument was harder to refute. Holguín, like Caro before him, contended that the Regeneration had stimulated the coffee industry, particularly through the system of paper money, which acted like an export bounty. Uribe Uribe's first response to that point was weak. Avoiding the issue that Colombia was a high-cost coffee producing nation, Uribe Uribe contended that if it were true that paper money caused the coffee boom in Colombia, how would Holguín explain the fact that coffee production had soared in nations not enjoying the alleged advantages of paper money. In fact, Uribe Uribe argued, paper money discouraged saving and disrupted normal, healthy economic activities. According to him, Holguín would have had to prove metallic currency would have doomed the coffee industry in Colombia. Uribe Uribe met with more success in attacking the contention of Holguín from a different angle, attempting to show that Regeneration governments had actually contributed to the high transportation and production costs that endangered the Colombian industry's very existence in the worldwide competition to come. River freight rates had risen as a result of governmental suppression of river transport competition. Worse, the Regeneration had demonstrated a "fundamental incapacity" to develop the railroad network. A classic example of the government's abominable maintenance of mule trails could be found in Viotá, one of the primary coffee-producing areas in the nation. The trail from Viotá to La Mesa was "a hellish neckbreaker, more than impassable, 'unflyable' [impajaretable]."

Many factors helped to account for high Colombian coffee production costs, all of which, according to Uribe Uribe, were exacerbated by unfriendly government policies. The scarcity and high cost of labor, major factors in production costs, were intensified by the government in three ways. A standing army of eight thousand men extracted scarce labor from the pool of able-bodied men. Through its onerous policies of military recruitment and heavy ecclesiastical contributions, the government encouraged the emigration of thousands of Colombians from Santander and Boyacá to Venezuela. Finally, according to Uribe Uribe, government officials frequently impeded the efforts of coffee growers to recruit [enganchar] extra labor during harvest time, or else engaged in the military recruitment of groups of contracted laborers en route to the coffee plantations. Most important, Uribe Uribe argued, the government damaged the vitality of the coffee industry through the air of insecurity, the constant threat of war, fostered by the Regeneration's policies of repression of civil liberties and political exclusivism. As a result credit operations were limited, expansion curtailed, and new endeavors put off.

Jorge Holguín had also argued that the coffee export tax was a tax on the rich: "today coffee producers comprise an aristocracy that lives in the midst of luxury, constantly traveling around Europe." Uribe Uribe's indignant response was that corrupt public officials and despoilers of the treasury were more frequent travelers to Europe and that "if coffee growers are in the habit of going, not for pleasure but on business, they do it with money honorably earned in arduous labor, not with the proceeds from extortion and graft." Besides, Uribe Uribe added, small producers, located primarily in Santander, Antioquia, and Tolima, produced about two-thirds of the coffee exported annually, and it was on their shoulders that the burden of the tax came to rest.

Fundamental to Uribe Uribe's position was his belief that the conflict between the Regeneration and its critics was a confrontation between two social types. On the one hand were the noble coffee farmers (who included Liberals and Conservatives): vigorous, intelligent, virtuous, hardworking men who earned their living honorably and contributed to the progress of the nation by braving inhospitable climates to open up new lands to export agriculture. On the other hand were the parasitic absentee gentlemen farmers of the cold country who had inherited their wealth, and the weak, immoral urban types who trafficked in influence, fed on intrigue in the capital, supported their families through dishonorable transactions, and contributed to the backwardness of the nation. The only remedy for Colombia's ills, warned Uribe Uribe, was a government composed of men of the first social type.[7]

For all of Uribe Uribe's efforts, the congress of 1896, still controlled by a Nationalist majority, did not abolish the coffee export tax, but it did reduce the tax to one-third of the original rate and empowered the chief executive to lower or eliminate the tax if he determined that the demand for coffee had suffered a great decline.[8] Despite the decline in prices after 1896, however, Caro made no move to eliminate the tax. On June 30, 1897, all the major coffee exporting firms submitted a petition to Caro that emphasized the alarming drop in international coffee prices and requested suspension of the coffee export tax. If the tax were not eliminated, the exporters warned, a grave commercial crisis could result leading to a decline in the value of paper money "and consequently, difficulties in the Government, which very well could bring with them, in a country excited by political passion, war itself, which would be the complement of all our maladies and misfortunes."[9] Caro bowed to the pressure and temporarily suspended the tax in his decree No. 301 of July 13, 1897.[10] The suspension was only tentative, however, and the threat of the tax still existed. It was only late in 1898 under a new chief executive and a lower house dominated by dissident Conservatives hostile to the previous policies of Caro and the Nationalists that the coffee tax established by Caro during the Revolution of 1895 was finally abolished.[11]

The success of the coffee interests in reducing and eventually abolishing the coffee export tax was not only the result of Uribe Uribe's campaign and the pressure exerted on the Caro regime by exporters. More directly it was the consequence of the political gains made by the dissident Conservatives between 1896 and 1898. In fact the drive to eliminate the coffee tax was but one aspect of a multi-pronged attack against Regeneration political and economic policies undertaken by the dissident Conservatives and their Liberal allies

7. Uribe Uribe, *Discursos*, pp. 233-34, 231-32, 277, 227, 248-49. To some extent Uribe Uribe's two Nationalist contenders in this congressional debate, Jorge Holguín and Ruperto Ferreira, resembled the negative stereotypes drawn by Uribe Uribe. Jorge Holguín inherited and married into considerable landed wealth and engaged in traditional agriculture. Palacio, "Historia," *El Tiempo*, March 9, 1941; Uribe Uribe, *Discursos*, p. 233. Ruperto Ferreira, a man of modest fortune, was a distinguished engineer, teacher and bureaucrat. Ospina, *Diccionario*, I, 793-94.

8. Law 37 of October 14, 1896. The delegation of the discretionary power to the executive represented a victory for Uribe Uribe's position that world price would fall considerably. For an indication of the dissident Conservative opposition to the coffee export tax, see Martínez Delgado, *Revistas*, II, 62-63, 72-73.

9. *Diario Oficial*, No. 10, 395.

10. *Ibid.*

11. Law 9 of September 21, 1898, *Anales de la Cámara de Representantes*, February 23, 1899.

after 1896. Representing economic and regional interests distinct from those represented by the Nationalists, occupying positions within the government bureaucracy and the military, and competing for the same Conservative constituency as the Nationalists, the dissident Conservatives constituted an especially powerful and insidious threat to the Regeneration.

The dissident Conservatives formally dissociated themselves from the Nationalists in January, 1896, with the publication of a manifesto entitled the "Motives of Dissidence."[12] Drafted by Carlos Martínez Silva, signed by twenty-one prominent Conservatives (all former collaborators in the Regeneration), and subsequently endorsed by Marceliano Vélez, the document was at once an indictment of virtually every aspect of the Regeneration and a declaration of the principles of the "historical" Conservative party. The dissidents acknowledged two great achievements of the Regeneration: the establishment of national unity and the settlement of the Church issue. But, they went on to argue, the Constitution of 1886 and the political and economic policies of subsequent government had been an exaggerated reaction to the extreme federalism and weakness of the national governments under the Constitution of 1863. The Regeneration had become authoritarian, systematically repressing dissent through arbitrary press decrees and excluding the Liberal party from government through electoral abuses and the unrestrained use of the extraordinary faculties granted the executive.

According to the dissident Conservatives the fiscal policies of the Regeneration had been disastrous. Tariff rates were too high and had retarded agricultural growth. Administration of the customs houses was inefficient and management of the salt monopoly was corrupt. Instead of improving the administration of existing taxes, the Regeneration had erected new, unsuccessful ones like the tobacco monopoly. The Regeneration had signed many railroad contracts, but they were carelessly written, and the projects suffered from the lack of an overall plan. The result had been dispersion of energies, piecemeal construction, and costly indemnifications paid by government. The Regeneration had made no attempt to arrange for payment on the foreign debt; it had reneged on the arrangement to settle the internal debt. Uncritical reliance on emissions of paper money to balance every deficit had led to the impossibility of returning a "normal and valid" monetary system. No attempt had been made to begin amortization. The Regeneration, the dissident Conservatives concluded, had the wrong priorities for expenditures. It had failed to develop the

12. The complete text is reproduced in Martínez Delgado, *A propósito*, pp. 157-78.

nation's educational system, while uselessly overspending on the military.[13]

The growing political strength of the Conservative dissidents and the magnitude of the threat perceived by Nationalists as they contemplated the possibility of Historical Conservatives' acquiring positions of power within the government was strikingly demonstrated in March, 1896. On March 12 Caro delegated power to his designate, Guillermo Quintero Calderón and retired to the village of Sopó near the capital.[14] Quintero proceeded to name his cabinet, which included Nationalists loyal to Caro, such as Minister of War Pedro Antonio Molina. But Quintero, a former governor of Santander and a man sympathetic to the Historical Conservatives, also named a supporter of Marceliano Vélez, Abrahám Moreno of Antioquia, to the powerful political post of minister of government, and a man opposed to the fiscal policies of the Caro regime, Francisco Groot, as minister of the treasury.[15]

Caro's response was immediate and severe. On March 15 he wrote to José Manuel Marroquín decrying Quintero's actions.

> The harmony of Christian elements is not obtained by the naming of Protestant cardinals.
>
> .   .   .   .
>
> These men can come into the government when they have a majority to win elections or the strength to win battles; not before.[16]

On March 17, after only five days, Caro resumed power and named an entirely new cabinet that reflected a hardening line against the Liberal and Conservative dissidents. After Quintero Calderón's ill-fated "Administración de los cinco días," the struggle between Regéneration forces and the Historical Conservative opposition revolved around the selection of Conservative candidates for the presidential election of December, 1897.

Like no other political event of the period, the presidential campaign of 1897 illustrates the extent of the ideological and programmatic

13. The phrases quoted are from *ibid.*, pp. 173, 174.

14. One factor in Caro's decision may have been the desire to maintain his eligibility for re-election to the presidency for the period 1898-1904.

15. One of the first large-scale coffee growers in Cundinamarca, Groot was also an important Bogotá merchant, publisher of the *Revista Mercantil*, commission agent, and small factory owner. A supporter of Núñez, Groot early became dissatisfied with the policies of Caro and after 1896 became a major leader of the Historical Conservative faction. Francisco Groot, *Datos históricos contenidos en las réplicas del Senador Groot al Senador Caro* (Bogotá, 1904), p. 76; Ospina, *Diccionario*, II, 243; Julio H. Palacio, "Historia," *El Tiempo*, January 11, 1942.

16. Caro, ed., *Obras completas*, VI, 171-72.

differences dividing Colombian upper-class factions by the end of the nineteenth century. Whether one looks at the public pronouncements or the private correspondence of party leaders, analyzes official party platforms, or probes the sociology of these political factions, one is struck by the divergence of upper-class ideological and economic interests. Moreover, despite the potential for opportunistic political maneuverings during the campaign and the inevitable compromises with political realities, these political factions consistently pursued their interests. Although for political reasons both the Nationalists and Historical Conservatives had to abandon their first choice for president, each faction's initial candidate as well as its final nominee were men whose career patterns and public statements admirably qualified them to represent their faction's interests.

Central to the politics of the election was Rafael Reyes, who returned to Colombia from his post as minister to France for the conclusion of the campaign. Reyes was a popular figure, a man of action who had worked in agriculture and commerce, explored the Colombian jungle, and become the hero of the Conservatives during the short-lived Revolution of 1895.[17] Reyes had a foot in each Conservative camp: a proven Nationalist in the past, he was reported to favor reform of the Regeneration in the future. Aware of Reyes's potential in the opposition, some Nationalists began to boost his candidacy for president in mid-1896. Other Nationalists, loyal to Miguel Antonio Caro, and aware of Reyes's demonstrated lack of commitment to Regeneration institutions and policies (and his rumored flirtation with the Historical Conservatives), declared in favor of Caro for a second presidential term.[18] In the meantime Historical Conservatives took advantage of the split in Nationalist ranks to woo Reyes into an unofficial candidacy on their ticket. The Historical Conservatives wanted to benefit from Reyes's popularity, but resolved to name him as their official candidate only if they could commit him to their reform platform.

In August, 1897, Historical Conservatives prepared a statement of principles to serve as a foundation for a union of Conservative elements against the Nationalist regime. Composed of nineteen points and termed a faithful translation of the "main currents of thought within the party" by a newly formed Conservative directorate, the

17. Reyes is given more detailed biographical treatment in Chapter VII. Here it is interesting to note that Reyes had participated in the quinine boom and by 1896 was tentatively planting coffee in company with his nephew Carlos Calderón, perhaps on his hacienda "Andorra" near Tocaima in southwestern Cundinamarca. Rafael Reyes to Carlos Calderón, Paris, October 25, 1896, Personal Papers of Carlos Calderón, Academia Colombiana de Historia (hereafter cited as Calderón, ACH).

18. Nationalist circular dated February 20, 1897, reprinted in Martínez Delgado, *Revistas*, II, 138.

"Bases," as they were called, summed up the Historical Conservative critique of the Regeneration. Several of the points sought to limit executive power, restore civil liberties, strengthen the separate powers of congress and the courts, and establish an electoral system absolutely free of official interference. The other points outlined fiscal, economic, and educational reforms demanded by the Historical Conservative opposition. These called for fiscal decentralization, increased congressional fiscalization of government expenditures, a ban on export taxes, elimination of national fiscal monopolies, a reduction of tariff rates, and an

> absolute ban on the issuance of paper legal tender, and the adoption of effective measures designed to retire, as soon as possible, and gradually, paper money currently in circulation, in order to return to metallic specie and to the spontaneous workings of private credit.

A final point advocated increased development of public education.[19]

As soon as Reyes arrived in Colombia, the Historicals began to pressure him to approve the substance of the "Bases." Reyes was reluctant to identify himself completely with either of the two Conservative factions. His assessment of the political situation had been carefully expressed in a "strictly confidential" letter written to his nephew in October, 1896, in which he noted the serious decomposition of all three Colombian parties and contended that the success of any president depended upon his attracting the support of "all men of goodwill who represent family, wealth, and honor." At the same time Reyes stated his belief that success in the presidency could be achieved only through commitment to the material progress of the nation, which he defined as the development of communications, agriculture, manufacturing, and mining. Reyes aspired to run compromised by no one,[20] but only three days after his arrival in Bogotá, he was pressured to issue a statement in accordance with the "Bases" of the Historical Conservatives. In that declaration he paid tribute to the positive aspects of the Regeneration, but stressed the need for legislative reform. He called for repeal of the grant of extraordinary powers to the executive, reform of the press law, and measures to assure pure elections that would permit the peaceful rotation of political parties in power.

19. The "Bases" were published in Carlos Martínez Silva, "Revista política de agosto 31, 1897."

20. Rafael Reyes to Carlos Calderón, Paris, October 25, 1896, Personal Papers of Carlos Calderón, Academia Colombiana de Historia (hereafter cited as Calderón, ACH). Unable to meet these conditions in 1897, Reyes won the presidency after the War of the Thousand Days with bipartisan support and proceeded to implement his political and economic policies with a relatively free hand. See Chapters VIII and IX.

Reyes placed great emphasis on the need for fiscal and economic reforms in his statement.

> Believing, as I do, that the greatest part of the permanent difficulties that we have are of economic and fiscal origin, more than of a political nature, I will devote preferential attention to the organization and administration of public finance, so that with order, honesty, and economy, and with severe and effective fiscalization, we can establish domestic and international credit on a solid basis, develop [the economy] . . . and return . . . to the gold monetary system to which all civilized nations aspire.[21]

Satisfied, the Conservative Directorate adopted the ticket Rafael Reyes for president, Guillermo Quintero Calderón for vice-president.

Before Reyes's arrival in Bogotá, the Nationalists had finally decided on their ticket. Despite some great drawbacks, the combination of Manuel Antonio Sanclemente for president, José Manuel Marroquín for vice-president was very cleverly chosen. Critics immediately emphasized the immoderate age of the Nationalist candidates and one pundit described their choice as an example of "political paleontology."[22] Sanclemente, a native of Buga, Cauca, was eighty-three years old in 1897. Given his age and poor health (critics said he was senile), it was generally assumed that Sanclemente would not exercise power. As a result, the nominee for vice-president was extremely important. A septuagenarian descended from an illustrious land-holding family of the Sabana de Bogotá, Marroquín was best known as a teacher, costumbrista novelist, and gentleman farmer. Like Miguel Antonio Caro, this deeply religious "prototype of the old Castilian hidalgo" had never traveled out of the Colombian interior.[23] While there were those who contended that Marroquín would not serve either, due to his age and disinclination toward politics, and that Caro planned to have himself elected designate in order to exercise executive power for an additional six-year period, the choice of the two men may have involved nothing more than a careful Nationalist appeal to a fractured Conservative constituency. As an opposition paper pointed out, the age, moderation, and lack of recent involvement in politics of both

21. Martínez Delgado, *Revistas*, II, 245-46.
22. *El Guasca* (Bogotá), October 23, 1895.
23. The quotation is from Palacio, "Historia," *El Tiempo*, June 7, 1942. Marroquín never saw the sea and was reported to have said that he desired " 'si Dios le daba vida, salud y licencia para ello, morir sin conocer el mar. . . .' " Quoted in José Joaquín Casas, *Semblanzas (Diego Fallón y José Manual Marroquín)* (Bogotá, 1936), p. 136. The life and character of Marroquín is treated more fully in Chapter VI. The best source for biographical data on Marroquín is José Manual Marroquín Osorio, *Don José Manuel Marroquín íntimo* (Bogotá, 1915). See also the sketch of the man in Luis Martínez Delgado, *Historia de un cambio de gobierno* (Bogotá, 1958), pp. 245-53.

candidates made the Liberals less hostile to them. These qualities, and the fact that both men were "solid Conservatives," would help to attract the Conservatives. The name of Sanclemente would secure the important department of Cauca, while Marroquín would attract the clergy.

At first glance, the Nationalists' concern with clerical opposition to their ticket seems curious indeed. The Regeneration had favored the Church in numerous ways. Besides the many advantages granted the Church by the Constitution of 1886, Núñez settled long-standing differences between the Holy See and the Colombian government by negotiating a concordat that was signed December 31, 1887. That formal agreement settled the question of compensation due the Church as the result of the Liberal disamortization of Church properties in 1861. According to the terms of the document, which was ratified February 27, 1888, the Colombian government agreed to pay the Colombian Church an annual subvention. In addition, the Concordat provided for the juridical personality of the Church, declared it independent from civil power, and gave it wide control over education. By terms of a special convention the Concordat was slightly modified in 1892. According to that agreement, ecclesiastics involved in criminal cases would be tried in civil courts, although they would be guaranteed numerous privileges in those trials and granted special considerations in cases of conviction. In another clause, ecclesiastical authorities were given custody of records of vital statistics.[24] Besides these legal manifestations of a new era of cooperation and good feeling between Church and State under the Regeneration governments, the tangible results of warm Church-state relations were everywhere evident. The Jesuits returned to Colombia in 1886 and took charge of the most important teaching establishment in the nation, the Colegio de San Bartolomé. Many schools run by religious communities received subventions from the government.[25] Regeneration governments also continually passed laws granting churches subventions or special import privileges.[26]

Nevertheless, Caro had incurred the opposition of some Church officials by his attitude toward a proposed constitutional amendment

24. José Joaquín Guerra's published doctoral thesis, *Estudio sobre los concordatos celebrados entre Su Santidad León XIII y el Gobierno de Colombia en los años 1887 y 1892* (Bogotá, 1895) provides a discussion of individual articles in the two agreements.

25. For a list of these subventions see Lorenzo Marroquín, *Las cosas en su punto. Ojeada sobre la situación de la iglesia en Colombia* (Bogotá, 1898), pp. 93-94. Marroquín's book, written in response to clerical opposition to Nationalists during the campaign in 1897, is a catalogue of benefits accorded the Church by the Regeneration, and particularly, by Miguel Antonio Caro.

26. A list of all laws aiding the Church under twelve years of Regeneration governments, 1886-1898, is provided in *ibid*, pp. 95-100.

that would have repealed Article Fifty-four of the Constitution of 1886. That article circumscribed the political rights of priests, denying them the right to hold all public political offices except those involved in education and charity. Rafael Reyes introduced and championed the proposed constitutional amendment in the Senate in 1894. Caro was finally forced to take a public stand against the amendment to the constitution he himself had largely written.[27] The issue was eventually dropped, but clerical sympathy for Reyes, and for Historical Conservatives in general, continued to influence Colombian politics.[28]

By mid-November, 1897, jockeying between the Nationalists and Historical Conservatives had reached an impasse. While Nationalists controlled the army, the bureaucracy, and the electoral machinery, Historical Conservatives enjoyed the considerable advantages of a popular candidate and the support of part of the clergy. In a desperate attempt at compromise in order to avoid an electoral battle that might fatally weaken both Conservative factions, Conservative leaders of different tendencies met in Bogotá on November 15.[29] Conspicuously absent from the meeting was Marco Fidel Suárez, Director of the Nationalist party and Caro's most loyal supporter.[30] By ignoring the

27. Miguel Antonio Caro, "Mensaje sobre el proyecto de acto reformatorio del artículo 54 de la constitución, 31 de agosto 1894" in Caro, ed., *Obras*, VI, 146-60.

28. Caro's decision to appoint a priest as minister of public instruction in March, 1896, reflected his concern over clerical opposition. In a telegram addressed to Reyes in Paris dated Bogotá, June 11, 1897, Caro accused the Historical Conservatives of abusing Reyes's name to incite the clergy and to promote "fanaticism, demagogy, and revolution." Calderón, ACH.

29. A draft of the minutes of this meeting, signed by Manuel Casabianca and Carlos Calderón, president and secretary respectively of the emergency junta, exists in Calderón, ACH.

30. Born out of wedlock to a washerwoman in Hatoviejo, Antioquia, in 1855, Suárez enjoyed a position of the highest social prestige by middle age. Unlike that of many other socially mobile Colombians of the period, Suárez's mobility owed nothing to success in private commercial or business affairs. Rather, his mobility resulted from his remarkable intellectual and academic achievements. Thanks to the interest of his parish priest, Suárez received his early instruction and was able to martriculate in the newly established Seminario de Medellín in 1869. He chose not to be ordained in 1877 and after two grim years clerking in a notary public and teaching, he managed to journey to Bogotá, where his intellectual capabilities soon catapulted him into the highest literary and academic circles. (The achievement most responsible for his phenomenal success was the winning of an essay contest sponsored by the Colombian Academy of Language on the occasion of the centennial of the birth of Andrés Bello in 1891.) In 1883 he went to work for Miguel Antonio Caro, who had been named Director of the National Library. Once the Nationalist party had established its hegemony of politics, Suárez, who depended all his life on bureaucratic salaries, began to fill high public posts, rising to minister of foreign relations in 1891. In 1895 he married into a Bogotá family of the highest social standing. Like Caro, Suárez was totally committed to the Regeneration and beginning in 1896 he defended Nationalist policies in the congress as a representative from Antioquia. The best biography of Suárez is Jorge Sánchez Camacho, *Marco Fidel Suárez, biografía* (Bucaramanga, 1955); another one is Bernardo Blair Gutiérrez, *Don Marco Fidel Suárez, su vida y su obra* (Medellín, 1955).

meeting, Suárez doomed the effectiveness of the measures proposed. These included the renunciation of all proposed candidates and the choice of new, compromise ones. The next day Reyes offered to resign as the Conservative candidate in a letter to the Directors of the Conservative and the Nationalist Directorates.

Reyes's analysis of the situation of the country and the reasons for his resignation merit close attention. Stressing the deteriorating economic and fiscal situation, Reyes warned against elite division and violent official manipulation of the coming elections. According to him the political crisis had contributed to a commercial crisis. Fear of an outbreak of armed hostilities had caused commercial transactions to be suspended, creditors to call in their accounts, and the exchange rate to rise. The lack of faith in the preservation of public order was exacerbated by the sorry and worsening state of the public treasury. But worst of all, Reyes contended, the steady decline in the price of coffee, "our principal and almost exclusive article of exportation," threatened Colombia with "general ruin." Falling wages in the coffee zones would leave workers ready to join "any revolutionary movement of the worst imaginable sort." Imposition of an official candidate with all the fraud and violence that could accompany it would only serve to "throw the country into a disastrous war with pernicious characteristics of social revolution which could carry us to dissolution."[31]

While the two Conservative factions hammered out their platforms, chose their candidates, and failed in their efforts to compromise and present a single presidential ticket at the polls, Liberals had called a convention to adopt a platform and determine the best course for the party as the election approached. That convention, attended by more tha twenty delegates representing all but two of the nine Colombian departments, met in Bogotá from August 15 to September 20.[32] The Liberal delegates struggled over ideological and tactical questions, but finally made several basic decisions. In one of the most important of these, the delegates voted to replace the plural leadership of the party with a single director and elected Aquileo Parra to fill that position. The delegates also adopted a comprehensive platform, which articulated their critique of Regeneration policies. It called for expansion of civil liberties (absolute freedom of the press, abolition of the

31. Rafael Reyes to General Juan N. Valderrama and Marco Fidel Suárez [and all the other members of the Conservative and Nationalist Directorates], Bogotá, November 16, 1897, Calderón, ACH. Without doubt Reyes sought to exaggerate the gravity of the situation in order to further his own candidacy. Nevertheless, in the light of the nature of the War of the Thousand Days, an event whose origins lay close to the political maneuverings of the presidential campaign of 1897, Reyes's analysis of the crisis may not have been too wide of the mark.

32. Neither Bolívar nor Magdalena was represented.

death penalty, effective suffrage) and curtailment of executive power (reduction of the president's term of office to four years, repeal of the extraordinary powers, prohibition of the re-election of either the president or the vice-president, reestablishment of the legal responsibility of the chief executive, restoration of judicial inviolability, and decentralization of administration and power). Other points called for the reorganization of public instruction to make it genuinely free and available to all social classes, and creation of a new department out of the southern portion of Cauca. Although somewhat more extreme in their content, political and administrative reforms outlined in the Liberal platform approximated those advocated in the "Bases" published a few weeks earlier by the Historical Conservatives.

It was on fiscal and monetary matters, however, that the two reform platforms most strikingly converged. The Liberals called for suppression of all export taxes, reduction of taxes on salt, meat, and "essential foreign imports," and abolition of all monopolies (without damage to previously acquired rights). Turning to the Regeneration's monetary system, Liberals called for an absolute ban on increases in the supply of paper money in circulation, gradual amortization of the paper money "debt" owned the public through the channeling of sufficient national income to this purpose, re-establishment of metallic currency and the free stipulation of money in contracts, and finally, the freedom to engage in banking and the consequent right of private banks to issue currency.

In an addenda to the platform the Liberal delegates attempted to put to rest the Church issue which had been used to alienate them from a large portion of the Colombian masses.

> The Liberal party, deferring to the religious sentiments of the majority of the nation, holds that relations between the State and the Catholic Church should be governed by means of a concordat that specifies the rights and obligations of the two powers.[33]

In addition to these public statements indicating the purpose of the Liberal party to participate in the peaceful conquest of political power, the convention also passed a secret resolution authorizing Parra to prepare the party for war. Although opposed by Sergio Camargo, Pablo Arosemena, and José Camacho Carrizosa, the resolution clearly reflected the wishes of the Liberal rank and file.[34] In fact, most Liberals thought that the real purpose of the convention was to perfect plans for revolt. War preparations had begun as early as April

33. *Convención Nacional Eleccionaria del Partido Liberal, 1897* (Bogotá, 1897), pamphlet, Manrique, ACH.
34. Rodríguez Piñeres, *Diez años*, pp. 51-52.

1897.[35] In subsequent months, at least in the department of Cundinamárca, Liberals took a complete inventory of war supplies at their disposal, collected money to finance the revolt, and organized themselves militarily at the departmental and municipal level.[36] At the same time, the National Directorate sent a commission composed of Luis R. Robles and Foción Soto abroad to procure arms and allies. At his own insistence, and despite the misgivings of the Central Directorate, Rafael Uribe Uribe joined the commissioners abroad in 1897. A matter of primary concern to the Liberal envoys was the need to secure permission from the friendly liberal governments of Venezuela and Ecuador to use their territory as a staging area for the invasion of Colombia.[37]

Despite all this warlike activity, Parra was determined to pursue peaceful means to achieve Liberal political and economic aspirations, and in late November he called together a special consultative junta that confirmed his suggested candidates for the Liberal presidential and vice-presidential nomination.[38] On the twenty-eighth of that month the junta announced the Liberal ticket: Miguel Samper for president, Foción Soto for vice-president.

The Liberal candidates were carefully chosen. Miguel Samper, whom Quijano Wallis called the "centurion of Colombian commerce," personified the Liberal critique of Regeneration economic philosophy, fiscal practice, and monetary policy.[39] Defending his choice in a letter to an influential Liberal in Boyacá, Parra stressed the fact that Samper had "the great merit of having mounted the most notable campaign against Regeneration finance."[40] Yet Samper's orthodox laissez-faire economic views were matched by a social conservatism and personal moderation. Cognizant of his reputation as a deeply religious man aloof from the petty concerns of partisan politics, Samper saw his nomination as a "pledge of political and religious peace"

35. Circular from National Liberal Directorate to departmental directors, Bogotá, April 11, 1897, Manrique, ACH.

36. Juan E. Manrique [untitled narrative of events, 1895-1899], pp. 40-42; Juan E. Manrique, "Circular to provincial chiefs," Bogotá, May 16, 1897, Manrique, ACH.

37. Diego Mendoza [for Aquileo Parra] to Pedro Lara, Bogotá, June 10, 1898; [Aquileo Parra], "Breve informe de las relaciones que el Director del Partido Liberal ha mantenido con el Sr. Rafael Uribe Uribe," Bogotá, August 11, 1898, Parra, ACH.

38. Parra's decision to name a separate Liberal slate may have been influenced by Caro's private assurances that he was determined to oversee peaceful, honest elections that the Liberals could win. At the same time, however, Caro warned that he could not be everywhere to avoid the excesses of his supporters, but he promised to listen to all complaints and take remedial action in case of abuses. Vicente Parra to Aquileo Parra, Bogotá, November 4, 1897, Parra, ACH.

39. Quijano Wallis, *Memorias*, p. 289.

40. Aquileo Parra to José Joaquín Vargas, Bogotá, November 30, 1897, published in Samper Brush and Samper Sordo, eds., *Escritos*, I, xiv.

given by the Liberal party to the nation and the Catholic Church.[41] In accepting the nomination, he vowed to work for every aspect of the Liberal platform except the plank calling for unlimited freedom of the press, and expressed the hope that Liberals and "republican" Conservatives would join in the effort to reform the institutions and administration of the country.[42]

An early and consistent opponent of Regeneration economic and political philosophy, Samper lost no opportunity to embarrass the Nationalist governments by exploring what he believed to be the consequences of their misguided, pernicious politics. The year before his nomination Samper had labeled the Regeneration "state socialism" since it attempted to make government the "motor and regulator of industrial activity." In founding the Banco Nacional, Samper argued at that time, the government had obtained a source of credit and a monopoly on money but had caused national and foreign capital to flee, and almost destroyed the great "industrial lever which is private credit." Samper granted the recent material progress of Bogotá, but claimed that the increase in construction fostered by paper currency occurred at the expense of capital for investment in productive endeavors. He called emphatically for a return to the gold standard through amortization of one million paper pesos a year. Such a plan could be implemented, he insisted, by curtailing government expenditures, eliminating government contracts, expanding the amortization fund, and resuming payment on the foreign debt. These measures would attract both foreign and domestic capital back into the country and assure the progress of the nation.[43]

Another of Samper's themes in 1896 was the failure of Regeneration railroad policy. Under the Regeneration railroads had not progressed beyond the flatlands to conquer the primary objective, which was to link the highlands to the Magdalena. The construction of the Carretera de Cambao (built to haul railroad equipment by ox cart from the Magdalena River near Honda to the Sabana) had been an expensive absurdity. The Regeneration, at great sacrifice, had built the railroads backwards. Samper's solution to the problem was to attract foreign capital by ending the system of paper money, resuming service on the foreign debt, and insuring public tranquillity. Once that was achieved government need only establish its priorities (only one railroad, Samper thought, should be built at a time) and carefully consider the

41. Miguel Samper to Aquileo Parra, *et al.*, Bogotá, November 30, 1897, *ibid.*, pp. ix-x.
42. *Ibid.*, p. xi.
43. Miguel Samper, "Restrospecto," in Samper Brush and Samper Sordo, eds., *Escritos*, I, 143, 144, 152-53, 176-77. In this essay Samper assesses changes in Bogotá since the publication in 1867 of his famous essay "La misera en Bogotá."

contracts it signed (a task suited to the congress, not the executive).[44]

The way in which Samper's views on Regeneration economic and fiscal policies related to coffee interests was amply demonstrated in an article by José Camacho Carrizosa, one of his strongest supporters.[45] Writing in January, 1898, before the final phase of the presidential election, Camacho Carrizosa argued that the outcome of the deepening Colombian coffee crisis depended upon which of the tropical coffee-growing nations produced most efficiently and survived the worldwide competition. According to Camacho Carrizosa, production costs depended on three factors: price of land, rate of wages, and availability and cost of credit. While Colombia, like many other tropical nations, was in good position with respect to the first two factors, the system of paper money, "besides banishing foreign capital due to lack of security, has had the effect of decreasing the amount of national capital loaned out at interest." But paper money was not the only way in which government hurt Colombia's chances for survival as a coffee-producing nation, Camacho Carrizosa asserted, for the government, by means of a "tyrannical and hateful" law, had deprived Colombians of the right to stipulate money in contracts. Moreover, the government had failed to foster the railroad construction needed to lower transportation costs. The contracts it had signed were poorly drawn up and the indemnifications it had been forced to pay would themselves have built any of the projected lines from the highlands to the river.[46]

Although Miguel Samper's laissez-faire economic philosophy clearly coincided with the interests of the Liberal elite involved in the export-import trade, a few of the more militant members of the party objected to his acceptance of the religious status quo and his lack of partisanship.[47] On the other hand, the Liberal candidate for vice-president, Foción Soto of Santander, was a favorite of the majority within the Liberal party that advocated armed revolt to redress Liberal grievances. In spite of his advanced age, Foción Soto retained a reputation for militancy earned during years of service to the party. For several years he had lived in Venezuela and he was thus well placed to support a Liberal revolt in Colombia. Although Carlos Mar-

44. Miguel Samper, "Los ferrocarriles en Colombia," in Samper Brush and Samper Sordo, eds., *Escritos*, II, 231-55.

45. José Camacho Carrizosa was nephew of Salvador Camacho Roldán and editor of the most influential Liberal newspaper of the period, *La Crónica*.

46. José Camacho Carrizosa, *Estudios económicos* (Bogotá, 1903), pp. 37-39. The article was first published in *La Crónica* (Bogotá), January 23, 1898. According to Camacho Carrizosa, of all the nations which had experienced the system of nonredeemable paper currency, Colombia was the only one in which the right to stipulate money in contracts had been denied.

47. Delpar, "The Liberal Party," p. 338.

tínez Silva insisted that Foción Soto placed more importance on good public administration than he did on political metaphysics, in fact his nomination for the vice-presidency constituted a symbolic threat of revolution if the Liberal demands for political power and economic and fiscal reforms were not met.[48]

The proclamation of candidates for a Liberal ticket on the eve of the election was matched by last-minute confusion among Historical Conservatives that caused them to abandon Reyes as their candidate and proclaim a new ticket. Reyes had never really given up his hope of attracting both Conservative factions to his banner, and he realized that without official backing he could not hope to triumph at the polls. In an effort to win over a group of influential Nationalists in the Caribbean port of Barranquilla, he wrote them on November 18 explaining that he had made his pro-reform declaration of November 3 only to prevent the Historical Conservatives from nominating Marceliano Vélez and Guillermo Quintero Calderón. That combination, Reyes contended in the letter, would certainly have won Liberal endorsement. Just before the election the letter was published by the Nationalist press in Bogotá. Thoroughly embarrassed, the Historical Conservatives were forced to disown Reyes and name their own ticket of Quintero Calderón for president and Marceliano Vélez for vice-president.[49] In Quintero Calderón and Marceliano Vélez, the Historical Conservatives found last-minute candidates with long and consistent records of support for party political and economic principles.

There is some evidence to suggest that the contrasting ideological and economic positions so clearly articulated in political platforms and revealed in the career patterns and policy statements of the presidential candidates also corresponded with the economic interests of a large group of each party's influential supporters. Lists of electors designated by each party to cast its votes in the second stage of the indirect presidential election of 1897 serve as a sample of important supporters of each party. For the district of Bogotá, each party named 95 electors and 95 alternatives.[50] The city directory for Bogotá published in 1893 shows the occupations of more than half of the 570 electors and alternates (see Table 3:1).[51]

48. Carlos Martínez Silva, "Revista política de noviembre 28, 1897," in Martínez Delgado, ed., *Revistas*, II, 252.

49. Carlos Martínez Silva, "Revista política de diciembre 26, 1897," in Martínez Delgado, ed., *Revistas*, II, 255-59.

50. The list of Nationalist electors was published in *El Nacionalista* (Bogotá), December 4, 1897. The Historical Conservatives published their list of electors in *El Correo Nacional* (Bogotá), November 11, 1897. The Liberal list can be found in *El Sufragio* (Bogotá), November 22, 1897.

51. Two editions of the *Directorio general de Bogotá*, compiled by Jorge Pombo and Carlos Obregón, were found. One, apparently the third annual publication, was issued

Table 3:1 Occupational distribution by party of presidential electors and alternates for the district of Bogotá, 1897

Occupation	Hist. Conserv.		Nationalists		Liberals	
	Electors	*Alternates*	*Electors*	*Alternates*	*Electors*	*Alternates*
accountant (*contabilista*)					1	2
agriculturalist (*agricultor*)	3	2				1
bank employee (*empleado de banco*)						1
blacksmith (*herrero*)		1			1	
bookseller (*librero*)		2				2
brazier (*latonero*)						1
cabinet maker (*ebanista*)		1				
carpenter (*carpintero*)		1	1			
chemist (*químico*)					1	
cobbler (*zapatero*)					1	1
commission agent (*comisionista*)	4	1	4	1	1	1
consul (*consul*)						1
dairyman (*dueño de lechería*)	1					
dependent (*dependiente*)		1		1		
educator (*institutor*)		1	2	1	3	
employee (*empleado*)	8	7	19	14	1	2
engineer (*ingeniero*)			3		1	1
general store owner (*dueño de pulpería*)						1
innkeeper (*hostelero*)		1				

	1	2	3	4	5	6
jeweler (*joyero*)	2	2	3			
journalist (*periodista*)	2	2	1			
landowner (*hacendado*)	5	2	3	1	3	3
lawyer (*abogado*)	5		6	5	13	7
man of letters (*literato*)	1			1	3	
manufacturer (*industrialista*)					4	
mason (*albañil*)		1	1	1	1	
mechanic (*mecánico*)	1			1		1
merchant (*comerciante*)	12	18	2	5	21	15
military man (*militar*)	6	2	2			
musician (*músico*)	1					
painter (*pintor*)	1				1	
peddler (*buhonero*)	1					
physician (*médico*)	3	1	2	1	6	4
priest (*sacerdote*)					1	1
publisher (*editor*)					1	
saddler (*talabartero*)						
student (*estudiante*)	2	2	1	1		2
tailor (*sastre*)	1	1	1	1		
tapestry maker (*tapicero*)					1	
trader (*negociante*)	3	9	1	5	1	4
typesetter (*tipógrafo*)	1	1				
Total identified	57	57	52	40	64	53
Total electors	95	95	95	95	95	95

One must be cautious in the use of these data. They are the product of an imperfect research tool and are geographically limited to the district of Bogotá. Moreover, problems arise in inferring economic interests from the occupational classifications listed in the table.[52] But despite all the difficulties involved in evaluating and interpreting the data, some very suggestive trends emerge from the table. The distribution shows "merchant" as the most common occupation among Historical Conservative electors. This tendency is much more pronounced in the breakdown of alternate Historical Conservative electors.

The distribution of occupations among Nationalist electors contrasts sharply with the data on Historical Conservatives. A glance at the breakdown reveals the high number of employees and professionals, the insignificant number of merchants and businessmen. While the contrast with the Historical Conservatives is not nearly so sharp in the breakdown of Nationalist alternate electors, roughly the same trend appears.

Analysis of the occupational distribution of Liberal electors reveals a pattern which, with its high percentage of merchants, diverges markedly from that of the Nationalists and approximates that of the Historical Conservatives.

Thus in a general way the occupational data, despite their obvious weaknesses, appear to support the contention that political parties in late nineteenth-century Colombia represented divergent economic

for the year 1889-1890, and is located in the library of the Colombian Academy of History. The other, published in 1893, was more useful to this study and is housed in the library of the Bogotá Municipal Council. The compilers attempted to list all of the city's residents along with their addresses and occupations. While the directory is probably hopelessly incomplete for the lowest strata of the population, it nevertheless includes large numbers of washerwomen, tavern owners, artisans, and owners of small general stores (*pulperías*) along with the ministers of state, lawyers, physicians, and merchants who figure prominently in the list.

The directory's incompleteness was magnified by the fact that it was already almost five years old by December, 1897, when the electoral lists were published. During the time elapsed since its publication the composition of the city had obviously shifted somewhat, and some people may have changed their occupations. Another problem in using the directory concerned the occasional ambiguities of names. Often more than one man is listed for a name appearing on the electoral lists. At other times one of the names or surnames given on the electoral lists does not appear in the directory. Only when a complete and single correspondence existed between the two was a positive identification assumed. (It is possible, however, that some false identifications were made. This would seem to be the explanation of the peddler listed in the table whose name, Justo López, is of common occurrence, making it quite possible that the elector and the man listed in the directory were not the same person.) Slightly more electors were identified in the directory than appear in the breakdown. This is true because the directory does not provide occupational information for quite all of the people listed.

52. While it is reasonable to assume, and contemporary newspaper advertising confirms, that virtually all "merchants" of the period sold foreign goods, it is not clear what kind of trade "traders" were engaged in. Likewise, although "employee" generally

interests. Clearly, additional research into the regional strengths of the three factions is necessary to test this generalization. But the pattern of socioeconomic interests revealed in the data on the electors from the district of Bogotá is consistent with the biographical data presented on leading spokesmen of the parties and the very clear philosophical and programmatic differences between the Nationalists on the one hand, and the Liberals and Historical Conservatives on the other.

The divergent economic and ideological interests separating the Nationalists from their Historical Conservative and Liberal political opponents did not preclude efforts by the two parties out of power to hammer out pre-election alliances with the incumbents. Liberals and Historical Conservatives were painfully aware of the slim chance of electoral victory given the Nationalists' control of electoral machinery and the customary fraud and violence practiced by political parties in power in Colombia throughout the century. Although both opposition parties engaged in negotiations with the Nationalists, these efforts to effect a political compromise capable of bridging the ideological and programmatic gulf separating the parties culminated in failure. Some Liberal and Historical Conservative political leaders also considered the possibility of bipartisan electoral alliance against the Nationalists. However attractive in terms of upper-class economic interests and world views, such an alliance across traditional party lines was not given very serious attention. Given the polarization of Colombian society into rival Liberal and Conservative patron-client groups, most politicians recognized the ineffectiveness of bipartisan political coalitions.[53]

---

meant government employee, presumably the term could also refer to a position in private enterprise (although the directory uses the additional classification "bank employee"). Conceivably, men listed as artisans could range from jewelers or tailors with their own prosperous businesses (which even sold imported merchandise) to modest craftsmen—although one assumes that only a well-to-do artisan would be named an elector. Another problem with the breakdown is that members of the upper class were rarely involved in one occupation, but often were landowners, lawyers, merchants, or military men at one and the same time. Since it is not clear how the directory was compiled, the compilers may have noted each resident's occupation or residents may have been given an opportunity to describe their occupations themselves. Whatever the method, the directory probably reflects the dominant occupation of those having several interests (i.e., the perception of the compilers) or the most coveted occupational self-image of the respondent (which one assumes would have the greatest relationship to his politics). In most cases where I was able to check the directory's classification with data gathered from other sources, the directory proved reliable. On occasion, however, the classification given in the directory appears to be arbitrary. For example, Francisco Groot was listed as a landowner, but he was also a merchant, newspaper editor, commission agent, and factory owner. Jorge Holguín, to give another example, was listed as a commission agent, but he was also a large landowner and had won the title of general.

53. The limitations on elite political strategy and maneuverability by party rank and file are discussed in Chapter V.

On December 5, 1897, the long-awaited election finally took place. First returns indicated an incredible Liberal victory. Liberals hailed the election in Bogotá as one of the purest ever held in Colombia, and Liberal voting inspectors reported that 3,788 votes had been cast for Liberal electors versus 2,385 for the Nationalists and 1,162 for the Historical Conservatives.[54] Returns from the provinces quickly changed the picture, however, as Nationalists triumphed over Historical Conservatives and Liberals in most areas and piled up a majority of the electors. Fraud, virtually absent in the capital, apparently was widespread in the provinces.[55] The final stage of the election took place on February 1, 1898. Historical Conservative leaders and Reyes instructed their electors to cast their votes for the Nationalist ticket.[56] Final results gave Sanclemente 1,606 votes and Marroquín 1,693; Samper 318 and Soto 324; and Reyes 121.[57]

The political costs of the Nationalists electoral victory were high. In order to defeat the Liberal and Historical Conservative reform candidates, the Nationalists had saddled themselves with a president-elect who could not be expected to take office and govern effectively, and a vice-president-elect who would soon succumb to the pressure of the reformers and acquiesce in the modification of some key aspects of the Regeneration. The Nationalist victory had also worked to discredit the Liberal leadership favoring peaceful solutions and strengthened the faction of the party advocating civil war.

During the remainder of Caro's administration the Nationalists' political problems were exacerbated by the steadily worsening economic and fiscal situation of the country. The precipitous fall in coffee prices begun in 1897 rapidly affected the volume of Colombia's imports and the public treasury suffered accordingly. Deprived of the ability to emit paper money, and unwilling or unable to secure domestic or foreign loans,[58] Caro's government attempted to expand

54. Delpar, "The Liberal Party," p. 339.

55. Carlos Martínez Silva, "Revista política de diciembre 26, 1897," Martínez Delgado, ed., *Revistas*, II, 260-61; Delpar, "The Liberal Party," p. 239.

56. At the time it was alleged that this was done to prevent a plan by the Nationalists to have their electors vote for Caro instead of Sanclemente. Another reason may have been to promote the good will of the newly elected officials, especially Marroquín, who it was assumed would take power.

57. Carlos Martínez Silva, "Revista política de julio 10, 1898," in Martínez Delgado, ed., *Revistas*, II, 318-19. These results, announced by the national electoral review board, which met on July 4, 1898, indicated that some 1,881 electors did not vote. According to Martínez Silva these electors either voluntarily abstained or their votes had been annulled at the local level.

58. Caro detested the option of an internal loan subscribed by local capitalists. Besides high interest rates, these loans generally provided that the government accept a large portion of the amount of the loan in documents of public credit. Since these documents of public credit often were bought up by private parties at a fraction of their face value, internal loans, with their opportunity to redeem documents of public credit

revenues through highly unpopular cigarette and match monopolies.[59] But expansion of fiscal monopolies could not offset the sharp decline in government income from the customs houses. During the last months of the Caro administration, many public officials went unpaid and even the army suffered delays in its rations. Public works were suspended, foreign obligations delayed, and payment of pensions and service on the internal debt was halted.[60]

Nevertheless, Caro defended Regeneration finance to the end. Much of his final message to congress justified the system of government monopolies, so vehemently attacked by the opposition, as a positive good. No monopoly, Caro contended, whether designed to produce government revenue, organized for the public good (like the manufacture and sale of arms and munitions), or established for public convenience (like the telegraph), no matter how poorly organized or administered, was as bad as the immoral and unregulated extremes of free competition. "Individualism is always less noble than collectivism," he went on; "the individual favored by nature or by the state never agrees to compensations nor does he seek compromise like governments representative of the general interest." Industrial monopolies were an appropriate means to foment manufactures in a young agrarian nation like Colombia.

Looking back on his six years in control of the executive, Caro marveled at the "ingenuity, cunning, tenacity, time, and money" employed by the opposition in an effort to discredit and destroy the system of paper money. Under the "appealing" name of free stipulation, the opposition proposed the repudiation of national currency, adoption of foreign money (which did not circulate in the country and was replaced by obligatory drafts), and "the tyranny exercised over domestic commerce by the import houses, which were tributaries of European firms." Even the "wealthy coffee growers," who had been especially favored by paper money, had blindly accepted the revolutionary indictment against paper money until the price decline on the world market demonstrated to them the virtue of cheap money in saving their endeavors from ruin.[61]

---

at full value, were a potentially lucrative venture for private capitalists (especially when payment was guaranteed through a lien on a source of government income). Moreover, the government acquired a relatively small amount of ready cash from such loans. Palacio, "Historia," *El Tiempo,* June 7, 1942. Given Colombia's credit position, a foreign loan, except under the most onerous conditions, was out of the question.

59. The cigarette monopoly in particular generated sharp criticism from Liberals and Historical Conservatives. Carlos Martínez Silva, "Revista Política de junio 26, 1897," Martínez Delgado, ed., *Revistas,* II, 202-5; Palacio, "Historia," *El Tiempo,* June 7, 1942.

60. Palacio, "Historia," *El Tiempo,* July 12, 1942; Martínez Delgado, ed., *Revistas,* II, 252-54, 275, 278-79, 295.

61. Miguel Antonio Caro, "Mensaje presidencial de julio 20," in Caro, ed., *Obras,* VI,

On August 7, 1898, Miguel Antonio Caro relinquished power and bequeathed the Regeneration's highly controversial fiscal system and budget deficit to his successor, José Manuel Marroquín, who assumed power in the absence of Sanclemente. In an effort to meet the first expenses of his government, Marroquín called together a group of leading merchants, composed almost entirely of Liberals and Historical Conservatives, to request a loan of 400,000 pesos. Marroquín reported that the treasury was completely empty, customs revenues were embargoed for 600,000 pesos, and the treasury was saddled with an exigible debt of about 7,000,000 pesos. In addition, he pointed out, many government employees had gone months without salaries while the judicial personnel of Panama had gone without pay for a full year. The merchants offered only 160,000 pesos, but called a new and more numerous gathering at which it was decided to propose a loan of 4,000,000 pesos to the government on the condition that the government economize and not issue any more paper money. The minister of the treasury responded that the administration was not authorized by congress to negotiate such a loan, and there the matter rested.[62]

This disappointing initial experience with the businessmen of Bogotá evidently led Marroquín to reconsider the idea of a large loan to keep his government afloat, and by the end of August he was arguing for a large emission of paper money. Justifying his position in a message to congress Marroquín indirectly rebuked the Bogotá merchants, declaring that under the circumstances any loan would be "ruinous, as are all loans consummated between him who urgently needs funds and him who, upon giving them, imposes his will."[63] It was vital that the government secure funds, Marroquín argued in the same message, since in a country like Colombia government provided thousands of citizens with their livelihood.[64] A large emission of paper money was the best solution. Government need pay no interest and

251-53, 258-60. I found no empirical evidence to support this last assertion. All things being equal, Caro's contention that a depreciating currency acted as an export bounty and should have won the support of coffee growers is correct. That coffee growers did not see the issue in this way can be explained not only by their doctrinaire commitment to orthodox liberal economic principles, but to the fact that most large coffee growers and exporters were also importers and all were vitally concerned with facilitating domestic and foreign private investment to expand export agriculture and build crucial railroads. These ends, they firmly believed, were unattainable as long as the regime of paper money remained in existence. There may in fact have been some divergence between large and small growers on the issue of paper money, but if there was, the politically ineffective small growers left no record of their position that I was able to find.

62. Carlos Martínez Silva, "Revista política de agosto 26, 1898," Martínez Delgado, ed., *Revistas*, II, 329-31.

63. Archivo del Congreso, Senado, 1898, XIX, f. 7.

64. "Millares de compatriotas nuestros que no pueden sustentar á sus familias sino merced á la distribución que de los fondos públicos hace el Gobierno, ya en la forma de

could redeem the paper when it was able.[65] The Senate complied with Marroquín's request and approved an emission of ten million pesos (two million more than Marroquín had requested), but the Chamber, controlled by the Historical Conservative opposition, demanded passage of a series of reforms as a condition for its acquiescence.

These reforms, championed by the Historical Conservatives, and supported by Uribe Uribe, the only representative of the Liberal party in congress, sought to implement key aspects of the oppositions' critique of the Regeneration and included: (1) passage of a less stringent press law; (2) enactment of an electoral law designed to eliminate abuses at the polls; (3) reorganization of the general accounting office with personnel appointed by the Chamber; (4) repeal of two measures which limited the independence of the judiciary and the primacy of the Constitution;[66] (5) revocation of the cigarette and match monopolies; and (6) repeal of the extraordinary powers granted the executive by the Law of the Horses.[67]

All but the first two of these reform measures had been passed by the Chamber by mid-September, but the reform program was hopelessly stalled in the Senate, which was controlled by the Nationalists. Caught between the two Conservative factions, and unable to secure the funds needed to govern effectively, Marroquín submitted his resignation to the Senate on September 20, 1898. Whatever the content of the negotiations which went on during the political crisis of the next few days, the Senate refused to accept Marroquín's resignation, he withdrew it, and on September 26 he sent a message to congress urging approval of the Historical Conservatives' reform program.

Liberals and Historical Conservatives were elated by the turn of events. After the message was read to the Chamber, the opposition majority, including Uribe Uribe, marched over to felicitate Marroquín. The following Sunday, October 2, a great "meeting" of merchants was called to congratulate Marroquín on his position. Miguel Samper addressed the rally and praised Marroquín in the name of the merchants; Marroquín modestly replied that to advocate the reforms involved no special merit since they were just in themselves.[68]

---

sueldos, ya en la de pensiones, ya de otras maneras, están padeciendo verdadera indigencia." *Ibid.*, f. 6.

65. *Ibid.*, f. 7.

66. The first was the so-called *ley de transhumancia* which enabled government to move judges from one district to another; the second was a section of law 153 of 1887 which held that any law in apparent conflict with the Constitution was to take precedence over the Constitution.

67. Carlos Martínez Silva, "Revista política de septiembre 24, 1898," Martínez Delgado, ed., *Revistas*, II, 348.

68. Carlos Martínez Silva, "Revista política de octubre 18, 1898," *ibid.*, 355-58.

Up to this point the concrete results of the opposition's program to dismantle Regeneration political and fiscal policies had been minimal. Historical Conservatives had succeeded in repealing the coffee export tax, and the Law of the Horses seemed certain of repeal, but the rest of their program remained deadlocked in the Senate.[69] Nationalist control of the Senate was tenuous, however, and now executive support of the reforms seemed to indicate the eventual success of the program of the Historical Conservatives. Moreover, on September 22 Aquileo Parra had officially encouraged Liberals to support the effort to secure congressional reforms. His published statement also included a list of reforms which he said would satisfy Liberal aspirations. These included repeal of the Law of the Horses, court jurisdiction over press offenses, curtailment of public spending and the gradual elimination of paper money, and electoral reform to guarantee honest elections.[70]

Confronted with the prospect of basic reform of the Regeneration by legislative means, and increasingly distrustful of Marroquín's abilities and intentions, doctrinaire Nationalists resorted to a desperate maneuver and in October convinced President Sanclemente to assume power. As the old man undertook the long journey to the capital, the political situation of the Nationalists continued to deteriorate. By the middle of the month the congress had definitively approved the repeal of the Law of the Horses and had passed a law which severely restricted the establishment of fiscal monopolies by requiring previous indemnification not only of immediate losses but of possible future damages as well.[71] The minister of war, an increasingly disaffected Nationalist, began shifting military commanders and placing dissident Conservatives in key positions.[72] Liberal and Historical Conservative leaders skillfully manipulated public demonstrations and friendly army commanders to discredit the Nationalist director of the thousand-man police force and cause the resignation of General Aurelio Mutis, a loyal Nationalist, from the powerful post of minister of government.[73]

Sanclemente arrived in Bogotá to find the capital in a state of great uncertainty and excitement. The Chamber planned to challenge his

---

69. Carlos Martínez Silva, "Revista política de septiembre 24, 1898," *ibid.*, pp. 348-49.

70. Parra's statement was criticized as an abdication of some important principles by some party militants, especially those associated with Uribe Uribe's *El Autonomista*.

71. Carlos Martínez Silva, "Revista política de octubre 18, 1898," Martínez Delgado, ed., *Revistas*, II, 362.

72. Palacio, "Historia," *El Tiempo*, August 23, 1942.

73. Charles Burdett Hart to William R. Day, Bogotá, October 24, 1898, United States, Department of State, Diplomatic Despatches from United States Ministers to Colombia, microfilm, United States National Archives (hereafter cited as USNA).

assumption of power and the threat of a military coup was very real. By November 3, the day Sanclemente indicated he would take possession, Historical Conservatives had cemented an alliance with Liberals to block Sanclemente and procure the reforms both groups advocated. According to Luis Martínez Delgado, the alliance was arranged by his father, Luis Martínez Silva, who was commissioned by a representative of the majority of the Chamber. Luis Martínez Silva met with Aquileo Parra and other Liberal leaders, secured their approval and the support of a secret Liberal military force, and awaited the announcement of support from General Rafael Ortiz, a leading Historical Conservative in command of major army units in Bogotá.[74] On November 3, as crowds milled through the streets and the Chamber met in frenzied discussion, Ortiz shuttled back and forth between Sanclemente's lodgings and the congress. Near the end of the day, he abandoned his Historical Conservative colleagues and threw his support to Sanclemente. According to his subsequent account of these events, he feared that support of the Historical Conservative-Liberal alliance would lead to civil war, and war to the "ascendancy of the most recalcitrant element within the Liberal party." In addition, he claimed that Sanclemente had promised him that all members of his cabinet would be Conservatives.[75] Ortiz's decision doomed the movement. Although the Chamber proceeded to pass a resolution declaring Marroquín the legal head of the government, it was an empty gesture. More appropriate was Uribe Uribe's advice to the crowd in the streets. Speaking from the balcony of the Hotel Blume, he urged the crowd to disperse, that all resistance was useless.[76]

Once again the Nationalists, largely as a result of their continued control of the army, successfully thwarted an attempt by the bipartisan opposition to reform the Regeneration and gain effective political power. It was true that Sanclemente initially retained Marroquín's cabinet officers, and congress eventually did approve a new press law which gave the courts jurisdiction over offenders. But despite an extraordinary session of congress which ran until December 6, the legislators did not pass the vitally important electoral reform bill. Failure to change the election law meant that the primary instrument for maintaining Nationalist control of the congress remained intact.

Just as in the election of 1897, the Nationalists' political victories of 1898 were achieved at great expense. Nationalists had placed in power a sickly old man unable to live in the cold rarefied air of the

74. Martínez Delgado, *A propósito,* pp. 189-90.
75. *La Crónica,* January 17, 1899. *La Crónica,* the official organ of the Liberal party, interviewed Ortiz after his resignation from the Sanclemente government in early January.
76. Martínez Delgado, *A propósito,* p. 190.

country's capital city. Moreover, they had completely alienated the Historical Conservatives and thoroughly discredited the reformist peace leadership of the Liberal party. As economic conditions in the country continued to worsen, the full implications of the Nationalists' intransigence began to reveal themselves. By 1899 the Regeneration was in crisis.

Chapter IV

The Liberal Party Drifts Toward War

One effect of the events of November 3, 1898, was to help tip the balance of power between the peace and war factions that had contended for control of the Liberal party throughout most of the 1890's. The failure of the Liberal-Historical Conservative alliance to prevent the re-imposition of Nationalist control of the government served to discredit the strategy of the peace Liberals led by Aquileo Parra and other members of the old Radical Olympus. At the same time the country's deteriorating economic situation and the government's growing fiscal difficulties worked to increase unrest within the country and strengthen the war Liberals' argument that revolution was not only a justifiable, but a viable course of action open to the party. Although the war Liberals had long counted a majority of the party's rank and file, they had suffered from the lack of a well-known, influential national spokesman. In 1898 Rafael Uribe Uribe emerged to capture that role, and by the end of that year he seemed to be succeeding in his campaign to replace the peace Liberal leadership of the party with men who would prepare the party for war.

Born of respectable Liberal parentage on a rural estate in southern Antioquia, Rafael Uribe Uribe early acquired a severe sense of morality, a love for hard work and discipline, and the need to excel in whatever he did.[1] As a student in Medellín, Uribe Uribe's younger brother Heraclio recalled, Rafael "had a weak constitution, cried with little cause, and had a twitch in his face."[2] If he did suffer from those characteristics, he learned to surmount them and in later life became

1. One of the two great martyrs of the Colombian Liberal party, the figure of Rafael Uribe Uribe has stimulated an abundant literature which diverges sharply on the nature of his personality and the meaning of his career. The best introduction to the secondary literature is Fernando Galvis Salazar, *Rafael Uribe Uribe* (Medellín, 1962). For an uncritical biography containing much useful information, see Eduardo Santa, *Rafael Uribe Uribe*, 2nd ed. (Bogotá, 1968). Martha Cleveland Child, "Politics, Revolution and Reform: The Liberal Challenge to the Colombian Status quo: Rafael Uribe Uribe (1859-1914)," (M.A. thesis, Vanderbilt University, 1969) synthesizes secondary materials for English readers. A venomous satire of Uribe Uribe emerges from Lorenzo Marroquín's popular novel, *Pax* (Bogotá, 1904). None of these works taps the wealth of material available in the voluminous personal papers of Rafael Uribe Uribe cited previously.

2. Heraclio Uribe Uribe, "El General Uribe," *Pan*, 11 (December, 1936), p. 50.

famous for his commanding appearance and his impetuous manner. Suggestive of this change was an incident recounted by another of Uribe Uribe's brothers. After graduating from law school in 1880, Uribe Uribe and his brother Julián left on a trip to Buenaventura to "see the sea for the first time." Waiting for boats to cross the Cauca River, Rafael recklessly threw himself into the water in an attempt to swim to the other side. Unable to continue after reaching mid-stream, he very nearly drowned before he was rescued by a boatman.[3]

At the age of seventeen, Uribe Uribe began his military career fighting for the government cause against the Conservative insurgents of 1876. At Los Chancos he was wounded in the knee, then came down with fever to recover only after the war was over. In 1885 he served as a colonel in the ill-fated revolutionary army. Faced with insubordination after Liberal hopes for victory appeared lost, he did not hesitate to shoot and fatally wound the leader of his mutinous troops. Jailed by the victorious Conservatives after that episode, he was exonerated the next year and returned to private life.[4]

Throughout his career Uribe Uribe was always engaged in a prodigious amount of activity. Before the war of 1885 he had practiced law in Medellín and taught law and political economy at the University of Antioquia. In 1884 he founded and ran single-handedly a paper appropriately called *El Trabajo* that was dedicated to the propagation of scientific industrial and agricultural information. Publication of the paper was suspended during the war of 1885, but resumed upon Uribe Uribe's release from jail in 1886. The next year, however, the paper was closed for political reasons by the governor of Antioquia. According to Galvis Salazar, at some point during these years, Uribe Uribe established an agency of the New York Life Insurance Company.[5]

By far the most impressive of Uribe Uribe's private endeavors was the founding of "Gualanday," a large coffee hacienda in the municipality of Fredonia, Antioquia. Carved out of uncultivated lands, Gualanday was evaluated at 80,000 pesos in 1897.[6] On the eve of the War of the Thousand Days, one-fourth of the estate was planted in coffee, containing, according to Uribe Uribe's possibly exaggerated estimate, 200,000 coffee trees, another one-fourth of the estate was planted in sugar cane, and half of the land was still uncleared.[7]

In the early 1890's Uribe Uribe moved to Bogotá, where he played

3. Julián Uribe Uribe, "Memorias inéditas" quoted in Santa, *Uribe*, pp. 47-48.
4. Ricardo Restrepo, *Defensa del coronel Rafael Uribe Uribe* (Medellín, n.d.).
5. Galvis Salazar, *Uribe*, p. 47.
6. Uribe Uribe to Members of the Liberal National Directorate, June 25, 1897, Parra, ACH.
7. This information comes from Rafael Uribe Uribe, "Conózcaseles" [Bogotá, 1904], a broadside accusing his wartime administrator of mismanagement, and from Luciano Arias F., "Calumnia," Medellín, January 30, 1905, Arias's response. Manrique, ACH.

an active role in national Liberal politics and served as administrator of Eustacio de la Torre Narváez's large Cundinamarcan coffee holdings. Uribe Uribe took part in the deliberations of the Liberal Convention of 1892, where, according to Rodríguez Piñeres, he proved himself a staunch defender of peaceful approaches to the conquest of power.[8] He drafted the memorial sent to congress by coffee interests in 1894 protesting the proposed coffee export tax. When the revolt planned by his employer broke out in 1895, Uribe Uribe assumed an important role in the military campaign in Cundinamarca. Imprisoned by the government in Cartagena for several months after the defeat of the Liberals in March, 1895, he emerged from jail a hero of his party, and in 1896 he was one of two Liberals elected to the congress. The only Liberal to take his seat,[9] Uribe Uribe found support for many of his positions among the dissident Conservatives in the Chamber of Representatives and became a leading spokesman for the anti-Regeneration forces in congress. During the session of 1896, as has been seen, he concentrated his energies on a campaign to repeal the coffee export tax and skillfully utilized the tax issue to mount an attack against the Regeneration itself.

Influential members of the Liberal Directorate recognized Uribe Uribe's potential as leader of the war faction of the party as early as 1897. In January of that year he had requested a commission to join Robles and Soto abroad in the search for allies and arms for the Liberal revolt. In that letter, Parra later claimed, Uribe Uribe promised to subordinate his activities to the directions of the other two emissaries and promised to act with prudence. Although some members of the Directorate doubted his sincerity,[10] and did not cooperate with his schemes for selling his coffee plantation before leaving the country,[11]

8. Rodríguez Piñeres, *Diez años*, pp. 7-10.

9. The other Liberal elected was Santiago Pérez, who still lived in Europe although his exile had been lifted soon after he left Colombia. The Liberal directorate discouraged Uribe Uribe from taking his seat out of protest of government fraud in the election of 1896. It seems fair to assume that the old Liberal leadership was also concerned with the potential challenge to their control that he could mount with such an excellent forum for his views.

10. [Parra], "Breve informe," Parra, ACH.

11. Unable to sell his coffee estate, which was saddled with a debt of 35,000 pesos, and afraid to leave it under poor administration and at the mercy of government expropriation in the event of revolution, Uribe Uribe had solicited help from the Liberal Directorate. He requested that the Directorate urge wealthy *antioqueño* party members to buy the farm so he could go abroad on party business. The Directorate apparently dragged its feet and *antioqueño* Liberals refused to cooperate. Rafael Uribe Uribe to Members of the Liberal National Directorate, Manizales, June 25, 1897, Parra, ACH. Eventually, Uribe Uribe was able to mortgage Gualanday to an English house, Arbuthnot Latham and Co. of London. By the terms of that arrangement, he received a loan of 4,000 pounds which he promised to pay within three years, although extensions were provided for. Notarized document, Medellín, June 10, 1897, and Uribe Uribe, "Conózcaseles," Uribe, Boxes 17 and 8, ACH. As early as February 1896 Uribe Uribe

they eventually agreed to grant him the commission he had solicited. According to Parra, the Directorate instructed him, however, not to visit Ecuador for fear that he would jeopardize previous commitments to the projected Liberal revolt made by Ecuadorian President Eloy Alfaro.[12] In reality the Directorate probably feared that Uribe Uribe planned to invade Colombia from Ecuador immediately and start a revolt which could not be adequately seconded in the rest of the country. This was, in fact, his intention, but when he was discovered in Quito in early November by a Colombian official, Alfaro was obliged to suspend his contacts with Colombian Liberals.[13] Uribe Uribe then traveled to Central America to court favor with the Liberal governments of Guatemala and Nicaragua. There too his mission met with little success.[14]

At some point during his stay in Central America Uribe Uribe decided to oppose openly the politics of the Liberal leadership and replace Parra with someone (perhaps himself) capable of taking the party to war against the Regeneration. Upon his arrival in Colombia in late July, 1898, he made a dramatic speech which catapulted him into the leadership of the war faction of the Liberal party. Addressing an overflow crowd of Liberals, who took advantage of the free admission to the Salón Fraternidad in Barranquilla, he wove his political passion, a thorough grasp of Colombia's alternatives in the expanding world capitalist system, and a flair for satire into a scathing indictment of both the Regeneration and the Liberal leadership.

Uribe Uribe began by declaring that revolution was no longer opportune nor possible. The time for successful revolt was right after an election. "Revolutionary raw material" was made up of passion more than conviction. Emotions were incensed after an electoral affront, but delaying a revolt allowed passions to cool, appeared to sanction the election, gave the opposition time to consolidate, and filled the neutral camp with the chimerical hope that the new administration would enact reforms.

---

received a negative reply to an offer to sell the farm or mortgage it to the French house Fould and Cía. William Gordon to Rafael Uribe Uribe, Medellín, February 24, 1896, Uribe, Box 5, ACH.

12. [Parra], "Breve informe," Parra, ACH.

13. Rafael Uribe Uribe to Eloy Alfaro, Quito, November 2 and November 3, 1898, Uribe, Box 13, ACH.

14. For an indication of Uribe Uribe's activities in Guatemala, see his review of the Colombian political situation dated Guatemala, December 8, 1897, Uribe, Box 10, ACH. He later claimed that he had secured promises of 80,000 pesos worth of elements of war. Rafael Uribe Uribe to Miguel de la Roche, Bogotá, September 3, 1899. The effective support he procured was probably very limited. Belisario Porras describes how an arms deal Uribe Uribe made with Guatemalan President Manuel Estrada Cabrera fell through at the last minute in his *Memorias de las campañas del istmo, 1900* (Panama, 1920), pp. 5-14.

For three years, Uribe Uribe went on, the party had been encouraged by its leaders to believe that war was imminent. These years of expectation and delay had been economically ruinous. Cattlemen had lost three years of pasture, afraid to expose livestock to the pillage of war. Merchants, hindered by tight credit and the reduction of consumption induced by the state of insecurity, had restricted operations. Entrepreneurs had ceased to embark upon projects that required time to produce a profit. Everyone in need of capital and credit had been hurt by rising interest rates and increasingly short terms for loans. "Youths and men of action," in order to be prepared for a revolt, had not wanted to take on any occupation and had consumed their capital while waiting. In short, all had been hurt by the expectation of a war which never came and which had turned out to be more costly than two lost revolutions.

But if the Liberal leadership had contributed to the economic ruin of many Liberals, Uribe Uribe argued, the policies of the Regeneration had brought the entire nation to the brink of an economic crisis that threatened the very existence of the nation. Foreign markets had become "tired of waiting for us" and had resolved to produce for themselves what little Colombia had sent them. Colombia now had to compete at a disadvantage with the new producers. Defeated some time ago in the competitive production of quinine, tobacco, indigo, cacao, sugar, hides, rubber, cotton, and other crops, Colombians were about to experience the same fate with coffee and precious metals. The nation was witnessing a "decisive moment" in its life as a republic, its entire economic organization was in a state of crisis. The difference between winning the competition, and losing it was as "little as a penny more or a penny less in [the cost of production of] a pound of coffee or an ounce of silver." Time, Uribe Uribe contended, was of the essence: a month gained or lost could be crucial in winning the competition.

> Whether the frightening crisis in which we find ourselves recedes completely, slows down, or hurries to its tragic conclusion depends on greater or less economy and speed in the production of those [export] items.

If Colombians diminished consumption (this contention placed Uribe Uribe in conflict with importers of foreign goods) and developed agriculture, salvation was possible, but if Colombians wasted the time in destroying and ruining themselves (that is, by tolerating the Regeneration), economic and social disaster would visit Colombia with such force that it could bring dissolution and the end of the nation. That possibility was not remote given the "visibly growing expansionist colossus to the North," the needs of the nations of the Old World to settle and protect their excess populations, and the incapacity Colombians had demonstrated in governing themselves. The Regeneration was the principal, if not the only, agent of this ruinous state of affairs and "the major obstacle standing in the way of economic improvement." The Regeneration had cost the country more than ten civil wars.

While Uribe Uribe believed that war was not possible at that time he left no doubt about the future course the party should take. His closing remarks sarcastically chided his audience to militant action. "[A]lthough they kill us with taxes, and although new issues of paper money, monopolies, and fiscal depradations complete our ruination," we will find a way to make a living and pay our taxes. As long as we refrain from thinking and give up the insane idea of criticizing and fiscalizing government, we can be sure that nobody will bother us and we can carry on an easy, contented life in the laps of our wives, dedicated to the care of our children and the development of our interests. Tongue-in-cheek, Uribe Uribe closed his speech exhorting those present to vote in the upcoming elections.[15]

Uribe Uribe's speech faithfully interpreted the sentiments of the majority of the Liberal party, which had long favored a violent solution to the Liberals' grievances.[16] In the words of one provincial Liberal leader sympathetic to Uribe Uribe, the speech, which was printed and distributed, appeared at exactly the right time. Threatened by deteriorating economic conditions, by government monopolies, and by emissions of paper money, Liberals had become convinced that war was the only way to change this state of affairs. "[E]verybody who reads the speech becomes an *uribista* [and] disowns the Directorate...."[17] Reaching Bogotá, Uribe Uribe continued his campaign against the Liberal leadership from the pages of *El Autonomista,* a paper founded September 20, 1898, under the nominal direction of Alejandro Rodríguez F. and Maximiliano Grillo. Although Uribe

15. This résumé of Uribe Uribe's Barranquilla speech is closely paraphrased from an unsigned, undated, twenty-four page document, written in Uribe Uribe's own hand and located in Uribe, Box 9, ACH. The speech was printed under the title of *Censura de la política liberal* by the Papelería de Samper Matiz in 1898 and circulated widely among Liberals. I was unable to consult a copy of the printed version.

16. Just as they had done since the early 1890's, the majority of articulate Liberals continued to favor war. As Quijano Wallis put it, "el elemento popular, el más numeroso, siguió animado de un espíritu belicoso, no buscando otro medio para la restauración de los principios liberales que la guerra," *Memorias,* p. 542. See also Palacio, "Historia," *El Tiempo,* August 2, 1942. Parra himself later admitted that he had not foreseen the way "la opinión liberal en masa" supported the War of the Thousand Days when it broke out in October, 1899. Aquileo Parra to Juan Evangelista Manrique, Bogotá, December 11, 1899, Parra, ACH.

17. Clodomiro F. Castillo to Aquileo Parra, Honda, September 22, 1898, Parra, ACH.

Uribe left open the door for reforms,[18] *El Autonomista* editorially argued that Parra overstated the degree to which Liberal demands would be met by passage of the reforms he outlined in his manifesto of September 22.[19] The debacle of the Liberal-Historical Conservative alliance of November 3 seriously undermined Parra's position, but he clung to the hope that Sanclemente and the congress would enact the all-important electoral reform before congress adjourned.[20] Nevertheless, Parra considered resigning as early as November 18, and when congress adjourned without having passed the election law, his resignation was only a matter of time.[21] By late December Parra himself conceded that war was the only means left the Liberal party in its struggle to secure its rights, but he continued to argue that the party's unpreparedness and internal division left it in no position to undertake a revolt at that time.[22] On February 4, 1899, the Liberal Advisory Council finally accepted Parra's insistent resignation. Uribe Uribe had won his first victory in his campaign against the Liberal leadership.

It was one thing to cause Parra's formal resignation, however, and quite another to wrest control of the party from the peace Liberals, whom Parra still led. During the next several months the war Liberals under the leadership of Uribe Uribe fought incessantly for control of the party. Yet as late as September, 1899, Uribe Uribe was forced to admit that the main hindrance continued to be the Olympus.

> They are only four clever men, yet they resist virtually the entire mass of the party. They are to the party what Nationalism is to the nation: a vile minority, but one that does not relinquish control.[23]

However small a minority nationally, the peace Liberals were nevertheless numerous and powerful in Bogotá. Even after the resignation of Parra, peace Liberals still maintained control of the party machinery through a majority on the advisory council. Another im-

18. See the excerpts from his speeches in the Chamber of Representatives on September 21 and 22 in Galvis Salazar, *Uribe Uribe*, pp. 93-95.

19. Delpar, "The Liberal Party," p. 348.

20. Aquileo Parra to Juan E. Manrique and Francisco de la Torre, Bogotá, November 30, 1898, Manrique, ACH. In this belief Parra was supported by the most influential members of the peace faction of the party in a statement dated Bogotá, November 17, 1898, which favorably reviewed his political decisions during previous months, Parra, ACH.

21. Manrique later confessed that from the time he touched Colombian soil upon his return from Europe (probably in December, 1898) every Liberal he talked to was in favor of war and against any further attempts at peaceful solution or alliances with the Historical Conservatives ["Relación"], Manrique, ACH.

22. Circular from the National Directorate, Bogotá, December 20, 1898, Parra, ACH.

23. Rafael Uribe Uribe to Miguel de la Roche, Bogotá, September 3, 1899, Uribe, Box 32, ACH.

portant political resource at their disposal was the newspaper *La Crónica*, edited by José Camacho Carrizosa and his brother Guillermo, nephews of Salvador Camacho Roldán and ardent supporters of the peace Liberal faction. Besides being the official organ of the party, *La Crónica* was the most popular and complete newspaper published in the capital.[24]

Recognition of the strength and tenacity of the peace Liberals led Uribe Uribe and other war Liberals to pursue a dual approach to the problem of carrying the party to war. On the one hand they continued to fight publicly to place men sympathetic to their cause in positions of leadership. On the other hand, however, war Liberals secretly planned for revolt. In February, 1899, war Liberals including Pablo E. Villar, José María Ruiz, Uribe Uribe, Ramón Neira, Cenón Figueredo, and Justo L. Durán met in Bucaramanga, Santander, to plan strategy and coordinate war preparations. In a pact signed on February 12, these and other leaders of the war faction pledged to revolt on a date fixed by Villar, director of the party in Santander. Villar in turn promised to give the order for revolt only when he had documentary proof that a "sufficient" number of responsible Liberal chiefs were prepared to back the movement in most of the country.[25]

The public struggle for control of the party preoccupied Liberals throughout 1899, and as the year progressed relations between the two factions became increasingly hostile. Parra was eventually replaced by a three-man directorate, dominated by peace Liberals, which ostensibly sought to chart a course acceptable to both Liberal factions. The Directorate published a strong plea for electoral reform and issued a directive calling for reorganization of the party from the bottom up. On June 18 the Directorate wrote Foción Soto in Venezuela urging him to accept stewardship of the party's funds, apparently totaling some £20,000. The Directorate did not instruct Soto to buy arms, however, and the move apparently resulted more from the Directorate's concern for the security of the funds than from its desire to ready the party for war.[26]

By late May the struggle between the two Liberal factions had moved from lofty ideological discussion to the level of personal attacks and recriminations. *La Crónica* began a hard-hitting press cam-

---

24. With a circulation of some three thousand copies in 1899, *La Crónica* exhibited a polished four-page format, was published every day of the week but Monday, and included a substantial amount of international news.

25. Joaquín Tamayo, *La revolución de 1899* (Bogotá, 1938), pp. 35-36. Leonidas Flóres Alvarez notes a similar meeting which he claims took place in Zipaquirá, Cundinamarca, in mid-1898. See *La campaña en Santander, 1899-1900*, p. 9.

26. Medardo Rivas, Juan E. Manrique, and José B. Gaitán to Foción Soto, Bogotá, June 18, 1898; Juan E. Manrique to Pablo Arosamena, Bogotá, September 24, 1899, Manrique, ACH.

paign designed to discredit Uribe Uribe for a position he had taken on the liquor monopoly in Tolima. Uribe Uribe had visited Tolima, and partly for local political reasons, had accepted the legitimacy of the monopoly.[27] *La Crónica* attacked him mercilessly for his deviation from orthodox Liberal laissez-faire economic policy, an embarrassing charge given the nature of the Liberal critique of government fiscal and economic policy since the start of the Regeneration. Uribe Uribe fought back vigorously from the pages of *El Autonomista*, but he found it difficult to explain his position.[28] Relations between the two Liberal factions reached the breaking point in late July. On July 28 Sanclemente's government became alarmed by information of a Liberal conspiracy and the outbreak of a liberal revolt in Venezuela and declared a state of siege in the departments of Cundinamarca and Santander. The same day Uribe Uribe and other prominent leaders of the war party were arrested, marched through the streets of Bogotá, and temporarily imprisoned. Uribe Uribe's supporters gathered in protest and blamed the government measures on an editorial denouncing the Liberal *impacientes* as war propagandists which had appeared in *La Crónica* on the 27th. That afternoon a crowd sympathetic to the imprisoned war Liberals stoned the offices of *La Crónica*.[29]

At the same time the electoral struggle to gain control of the party machinery continued. In July and August elections were held to choose new leaders at all levels of the party. *El Autonomista* claimed large majorities for the so-called *impaciente* or war Liberal candidates in the Bogotá district elections and predicted that these victories would insure the election of General Gabriel Vargas Santos as the new head of the party. A military man over seventy years old, Vargas Santos lived in retirement on his cattle estate near Tame on the eastern plains of Boyacá. Long aloof from active politics, Vargas seemed to offer the possibility of union between the two Liberal factions. Although Parra initially sought to work behind the scenes to impose formal conditions in exchange for his acquiescence in favor of Vargas Santos, he subsequently became convinced that Vargas Santos was not the pawn of the war faction. On September 30, 1899, he advised Liberals of his

27. According to a peace Liberal in Ibagué, the provincial capital of Tolima, many Liberals, "predominando un grupo de antioqueños adictos a Uribe U," had interests in the "compañía rematadora." Sharing a common interest in the monopoly, the Nationalist government had cooperated with these Liberals, favoring and protecting them. Thus strengthened, *uribistas* were about to dominate Liberal politics in the department. Belisario Esponda [?] to Juan E. Manrique, Ibagué, August 14, 1899, Manrique, ACH.

28. The debate fills the pages of both papers during the end of May. See also *La Crónica*, September 29, 1899.

29. *El Autonomista*, July 29, 30, and August 1, 1899; *La Crónica*, July 29, and 30, 1899.

approval of the new head of the party.[30] In early October Uribe Uribe and José María Ruiz journeyed to Tame to convince Vargas Santos to accept the position.

The division among Liberals that dominated party politics during the last years of the Regeneration and reached the breaking point in 1899 was not only the reflection of differing opinions on political strategy or the result of personal sympathies or antipathies toward individual leaders, although both of these factors played a part in the split. At the heart of the Liberal division were sociological differences. Although at one point Uribe Uribe stressed the lack of social, economic, or generational differences between the Liberal factions,[31] the war Liberals, Uribe Uribe included, generally distinguished the Liberal factions on sociological grounds. War Liberals tried to characterize peace Liberals as rich old Bogotá merchants who had enjoyed political power and the advantages of office during the period of Liberal hegemony. At the same time they cast their own faction as young, idealistic, deprived representatives of "the people." Illustrative of this tendency was the analysis of the division within the party made in November 1898 by Max Carriazo, an ardent supporter of Uribe Uribe and a future general in the Liberal army during the War of the Thousand Days. Twenty-eight years old at the time, Carriazo managed the branch of an export-import house, Rocha Brothers, located in the river port of Girardot, Cundinamarca. "Naturally," Carriazo argued, the reformist, peace wing that supported the politics of the Directorate was made up of "merchants and faint-hearted men" while the war faction counted as its supporters "[m]en of action, most of them youths, artisans, and members of the mass."[32] Echoing Carriazo's views was a group of Liberals from Palmira who complained to Uribe Uribe that the regional directors of the party were chosen by the "Olympus," not the "people." Casting themselves as "men of the people," they stressed that their sole aspiration was to procure the "rapid resolution of our terrible state of expectation." They were, they wrote, "what is called 'cannon fodder'" and spoke not from the mind but expressed the "unanimous cry of the poor in the countryside and the artisans."[33] In a similar vein Liberals from Honda deplored the "cruel indifference" with which the "men of wealth" contemplated the future of the country. While peace Liberals alleged a lack of means

30. *La Crónica*, September 20, October 3, 1899.
31. Attempting to show that he sought unity of the party, Uribe Uribe argued in an *Autonomista* editorial on July 14, 1899, that "pobres y ricos, viejos y jóvenes, ignorantes y sabios, civiles y militares" had figured in both the pacifist and militant branches of the party.
32. Max Carriazo to Rafael Uribe Uribe, Girardot, November 6, 1898, Uribe, Box 27, ACH.
33. Manifesto to Uribe Uribe dated Palmira, November 18, 1898, Uribe, Box 27, ACH.

to wage war, "Liberal merchants" offered the government a four million peso loan in exchange for a promised ban of future emissions of paper money.[34] Uribe Uribe himself appreciated the kind of man favorable to his prowar position. In a remarkably candid circular he advised his supporters on the criteria for choosing men to represent the party at a proposed national convention.

> [E]xperience shows that men who . . . have a position to risk, and perhaps lose, are not the best to lead the party on certain paths, and by preference we should place our trust in men who, endowed with abilities and courage, have a reputation to acquire or conquer. . . .[35]

One of Aquileo Parra's correspondents accused the Liberal leadership of planning a "scientific war, with victory mathematically assured beforehand," which demanded a state of preparedness beyond the capabilities of the party. He accused Parra of being surrounded by "great, affected gentlemen . . . loaded with comforts and prehistoric honors" and "little gentlemen, petty personages, and empty-titled doctors whose aspirations are satisfied with being pretentious nobodies on a party advisory board." Both of these types were horrified by the idea of a revolution and both were oblivious to the people's state of unrest and desperation. Liberals had to "open the valve of political movements"; otherwise the country could "explode in a frightening social movement."[36]

Uribe Uribe himself most clearly expressed the frustrations of those Liberals who had reached maturity just as their party lost power. In an editorial published in *El Autonomista*, Uribe Uribe reflected on the different fates of his own generation of Liberals and the one which preceded it. The previous generation had developed while the Lib-

34. Clodomiro F. Castillo, *et al.* to Aquileo Parra, Honda, October 29, 1898, Parra, ACH.

35. Circular from Rafael Uribe Uribe, Bogotá, December, 1898, Uribe, Box 27, ACH. Peace Liberals seem to have shared the view that supporters of the war faction were of lower social and economic status. This was usually expressed by calling the war faction "personalista" or "draconiano," an allusion to the Liberal military-artisan alliance which backed José María Melo in 1854. A provincial leader loyal to Aquileo Parra's leadership was more direct. He characterized the few vociferous supporters of Uribe Uribe in his district as "seres despreciables por su ninguna honradez política y social," men who were "pobres y mui impopulares." Daniel de la Pava to Aquileo Parra, Salento [Cauca], November 9, 1898, Parra, ACH.

36. Saúl Cortissor to Aquileo Parra, Ubaté, Cundinamarca, February 8, 1898, Parra, ACH. Cortissor's insistence on imminent social revolution, like that of Rafael Reyes noted previously, may reflect a contemporary European obsession with social revolution. Cortissor's letter is sprinkled with references to European revolutionaries. Cortissor, like Reyes, may have also exaggerated the social tensions of the time for his own political ends. Still, the quotation raises the possibility that some Liberal leaders conceived of traditional political revolt as the safest means to channel mass unrest during a period of economic crisis.

eral party was in power, its members nurtured their intelligence in an era of absolute freedom of the press, practiced jurisprudence as judges and prosecutors, developed their military skills as men in uniform with pay and commanding veteran troops in the service of the government, learned oratory in university professorships and in provincial and national legislatures, became statesmen as state governors and cabinet ministers, and mastered diplomacy in the legations of the nation. "[W]ith the tranquillity and time afforded by the possession of public office, they cultivated literature and other branches of knowledge." His own generation, on the other hand, had suffered "something like the ablation of half its cerebrum under the knife of press repression." Members of his generation either had to practice law under a system of partisan justice or resign themselves to a miserable existence transcribing legal commentaries in the solitude of their offices. They had learned the art of war fortuitously in the ranks of the revolution and by reading the works of specialists. Members of the younger generation had received neither honors nor perquisites from the party; they had been deprived of the opportunity to serve and develop in public office.[37]

There is some evidence to support the impressions of contemporary observers concerning the sociological differences between the Liberal factions. Although relatively young men such as Juan E. Manrique and José Camacho Carrizosa did figure prominently among peace Liberals, important figures like Aquileo Parra, Miguel Samper, Salvador Camacho Roldán, Sergio Camargo, and José B. Gaitán were all septuagenarians. Conversely, leaders of the Liberal war faction in Bogotá were considerably younger. Uribe Uribe was forty years old in 1899. Max Grillo was thirty-one and Ricardo Tirado Macías, Uribe Uribe's other collaborator on *El Autonomista,* was about the same age. Juan Félix de León and Pedro Soler Martínez were exceptionally old at sixty-one and about fifty-nine, respectively. Cenón Figueredo was about thirty-five in 1899, while Juan Manuel Rudas was fifty. Scattered information on important provincial leaders of the war faction of the party supports this trend. Luis E. Villar and Justo L. Durán, organizers of the revolt in Santander, were fifty and forty years old respectively in 1899. Ramón Neira of Boyacá and Avelino Rosas of Cauca were both fifty when the war broke out.

It appears that most of the young men of the party identified with the leadership of the war faction. At least that is the impression con-

37. *El Autonomista,* September 13, 1899. Uribe Uribe had emphasized the same theme in 1896 when he explained that the hatred of "los hombres nuevos" toward the Regeneration was not gratuitous. "Ella [La Regeneración] ha impedido en nosotros el funcionamiento de toda facultad y ha matado en germen toda aptitud. . . ." Uribe Uribe, *Discursos,* p. 3.

veyed by many of Uribe Uribe's correspondents.[38] The depth of the hostilities that some Liberal youth came to hold toward the leaders of the peace Liberal faction was revealed in a protest letter that a number of Liberal youths planned to deliver to the offices of *La Crónica* during a public demonstration to be held on July 29, the day after Uribe Uribe's imprisonment. In their protest, the young Liberals disavowed the peace Liberal leaders, declared they no longer considered them as countrymen, denied them the authority to speak to them of their beliefs and ideals, and stated that they "dishonored and perverted" Liberal youth.[39]

In an effort to determine the occupations of representatives of the two Liberal factions, lists of partisans were checked in the 1893 Bogotá city directory used previously. Peace Liberals were identified by their signing of a manifesto which indirectly, but strongly, criticized Uribe Uribe in July, 1899.[40] Although over 400 people signed the manifesto only the first 200 names were checked in the directory; 132 of these were identified. Of those, well over a third were listed as merchants, while lawyers and physicians were well represented (see Table 4:1). Finding a comparable published list of war Liberals was difficult. The most appropriate list uncovered was an exhortation signed by 56 partisans of Uribe Uribe urging provincial supporters to begin to organize for the coming party elections.[41] The unavoidably small number of war Liberals was then searched in the city directory and 25 of the 56 signers were identified. Ten of those were lawyers, while only four were merchants (see Table 4:2).

While this limited and crude statistical information is only suggestive, comparison of the breakdowns does support the contention that a much higher proportion of export-import merchants were identified with the peace Liberal faction. Indeed the concerns of merchants correlate nicely with the nature of peace Liberal politics. Peace Liberals were primarily interested in dismantling Regeneration finance, and only secondarily concerned with the acquisition of formal political power by the Liberal party. Certainly, as men of wealth depen-

38. See, for example, Adriano Páez to Rafael Uribe Uribe, Cafetal de Balunda, cerca de Fusagasugá [Cundinamarca], September 8, 1898; Alonzo Alvarez to Rafael Uribe Uribe, Medellín, February 15, 1899; Calixto Gaitán to Rafael Uribe Uribe, Utica [Cundinamarca], February 14, 1899, Uribe, Box 13, 31, and 5, respectively, ACH.

39. When the demonstrators' protest march, planned for mid-day on July 29, was prohibited by the governor of Cundinamarca, they submitted the letter for publication in *El Autonomista*. Uribe, Box 17, ACH.

40. The manifesto was published in *La Crónica*, July 15, 1899, and supported the position taken by the Provisional Directorate against the liquor monopoly in Tolima. Since by July the debate over Uribe Uribe's position condoning the Tolima monopoly had become a major battleground in the struggle between the two factions, the manifesto provides a good index of peace Liberals.

41. The document was published in *El Autonomista*, July 12, 1899.

Table 4:1 Occupations of two hundred sample peace Liberals, Bogotá, 1899

comerciantes (merchants)	50
abogados (lawyers)	27
negociantes (traders)	14
médicos (physicians)	10
empleados (employees)	7
hacendados (landowners)	6
agricultores (agriculturalists)	3
ingenieros (engineers)	2
institutores (educators)	2
farmacéuticos (pharmacists)	2
dependientes (dependents)	2
sastre (tailor)	1
periodista (journalist)	1
industrial (manufacturer)	1
sacerdote (priest)	1
sombrerero (hatter)	1
contabilista (bookkeeper)	1
estudiante (student)	1
Total identified	132
Unidentified	68
Total	200

Table 4:2. Occupations of fifty-six sample war Liberals, Bogotá, 1899

abogados (lawyers)	10
comerciantes (merchants)	4
negociantes (traders)	2
ingeniero (engineer)	1
sastre (tailor)	1
industrial (manufacturer)	1
estudiante (student)	1
agricultor (agriculturalist)	1
Cónsul de Venezuela (Venezuelan Consul)	1
empleado (employee)	1
prestamista (money lender)	1
librero (book dealer)	1
Total identified	25
Unidentified	31
Total	56

dent upon international trade, merchants found the idea of civil war with its attendant risks of expropriation of property and disruption of commerce abhorrent. Although war Liberals generally shared the laissez-faire critique of Regeneration economic and monetary policy, they reversed the priorities of the peace Liberals. For them the paramount issue was control of the government. Often well educated, as the number of lawyers in the sample indicates, many war Liberals in Bogotá may have believed, as did Uribe Uribe, that their opportunities for social and economic mobility were unacceptably limited under the political exclusivism of the Regeneration governments. But while it is useful to explore the occupations of the war Liberal leadership resident in Bogotá, in one sense such an exercise is misleading, for the bulk of the war faction's strength and leadership lay in the provinces, and it is in the consideration of the differences between politics in the capital and politics in the countryside that the fullest meaning of the Liberal split can be found.

Historically there has been a striking cleavage between city and rural politics in Colombia. The literature on *la violencia* documents the extremes of political exclusivism on the local level in the mid-twentieth century, while the masterful writings of Gabriel García Márquez convey the human dimensions of the pervasive political tensions in small Colombian towns.[42] At the end of the nineteenth century political commentators often reminded themselves and their readers of the gulf separating the genteel, urbane politics practiced in a city like Bogotá and the violent political exclusivism characteristic of the rural areas and small towns where the vast majority of the Colombian people lived. During the election of 1897 Carlos Martínez Silva noted that the elimination of the opposition's right to vote was still considered indispensable in "small town politics," where everything "is determined by personalities" and the fight for the "exercise of brutal *cacicazcos* [local spheres of influence]." In the capital, Martínez Silva went on, personal matters were of relatively small importance and "all cultured people treat each other with cordiality and respect."[43] Uribe Uribe continually stressed the contrast between the niceties of urban politics and the naked abuses typical in the countryside[44] and Miguel Antonio Caro acknowledged his inability to con-

42. Although García Márquez's famous novel *Cien años de soledad* and the novella *El coronel no tiene quién le escriba* contain much insight into the nature of local Colombian political violence, the powerful novella *La mala hora* and the author's earliest short stories most successfully convey the way in which national political rivalries are played out in inter-personal relationships in the hot, dusty monotony of Colombian small towns. Márquez's works are available in numerous Spanish editions and most of them have been translated into English.

43. Carlos Martínez Silva, "Revista política de noviembre 28, 1897," Martínez Delgado, ed., *Revistas*, II, 249-50.

44. See *El Autonomista*, March 9, 1889, April 19, 1899, September 12, 1899.

trol local government officials in his electoral pledge to the Liberals in 1897.

The different quality of rural politics became especially notable near election time when petty government officials and local strongmen mobilized their resources to defeat the political opposition. The crucial presidential election of 1897, for example, provides a wealth of data to support the observations of Carlos Martínez Silva, Rafael Uribe Uribe, and others on the dichotomy between rural and urban politics.[45] As has been noted, Liberals won that election in Bogotá, declaring it one of the fairest and cleanest elections in Colombian history. Voting conditions were quite different in the provinces. Although most electoral abuses outside the capital were accomplished through peaceful means, the potential for violence was great. The restricting of voter registration was the most common method used to limit Liberal access to the polls. Registrars were either never in their offices for Liberals or simply found some pretext for refusing to inscribe Liberals. Government officials abused the literacy requirement as in the case of one district in southern Tolima where Liberals were disqualified because they could not spell such words as "particularísimamente." Alternatively, the property requirement could be unjustly applied.[46] In addition, the government could vote the army, its ranks often swollen with pre-election recruits.[47] These quasi-legal methods were sometimes accompanied with overt intimidation and violence. Witness the report of one Liberal on the nature of the presidential elections held on December 5, 1897, in the municipalities of the Río Negro basin in western Cundinamarca. Nationalists won in La Palma, he claimed, because of the arrival of a detachment of troops in time to cast their ballots. In La Peña no elections were held because several armed individuals led by Anastacio Martínez, an associate of the brother of the prefect of Guaduas, forced the mayor and the electoral judges to flee the city. In Utica the mayor, Pedro Saavedra, the judge, Anastacio Ramírez, and Pedro Murillo Frío shot up the town on the night of the fourth damaging the house of Heliodoro Rubio, wounding one man, and killing a donkey that was mistaken for a person. In Nocaima irregularities occurred, and in Villeta the lists of

45. In a typical letter one of Parra's correspondents commented on the Liberals' inability to register to vote due to the abuses of local officials. The situation in Ubaté, Cundinamarca, was similar to that of the entire republic "fuera de las ciudades grandes en donde se puede ejercer sanción y los agentes del Gbo. tienen una honorabilidad relative ó impuesta, pero por acá, las cosas pasan de manera muy distinta." Cenón Solano R. to Aquileo Parra, Ubaté, November 15, 1898, Parra, ACH.

46. In order to be eligible to vote citizens had to be at least twenty-one years of age and either be able to read and write or have an annual income of at least 500 pesos or real property worth at least 1,500 pesos.

47. These abuses are amply documented in the papers marked, "Correspondencia de 1897" in Parra, ACH.

registered voters were not to be found. In short, the informant concluded, "everything has transpired as in the other elections."[48]

In the light of such abuses the reasons for the extreme reluctance of provincial Liberal leaders to follow the directives of the national Directorate and urge the rank and file to go the the polls and vote become clearer.[49] Uribe Uribe probably spoke for many provincial Liberal party members when he editorialized in early 1899 that it was easier and less dangerous for Liberals to take up arms than to participate in electoral politics under the Regeneration. One went to war resolved to die if need be, Uribe Uribe argued, but risking one's life against that of one's adversary in a fair fight, and hoping to win through greater valor, ability, or numbers. But to have to go to the polls peacefully, knowing full well that one's adversaries, civil as well as military, were armed, knowing that one's opponents were ready to use force to implement previously planned frauds, and knowing that one must remain patient and resigned as instructed in the face of verbal insults and physical affronts, this was a sacrifice greater than most men could bear. Small wonder, Uribe Uribe concluded, that Liberals in the provinces would be reluctant to exercise the vote even under a new electoral law.[50]

Elections were only one aspect, and perhaps a superficial one, of the dichotomy between rural and urban politics. Outside the major cities, control of politics more seriously affected not only access to the polls, but access to government jobs and favors, to police protection, and to justice in the courts. Identification with the man or party in control of local politics significantly increased one's life chances. Opposition to those in control not only eliminated opportunities but threatened one's property as well as one's life. A vivid and certainly biased description of the impact of national political hegemony on local affairs was sent to *El Autonomista* in April, 1899, by C. N. Rodríguez, a resident of La Paz, a subdivision of the municipality of Guaduas in western Cundinamarca. Rodríguez described how a local conservative strongman, with the help of Nationalist authorities ranging from the mayor to the departmental governor, had successfully and massively enlarged his landholdings until he owned thousands of hectares, and made of La Paz his own bailiwick, imposing his will on those who lived on his lands making them "render vassalage." Smaller landowners lodged protests against his encroachment on their lands, "but the governor at the very least is deaf, the prefect at the very least is tolerant, and the mayor is always loyal."

48. Ramón Calderón to Aquileo Parra, Villeta, December 10, 1897, Parra, ACH.
49. José del C. Montenegro to Juan E. Manrique, Chocontá, October 5, 1897; Juan E. Manrique to Aquileo Parra, Bogotá, October 2, 1897, Manrique, ACH.
50. *El Autonomista*, April 8, 1899.

Those who carried their complaints to the national authorities in the capital were undercut by the local strongman who labeled them as Liberal conspirators whom it was necessary to "hold at bay."[51]

A better illustration of the implications of political partisanship in small towns emerges from the events surrounding the murder of Proto Ramírez, a provincial Liberal chief whose life was typical in many ways of other war Liberals' careers and whose death in April, 1899, became a sort of cause célebre among party militants. Proto Ramírez was born in the municipality of Susa in northern Cundinamarca on March 15, 1868. According to *El Autonomista,* his birth came two months after his father had been "barbarously murdered" in circumstances "identical" to those surrounding Ramírez's own death in 1899.[52] Somewhat later Ramírez's mother died and he moved to Bogotá, where he studied in the elite Liberal school of El Colegio del Rosario, at that time under the rectorship of doctrinaire Liberal Juan Manuel Rudas. Ramírez left his studies to fight in the civil war of 1885. In 1895 he again joined the Liberal ranks distinguishing himself in battle and rising to the rank of colonel. After the Revolution of 1895 he found it impossible to live in Susa for political reasons and worked in Bogotá as an employee for the newly established Bavaria beer factory and the recently founded Bogotá Tramway. Ramírez never married, but he supported the large families of two widowed sisters. He had returned to live in Susa when he was murdered on April 15, 1899.

For two years prior to his death Ramírez had been engaged in a land dispute with Conservatives Mario, Parmenio, and Aristides Pinilla over ownership of part of a pasture called *El Chequín* in the municipality of Susa. Ramírez claimed to have legally acquired the land in question, having purchased it from Ismael Pinilla, brother of the men who later killed him. Several days before Ramírez's death, the two parties seemed on the verge of reaching a settlement, but for some reason their proposed deal fell through and Ramírez appealed to the mayor for protection. The mayor isued an order requiring the Pinillas to appear before him, but they ignored it. At that point the question was complicated by the arrival of Delfín Medina, Prefect of the Province of Ubaté, which included the municipality of Susa. An uncle of the Pinilla brothers, Medina visited the piece of land in question and promised his nephews he would take care of the problem. Fearing that Medina would be able to gain possession of the land through use of his authority, Ramírez resolved to plow the land, thereby strengthening his claim to ownership. He was in the act of plowing

51. *El Autonomista,* April 19, 1899.

52. *Ibid,* July 9, 1899. The story which follows is adapted from this issue and several previous issues of *El Autonomista* including those of April 21, 1899, April 23, 1899, and May 27, 1899.

when the Pinilla brothers moved in and shot him, in the passionate language of *El Autonomista,* "just as one shoots a deer." Then, as Ramírez lay dying on the ground, "they finished him off and cruelly vented their passion on his cadaver." The perpetrators of the crime were quickly apprehended and confessed to the mayor that Medina had sent them to kill Ramírez, that he, Medina, was responsible. Ramírez's supporters were dismayed to learn, however, that the judge in charge of the case had as his secretary one Ahumada, son-in-law of Delfín Medina. Presuming the complicity of Ahumada, they requested that he be replaced, but the judge refused. *El Autonomista* doubted that justice would be done and urged that Liberals from the eight surrounding municipalities contribute to a fund to secure a private prosecutor. Liberals should watch over the handling of the case, the paper editorialized, bombarding public officials with memorials urging justice and, in the event they were ignored, they should carry out their own investigation in the certainty that some day it would be possible to judge the murderers of Ramírez and punish them. On April 23, Jorge Franco, secretary of government of Cundinamarca, announced that the government's preliminary investigation of the case had confirmed the apparent innocence of Delfín Medina. The Pinilla brothers, however, were still in jail when the case was last mentioned in the press in July, 1899. Proto Ramírez was buried in Susa on April 17, 1899. According to three local Liberal observers his funeral was an impressive affair attended by a large number of Liberals, many of them from Chiquinquirá, Ubaté, and neighboring towns. Six months later, the province of Ubaté became one of the major foci in Cundinamarca of the Liberal uprising which mushroomed into the War of the Thousand Days.

Part Two

The War of the Thousand Days

Chapter V

The Outbreak of War

It is difficult 'to overemphasize the magnitude of the economic and political crises confronting Colombia and its Nationalist government by 1899. The origins of both these crises lay ultimately in the changes wrought in Colombia by the rise of the coffee export economy, yet if they could have been handled separately they might have proved manageable. But during 1899 each crisis influenced and intensified the other, creating a problem that was much greater than the sum of its separate parts, and generating the conditions which led, seemingly inevitably, to civil war.

World coffee prices fell sharply after 1896, and by 1899 they averaged only 8.6 cents per pound, or half the level maintained during the first half of the decade (see Figure 2:1). In many areas of Colombia where coffee production or transportation was especially costly, or the quality of coffee beans grown was inferior (as was the case, for example, in much of Santander), coffee growers began to operate at a loss or ceased production altogether by 1899. In most other coffee-producing areas profits were marginal.[1] Hard times in the coffee zones led many people to countenance the idea of revolt which, despite its attendant risks, offered opportunities for pillage and sustenance. Commenting on persistent rumors of impending revolt in Colombia in a telegraph he sent high government officials a day before the War of the Thousand Days broke out, the governor of Santander described the clandestine movement within the department of "many unemployed and probably hungry people . . . in search of adventure," but mistakenly assumed they were en route to the neighboring province of Táchira, Venezuela, where a revolt was already in progress.[2]

The massive decline in imports resulting from the coffee crash drastically reduced customs revenues and placed the government in a

1. As noted in Chapter II, average Colombian production and transportation costs were estimated by contemporaries at about eight cents per pound.
2. Vicent Villamizar to the Ministers of Government and War, Pamplona [Santander], October 17, 1889, AMD, vol. 05694. For an introduction to conditions in neighboring Venezuela and some indication of the interrelatedness of Colombian and Venezuelan politics at this time, see Domingo Alberto Rangel, *Los andinos en el poder* (Caracas, 1964).

fiscal crisis of mammoth proportions.[3] By June Minister of Finance Carlos Calderón wrote President Sanclemente that the deficit was "terrifying" and claimed that government income was only meeting two-thirds of the ordinary expenses, not including many extra obligations already incurred.[4] As the year progressed the government began to experience difficulties in paying even such crucial employees as telegraph operators, military personnel, and police. Instructed by the president in July to give payment of the army first priority, by September Calderón declared that government revenues were no longer sufficient to pay even the army and added that he was borrowing at a discount on future customs receipts to meet the most crucial expenses of the government. At that Sanclemente threw up his hands in despair and admitted that his government was in a state of virtual bankruptcy with the fiscal situation getting worse each day.[5] Any hope government officials might have still entertained for a solution to the fiscal crisis was soon dashed by news presaging an even greater decline in imports. In late September the important New York commercial house Punderford and Co. announced that it was suspending the credit of its Colombian clients and *La Crónica* reported that other foreign commission agents had begun to call in their Colombian accounts.[6] By mid-October the government was being deluged daily by telegrams from all parts of the country pleading for shipments of funds to pay back salaries of public officials.[7] Telegraph operators in several areas threatened to resign if not paid, and delays in pay compromised the loyalty of the police in Bogotá as well as key army garrisons around the country.[8]

3. McGreevey's estimates only partially confirm the very large decline in trade perceived by contemporary Colombian observers. His data indicate that exports fell off from 16.9 million current United States dollars in 1898 to 15.2 million in 1899. Imports, on the other hand, did fall rapidly after 1896 according to McGreevey's estimates, declining from 22.9 million in 1896 to 13.7 million in 1899. McGreevey, *An Economic History*, p. 210. Figures for 1899 tend to exaggerate the prewar slump somewhat since trade was greatly curtailed after the war began in mid-October.

4. Carlos Calderón to Manuel A. Sanclemente, Bogotá, June 3, 1899, Correspondencia del Presidente Manuel A. Sanclemente, Archivo Nacional de Colombia, 5, f. 777 (hereafter cited as Sanclemente, ANC).

5. Manuel A. Sanclemente to Carlos Calderón, Anapoima, July 19, 1899, September 5, 1899, Calderón, ACH. Calderón gave some figures to support his contentions concerning military expenditures and government revenues in a letter to Sanclemente on September 11. He estimated that the armed forces cost about 600,000 pesos a month, about the same as the "producto bruto de todas las aduanas en las cuales se paga en primer término a los empleados de las mismas oficinas y de los resguardos." Carlos Calderón to Manuel A. Sanclemente, Bogotá, September 11, 1899, Calderón, ACH.

6. The company cited fear of imminent civil war as the reason for its action. *La Crónica*, September 28 and 29, 1899.

7. See for example the telegrams received on October 9, 1899, in AMD, vol. 05783.

8. AMD, vol. 05694. See especially Inocencio Madero [?] to Director of the National Police, Bogotá, October 16, 1889, and Eduardo Gerlein to Minister of the Treasury, Bogotá, October 14, 1899.

Two months before the war broke out, the minister of finance captured the essence of the crisis which had befallen the Nationalist government. "[A] poor government," he explained, "is a weak government, a government without moral authority, incapable of inspiring fear or affection." Moreover, the Nationalist government was caught in a vicious circle. The government's inability to meet its financial obligations was generally, and daily, perceived. The result was widespread distrust of the government's ability to maintain order, the consequent paralysis of commerce, and therefore, a continuing fall in the customs receipts, the main source of government revenues.[9] The economic and fiscal crisis materially weakened the government but perhaps its greatest impact was psychological. Nationalists became less sure of the political and economic institutions and policies of the Regeneration, while their political opponents, both Liberal and Conservative, became ever more convinced of the validity of their critique of Nationalist policies and emboldened in their choice of tactics to combat the regime.

The Liberal campaign against Regeneration fiscal and monetary policies escalated during 1899, forcing the supporters of paper money onto the defensive. Miguel Samper, the great critic of Regeneration finance, died on March 16, 1899, but José Camacho Carrizosa maintained a constant barrage of criticism of government economic policies from the pages of *La Crónica*. A newcomer to the ranks of Liberal economic polemicists was Lucas Caballero, a young man from Santander whose detailed descriptions of the impact of the fall in coffee prices on every aspect of the Colombian economy gave his articles published in *La Crónica* an immediacy often wanting in the more abstract writing of other Liberals.[10]

Caballero argued that during the boom in the coffee industry, everyone—workers, merchants, priests, cattlemen, cane growers—had

9. Carlos Calderón made this statement in an address to the secretaries of finance of the departments in Bogotá. See *El Autonomista*, September 2, 1899.

10. Born into the landed elite in the town of Suaita, Santander, on January 20, 1868 or 1869, Caballero studied in the school run by Santiago Pérez and graduated from the Externado in jurisprudence in 1889. Along with Eduardo Rodríguez Piñeres he was a partner in the law firm Nicolás Esguerra y Cía. In August, 1899, he left *La Crónica* and joined Alejo de la Torre in founding *El Diario*, a paper backed by prominent peace Liberals and merchants. (A list of wishers-well was published in the first issue of *El Diario*, August 19, 1899.) During the paper's short existence the editors devoted themselves to careful criticism of the government's attempts to deal with the fiscal crisis. They steadfastly opposed war and ceased publication after a call for peace on October 18, 1899. After forming part of an unsuccessful peace mission, Caballero joined the revolution and came to play an important role in the war as chief of staff of Benjamín Herrera, the most successful of the Liberal generals. On Caballero see Ospina, *Biografía*, I, 366, Luis Eduardo Nieto Caballero, "Recuerdos de Lucas Caballero," *El Tiempo*, Suplemento Literario, November 2, 1942, and Caballero's own book, *Memorias de la guerra de los mil días* (Bogotá, 1939).

benefited. In those days to be a "coffee grower was a glorious achievement for individuals, and a title of respect among the people." But the fall in world prices had ruined the coffee industry and depressed other sectors of the economy as well. Although it was true that coffee prices for the best grades had remained high, exporters had painfully learned that only a small portion of their shipments were classified in that category. Prices had dropped to almost a third of their former levels in less than three years and had made it unprofitable to harvest coffee in some areas, and cases of satisfactory return on large initial capital investments in the coffee industry had become "phenomenally rare." For those coffee growers paying off loans the drop in prices had been disastrous; often they had been forced to borrow against the next harvest and pay interest on that money of up to 3 or 4 percent monthly.[11]

Caballero attempted to show that paper money made the situation of the Colombian coffee grower even worse. Most growers had arrangements with commercial houses that allowed them to draw on accounts in gold currencies, and cover these drafts with coffee shipments, usually within a period of four months, although extensions were possible. Thus, he contended, a coffee grower who received a certain quantity of paper pesos in Colombia for a draft in gold against his account would have to pay back a much larger quantity of pesos a few months later as a result of the rising exchange rate produced by the constant emissions of paper money.[12]

While it was true, Caballero admitted, that coffee growers who were already in production when coffee prices rose had made a fortune, for most producers coffee growing had been "a real fiasco; more: a burying ground for illusions, health, the best years of life, and capital." This had happened because most growers had joined the boom in the 1890's. They paid high prices for land, gave little attention to the problems of transportation and labor supply, and failed to realize that it took seven years for coffee trees to reach maximum production.

During the period of growing coffee exports, coffee had become the foundation of Colombia's commerce; when the industry collapsed it had "ruined practically every other industry." The sugar cane industry had been severely hurt by the decrease in consumption of syrup and rum in the coffee zones caused by the decline in the number of

11. Lucas Caballero, *Bancarrota nacional* (Bogotá, 1899), pp. 40, 35, 36. This book is a collection of articles published previously in *La Crónica*.

12. *Ibid.*, p. 37. This argument appears to have held only for small producers who sold their coffee to export merchants within Colombia. Large growers shipped their coffee directly abroad and for all practical purposes bypassed the Colombian monetary system by dealing directly in gold-based currencies. But since most large exporters were also importers they were hurt by the rising exchange rate, and import merchants appear to have been the main constituency of Lucas Caballero.

workers employed on the coffee plantations. In many areas sugar cane syrup could not be sold and usually its selling price, far from providing a return on investments, barely covered production costs. Commerce was in a similar state. Consumption of imported goods had greatly diminished, leaving merchants in the dilemma of not selling on credit and having few purchasers, or extending credit and losing because of currency depreciation. Alternative means for making a living were not available. Mining required too much capital, cotton had serious drawbacks in Colombia, rubber collection was too risky to health.

Caballero admitted that many elements of the country's economic and fiscal crisis were beyond the control of the government; nevertheless, he argued, the Regeneration had been guilty of political errors and economic improvisation. The Nationalists had mishandled relations with foreigners and as a result had had to pay costly indemnifications. They had imposed monopolies, failed to service the foreign debt, and tolerated graft and corruption. Reflecting the regional interests of Santander, which lacked rail as well as adequate trail communication with the Magdalena River, Caballero criticized not only the Regeneration's poor handling of railroad contracts, but the very idea of constructing railroads when the country still lacked an adequate mule trail system. Railroad construction was wasteful and unproductive in Colombia's mountainous terrain. The lack of sufficient mule trails had almost placed Colombia "outside the world market," he contended, and was in great part the cause of the economic and fiscal crisis facing the nation at the end of the century. With one-fifth of the money the Regeneration had spent on the military or on indemnification for unfulfilled contracts, the economic situation could have been transformed through improvement and construction of mule trails.

Caballero capped his criticism of Regeneration fiscal and economic policies with a program for reform which closely paralleled previous Liberal and Historical Conservative platforms. He called for a minimum of government by honest, capable men responsive to public opinion and capable of establishing security and stability. He advocated tax reform to remove impediments to the free exchange of goods and services. He called for effective freedom of enterprise and improvements in education. He demanded an end to emissions of paper money in order to rehabilitate the institution of private credit. Finally, he stressed the need for punctual payments on the foreign debt. If that were done, foreign capital would flow into Colombia and usher in a new era of material progress.[13]

13. *Ibid.*, pp. 38, 39-40, 47-49, 10-14, 53-54, 61-64.

Another Liberal indictment of Regeneration monetary policies, more theoretical than Caballero's work, was Roberto de la Torre's *Estudio sobre nuestra circulación monetaria*, a thesis submitted to the Liberal school El Liceo Mercantil in June, 1899, and published later in the year as a book by José Camacho Carrizosa's press, La Crónica. Like the other Liberal economists, de la Torre argued that paper money caused a constant rise in the rate of exchange, forced capital out of productive investment, dried up sources of private credit, encouraged investment in buildings and land, produced only temporary well-being among workers, ultimately caused property (especially property like coffee farms which required capital investments to make it productive) to decline in value, stimulated the flight of capital abroad, discouraged foreign investment in Colombia, caused prices to rise, and made the export-import business risky. While coffee prices were high many of those pernicious effects had been neutralized, de la Torre contended, but once coffee prices fell, the economic crisis had been "aggravated and accelerated" by the regime of paper money. The economic rehabilitation of the country depended upon the immediate cessation of the printing of paper money, the reversion of the power to issue money to private banks, and the restoration of the right to stipulate hard currencies in contracts.

The originality of the thesis lay in its novel plan for conversion of paper to gold. De la Torre called for the integral participation of merchants in the process, formalized by legal contract. A syndicate of merchants would collect the tax revenues designated for amortization and enjoy all powers necessary to implement the conversion. Government would cease issuing paper money, but could expect loans from the merchant syndicate. If the interests of the merchant guild and government were thus harmonized, political stability and a new era of material progress would result.[14]

Responding to a growing consensus against Regeneration monetary policies, *La Crónica* shifted its emphasis from criticism of the evils of paper money to a search for the best solution to the problems of conversion to metallic currency. In September, 1899, *La Crónica* asked prominent merchants, bankers and other men reputed to have a special understanding of economic and financial affairs to state their opinions on three questions. Assuming a general desire to rid the country of paper money, *La Crónica* asked: (1) Should the country return to a gold or to a silver standard? (2) Should the depreciated paper be redeemed at its nominal or market value? And (3) Should private banks be given the right to issue money? Some fifty-seven

14. Roberto de la Torre, *Estudio sobre nuestra circulación monetaria* (Bogotá, 1899). The phrase quoted is taken from p. 14.

men responded to *La Crónica's* query, virtually all of them peace Liberals or Historical Conservatives. Although the respondents divided on the first question, a majority favored gold. Most supported the idea of redeeming paper money at face value and virtually all passionately defended the right of private banks to issue money. Only one response, that of J. de D. Uribe R. Alvarez, argued in favor of paper money.[15] That view was vigorously rebutted by Quijano Wallis, who contended that it was true that as long as a nation had only internal commerce, anything, even the "dirty" paper money in use in Colombia would do as a medium of exchange. But from the moment nations progressed beyond the "savage and primitive" state to take part in "the concert of world civilization," they had to adopt money of intrinsic international value.[16]

Nationalists resisted these arguments, blaming the drop in coffee prices for the economic and fiscal crisis and denying the pernicious influence of paper money.[17] The scrappy Nationalist paper *Bogotá* in language reminiscent of Miguel Antonio Caro continued to denounce "free stipulation." At a time when the value of Colombian currency was declining, *Bogotá* editorialized, free stipulation favored the big capitalist, invariably a creditor, over the small retailer who lived on credit. It was hard to understand how those who claimed to defend the interests of the people could seek to oppress and exploit the poor through free stipulation.[18] One of the most intelligent Nationalist defenders of paper money was Carlos Calderón, the man who served both as minister of finance and minister of the treasury during much of 1899. A long-time apologist of paper money, Calderón had served as minister of the treasury under Miguel Antonio Caro. As late as 1898 Calderón audaciously proposed a large emission of paper to be used by the state to foment the textile industry in Colombia. Calderón appreciated how paper money could act as an over-all protection against foreign imports and thereby stimulate national industry. He believed that returning to the gold standard would benefit only importers of foreign goods, and insisted that the economic crisis faced by Colombia was a result of deficient production, not the country's monetary system.[19] By 1899 however, even the apologists for paper money in Co-

15. *La Crónica,* September 14, 1899.

16. *Ibid.,* September 15, 1899.

17. Liberals were alarmed at the political implications of this argument and even went to the extreme of arguing that coffee prices had begun to rise. See *El Autonomista,* June 28, 1899.

18. *Bogotá,* December 1, 1898.

19. Calderón, *La cuestión monetaria,* Appendix A, pp. 163-76. Calderón's book, compiled from articles written just after the conclusion of the War of the Thousand Days, at a time when the depreciation of the Colombian paper peso was greatest and the prestige of paper money reached its lowest ebb, ranks along with Jorge Holguín's *La bestia negra* (Bogotá, 1892) and Miguel Antonio Caro's messages to congress as one of the most

lombia were on the defensive, and Calderón returned to the cabinet in 1899 to spend his time juggling government revenues to meet the most pressing expenses while casting about for new sources of revenue in a desperate attempt to keep Sanclemente's government afloat financially.

Deprived of sufficient revenue, discredited in its economic and fiscal policies, the Nationalist government found itself besieged on all sides by dissident factions demanding major political and economic concessions as the price for their continued support of the government. Historical Conservatives, Liberals, and even many erstwhile Nationalists pressured the government to adopt political and fiscal measures which, had they been implemented, not only would have repudiated past Regeneration policies, but would have gravely compromised the Nationalist hold on political power. Although at various times during the year the Nationalist government made minor concessions or indicated a willingness to negotiate with the opposition, it proved unwilling to make concessions which threatened its very existence.

From the first, the political strength of Sanclemente's government had been seriously compromised. An old man, unable to govern from the capital, Sanclemente was often described by his critics as mentally and physically unfit for his position and subject to manipulation by unscrupulous men around him. Critics were supported in the contention by the fact that Sanclemente's signature was often stamped on important documents.[20] Sanclemente's unexpected assumption of power on November 3, 1898, had alienated Liberals and Historical Conservatives alike, and although most leaders of both parties adopted a wait-and-see attitude toward the new regime, as the months went by the opposition to Sanclemente grew while his support steadily dwindled.

Fortunately for Sanclemente, his government was early able to conclude on agreement with the Nationalist-Conservative faction led by Rafael Reyes. Reyes continued as presidential designate and the *reyistas* Jorge Holguín, Carlos Calderón, and Carlos Cuervo Márquez were given cabinet posts in Sanclemente's government, which reserved the powerful post of minister of government to the trusted Nationalist Rafael María Palacio. The *reyistas* saw themselves as occupying a pragmatic middle ground between the extreme positions of the Nationalists and the Historical Conservatives, and, true to the

comprehensive and intelligent defenses of the Regeneration's monetary system. See also Calderón's impressive explanation of the Colombian economic and fiscal crisis published in *El Autonomista,* September 2, 1899.

20. A facsimile of the stamp is published in Martínez Delgado, *Historia,* between pp. 56 and 57.

aspirations of their mentor, they attempted to unify the Conservative party by bringing the Historical Conservatives into the government.[21] The Historical Conservative leadership based in Bogotá apparently rejected these overtures. On February 8, 1899, the leading Historical Conservative paper in Bogotá, José Joaquín Pérez's *El Heraldo*, publicly speculated on the possibility of an alliance of Historical Conservatives and Liberals against Sanclemente's government, and on February 23 the paper editorialized that if reforms were not forthcoming a Liberal revolt would be justified.[22]

The *antioqueño* leadership of the Historical Conservatives expressed a willingness to support Sanclemente's government, but only under certain conditions. Their position was framed in a memorial dated February 1, signed by Marceliano Vélez and twelve other prominent *antioqueño* Historical Conservatives and sent to the three *reyista* ministers.[23] Raising the specter of a Liberal revolt within a year, the *antioqueños* demanded a greater share of power and positions within the government as the price for their support. The petitioners wanted above all to exercise a decisive influence in the selection of candidates for nationally appointed posts within their department including everything from governor to telegraph operators.[24] The memorial was published much later and inspired the ridicule of Uribe Uribe, who declared that the *antioqueño* Historical Conservatives had "revealed their hunger for jobs."[25] The memorial did seem to indicate that the petitioners were more interested in jobs than in political and economic reforms. It is hard to separate the question of power from positions, however, and certainly the *antioqueños'* desire for control over their own affairs is reflected in the demand for an end to the imposition of national appointments.

The *antioqueño* Historical Conservatives' vital interest in political, and above all, economic reforms, is demonstrated by a letter sent by Guillermo Restrepo, one of the signers of the memorial of February 1, to Carlos Calderón, Sanclemente's minister of finance, a few days

21. See Reyes's confidential instructions to Jorge Holguín dated Anapoima, January 10, 1899, MDT, ACH.

22. In his editorial of February 9, 1899, Pérez claimed he had received wide support for his proposed alliance with Liberals. One of the signers of the Motives of Dissidence in 1896, Pérez was the son-in-law of Sixto Durán, a prominent Liberal merchant and coffee grower.

23. Marceliano Vélez, *et al.* to Jorge Holguín, *et al.*, Medellín, February 1, 1899, Calderón, ACH.

24. In his covering letter, Vélez discounted any desire for public positions in the part of the petitioners and attributed their demand for jobs to pressure from party rank and file. Marceliano Vélez to Jorge Holguín, *et al.*, Medellín, February 5, 1899, Calderón, ACH.

25. *El Autonomista*, May 9, 1899. This is the document obliquely defended by Carlos Martínez Silva referred to in Chapter I.

later. The two men had recently consulted in Bogotá, and Restrepo began by noting the results of their conference. "Happily," he said, "we agreed on almost all political and financial matters, except the question of banks of issue." Restrepo confessed that he nourished the secret hope that they would some day agree on that important issue "just as we have come to agree on the transcendental matter of free stipulation." Restrepo went on to express his compassion for those of his friends who had to navigate in the agitated sea of politics, especially in Colombia, where politics was "so tortuous and insidious," but ended his letter urging Calderón to continue the fight.

> Marceliano [Vélez] thinks a great deal of you. . . . You constitute a great hope for us: your mission is one of struggle: don't do what our friend Megía [*sic*] Alvarez did.[26]

Restrepo's reference was to Luis María Mejía Alvarez, appointed by Marroquín to the ministry of the treasury in August, 1898. The Historical Conservatives had placed high hopes in Mejía Alvarez's fiscal orthodoxy. Carlos Martínez Silva described him as well versed in financial matters, "very honest and very much of the *antioqueño* school." Before taking his post Mejía Alvarez had notified Marroquín of his orthodox views on paper money, and the need for drastic economies and strict accounting, but by September, 1898, he had bowed to the political and economic pressures of the situation and recommended to the congress an issue of eight million paper pesos.[27]

In March Reyes himself journeyed to Anapoima to join the three *reyista* ministers in pushing for the designation of a Historical Conservative as governor of Antioquia as proof of their influence and the government's good-will toward the Historical Conservatives. Sanclemente and his strong-willed Nationalist minister of government, Rafael Palacio, refused to accede to the plan. To have shared political power and the spoils of government with the *antioqueño* Historical Conservative leadership that had steadfastly opposed Nationalist political and economic policy throughout the Regeneration would have constituted both an ideological and material defeat for the government. As events were to show, the Nationalist government realistically assessed the importance of the support of the Historical Conservative elite. Once the Liberals revolted against the government, Conservative party rank and file disobeyed the instructions of the Historical Conservative leaders and lent their support to the Nationalist regime.

26. Guillermo Restrepo to Carlos Calderón, Medellín, February 19, 1899, Calderón, ACH.
27. Carlos Martínez Silva, "Revista política de septiembre 24, 1898," in Martínez Delgado, ed., *Revistas*, II, 346-47.

The government may have been confident of the political impotence of Historical Conservative leaders, but it must have been greatly alarmed in May, 1899, when many former Nationalists joined with influential Historical Conservatives to petition the president to return to Bogotá, where he could govern effectively. Since the president's health would not permit him to live on the cold Sabana de Bogotá, the petition in effect constituted a declaration in favor of Marroquín's assumption of power.[28] A large proportion of the document's more than one hundred signers were defectors from the Nationalist camp, grouped behind the leadership of Army Chief of Staff Próspero Pinzón.[29] The Nationalist government reacted immediately to this impossible demand. It denounced the petitioners and removed Pinzón from his post. Pinzón went on to found *El País*, a Conservative newspaper backed by a meld of Historical Conservatives and former Nationalists,[30] from which he criticized government policies until he was forced to suspend publication with the advent of the declaration of the state of seige in Cundinamarca on July 28. Pinzón and his followers, however, continued to oppose the government until well after the outbreak of the war.

In July and August Historical Conservatives sought to escálate their pressure on the Nationalist government. At Marceliano Vélez's urging, a small convention of ten prominent Historical Conservatives (one to represent each department plus a secretary) met in Bogotá to formalize their opposition to government political and economic policy and to serve official notice of their oft-stated position of nonsupport for the government, even in the event of Liberal revolt.[31] Some of the delegates favored an even more radical stand and had proposed alliance with the Liberal party against the government.[32] After weeks of debate, on August 17, 1899 the delegates issued a statement, called the Acuerdo No. 3, in which they formally blamed Caro's and Sanclemente's policies for the fiscal and economic crisis, denounced as unjustified the declaration of martial law in Cundinamarca and Santander of July 28, 1899, deplored recent changes in military and government personnel which favored the Nationalists over the Con-

28. The petition was published in *El Heraldo*, June 9, 1899.

29. Born in Boyacá, Pinzón had acquired a military reputation during the Revolution of 1895. He had served in several high bureaucratic posts under subsequent Regeneration governments. Cayo Leonidas Peñuela, *El Doctor y General Próspero Pinzón* (Bogotá, 1941).

30. Lists of these collaborators and supporters appear in *El País*, June 23, 1899, and *El Heraldo*, June 6, 1899.

31. *El Heraldo*, February 8, 9, 23, 1899; Carlos Martínez Silva, "Revista política de abril 28, 1899," in Martínez Delgado, ed., *Revistas*, II, 432; Euclides de Angulo to Jorge Holguín, Bogotá, March 29, 1899, MDT, ACH.

32. Carlos Martínez Silva, "Revista política de agosto 30, 1899," in Martínez Delgado, ed., *Revistas*, II, 490-91.

servatives, and scored the government's unwillingness to cooperate with the Conservatives in reforming government policies. Declaring that they had a responsibility to make their position known, the Historical Conservatives hinted that they were contemplating alliance with Liberals. They declared that in the event constitutional order were disrupted, it was the duty of all Conservatives to seek every means at their disposal to reestablish it, without waiting for instructions from anyone, "and earnestly uniting their efforts with those of all other republicans who have the same aspiration."

As the political opposition to Sanclemente's government gathered momentum and the economic and fiscal crisis deepened, the Liberal factions were forced to define their position toward Sanclemente's embattled government and its Conservative opponents. There was never any question of the war Liberals' attitude toward the government. From the first they planned to revolt, secretly organizing for war, while publicly seeking to discredit the government. Peace Liberals, on the other hand, continued to work for peaceful reform of the economic institutions and policies inimical to their interests while lobbying for passage of the election reform law they felt would stem the tide carrying their party toward war.

Peace Liberals, represented by the Provisional Directorate which replaced Parra, initially placed great hope in the possibility of the government's convoking an extraordinary session of congress to pass an electoral law satisfactory to the political opposition. Liberal José C. Borda and President Sanclemente's son, Sergio, had conceived of the idea of a special session of congress to pass the election reform bill and the plan apparently had the initial approval of Sanclemente.[33] But in June Sanclemente seemed to renege on his promise by delaying his decision to convoke the congress and noting vaguely that future circumstances would determine the advisability of convoking an extraordinary session. The Provisional Directorate of the Liberal party, its reformist strategy once more discredited, denounced the president's decision and disclaimed any responsibility for the future course of national politics.[34]

Although unsuccessful in these efforts to secure political reforms, peace Liberals were encouraged by their ability to influence Sanclemente's fiscal policies. In May, the leading merchants of Bogotá, primarily peace Liberals and Historical Conservatives, organized to protect their interests in the face of a new and threatening manifestation of the economic and fiscal crisis confronting the nation.

33. Carlos Martínez Silva, "Revista política de junio 20, 1899," in Martínez Delgado, ed., *Revistas*, II, 472.

34. Unsigned draft of telegram sent by Liberal Provisional Directorate to President Sanclemente, Bogotá, June 10, 1899, Manrique, ACH.

The merchants were alarmed by the rapid rise and wide fluctuations in the exchange rate that occurred during the month of May, 1899. This kind of short-term fluctuation especially disturbed import merchants, who needed a fairly stable, predictable exchange rate to carry on long-term business transactions based mainly on foreign credit. Alarmed by a steep rise in the rate from April to May and an especially abrupt increase on May 25, leading merchants called a meeting for Sunday, May 28, to chart strategy to protect their interests. José María Quijano Wallis, a peace Liberal, was acclaimed chairman of the meeting attended by some two hundred merchants. He gave a brief review of the situation, stressing emissions of paper money and falling coffee prices as dual long-term causes of the rising exchange rate, but blaming speculators for the sudden changes in the value of Colombian currency. Affirming the strength of the merchant guild and its ability to influence government, Quijano Wallis proposed a twofold solution to the situation confronting the nation: (1) formation of an organization of merchants to be called the Liga de Comercio de Bogotá and run by an executive committee with wide powers, and (2) foundation of a commercial bank through which merchants could join forces to insure a stable exchange rate. The first resolution passed easily, but there was considerable opposition to the second. Some merchants, notably Abel Camacho, argued that the blame for rising and fluctuating exchange rates lay squarely with the government. The abrupt rise of May 25, Camacho argued, was the result of a panic triggered by *El Autonomista's* publication of an interview with the minister of the treasury in which he acknowledged a monthly deficit of 200,000 pesos. A bank, Camacho concluded, would attack a symptom but not cure the disease, which emanated from the government itself. An impasse developed over the issue, but by the next Sunday the merchants had reached a compromise. The question of a bank was submitted to a committee for study, and the Liga de Comercio was founded.[35]

One of the first acts of the Liga was to send a mission led by Quijano Wallis to Anapoima for an interview with President Sanclemente. According to the optimistic report which the commissioners telegraphed to Bogotá, the president and his minister of government had received them cordially and planned to cooperate with the merchants. The government had promised to implement important economies including reduction in the size of the army and the elimination of most Colombian legations abroad. The government would abstain from buying letters of exchange and gave its solemn promise to refrain from asking for authority for new emissions of paper money. In addition, the commission reported, Sanclemente had endorsed the merchant's

35. *El Autonomista,* May 30, May 31, June 7, 1899; *El Heraldo,* June 9, 1899.

plan to convert paper money to silver with the cooperation of merchants.[36] Years later, Quijano Wallis recounted in his memoirs that Sanclemente had promised political as well as fiscal reforms and government economies to the representatives of the Liga. Sanclemente, he wrote, had told him that he would cut off his hand before authorizing new emissions during peacetime and went on to guarantee a peaceful Liberal party effective political power through one-third of the seats in congress. Quijano Wallis recalled that he was deeply impressed by the sincerity of the old man.

Quijano Wallis's optimism over the government's response to the merchants' commission was not shared by the war Liberals. *El Autonomista* argued editorially that of all the demands made by the commission—economies in government, an end to new emissions, conversion of paper money—the only measure actually implemented was an agreement by the representatives of the merchants to aid the government in floating a ruinous loan.[37] For war Liberals the loan was only a palliative that kept the government afloat while ignoring the basic causes of the crisis.

War Liberals, at least publicly, were equally critical and distrustful of the possibility of an alliance with Historical Conservatives. When the Historical Conservatives' manifesto of nonsupport for the government (the Acuerdo No. 3) was published in mid-August, *El Autonomista* openly doubted the sincerity of the signers of the document.[38]

Peace Liberals, on the other hand, reacted more favorably toward the possibility of a peacetime alliance with Historical Conservatives against the government. The peace Liberal editors of *La Crónica* supported the content of the Historical Conservatives Acuerdo No. 3, although they expressed some doubt that the Conservative rank and file would obey the instructions of their leaders and thus renounce all hope of "perquisites, jobs, and distinctions" from the Nationalist government.[39] A bipartisan appeal for an alliance of moderates from both traditional parties behind a concrete program of reform was contained in a study commissioned by the Historical Conservatives' convention and approved by that body ten days after the publication of the Acuerdo No. 3. Written by two prominent Historical Conservatives, Carlos Martínez Silva and Guillermo Uribe, and peace Liberal Santiago Samper, brother of Miguel Samper, the study called for the formation of a "great League" including men of good will and intelligence from both political parties who could agree on a program of

36. *El Conservador*, June 21, 1899.
37. *El Autonomista*, June 6, 1899.
38. *Ibid.*, August 23, 1899.
39. *La Crónica*, August 22, 1899.

general interest and immediate application to solve the frightening crisis facing the nation. The report blamed paper money as the primary cause of the rising exchange rate and called for drastic government economies, including a reduction of four thousand men in the army, coupled with popular political reforms as the only viable solution to the crisis.[40]

Theoretically, the Nationalist government could have implemented the steps proposed by the bipartisan commission or it could have pursued a number of alternative solutions to the fiscal crisis. It could have raised taxes or established new ones, instituted economies in government, negotiated internal or external loans, or resorted to new issues of paper money. Given the gravity of the situation, however, the measures taken had to provide or save a great deal of money. Such drastic measures inevitably involved a high political price, a price the last Regeneration government proved unwilling to pay.

The Nationalists' tenuous political situation precluded large hikes in established taxes or the adoption of significant new taxes. The explosive reaction to Caro's earlier attempts to establish export taxes and fiscal monopolies was fresh in mind, and Sanclemente's government was in a much weaker position in 1899 than was Caro's before it. An easier line of attack was a plan proposed and partially implemented by Carlos Calderón that forced the departments to take on some of the administrative expenses assumed by the central government at the start of the Regeneration.[41]

Such minor savings helped, but the problem was of such magnitude that any serious plan for balancing the budget required drastic reductions in the number of public employees and men under arms, the two major items in the Colombian budget. Yet reductions in the bureaucracy would weaken the government's ability to attract loyal supporters, while large cuts in military expenditures would leave the government more vulnerable to a Liberal revolt. Nevertheless, the government took a small step in that direction in June, announcing the discharge of one thousand men from the army.[42] The scale of economies required was much greater, however. The bipartisan fiscal study produced by Carlos Martínez Silva, Santiago Samper, and Guillermo Uribe recommended a reduction of four thousand men in the army, the halving of the police budget, and a scaling down of monies devoted to arms acquisitions and the navy. According to their proposal, the bureaucracy would have to be trimmed with the largest savings achieved by virtually eliminating public works and sharply

40. The lengthy study was published in the August, 1899, edition of *El Repertorio Colombiano*.

41. *El Autonomista*, August 20, 1899.

42. Decree No. 251 (May 31, 1899), *Diario Oficial*, No. 10,987 (June 7, 1899).

reducing expenditures on mail and telegraph service. Some members of Sanclemente's government shared the belief that economies approaching this magnitude constituted the only solution to the crisis. A hotly debated decree drafted by Jorge Holguín would have reduced the army by four thousand men, made other significant economies, and raised taxes moderately. The decree was being considered as early as September, 1899, but was still being debated when the war broke out on October 18, 1899.[43]

Loans represented another alternative solution to the fiscal crisis, and in July Sanclemente's hard-pressed government attempted to negotiate an internal loan with the Bogotá merchants. The merchants expressed their willingness to do business, but their terms were difficult. They insisted on covering a large proportion of the loan in documents of public credit and a monthly interest rate of 10 percent. Sanclemente was scandalized at these terms, declaring that the arrangement would be "greatly usurious," especially given the depreciated value of the public credit certificates on the open market. Furthermore, Sanclemente cautioned, such a deal would engender "sharp criticism to which we should not submit ourselves."[44] Sanclemente instructed his minister of the treasury to procure better terms, but Calderón was evidently unsuccessful, for a few days later Sanclemente lamented the attitude of the merchants and asked Calderón for an opinion on preparations for an emission of five million pesos in the event of a disruption of public order.[45]

Of all the courses available to the government perhaps the most costly in political terms would have been an issue of paper money, an illegal procedure except during the disruption of public order (a condition hardly fulfilled by the much criticized state of seige declared in two departments on July 28). On August 11 Sanclemente mentioned another possible recourse available to the executive under a state of seige: an increase in the tariff accomplished by executive decree. Like an emission of paper money, the legality of such a decree was questionable because of the limited nature of the state of seige in effect in the country. Such a measure would also have stiffened political resistance among import-export groups.[46]

In August Sanclemente's government began to take practical steps to undertake negotiations of a large foreign loan as a solution to its monetary and fiscal troubles. The idea of a foreign loan had been

43. Sanclemente, ANC, 4, ff. 506-16.

44. Telegram from Manuel A. Sanclemente to Carlos Calderón, Anapoima, July 28, 1899, Calderón, ACH.

45. Telegram from Manuel A. Sanclemente to Carlos Calderón, Anapoima, August 2, 1899, Calderón, ACH.

46. Manuel A. Sanclemente to Carlos Calderón, Anapoima, August 11, 1899, Calderón, ACH.

suggested by the Liga de Comercio, and in August Sanclemente instructed Calderón to seek the cooperation of the Liga in drawing up a
proposal for such a loan, authorizing him to offer the income from the
rent of the emerald mines and the revenues from the match monopoly
as a guarantee for the loan and urging him to avoid compromising the
customs receipts and the income from the salt monopoly.[47] On August
18 the government issued two decrees implementing the decision to
negotiate a foreign loan. Decree No. 361 authorized the government to
procure a loan of up to three million pounds sterling to redeem paper
money. The loan was to be guaranteed by the rent of the emerald
mines, the match monopoly, and the income from the railroad in
Panama. Decree No. 362 called for the establishment of a national
bank with private capital to administer the loan and eventually redeem the paper money in circulation.

Prospects were dim for the successful negotiation of a foreign loan
except under the most unfavorable circumstances and after a long
period of discussion. Colombia's credit rating abroad was very low.
Although the foreign debt itself (largely composed of interest accrued
on loans contracted during the first years of independence) was quite
small when compared on a per capita basis with other nations of Latin
America, Colombia had often been delinquent on her payments.[48]
Optimism caused by the coffee boom led the government and the
foreign bondholders to renegotiate and scale down the debt in an
agreement signed in 1896, but deteriorating economic conditions soon
after caused Colombia's Nationalist government to default once again
in the payments. In 1899 the debt stood at some 12.5 million pesos
gold and the current market value of the bonds held by creditors was
about one-fifth of the face value.[49] Although most Colombian commentators approved of the idea of the loan, many doubted it could be
successfully negotiated. Silvestre Samper heartily approved of the
plan to redeem the paper currency and thought three million pounds
was enough to do it, but he thought the Europeans would demand
much greater assurances of payment than the government had offered.[50] Jorge Holguín predicted that even if the terms were accepted
such a loan could not be negotiated in less than eight months.[51]

47. Manuel A. Sanclemente to Carlos Calderón, Anapoima, August 11, 1899, Calderón, ACH.
48. In 1896 the United States minister to Colombia claimed that the public debt,
which included foreign and internal debts, amounted to less than five dollars gold per
capita, the "smallest public debt owed by any nation in the world." Luther F. McKin-
ney to Richard Olney, Bogotá, October 17, 1896, USNA.
49. A. Held to R. María Palacio, Bremen, October 4, 1899, Sanclemente, ANC, 10,
ff. 40-45.
50. *La Crónica*, September 1, 1899.
51. Jorge Holguín to Manuel A. Sanclemente and Rafael M. Palacio, Bogotá, August
11, 1899, Sanclemente, ANC, 7 ff. 832-36.

In the meantime the government needed a short-term loan to sustain itself until the projected foreign loan could be consummated. Once again Sanclemente sought to negotiate a small internal loan of one million pesos with the Bogotá merchants offering an interest rate of 1 percent per month and guaranteeing payment with 20 percent of the income from the custom houses and the salt monopoly.[52] Apparently these negotiations were not successful, for on August 18, 1899, the minister of government, Rafael Palacio, included the following warning in a circular to the governors of the departments. The government had acted in good faith, Palacio argued: it had instituted economies, refrained from raising taxes, and refused to resort to emissions of paper. If the merchants, capitalists, and property holders remained indifferent to the plight of the government, high officials would not hesitate to take whatever action necessary to accomplish their "mission of redemption." Palacio implied that any member of the government who could not agree to support measures necessary to preserve the Regeneration should resign.[53]

The hardening political line and threat embodied in Palacio's circular reflected the government's growing frustration in handling the fiscal and political crisis. The fiscal situation worsened during September, and speculation increased that despite the political costs the government would resort to the only remaining resource available to it: an issue of paper money. By the end of the month rumors of an issue became so insistent that prominent members of the Liga de Comercio telegraphed Sanclemente urging him to reaffirm the government's stated commitment to avoid issuing paper money at all cost.[54] If the government broke its word on issuing paper money "it would mean disaster," *La Crónica* editorialized.[55] By October Sanclemente was under extreme pressure from some quarters to authorize a new issue, but he continued to honor his promise to the merchants, and pressed on with his efforts to obtain a small internal loan. Unable to secure additional credit from private bankers in Bogotá, the government sought a small loan in *antioqueño* financial circles.[56] Finally, just as the war broke out the government concluded a deal with the *an-*

52. Manuel A. Sanclemente to Carlos Calderón, Anapoima, August 11, 1899, Calderón, ACH. Manuel A. Sanclemente to the Liga de Comercio, Anapoima, August 11, 1899, Sanclemente, ANC, 4, ff. 495-96.

53. The circular was published in *El Autonomista*, August 24, 1899. One of Palacio's correspondents urged him to make government employees sign a loyalty oath since they would not "comer y callar." Rudesindo Arango [?] to Rafael M. Palacio, Tunja, August 30, 1899, Sanclemente, ANC, 7, f. 145.

54. The telegram is published in *El Autonomista*, September 28, 1899.

55. *La Crónica*, September 27, 1899.

56. Manuel A. Sanclemente to Carlos Calderón, Anapoima, September 7, 1899, Calderón, ACH.

tioqueños for a loan which included half a million pesos in cash.[57]

President Sanclemente may have had a special reason for resisting an emission of paper money. During September representatives from the Nationalist and Liberal directorates were attempting to negotiate the terms of an alliance between the two parties. It is not known how seriously these negotiations were taken by the leaders of the two parties, but both sides had good political reasons for pursuing such an agreement, despite their mutual hostility in the past. Nationalists could argue that such an alliance would not only strengthen their political position, but encourage division within the Liberal party and undercut the support of the war Liberals in the event they revolted. Peace Liberals, on the other hand, struggling to maintain control of their own party and avoid a civil war, could find the idea of an alliance involving electoral guarantees extremely attractive.

By the end of September the negotiations between Juan E. Manrique, representative of the Provisional Directorate of the Liberal party, and José Manuel Goenaga, representative of the Directorate of the Nationalist party, yielded an agreement. Composed of six articles, the understanding called for the Nationalist government to: (1) make a public statement in favor of such Liberal-patronized reforms as administrative decentralization, presidential accountability, effective suffrage, and other secondary measures which were not incompatible with Nationalist principles; (2) issue the necessary directives to insure that through redistricting and the participation of Liberals on electoral boards, all parties might be represented in congress; and (3) adopt a harmonious political attitude toward the Liberal party demonstrated by positive administrative acts, such as in the filling of public posts, to show that the Liberal party was not an adversary, but an ally. For its part the Liberal party promised to: (4) support morally and materially the Nationalist party, the government, and the Constitution of 1886, especially the centralization of power and the sections concerning civil liberties, including the clause regulating freedom of the press; and (5) accept and support the status quo on religious and ecclesiastical questions. The final article (6) addressed the crucial question of economic and fiscal policy. Both parties agreed to develop a plan that would balance the budget and achieve the "normalization" of the economic situation chiefly through the orderly and economic administration of public monies and the adoption of measures designed to solve the economic problems "in consonance with public opinion and in accordance with, and to the benefit of, general, long-term interests of the community." This last phrase was sufficiently vague to be in-

57. Carlos Cuervo Márquez to Manuel A. Sanclemente, Bogotá, October 17, 1899, Sanclemente, ANC, 9, ff. 208-09.

terpreted as a victory for the economic policies advocated by either party. In essence, by the terms of the document, the peace Liberals agreed to support the Nationalists and the noneconomic aspects of the Regeneration in exchange for access to power and spoils through electoral reform. The two parties agreed to disagree on the fiscal and monetary policies of the Regeneration.[58]

The reaction of the Nationalist and Liberal parties to this last-minute attempt at alliance between the two parties cannot be adequately documented at this time.[59] Manrique later claimed that both José María Quijano Wallis and José María Ruiz supported his efforts and that Uribe Uribe knew of the negotiations before traveling north to his interview with Vargas Santos in early October.[60] Uribe Uribe publicly denied such knowledge.[61] Certainly war Liberals would have never accepted the agreement signed by Manrique. Distrustful of electoral promises war Liberals aimed at control of government not a promise of limited access to power and positions. Moreover, by October, 1899, events had assumed a momentum and logic of their own.

Acting in accordance with the terms of the pact of war Liberals signed in February, 1899, Pablo E. Villar had set the date of October 20 for the outbreak of the Liberal revolt. Villar's timing was questioned by many war Liberal leaders including Uribe Uribe and Cenón Figueredo, who were appalled by the pathetic state of preparedness of Liberal forces in most of the country. There was no doubting the favorable conditions for revolt in Santander, however. The newly established and sympathetic liberal regime of Cipriano Castro in neighboring Venezuela augured well for the importation of war supplies into Santander. Moreover, Santander's civil and military personnel were behind in their pay and discontented. Finally, the collapse of the coffee market had hit Santander harder than any other department. In the rest of the country, however, organization was poor, arms practically nonexistent, and except for centers of Liberal enthusiasm in Bogotá, western Cundinamarca, and Northern Tolima, sentiment in favor of war was limited. On October 5, 1899, Uribe Uribe and Figueredo, despairing at the party's unpreparedness, sought to delay the coming revolt by taking the unprecedented step of telegraphing Villar in Bucaramanga informing him that everyone in Bogotá was talking about his planned revolt due to begin on the twentieth and asking him to authorize them to deny the rumor. Villar tele-

58. The document, bearing the signatures of Manrique and Goenaga, is located in Manrique, ACH.

59. None of the accounts of the war or memoirs of contemporaries even mention the agreement.

60. Juan E. Manrique to Rafael Uribe Uribe, Bogotá, June 3, 1903, Manrique, ACH.

61. *El Constitucional,* June 13, 1903.

graphed back on the sixth that he had not been aware of the rumor, formally authorized Uribe Uribe and Figueredo to deny it, and noted that fortunately the very publicity given the rumor had served to squelch it.[62] In reality Villar resolved to advance the proposed date of revolt to October 18. Explaining his decision to Benjamin Herrera, Villar claimed that he had no other choice. He assumed that Siervo Sarmiento had already embarked with a shipload of arms from Europe, believed that the party leaders in Bogotá would never approve of revolt, and felt that even if he had wanted to he could no longer stop the planned revolt.[63] On October 8 Uribe Uribe left Bogotá for the north ostensibly to convince Vargas Santos to take the directorship of the Liberal party. According to his own account, however, Uribe Uribe's primary purpose was to enlist the support of Vargas Santos in an effort to convince Villar to delay the revolt.[64] Before Uribe Uribe could reach Bucaramanga from Salinas, however, the revolt in Santander began. Like all other war Liberals Uribe Uribe was faced with the dilemma of joining the enthusiastic but badly armed and poorly organized revolutionaries who had only a limited chance of success, or abandoning those who had begun the fight and facing the recriminations and long delays involved in organizing a new revolt. Uribe Uribe, like most other war Liberals who had opposed the timing of the revolt, chose to join the insurgents.

By the fifteenth imminent Liberal revolt was the only topic of conversation in Bogotá.[65] Peace Liberals debated their course of action then hammered out a strong statement against the revolt that urged Liberals to remain peaceful and obey only orders from the directorate. The statement, dated October 17, was signed by forty-one important peace Liberals and telegraphed to all parts of the republic.[66] It is difficult to gauge the effect of the peace Liberal's telegram. War Liberals subsequently blamed the "mortal telegram" for the defeat of the revolution, and it is true that many local Liberal leaders responded to the telegram pledging their support of the peace Liberals and the directorate.[67] Although war Liberals tended to exaggerate the impact

62. Both telegrams were published in *El Autonomista*, October 8, 1899.
63. Pablo E. Villar to Benjamín Herrera, Bucaramanga, October 9, 1899; Tamayo, *Revolución*, p. 52.
64. *El Constitucional*, June 13, 1903. This episode as well as the subsequent actions of Uribe Uribe during the war years are narrated and justified in Carlos Adolfo Urueta, ed., *Historia de la guerra; documentos militares y políticos relativos a las campañas del general Rafael Uribe Uribe* (Bogotá, 1904).
65. A. Dulcey to Marceliano Vargas, Bogotá, October 16, 1899, AMD, vol. 05694.
66. The telegram was published in *La Crónica*, October 17, 1899.
67. "Carta abierta de unos liberales a los señores Juan E. Manrique, Venancio Rueda y José Benito Gaitán (en donde se hallen escondidos)," Bogotá, November, 1899, Manrique, ACH. Many examples of the response from local Liberal leaders are published in Santa, *Uribe Uribe*, p. 158.

of the telegram to account for the subsequent failure of the revolt, it does appear that the telegram reinforced the position of local peace Liberals and may have convinced some who were undecided.[68] Perhaps the most damaging effect of the official Liberal disapproval of the revolt was to make it easier for the government to deny the insurgents belligerent status, a legal position which allowed it to consider them bandits subject to punishment for common crimes.[69]

Despite the peace Liberals' position, many *bogotanos* joined the revolt. The news of the revolt in Santander reached Bogotá on the eighteenth and was followed by reports of *pronunciamientos* or declarations of revolt in northern and western Cundinamarca and northern Tolima. During the next few days hundreds of Liberals, primarily artisans and young men, many of them students, streamed out of Bogotá to join the revolt.[70] One government official, alarmed by reports that two thousand people had left Bogotá in different directions during the previous two days, telegraphed Palacio urging him to issue orders to stop the exodus by requiring all travelers, especially those using trains, to have an official passport.[71] After the declaration of state of seige on October 18, security measures increased on the trains.[72]

As thousands of Liberals disobeyed their official leaders and joined the revolt, and the Nationalists girded for war, all eyes concentrated on the Conversatives, whose decision to join one side or the other or remain neutral could very well determine the success or failure of the revolution. There was no doubt about the attitude of the Historical Conservative leadership based in Antioquia and Bogotá that had fought Regeneration policies for years and committed itself publicly to neutrality, if not support, of the Liberal revolt. On October 20 printed copies of the Acuerdo No. 3 appeared on street corners in Bogotá. The governor of Cundinamarca reported he was certain that those responsible were the same "impenitent and fratricidal" group associated with *El País* and *El Heraldo* and promised to proceed

68. Tobías Hernández C. to Minister of War, Villavicencio, October 22, 1899, AMD, vol. 05787.

69. Circular from Rafael M. Palacio to "Jefes civiles y militares de los departamentos," Anapoima, December 12, 1899, Sanclemente, ANC, 15, ff. 169-70.

70. Telegram from Arcadio Dulcey to the Minister of Government, Bogotá, October 17, 1899, AMD, vol. 05694; General Manuel A. Castro to the Minister of War, Tocancipá vol. 05786; Justo Sánchez O. to the Minister of War, La Mesa [Cundinamarca], October 20, 1899, AMD, vol. 05786.

71. Roberto Ramírez to Rafael M. Palacio, Bogotá, October 17, 1899, AMD, vol. 05694.

72. Max Grillo, *Emociones de la guerra* (Bogotá, 1934; 1st ed., 1903), pp. 43-44. Close inspection of the available official documents sheds no new light on the charge that the Nationalist minister of defense, José Santos, promoted the Liberal revolt as a solution to the government's fiscal and political difficulties. Santos had been involved in an abortive alliance with Liberals in Santander the year before and according to Lucas Caballero had come to some kind of understanding with Uribe Uribe to aid the Liberal revolt in 1899. Caballero, *Memorias*, pp. 51-52.

against them "as with the rebels in arms." The same day government police closed *El Heraldo*.[73] First indications of the attitude of Conservatives around the country were not encouraging to the government.[74] Lack of Conservative support was pronounced in Bogotá, where Jorge Holguín noted "extreme coolness in the Conservative ranks."[75] The situation was worse in Antioquia. Reacting to reports that the majority of government officials had remained passive and were awaiting orders from local juntas, Palacio directed the governor of the department to remove any official not actively raising forces and supplies.[76] In Santander there were several cases of Historical Conservatives signing treaties of mutual neutrality with local Liberal forces.[77] There were also isolated instances of Historical Conservatives joining forces with the Liberal revolutionaries.[78] Within a few days, however, the government became more optimistic as it perceived the growing isolation of the Historical Conservative leaders from the Conservative party rank and file. "Everything indicates," Rafael M. Palacio telegraphed José Santos on October 22, "that certain Bogotá politicians remain alone."[79] The next day he happily informed Santos that the Conservative party had reacted "as was to be expected."[80]

Despite the continuing efforts of Marceliano Vélez and other Historical Conservative leaders to encourage the neutrality of their compatriots in the Conservative party, theirs was a losing battle.[81] Local Conservative leaders and rank and file in most of the country disregarded the instructions of the Historical Conservatives and flocked to support the Nationalist government. On November 11 more than sixty important Conservatives, all previous critics of Sanclemente's government, many of them identified with Próspero Pinzón, recognized the mood and drift of the party and moved to retain their positions of leadership by pledging their loyalty and willingness to serve the in-

73. Marceliano Vargas to General Palacio, Bogotá, October 20, 1899, AMD, vol. 05786.

74. Ramón Acevedo to the Minister of War, Tunja, October 18, 1899, AMD, vol. 05694; Marceliano Vargas to General Palacio, Bogotá, October 19, 1899, AMD, vol. 05686; General Brigard to Dr. Losada, Zipaquirá, October 19, 1899, AMD, vol. 05786; Francisco Cucalón to General Sanclemente, Bogotá, October 20, 1899, AMD, vol. 05786.

75. Jorge Holguín to Rafael M. Palacio, Bogotá, October 22, 1899, AMD, vol. 05787.

76. Rafael M. Palacio to Alejandro Gutiérrez, Anapoima, October 21, AMD, vol. [no number assigned].

77. Flórez A., *Campaña*, p. 10.

78. Brigard to Minister of War, Zipaquirá, October 23, 1899, AMD, vol. 05787; Flórez A., *Campaña*, p. 12.

79. Rafael M. Palacio to José Santos, Anapoima, October 22, 1899, AMD, vol. 05787.

80. Rafael M. Palacio to José Santos, Anapoima, October 23, 1899, AMD, vol. 05787.

81. Abraham Moreno, Alejandro Botero U. and Guillermo Restrepo to José A. Pinto, Medellín, November 7, 1899, and Marceliano Vélez to José A. Pinto, Medellín, November 7, 1899, MDT, ACH.

cumbent regime.[82] The core of the Historical Conservative leadership shunned the petition and Carlos Martínez Silva reacted indignantly to the suggestion that he sign. In the last analysis, he wrote, the petition was nothing but "a reminder to the government that those who sign it are willing to accept jobs and positions, not without recompense of course."[83]

As the weeks went by the Historical Conservative leadership became increasingly isolated and the pressure to join the mainstream of the party grew. Attempting to talk sense to the *antioqueño* Historical Conservative leadership, two Historical Conservatives residing in Bogotá clearly analyzed what had happened since the war broke out and urged the *antioqueños* to reconsider their politics. At first, they wrote, Conservatives in Bogotá had obeyed the directive of the Historical Conservative convention and abstained from offering their support to the government. Unfortunately, however, "Conservatives in the small towns," especially in Cauca, Tolima and Boyacá, were not well enough informed of the political decisions made in the capital. Seeing nothing more than the "threat of the victory of the eternal enemy of their principles and their tranquillity . . . they hurried to take up arms." The "contagion" had subsequently spread to the capital, where, after a serious government reverse in the north in mid-December, "it was no longer possible to contain the masses." Given this state of affairs, the informants concluded, it was vitally important to modify the original policy of neutrality "in order to channel that current so as to take advantage of it and so that it will not leave us to one side."[84]

The dilemma in which the Historical Conservative leadership found itself after the war broke out was perceptively foreseen by Jorge Holguín a year and a half earlier. A gifted politician with a profound sense of Colombian realities, Holguín had warned Vélez of the fruitlessness of his threat to withhold support from Marroquín's government in the event of a Liberal revolt, unless his demands for fiscal, political, and administrative reforms were met.[85] Holguín argued that Vélez had better support the regime since "the mass of the party" would back the government against the Liberals "even in defiance of contrary orders from the leadership."[86]

82. The manifesto of support, coupled with Sanclemente's short acceptance, was printed and distributed in the capital. A copy exists in Manrique, ACH.
83. Martínez Delgado, *A propósito*, p. 266.
84. Wenceslao Pizano and Rufino Gutiérrez to Marceliano Vélez, Abraham Moreno, Alejandro Botero U., Guillermo Restrepo I., Carlos Restrepo, y Pedro Nel Ospina, Bogotá, January 11, 1900, MDT, ACH.
85. Vélez's position is expressed in Marceliano Vélez to Jorge Holguín, Medellín, March 1, 1898, MDT, ACH.
86. Jorge Holguín to Marceliano Vélez, Bogotá, March 22, 1898, MDT, ACH.

To a great extent the motivations of large numbers of Conservatives in ignoring the directives of their national leadership and pledging their immediate support of the Nationalist government paralleled those of the provincial Liberals. Conservative partisans in the provinces were very much aware of the stakes involved in a civil war. Having enjoyed the advantages of political hegemony at the local level during fifteen years of Regeneration, rural Conservative bosses in much of the country were not inclined to watch passively the tables turned for the sake of the personal political aspirations of some elite politicians, the regional concerns of a fraction of the party, or the economic interests of some bankers, import-export merchants, and coffee growers within the party. It is significant that in coffee-growing zones such as Antioquia, Santander, and Cundinamarca many local Conservative leaders initially followed the instructions of the Historical Conservative leadership, maintaining their neutrality, entering into nonaggression pacts with local Liberal chiefs, or, in rare cases, actually joining with Liberals in the fight against the Nationalist regime. Neutrality was an extremely risky course of action, however, especially as the conflict took on major proportions in the months following its outbreak. Conservatives claiming neutrality were labeled as traitors by fellow Conservatives under arms, as enemies by war Liberals. Their property became subject to expropriation by both government and revolutionary forces. Moreover, they appeared to gain nothing for the risks they incurred; they seemed doomed to lose no matter which side won.

Holguín himself explained his prediction that the mass of the party would support the government against a Liberal revolt by reminding Vélez that in Colombia the differences between the parties were not "simply political, but social, and above all, ethical." Many years would pass, Holguín concluded, before these differences were erased, and it would be centuries before harmony was established and suspicion and fear destroyed.[87] Holguín seemed to be pointing to at least two underlying characteristics of Colombian politics that worked to channel the impact of social and economic forces and limit the maneuverability of political elites. The first was the deep mutual distrust and suspicion with which most Liberals and Conservatives regarded each other, a feeling passed from one generation to another, the product in part of the intermittent civil strife which had characterized Colombian politics for decades. The second was the so-called Church question.

The Church appears to have helped mobilize mass Conservative support for the war, especially in highland areas of traditional ag-

87. *Ibid.*

riculture.[88] Nevertheless, religious fervor did not translate into volunteers for the government armies; most of the common soldiers in the government forces were forcibly drafted into service.[89] But the Church played a major role in legitimizing the draft, indeed the entire Conservative cause, and probably helped to improve morale among rank and file already incorporated into the army. The Catholic Church was a part of the Conservative world view capable of arousing emotional and moral fervor and at the very least provided upper-class Conservative politicians with a rationale for joining the struggle against Liberals.[90] Indicative of attitudes toward the Church and their place in the world views of Colombian upper-class groups was a relatively insignificant incident that occurred in Bogotá in June, 1899, but that nevertheless had great symbolic value and received wide attention in the press.

The incident involved two young European ladies, Sofia and Berta Feuerhoff, who were prohibited from entering the Church of Santa Clara in central Bogotá by Father Eulogio Tamayo, an aged Catholic priest. According to most accounts, Tamayo treated the ladies in an abusive manner and barred their entrance to the church because they insisted on wearing hats instead of conforming to the practice of using the mantilla that was customary in Colombia. The Feuerhoff sisters indignantly published a sharp protest in the Historical Conservative paper *El Heraldo*. The protest initiated a heated debate among the newspapers of the capital over the propriety of Tamayo's act. Most editors criticized the priest's actions and sided with the Feuerhoffs in demanding an apology, but some Conservative writers accused the Liberal, Historical Conservative, and even Nationalist press of using the incident as an excuse to discredit the clergy.

The most vehement apologist for Tamayo was Próspero Pinzón, editor of *El País*. Pinzón questioned the motives and values of the priest's detractors and affirmed the continuing Liberal threat to the Church in Colombia. One contributor to the paper, identified only as

88. An unusually candid correspondent of Aquileo Parra in Ubaté, Cundinamarca, affirmed that since the masses in that cold-climate town to the north of Bogotá were "indios pusilánimes é ignorantes" they acted either out of fear of "poder ó del Infierno," Cenón Solano R. to Aquileo Parra, Ubaté, November 15, 1897, Parra, ACH. Luis Martínez Silva considered the Church, which put "las multitudes sencillas e iletradas" at the disposal of the Regeneration, to be the best explanation for the Nationalists' strength during the waning years of the nineteenth century. Martínez Delgado, *A propósito*, p. 84.

89. The forced recruitment policies of the government are treated in detail in the next chapter.

90. The need to protect the Constitution of 1886, which embodied "los principios fundamentales de nuestras aspiraciones y creencias religiosas" was the primary reason given by the Conservatives who pledged their support to Sanclemente on November 11.

"C," was warmly applauded by the editor for his statement that the religious question was still very much alive in Colombia, in spite of the legal prerogatives and government favor enjoyed by the Church. There were groups in Colombia that disagreed with the country's institutions, preached total separation of Church and State, sought to combat Catholic dogma, and aimed at publicly embarrassing the clergy. Father Tamayo's possible excesses could be attributed to his advanced age; the record showed that he was a hard-working, devoted, and venerable priest. As far as the question of proper attire was concerned, "C" concluded, a hat was just as good as a mantilla, but it would seem that in matters of custom it was "more natural that foreigners yield to the [customs] of the nation, than the other way around."[91] Pinzón agreed completely with this view. In passionate, convoluted prose he deplored the fact that Catholics, "who as a rule espouse Colombian Conservatism," were denounced as fanatics who never forgot anything simply because they raised their voices in warning. It was possible that Colombians could witness once more "barefooted nuns and friars on the road to exile, their property the prey of a new disamortization." But how could a child forget, Pinzón concluded, the tradition of his family—a family which had been unable even to take him to Church to baptize him thanks to the so-called tolerance of the Liberals.[92]

That kind of language greatly alarmed Uribe Uribe, who was very much aware of the potential strength of the Church issue in combating Liberal strength among the lower classes. "Religious wars at the end of the nineteenth century!" Uribe Uribe scoffed in an editorial; "among modern men only a Turk could conceive of such a thing!" Uribe Uribe accused the leaders of the Regeneration of reviving the religious question when all other bases of its support were crumbling, and added, as if to convince himself, that the poeple "no longer hear them and their preachings are lost in the void."[93] Several years later Uribe Uribe expressed his constant preoccupation with the fate of Liberals subject to "politico-religious" persecution in small towns and rural areas. Liberals in the cities, given their greater education and means of defense, were not subjected, "at least brutally," to such oppression since potential persecutors either did not dare to proceed against them, or, if they did, they encountered organized resistance.

91. *El País*, June 30, 1899. This view was echoed in *El Conservador*, edited by Rafael Ortíz, the general who had thwarted the Liberal-Historical Conservative coalition of November 3, 1898. Ortíz criticized *La Crónica* for censoring Tamayo's actions. Such an attitude, he wrote, encouraged foreigners to "humillarnos y exigirnos reclamación por cualquier pequeñez. . . ." *El Conservador*, July 1, 1899.
92. *El País*, August 4, 1899.
93. *El Autonomista*, July 6, 1899.

But "upon the villagers and ignorant, innocent country people there weighs here in Colombia a tyranny equaled only in the European Middle Ages."[94]

The kind of conflict Uribe Uribe called "politico-religious" persecution was illustrated by a letter sent to *El Autonomista* in September, 1899, from the western Cundinamarca town of La Vega. The author, a Liberal named Emilio Matíz and an acquaintance of Uribe Uribe, complained of how the parish priest, Presbítero Pío Medrano, had attempted to collect a debt which Matíz owed a third party. Matíz claimed to be contesting the debt as unjust and refused to pay. In retaliation, the priest ordered him to remove his four children from school immediately. According to Matíz's version, Medrano justified his action exclaiming that the children had been tolerated long enough since neither they nor Matíz fulfilled the religious obligations of the Catholic Church, and consequently, to allow them to attend school was a violation of the educational code. As an agent of the government in charge of the school, Medrano claimed he was responsible for enforcing the code. Matíz said he complied with the order, fearing his children might suffer some "barbarous act" similar to ones the priest had committed in the past. He concluded his letter declaring that his constitutional rights had been violated and lamenting that he had to witness such "farces, so inappropriate of the progress attained by civilization in the last stages of the century of light."[95]

Although there were probably many impassioned clergymen who participated in the persecution of Liberals, these abuses, like electoral and other excesses of local government officials, were discouraged by officials at the highest levels. At least that is the conclusion drawn from the cryptic prose of a telegram sent by Archbishop Bernardo Herrera to the parish priest of La Vega, Cundinamarca, just as the War of the Thousand Days began.

> Go to Nocaima [a contiguous and predominantly Conservative municipality], and stay there a few days, try to calm the citizens telling them in our name to abstain from committing what are in reality wrongs against others under the pretext of sustaining the prerogatives of the Church; if they do not we will not send them a new priest. Keep us informed.
>
> Bernardo, Archbishop[96]

94. Rafael Uribe Uribe, *De cómo el liberalismo político colombiano no es pecado* (Bogotá, 1912), p. 3

95. Emilio Matíz to Rafael Uribe Uribe, La Vega, September 10, 1899, published in *El Autonomista*, October 13, 1899.

96. Bernardo [Herrera], Arzobispo to Cura, La Vega, Bogotá, October 17, 1899, AMD, vol. 05694. According to a lecture given by Monseñor José Restrepo Posada to the Colombian Academy of History in Bogotá on March 23, 1971, Archbishop Herrera also

Soon after the war broke out, the archbishop lent his support to efforts to reach a negotiated settlement. There was never any question of where the Church's sympathies lay, however, and as the war dragged on hardline Conservatives used the Church issue to mount a crusade against the Liberal revolutionaries.

At the end of the nineteenth century the intricate counterpoint between an international economic system and domestic Colombian politics reached a climax. Conflict between upper-class groups was never absent during the whole of the Regeneration, but it became more intense as the period progressed. Although personal and political ends certainly influenced politicians, cleavage between upper-class groups was largely determined by their relationship to the export-import economy. Biographical information on important national political leaders, the sociology, regional strengths, and world views of the various political factions, and the importance of the debate over Regeneration fiscal and economic policies all tend to support this conclusion. Throughout the Regeneration attempts at coalition between upper-class factions through compromise and reform were unsuccessful. Deepening divisions within the upper class and the strident public controversy they generated helped to undermine the authority and consensus enjoyed by Núñez at the start of the Regeneration. Ironically, the Nationalist government's declining legitimacy, largely brought about by the rise of the coffee-export economy, was hastened by the crash in coffee prices after 1898. The coffee crisis combined with the political crisis left unresolved throughout the Regeneration to cripple government effectiveness while simultaneously augmenting unrest around the country, especially in the coffee zones.

When the war broke out in October, 1899, many factions within the Colombian upper class were not unhappy with the turn of events. Some Nationalists undoubtedly welcomed the war as an escape from the fiscal straitjacket imposed upon the government by the illegality of peacetime emissions of paper money. Nationalists also must have viewed the war as a means of reuniting the Conservative party under their leadership without concessions to the Historical Conservatives. For Historical Conservatives themselves, the outbreak of the Liberal revolt vindicated their predictions concerning the consequences of the Nationalists' uncompromising politics. The Historical Conservative leadership, particularly in Antioquia, envisioned substantial concessions from the Nationalists in exchange for their support of the government, and barring that, may even have contemplated some kind

attempted to limit partisan violence between Nationalists and Historical Conservatives during the election of 1897. Restrepo's information came from notes he took from the archive of the Archbishopric prior to its burning during the *bogotazo* of April 9, 1948.

of arrangement (perhaps an entente similar to that of the 1860's) with a triumphant Liberalism whose economic and political views paralleled their own. But the Historical Conservatives were soon forced to adjust their plans as party rank and file ignored the directions of their leaders and rushed to the support of the government in the battle against their perennial Liberal enemies. War Liberals, of course, initiated the war as a means for achieving political power and economic reform while gaining control of their own party. Some peace Liberals, on the other hand, had favored splitting the party before the war and believed that unsuccessful revolt would discredit the war Liberal leadership, leaving the peace Liberals a free hand to pursue their reformist policies unchallenged after the war.

But if political leaders of all persuasions sought to use the war to justify past positions and further their political fortunes, they were to learn to their dismay that the conflict unleashed by their political contention and the crisis in the coffee economy quickly carried events beyond their control.

Chapter VI

The Gentlemen's War

As the War of the Thousand Days began, most indications were that it would be a short civil conflict of the kind witnessed so frequently in Colombia during the nineteenth century. Indeed, the events of the first few months of the war reveal little at variance with the ordinary pattern of civil conflict in the country. While elite politicians and local strong men volunteered their services as officers, often bringing with them their clients and dependent laborers as common soldiers, the government resorted to time-tested methods of forced recruitment of lower-class men to fill its armies. In financing their efforts both sides followed customary and moderate procedures that had been used in previous civil wars. Although fighting was often desperate during the first few months of the war upper-class generals displayed a chivalrous concern for the dignity of their opponents. Meanwhile, traditional political leaders not engaged in the fighting worked feverishly to effect a compromise between the opposing factions that would bring the fighting to an end. These efforts, which culminated in a coup against President Sanclemente, ultimately failed to bridge the gap between upper-class factions deeply divided by economic interest and ideological conviction, and circumscribed in their efforts at conciliation by the expectations and demands of their militant followers. After seven months of fighting the "gentlemanly" phase of the war came to an end and a new and more desperate struggle began that was to drag on for more than two and one-half more years, raise the war's death toll to perhaps a hundred thousand men,[1] and threaten the social foundations of Colombian life.

1. This figure, commonly cited in the literature, is no more than a guess. Combat was most intense during the first year of the fighting when, according to one contemporary estimate, 13,492 men died in combat on both sides in battles involving more than 200 men. The same source estimated total deaths "including those resulting from wounds and epidemics" at about 20,000. L. Paláu, "Cuadro sinóptico de los combates librados hasta la fecha en la presente guerra, octubre 18, 1900," Archivo Manrique, ACH. Disease, particularly yellow fever and dysentery, probably caused more deaths than combat, especially during the last year of the war when government armies sent from the interior highlands were decimated by epidemics upon their arrival on the Isthmus of Panama. Whatever the exact number of deaths resulting from the war, it was certainly a very high proportion of the total Colombian population of some four million people at the turn of the century. V. J. de D. Higuita estimates total population in 1900 at some-

From the beginning Liberals realized that they were greatly out-numbered and outgunned by the relatively well-trained and well-armed government armies. Consequently, their strategy hinged on the success of bold initial maneuvers. Simultaneously with the first *pronunciamientos* in Santander and Cundinamarca, Liberals in Barran-quilla executed an audacious plan that almost gave them control of the lower Magdalena River. Taking advantage of the fact that most of the rivermen were Liberals, revolutionaries seized control of several river boats docked at Barranquilla, sank a dredge to block the channel and impede pursuit, and proceeded up the Magdalena, capturing the river ports of Magangué and El Banco on the way. On October 24, however, the Liberal flotilla was overtaken by the well-armed government gun-boats *Hercules* and *Colombia*, and in a violent nighttime battle the government gunboats sank most of the Liberal flotilla. The naval vic-tory preserved government control of Colombia's vital water link with the outside world. During the entire course of the war the rev-olutionaries never again seriously threatened control of the river, which not only constituted the primary avenue for shipments of arms and supplies into Colombia from abroad, but also provided, through the customs houses at Barranquilla and Cartagena, an important source of revenue for financing the war effort.[2]

Liberals were also defeated in important early battles in Cun-dinamarca and Santander. In Cundinamarca initial Liberal hopes were shattered when Cenón Figueredo's hastily formed army was boxed in by government troops and decisively defeated at Nocaima, but the most serious reverse occurred in Santander, where a large Liberal army under the command of Uribe Uribe failed in its attempt to take the important town of Bucaramanga and was forced to retreat to Cúcuta.

These early Liberal defeats convinced some peace Liberals that the revolutionaries might consider an honorable surrender, and they ap-proved a plan conceived by the Ecuadorian minister to Colombia, Luis F. Carbo, and supported by Vice-president Marroquín and Arch-bishop Herrera, to send a delegation of Liberals respected by the war faction to negotiate the terms of surrender. A commission composed of Lucas Caballero and Generals Rafael Camacho and Celso Rodríguez O. journeyed to Santander, but once they learned that Liberal gener-

what less than 4 million, "Estudio histórico-analítico de la población colombiana en 170 años," *Anales de Economía y Estadística*, III: 2, Supplement (April, 1940), graph fol-lowing p. 2. O. Andrew Collver, *Birth Rates in Latin America* (Berkeley, 1965), p. 86, estimates total Colombian population at the same time at somewhat more than four million.

2. Julio H. Palacio, Historia, *"El Tiempo,"* October 11, 1942, October 18, 1942, November 2, 1942; Tamayo, *Revolución*, pp. 54-56; Justo L. Durán, *La revolución del 99* (Cúcuta, 1920), pp. 13-14.

als Uribe Uribe, Herrera, and Durán had managed to join forces and that Conservative commanders demanded unconditional surrender, they realized there was no hope for a peaceful settlement and denounced the attitude of the Conservative generals. Jailed for their impertinence, the Liberal commissioners subsequently escaped and joined the revolution. The attitude of government officials in the field toward the Liberal mission faithfully reflected the policy of the government, which had been forcefully stated even before the battle of Bucaramanga in a telegram from Sanclemente to the Liberal Directorate. The revolution, the president declared, was "the most unjustifiable" ever fought in Colombia. To request that he make a solemn promise to reform current laws and institutions was to ask him to violate his oath of office. To negotiate with the revolutionaries, moreover, would accord them the status of belligerents when in fact they were rebels subject to punishment under the penal code.[3] These arguments would form the basis of the government's legal attitude toward the revolution throughout the war. Consistent with the Nationalists' prewar ideological and political position, they also revealed the government's confidence in its ability to defeat the Liberal revolt.

When the war broke out, the military resources at the command of the government were relatively large. In October, 1899, the Colombian army officially numbered just under nine thousand officers and men. Although slightly smaller in size than during the last years of the Caro government, the army was probably better trained and equipped. In 1896 an officers' training school had been established in Bogotá, and a French military mission had been brought to Colombia to staff the school and to advise the government on ways to improve the military establishment.[4] The army appears to have been moderately well-armed at the outbreak of hostilities and government control of the Magdalena and the Honda road to Bogotá meant that new supplies purchased abroad moved easily into Bogotá, the staging area for the armies sent to the North.[5]

Once the war began, the government moved rapidly to expand the number of men under arms. As in previous civil wars, the government depended heavily on the conscription of men from the working classes to fill its armies. In order to catch, in the words of one general, "Indians appropriate for military service," squads of armed men de-

3. Manuel A. Sanclemente to the Liberal Directorate, Anapoima, November 9, 1899, Manrique, ACH.

4. Flórez A., *Campaña*, pp. 16-19. The mission made a concerted effort to improve the quality and lower the price of munitions manufactured in Bogotá, but because of the lack of supporting industries, met with little success, *ibid.*, p. 29.

5. See the inventory of rifles dated March 17, 1899, and the guidelines for arms purchases dated April 6, 1899, in Sanclemente, ANC, 3, ff. 333-37.

scended on market places, general stores that dispensed alcoholic beverages, and other public places where common people congregated.[6] Laborers employed by the government such as road gangs were automatic targets for conscription.[7] Groups of farm workers were seized in the field, bound together and marched off to war without recourse to legal procedures or time to arrange their affairs or say farewell to their families.[8] Once caught, conscripts had little chance of regaining their freedom unless they deserted or their landlords or employers could bring special influence to bear on the government.[9]

Resistance to conscription generally took the form of flight. Families would leave their homes, often taking utensils and livestock along with them, and seclude themselves in surrounding forests. By December, 1899, government officials in Cundinamarca began to experience some difficulty in securing additional recruits because of the "precautions" taken by the people.[10] During the war there were also a few isolated cases of violent resistance to recruitment,[11] but as a rule government agents encountered little organized opposition to conscription.

Although most of the rank and file in the government armies were coerced into service, some joined the war effort voluntarily. Local Conservative caudillos, like their Liberal counterparts, attracted groups of volunteers from among their friends, relatives, and workers, and either joined regular government forces or formed Conservative guerrilla bands.[12] The motivations of lower-class volunteers in joining

6. Gral. Brigard to Dr. Losada, Zipaquirá, October 18, 1899, AMD, vol. 05694.

7. See for example M. Vargas to Prefecto, Chocontá, Bogotá, October 21, 1899, AMD, vol. 05787.

8. Julio Holguín Arboleda, *Mucho en serio y algo en broma* (Bogotá, 1959), p. 150.

9. The military governor of Cundinamarca instructed the prefect of Facatativá at the start of the war to release only "los inútiles." Marceliano Vargas to Prefect, Facatativá, Bogotá, October 20, 1899, AMD, vol. 05786. Special favors granting immunity to the workers of friends of the government and foreigners were common. See for example, E. Ch. Argáez to Prefecto, La Mesa, Bogotá, October 19, 1899, and C. Cuervo Márquez to Capitán Eduardo Mendoza y Alcalde de Soacha, Bogotá, October 19, 1899, AMD, vol. 05786. According to Decree No. 66 of October 18, 1899, issued by the government of Cundinamarca, every male citizen under sixty not a member of the clergy or actively serving the government in another capacity was liable for military duty unless he paid an exemption fee of twenty-five pesos. See AMD, vol. 05787. Deas, "Una finca," demonstrates how one Liberal coffee farmer sought to conserve his labor force in this way.

10. Telegram from Federico Tovar to the Minister of Government, La Mesa [Cundinamarca], December 21, 1899, Sanclemente, ANC, 14, f. 508. Nevertheless a telegram sent on the same day reported the capture of forty-four conscripts in two days in Viotá, Cundinamarca. [?] Fierro to Rafael M. Palacio, Viotá [Cundinamarca], December 21, 1899, *ibid.*, f. 814.

11. Medardo Perilla, Prefecto, to Minister of War, Guateque, October 19, 1899, AMD, vol. 05786.

12. Typical was a band of un-uniformed Conservative volunteers which worked out of Vergara [Cundinamarca] and was led by Tobías Vásquez, Tobías Vásquez to Minister of War, Guaduas [Cundinamarca] March 24, 1900, Sanclemente, ANC, 21, ff. 51-52.

the war effort are difficult to deduce from the historical record. There is a consensus among Colombian writers that the unthinking lower classes were duped by caudillos and sacrificed in the war like innocent sheep. One contemporary wrote that the masses, the "antithesis of thinking mankind," were marched to battle "like the steer is led to slaughter."[13] Another writer who witnessed the war as a young man recalled that neither the Liberal nor the Conservative rank and file had any notion of the principles or ends for which their leaders fought, but killed one another "with a dull, savage hatred."[14] In his history of the war, Joaquín Tamayo casts the common people as faithful servants of a minority little concerned with their welfare. According to him, common people sacrificed

> their blood without complaint, aroused by the cries of savage enthusiasm that awakened in their sleeping minds similar cries, shouted in previous years by their fathers, cannon fodder like themselves.[15]

It is not necessary to conclude, as does Tamayo, that lower-class participation in the War of the Thousand Days, as in all of the civil wars of "tropical America," obeyed "a romantic, emotional impulse."[16] Certainly the potential for feelings of loyalty and identification with superiors inherent in any dependent economic relationship helps explain the attitude of many workers in following their landlords and employers to war, particularly if the boss was successful in his role as paternalistic protector of his workers. But the tremendous economic power at the heart of this relationship was of primary importance. Through their monopolization of the land and the judicious manipulation of economic sanctions and incentives, large landowners could decisively influence political behavior. On the cold country estates where Conservatives found much of their support, workers were required to work if needed for the landowner at a rate one-third less than the going wage for day laborers. Landowners determined the size, location and fertility of plots and had the power to expel uncooperative workers from the land, an especially fearful prospect for those with families during periods of civil war.[17] Routine advice

13. Carrasquilla, "Recluta" in Medardo Rivas, *et al., Cuadros de costumbres* (Bogotá, 1924), pp. 65, 67.

14 Holguín Arboleda, *Mucho en serio,* p. 149.

15. Tamayo, *Revolución,* p. 89.

16. *Ibid.,* pp. 88-89.

17. Their huts were generally windowless, one-room, wattle-and-mud constructions, measuring, according to one meticulous observer, 4.5 meters by 3 meters. The plots of land ranged from 2,000 to 3,000 square meters, level land to 6,400 or more on the sides of hills. "Régimen alimenticio de los jornaleros de la sabana de Bogotá" in *Anales de la Academia Nacional de Medicina,* I, 121. This remarkable study provides material on

given Rafael Uribe Uribe upon assuming the management of an hacienda in Cundinamarca in 1894 included this revealing dictum on the use of economic power to insure worker conformity. "It is advisable to make an example of one of those considered invulnerable on the hacienda and who perhaps encourages rebellion. Once one is expelled, the rest resign themselves."[18] Even where workers perceived a choice they had to weigh the danger and opportunities for adventure and pillage on campaign against the prospect of hard times, monotonous labor, and possible recruitment or despoilation at the hand of strangers if they remained behind. Because of the relatively wide identification with one of the two traditional political parties and the pervasiveness of the Church issue characteristic of Colombian political culture, the means for rationalization of participation in war were readily available to lower-class volunteers as well as to their social superiors. Conservatives could champion the cause of God and the Church and defend the Colombian nation from an international liberal conspiracy.

The government's capacity to coerce and attract men into service was matched by its ability to secure the supplies and transportation necessary to field an army in Santander within days after the outbreak of hostilities in October. The mobilization of men and supplies was greatly speeded by government control of the telegraph system, which extended by the end of the century to major towns and cities throughout the country.[19] Despite successful Liberal efforts to cut some lines, the government generally enjoyed communication with most parts of the country. The small railroad network fanning out in three directions from Bogotá was also a great aid to the government in moving men and supplies to Zipaquirá, the staging area for the army of the north.

Among the most pressing needs of the army forming in Zipaquirá were mules and horses for transport and cattle for food. In order to secure the livestock demanded by the army the government often resorted to confiscation, usually issuing promissory notes in lieu of payment in cash. As soon as the war broke out owners of haciendas took precautionary measures to protect their property from abuses at the hands of local government officials charged with raising and equipping the government armies. Conservatives attempted to obtain

dress, health conditions, wages, and prices, as well as diet, its primary concern. See also Great Britain, Foreign Office, "Report on the Agricultural Condition of Colombia," p. 18.

18. Antonio Suárez M. to Rafael Uribe Uribe, Ubaté, November 8, 1894. Uribe, Box 6, ACH.

19. República de Colombia, Dirección General de Correos y Telégrafos, *Informe del Sr. Manuel José Guzmán, Director General de Correos y Telégrafos, relativo a los años de 1899, 1900, 1901, 1902, y 1904* (Bogotá, 1904).

safe-conduct passes for the few trusted workers needed to care for their haciendas; other workers were dismissed for service in the government army. Hacienda owners also issued orders to hide mules and horses, which were always vulnerable to requisitions by the government.[20] The main target of government expropriations was the Liberals, but hard-pressed local officials often took animals from any source available in order to meet their quotas. Of course influential Conservatives could secure special consideration amounting to immunity from expropriation from government agents.[21] Other Conservatives sought to make the best of the situation by offering to sell their animals to the government at a good price. One influential Conservative sent a telegram to the minister of war spontaneously offering all the animals on his hacienda in Fusagasugá to the government. That communication was followed by another marked "confidential" to the mayor of Fusagasugá instructing him to proceed secretly to name a "friendly appraiser."[22] In areas where Conservatives were threatened by expropriation at the hands of Liberal forces, government officials could operate on the principle of buying livestock belonging to Conservatives first.[23] Liberal hacienda owners did not enjoy these privileges accorded to Conservatives through government favor, but they often managed to protect their interests by transferring their property to foreigners, who were relatively safe from expropriation.[24]

Expropriation was used primarily to equip armies, not to finance the war effort. From the beginning war finance turned on the government's power to issue unlimited quantities of paper money.[25] Other early government measures designed to produce revenue included the establishment of a national tax on the slaughter of livestock and

20. Aparicio Perea to Zoilo García (Hacienda Perea), Sasaima [Cundinamarca], Bogotá, October 18, 1899, AMD, vol. 05694; Florens [?] to Adolfo Rodríguez, Nocaima (Tobia), [Cundinamarca], Bogotá, October 19, 1899, AMD, vol. 05786; Miguel Montoya to Dolores Payán, Buga [Cauca], Bogotá, October 20, 1899, AMD, vol. 05786.

21. Marceliano Vargas to Prefecto, Anapoima, Bogotá, October 21, 1899, AMD, vol. 05787; A. Dulcey to Alcalde de Girardot, Bogotá, October 20, 1899, AMD, vol. 05786; Marceliano Vargas to General Rebollo [?], Bogotá, October 19, 1899, AMD, vol. 05786; A. Dulcey to Alcalde, Nocaima, October 18, 1899, AMD, vol. 05694.

22. Dr. Enrique de Argáez to Minister of War, Bogotá, October 18, 1899; Dr. Enrique de Argáez to Alcalde, Facatativá, Bogotá, October 18, 1899, AMD, vol. 05694.

23. Carlos Calderón to Rafael M. Palacio, Bogotá, December 7, 1899, Sanclemente, ANC, 15, f. 637.

24. Many Liberals may have done as Uribe Uribe did and transferred their properties to foreigners months or even years before the war broke out; others apparently did it soon after the revolt began. See Antonio U. Robayre [?] to General Palacio, Bogotá, October 20, AMD, vol. 05786. On the immunity of foreigners, see Carlos Cuervo Márquez to Capitán Eduardo Mendoza y Alcalde de Soacha, Bogotá, October 19, 1899, AMD, vol. 05786.

25. Once public order was officially declared disrupted, the government acquired the legal authority to issue paper money in the amounts necessary to meet the crisis. Decree No. 520 of 1899 (October 28), *Diario Oficial*, No. 11,134 (November 7, 1899).

the raising of the price of salt sold through the government monopoly.[26] Individual departments also adopted extraordinary measures to meet wartime expenses. In Cundinamarca Governor Marceliano Vargas reported he was doubling departmental taxes on liquor, property, and the slaughtering of livestock, suspending expenditures on public instruction and material improvements, and making up a list of men to be subjected to a forced loan.[27]

The question of forced contributions by Liberals was early debated by the national government, but President Sanclemente declared his opposition to the idea, preferring to finance the war with paper money.[28] Nevertheless, a decree calling for what was termed a *contribución extraordinaria* was signed on December 1. Declaring that it was not advisable to finance the war exclusively by emissions of paper, the decree assigned a quota to each department and instructed the respective governors to raise the money from among the "sympathizers, authors, accomplices, and abettors of the rebellion." The sum assigned each department varied in rough proportion to the degree of support each had furnished the revolution. Thus Santander and Cundinamarca were each assigned 1,500,000 pesos; Tolima, 600,000; Boyacá, 550,000; Bolívar, 300,000; Antioquia, 250,000; Cauca, 150,000; Magdalena, 100,000; Panama, 50,000.[29] Although after some delay the decree was published, it had still not been implemented in Cundinamarca eight months later.[30]

The decision not to follow through with the forced loan on Liberals, like the earlier decision to finance the war by printing paper money, was part of a general pattern of moderation, characteristic of government policy during the first few months of the war. Reacting to reports that contrary to general practice the property of peace Liberals had been expropriated by local government officials in Tolima, Historical Conservative Indalecio Saavedra counseled Rafael M. Palacio to pursue a policy of restraint. The government had an excellent opportunity, he reminded Palacio, to "lay the foundations for a solid and enduring peace" by protecting the economic interests of the peace Liberal faction. Such a policy would not only deepen the split in the Liberal party, Saavedra maintained, but would discredit the revolu-

26. Decree No. 485 of 1899 (October 20), *Diario Oficial*, No. 11,124 (October 25, 1899) and Decree No. 494 of 1899 (October 23), *Diario Oficial*, No. 11,126 (October 27, 1899).

27. Marceliano Vargas to General Palacio, Bogotá, October 19, 1899, AMD, vol. 05786.

28. Marceliano Vargas to General Palacio, Bogotá, October 22, 1899, AMD, vol. 05787; Manuel A. Sanclemente to Minister of the Treasury, Anapoima, October 31, 1899. Sanclemente, ANC, 9, f. 940.

29. Decree No. 582 of 1899 (December 1), *Diario Oficial*, No. 11,173 (December 23, 1899).

30. Decree No. 29 of 1900 (August 19), *Diario Oficial*, No. 11,314 (August 23, 1900).

tion, since only men who "have nothing to lose" would be willing to take up arms against the government.[31]

Although combat was often bloody during these early months, taking the lives of officers as well as men, the war was conducted in a gentlemanly manner between elites. "Allow me to recommend to you," the minister of public instruction, Marco Fidel Suárez, telegraphed the military governor of Cundinamarca on November 22, 1899, "the youth Enrique Olaya taken prisoner in Nocaima, whose mother is ill. If you could accept the necessary guarantees and confine him to his house instead of jail, I would be especially grateful to you for it."[32] The chivalry characteristic of relations between elite contenders during the first months of the war was noted by Julio H. Palacio, who was captured along with members of his family on a Magdalena riverboat that went over to the revolution on October 18. Palacio and his party were treated with utmost consideration by the revolutionaries and placed ashore in exchange for their word as gentlemen to avoid participation in the war.[33] Palacio went on to comment about conditions in general on the Atlantic coast during the first phase of the war. There was none of the cruelty and "ferocious reprisals" that characterized later stages of the conflict. Hardly any political prisoners could be found in the jails, and prisoners of war were not treated badly.[34] While Palacio had reason to exaggerate the moderation of the period (his father was military commander of the coastal zone), his description is confirmed by the tenor of official decrees and the content of official communications. As long as the war was fought between organized armies led by upper-class officers conventional means of waging civil war in Colombia were generally observed by both sides.

The first phase of the War of the Thousand Days lasted roughly six months.[35] After the initial Liberal defeats at Los Obispos, Nocaima,

31. Indalecio Saavedra to Rafael M. Palacio, Bogotá, December 17, 1899, Sanclemente, ANC, 15, ff. 699-704.

32. Marco Fidel Suárez to Marceliano Vargas, Anapoima, November 22, 1899, Sanclemente, ANC, 11, telegram following f. 679. Enrique Olaya Herrera, eighteen years old on the day Suárez penned his request to Vargas, apparently was granted a conditional release and did not return to the battlefield during the rest of the war. In 1902 he co-founded the newspaper *El Comercio* and began his ascent toward leadership within the Liberal party which led to his successful bid for the presidency of the nation in 1930.

33. Palacio, "Historia," *El Tiempo*, October 18, 1942.

34. Palacio, "Historia," *El Tiempo*, December 6, 1942.

35. The portions of this and the following chapter which deal with the military course of the war are drawn from the many accounts furnished by observers and participants, but seek to avoid the controversies over the responsibilities for victory and defeat which have preoccupied most writers. In addition to the information furnished by Tamayo, Peñuela, Flórez A., Grillo, Caballero, and Uribe Uribe in the books cited previously, the campaign in Santander is treated in detail in José María Vesga y Avila, *La guerra de los tres años* (Bogotá, 1914), Henrique Arboleda Cortés, *Palonegro* (Bucaramanga, 1953, 1st ed., 1900), and Justo L. Durán, *La revolución del 99* (Cúcuta, 1920).

and Bucaramanga, Liberal forces under Uribe Uribe, Benjamín Herrera, and Justo L. Durán congregated in Cúcuta near the Venezuelan border.[36] While the revolutionary army waited vainly in Cúcuta for arms shipments that they hoped would arrive via Venezuela, Conservative forces converged on northeastern Santander. Although superior to the Liberal forces in numbers and equipment, the Conservative army lacked unity of command. No less than thirty-nine generals, representing every faction of the splintered Conservative party, accompanied the approaching government army. Since a decisive victory for the general in command could spell predominance for his faction and the presidency for himself, political considerations tended to have an inordinate influence over military matters in the Conservative army.

On December 15 elements of the two armies came into contact in the Peralonso River valley west of Cúcuta. The encounter quickly generalized, and for two days the battle swirled inconclusively around a bridge across the Peralonso separating the two armies. By the afternoon of the sixteenth the undersupplied Liberals had began to consider breaking off the engagement when Uribe Uribe, in a characteristically desperate maneuver, led a group of ten volunteers in a daring charge across the bridge, routing the surprised Conservative defenders. The Liberal army pursued its advantage, and by nightfall the entire Conservative army was in disorderly retreat, its men abandoning arms, supplies, and horses in their flight and deserting by the hundreds.

Peralonso constituted a tremendous material and psychological victory for the revolution and initiated a five-month period of quiescence on the battlefield as both sides worked to organize an army capable of winning a decisive victory. Rising Liberal fortunes caused many previously undecided or hesitant party members to join the revolutionaries in arms or contribute financially to the revolutionary cause. Skeptics, including some prominent peace Liberals, began to reconsider their prediction that any attempt to topple Sanclemente's government by force was doomed to failure. Some peace Liberals complained to Parra that had they known of the money and instructions sent Foción Soto, they would have never signed the telegram

36. Born in Cali, Cauca, about 1848, Herrera pursued a military career during the years of Liberal hegemony. After 1885 he established himself permanently in Santander, where he engaged in the cattle business. Information on Herrera is scattered; the best single source is Gustavo Humberto Rodríguez, *Benjamín Herrera en la guerra y la paz* (Bogotá, 1973). Durán was born in Oiba, Santander. Like Herrera he had a limited formal education and devoted himself to commerce and agriculture, becoming one of the most important coffee growers in the department by the 1890's. Some information on his career is contained in his *La revolución del 99*, cited above.

counseling peace on October 17, 1899.[37]

Although the Liberals captured substantial amounts of arms and supplies from the retreating government troops, the Liberal high command elected to mop up pockets of Conservative resistance and reorganize the revolutionary army rather than risk a precipitous campaign against Bogotá. The decision to consolidate was taken by Vargas Santos, who had joined the Liberal forces with a small army recruited on the eastern plains after the victory at Peralonso. Proclaimed provisional president and supreme director of the war in a temporary show of unity by Uribe Uribe and Herrera, Vargas Santos rejected plans for a bold strike at the capital and argued convincingly that forthcoming arms shipments sent by Foción Soto through Venezuela would insure a Liberal victory.

In the months following the government's ignominious defeat at Peralonso, alarmed officials sent thousands of new men and a flood of supplies to bolster the Conservative army in the north. Despite the magnitude of the threat perceived by Conservatives, however, the division between Nationalists and Historical Conservatives continued to fester, undermining the effectiveness of the government's war effort. In late December reenforcements recruited in Cauca and Antioquia whose officers held little sympathy for the Nationalist government began to arrive in Bogotá, lending credence to reports of a projected coup by Historical Conservatives.[38] While the possibility of a coup may have seemed remote at that time, many Conservatives believed that the northern campaign would determine not only the fate of the Liberal revolution, but would greatly influence the outcome of the inevitable struggle between the two Conservative factions for control of the postwar government.[39] Pressured to choose between the cautious plans of Manuel Casabianca, nominal head of the northern army, and the bolder attack strategy of Casabianca's second in command, Próspero Pinzón, Sanclemente tried to conciliate Pinzón while supporting Casabianca in his demands for more troops and supplies.[40] In the end, however, Sanclemente changed his strategy and on May 2, 1900, he named Casabianca to replace José Santos as minister of war, and gave Pinzón command of the army, which would

37. Aquileo Parra to Juan E. Manrique, Bogotá, March 2, 1900, and March 3, 1900, Manrique, ACH.

38. Emiliano Izasa to Juan de Dios Jaramillo, Bogotá, December 28, 1899, MDT, ACH. As early as December 12, 1899, President Sanclemente was warned that Vicepresident Marroquín was involved in planning for a coup by Historical Conservatives. Juan A. Zuleta to Manuel Antonio Sanclemente, Bogotá, December 12, 1899, Sanclemente, ANC, 15, ff. 676-677.

39. M. Montoya to Sergio Sanclemente, Soatá [Boyacá], March 25, 1900, Sanclemente, ANC, 19, ff. 660-662.

40. Manuel Antonio Sanclemente to Próspero Pinzón and Manuel Casabianca, Tena [Cundinamarca], March 27, 1900, Sanclemente, ANC, 19.

engage the Liberals at Palonegro less than two weeks later.[41]

The financial demands of the stepped-up war effort following Peralonso, coupled with the fear of eroding political strength, worked to produce some modifications in the government's policies for financing the war. Although continuing to depend primarily on the printing of paper money,[42] the government reduced its initial increases in the tax on the slaughter of livestock and salt in order to cut the price of these sensitive food items.[43] While emissions of paper money provided the government with funds to meet its obligations within Colombia, paper currency could not be used to cover debts for arms and supplies contracted abroad. Of course the government could buy drafts on foreign banks from agents in Colombia, but several considerations made that course undesirable. Drafts were scarce, and given Colombia's precipitously rising exchange rate, expensive (see Table 6:1). Moreover, heavy government purchases only tended to drive the exchange rate up when the government greatly hoped it would decline.

An alternative solution available to the government was to secure additional income in gold. The government's first move in that direction came late in January, 1900, when a decree was passed which authorized the government to contract a small foreign loan of one and one-half million pesos gold offering the nation's interest in the Bogotá-Facatativá Railway as a guarantee.[44] A few days later another decree empowered the government to rent sections of the public domain for periods of up to three years. Rent was to be paid in gold or some exportable item.[45] Apparently these measures were not successful, and in April the government's quest for gold revenues to meet wartime financial needs led it to take two important steps which were to have profound ramifications in Colombian politics.

The first of these was the promulgation of a complicated decree governing exports that was immediately denounced by the powerful import-export interests. Lengthy, complicated, confusing, and probably unenforceable, Decree 731 of 1900 (April 24) gave exporters a choice. They could either sell a portion of the shipment they planned

41. Decree No. 741 of 1900 (May 2), *Diario Oficial*, No. 11,277 (May 5, 1900).

42. New emissions totaling nine million pesos were decreed in March and April. Decree No. 672 of 1900 (March 9), *Diario Oficial*, No. 11,239 (March 14, 1900), and Decree No. 755 of 1900 (April 30), *Diario Oficial*, No. 11,286 (May 22, 1900).

43. Resolutions Nos. 1 and 12 of the Minister of Finance, Carlos Calderón, in *Diario Oficial*, No. 11,190 (January 15, 1900), and No. 11,264 (April 20, 1900). The reason given for reducing the tax on salt was the plight of "clase obrera," hard pressed to provide for its subsistence given the "paralización casi total de todo trabajo" in the war situation. Decree No. 675 of 1900 (February 28), *Diario Oficial*, No. 11,242 (March 17, 1900).

44. Decree No. 676 of 1900 (January 27), *Diario Oficial*, No. 11,242 (March 17, 1900).

45. Decree No. 645 of 1900 (February 9), *Diario Oficial*, No. 11,221 (February 21, 1900).

Table 6:1. Average monthly exchange rate of Colombian pesos, 1899-
1902

	1899	*1900*	*1901*	*1902*
January	235	714	1,123	4,100
February	237	776	1,240	3,900
March	241	993	1,437	4,100
April	243	1,116	1,750	4,400
May	260	1,242	2,159	4,150
June	293	1,163	2,072	4,250
July	334	979	2,400	4,600
August	412	903	2,500	6,900
September	388	792	2,800	10,900
October	402	910	4,800	18,900
November	457	966	4,800	10,900
December	550	992	4,600	9,100

Source: Adapted from Guillermo Torres García, *Historia de la moneda en Colombia* (Bogotá, 1945), p. 276.

Note: Procedure for finding equivalencies in U.S. gold is explained in note to Table 2:2.

to export to the government for paper money, or they could avoid the red tape involved in that procedure and pay an export tax of 20 percent ad valorem (or its equivalent in the product being exported). If they chose the first alternative, the proportion sold to the government depended on the product being exported. Exporters of coffee were required to sell the equivalent of 10 pesos gold per 125 kilograms of coffee, exporters of hides the equivalent of 10 centavos gold per kilogram of hides, exporters of precious minerals and forest products the equivalent of 30 percent of the value of their goods. The current market value of each export item was to be derived from trade journals, while the official exchange rate of Colombian paper currency was to be determined each month by a special government commission.[46]

Decree 731 apparently represented a compromise within the administration. A month before its promulgation, the United States minister in Colombia, Charles Burdett Hart, reported to Washington that the minister of foreign relations had confirmed for him rumors that the government was considering expropriation of all the coffee, hides, and other exportable items within the country, including those belonging to foreigners. At that interview, and at a subsequent meeting that the ministers of Great Britain, France, and Germany had urged him to request, Hart reminded the minister that many of the exportable articles in deposit or transit, whose exportation had been interrupted by the fighting, were foreign property since they had either been purchased with the money of foreign houses or with

46. *Diario Oficial,* No. 11,272 (April 30, 1900).

money drawn against foreign houses. Agents for those houses were not authorized to sell, Hart went on, warning that he and his colleagues "foresaw endless trouble" if the edict of expropriation were issued and put in force. Implementation of the decree, Hart concluded, would severely and adversely affect the credit of Colombia and occasion a severe protest from him and his colleagues. According to Hart, Minister of Foreign Affairs Carlos Calderón admitted that the diplomats' position was "entirely right" and assured him that despite a strong disposition within the government in favor of the expropriation, he felt certain that the decree would not be issued.[47]

When the watered-down decree on export revenue (No. 731) finally was published on the last day of April, 1900, it aroused severe opposition. Soon thereafter, Calderón, who was then serving as minister of finance and was apparently one of the supporters of the measure, proposed minor modifications in the decree, and by May 17 he frankly admitted that the decree was causing serious unrest among exporters and was being used as a political weapon to discredit the government.[48] A few days later he was relieved of his duties as minister of finance.

One of the most vigorous and comprehensive attacks on the decree was addressed to Sanclemente and his cabinet by Historical Conservative Rafael Ortiz from Antioquia. Ortiz agreed with the ends of the decree, designed to meet the legitimate needs of a constitutional government dependent on foreign purchases to preserve itself in power, but he argued that the means outlined in the decree were counterproductive. Confining his remarks specifically to the impact of the measure on coffee exports, Ortiz argued that small producers would be forced to abandon production while large growers would stop exporting and wait for better days. Moreover, he argued, the proposed tax would further diminish the volume of exports, already down as a result of the civil war, and thus contribute to a rise in the exchange rate. As a result the domestic price of many imported goods "of popular consumption" would rise and Colombian commerce would be destroyed. Added to these purely economic disadvantages of the decree was the fiscal consideration that reduced exports inevitably meant reduced imports and a consequent decline in customs revenues. But the greatest drawback to the measure, according to Ortiz, was political. The decree would harden the attitudes of those in opposition to the government, alienate half-hearted supporters, and dampen the support of "many of those who today, with their persons and their resources, are lending important services to our cause." Ortiz assured

47. Charles Burdett Hart to John Hay, Bogotá, March 25, 1900, USNA.
48. Carlos Calderón to Rafael M. Palacio, Bogotá, May 17, 1900, Sanclemente, ANC, 26, f. 40.

the government that he was "experiencing many examples" of this last phenomenon "at this very moment."[49]

Ortiz's petition was sent to Sanclemente under a cover letter from Marco Fidel Suárez, the minister of public instruction. As an *antioqueño* Nationalist, Suárez seemed well-suited to serve as a bridge between the government and the Conservative critics of the decree. Affirming his lack of special knowledge concerning such matters, Suárez noted that Ortiz's argument made sense to him. Exporters would be willing, Suárez predicted, to pay an export tax as they had done in 1895, but the buying of a portion of goods exported seemed to him to be difficult and impractical. Suárez was most concerned, however, with the political impact of the measure.[50]

A few days after lending his support to those favoring modification of the decree, Suárez was named acting minister of finance charged with resolving the controversy over the export decree. According to Suárez, his preliminary investigation revealed that Calderón, confronted with the "absolute refusal" of exporters to cooperate and the administrative impossibility of implementing key aspects of the measure, had been unable to put the decree into effect. Suárez then requested authority to remove the decree's objectionable parts or find a new, practical formula that would serve the dual purpose of providing for the government's needs while satisfying the exporters. After consultation with the governor of Antioquia, Alejandro Guitérrez, and "several respectable merchants and bankers," Suárez, in conjunction with "competent and reputable merchants," drafted a new measure to replace decree No. 731. Suárez's proposal called for revocation of that controversial decree and established what he termed an equitable export tax, acceptable to exporters and yet capable of producing five million pesos in government revenues a year.[51] But Suárez's proposed decree failed to retain the vital gold-procuring feature of the original plan, and Rafael M. Palacio was quick to object. Suárez responded by offering to make minor increases in the rate of tax and suggested that the government reserve its right to exact an export tax in gold if the exchange rate did not fall. Suárez suspected that such a threat would encourage merchants to desist from attempts to maintain an artificially high exchange rate. Suárez also noted that even his watered-down

49. Rafael Ortiz to President Sanclemente and his ministry, Manizales, May 13, 1900, Sanclemente, ANC, 24, ff. 933-940. Ortiz recommended that the government allow free exportation of stored up goods, which he calculated worth two million pesos in gold and one million in coffee in Antioquia alone. Increased exports, by bringing down the exchange rate, would encourage importation and increase customs revenues.

50. Marco Fidel Suárez to Manuel Antonio Sanclemente, Bogotá, May 25, 1900, Sanclemente, ANC, 24, ff. 963-964.

51. Marco Fidel Suárez to Manuel A. Sanclemente, Bogotá, June 7, 1900, Sanclemente, ANC, 25, ff. 526-28.

decree had been accepted "against his will" by Minister of War Manuel Casabianca and added that Casabianca had practically refused to sign the first decree on exports.[52] The compromise measure hammered out by Suárez, Decree No. 777, was signed June 11, 1900, and provided for the following export tax rate, payable in paper currency:

Product	Tax per hundredweight in paper pesos
rubber	$5.00
coffee (husked)	3.20
coffee (unhusked)	2.40
cowhides	3.20
goat hides	4.50

The decree provided for taxation of precious minerals according to a more elaborate procedure and authorized the government to raise or lower the established rates. More important, the decree granted the government the power to substitute these rates with an export tax "payable in gold."[53] The Nationalist government's unprecedented scheme and continuing threat to procure gold revenue by taxing exports proved to be very costly in political terms. The move aroused the opposition of many nominal supporters of the government, especially among the powerful commercial interests centered in Antioquia and the Historical Conservative faction, and probably contributed in large degree to the Historical Conservative decision to mount a coup against Sanclemente a few weeks later.

In revoking its original decree on exports the government noted that it had secured gold income from an alternative source.[54] The government had in fact eased its financial situation by negotiating an extension of the concession held by the French-owned New Panama Canal Company. The terms of the agreement provided for a six-year extension of the concession beginning October 31, 1904, if the Company deposited five million francs gold in the account of the Colombian government within a period of 120 days.[55] The extension had been recommended, albeit in exchange for a much larger sum, by a bipartisan commission composed of Conservatives Rafael Reyes and Clímaco Calderón and the Liberal Nicolás Esguerra. The agreement was consummated for purely financial reasons; neither party seriously believed that the Company would complete the canal.[56] Although the

52. Marco Fidel Suárez to Rafael M. Palacio, Bogotá, June 9, 1900, Sanclemente, ANC, 25, ff. 554-55.

53. *Diario Oficial*, No. 11,291 (June 18, 1900).

54. Decree No. 777 of 1900 (June 11), *Diario Oficial*, No. 11,291 (June 18, 1900).

55. Decree No. 721 of 1900 (April 23), *Diario Oficial*, No. 11,278 (May 7, 1900).

56. Thomas R. Favell, "The Antecedents of Panama's Separation from Colombia: A Study in Colombian Politics" (Ph.D. diss., Tufts-Fletcher, 1950) suggests that the Company entered into the agreement in order to increase the salability of its interests in the canal (p. 145) and notes that members of the Colombian commission doubted the Company would finish the canal (p. 166).

deal furnished the government with desperately needed hard currency for military supplies abroad, the agreement greatly weakened the Colombian position when United States pressure for a canal increased in the postwar period. In the end, the New Panama Canal Company dealt directly with the United States, while one of the Company's officials, Philippe Bunau-Varilla, was a prime mover in the conspiracy to separate Panama from Colombia.

Ironically, these politically costly schemes to secure hard currency for military purchases abroad came too late to aid the government materially in its preparation for the decisive battle with the Liberal revolution in Santander. By early May, 1900, the contending armies had begun to maneuver for position in the warm mountainous coffee lands near Bucaramanga, and on May 11 the Liberal and Conservative forces clashed at a site called Palonegro. Palonegro proved to be the longest and bloodiest battle ever fought on Colombian soil. Although the well-equipped Conservative forces, variously estimated at between fourteen and twenty thousand outnumbered the Liberals by perhaps two to one, they found themselves on the verge of defeat by the end of three days of savage Liberal attacks on their positions.[57] On the fourteenth, however, the superior numbers and equipment of the Conservative forces and the conviction and determination of the Conservative commander, Próspero Pinzón, began to turn the tide.[58] By the fifteenth the Conservative forces had beaten back the desperate Liberal offensive, and the battle took on a new and terrifying aspect.

As each army dug in, stubbornly refusing to abandon the field of battle, the large-scale offensives of the first few days gave way to limited, intensive probing attacks by day and murderous silent patrols of *macheteros* by night. As the days passed and the inconclusive fighting continued, the bodies of hundreds of dead men and animals lay bloated and decomposing between the lines, filling the air with their nauseating stench. Water supplies became polluted and fever and dysentery began to claim more lives than combat. Despite the efforts of several score of doctors and nuns serving as nurses, many of the wounded, especially on the revolutionary side, went unattended.[59]

The seemingly interminable stalemate on the battlefield was broken after Conservative forces were resupplied with ammunition on

57. The higher estimates include Conservative reserve forces which arrived on the scene during the last days of the battle.

58. Pinzón, a deeply religious man, was convinced that Providence was on his side. During the battle he attended mass almost every day, and, according to his biographer, his aides often found him "rezando el rosario en algún cafetal" while the battle raged around him. Peñuela, *Próspero Pinzón*, p. 263.

59. The horror of Palonegro from a doctor's point of view is described by Carlos E. Putnam, "Los horrores de Palonegro," *La Opinión*, October 23 through October 26, 1900.

May 23. Appraised of the changed situation, on the night of May 25 the Liberals retreated from the battlefield, intent on continuing the war effort elsewhere. But the Liberal army never recovered from Palonegro. Decimated in numbers and lacking in arms and munitions, the demoralized Liberals were further handicapped by the depth of the personal animosities between Uribe Uribe on the one hand and Herrera and Vargas Santos on the other.[60] Although the Liberals, especially those commanded by Uribe Uribe, had some temporary success on the Atlantic coast after Palonegro, by the end of the year even these Liberal forces had been defeated and Uribe Uribe, Herrera, and Vargas Santos had been forced to flee the country in search of support abroad with which to renew the war.

With the destruction of the Liberal army following Palonegro, the war entered a new stage. During the remaining two and one-half years of the conflict, with the major exception of the conventional campaign mounted by Herrera on the Isthmus of Panama in 1902, Liberals depended primarily on guerrilla tactics. Guerrilla warfare was concentrated in the mountainous interior of the country, predominantly in the departments of Cundinamarca and Tolima. Liberals in Cundinamarca, aware of the difficulties of supplying their landlocked department with arms from abroad, had drawn up sophisticated plans for a guerrilla campaign long before the fighting broke out.[61] Even before the battle of Palonegro sizable guerrilla bands were operating in the coffee zones of southern and western Cundinamarca and northern Tolima.[62] The shift from conventional military tactics to guerrilla warfare threatened to prolong the conflict indefinitely, began to erode the respect for property and authority vital to upper-class social control, and brought a new savagery to the war which greatly alarmed traditional political leaders.

Upper-class concern with the implications of the changing nature of the conflict was apparent in a petition submitted by peace Liberal leaders in July, 1900, urging the government to grant belligerent

60. For a summation of charges and countercharges involved in the poisonous relations between the two war Liberal factions during the course of the war see Rafael Uribe Uribe, *Querella* (Bogotá, 1904) and Gabriel Vargas Santos, *La razón de mi dicho* (Bogotá, 1904).

61. See the unsigned, undated manuscript entitled "Bases de Operaciones" amidst letters dated July, 1899, in Manrique, ACH.

62. Western Cundinamarca and northern Tolima, divided by the Magdalena River, were really parts of one military theater. Guerrillas spawned in one department frequently campaigned for long periods of time in the other. These campaigns are described in Tulio Arbeláez, *Episodios de la guerra de 1899-1903; campañas del General Cesário Pulido*, 2nd ed. (Bogotá, 1936); Aurelio Masuera y Masuera, *Memorias de un revolucionario* (Bogotá, 1938); *La Guerra en el Tolima, 1899-1902; apuntes y relaciones de la compaña recopilados por El Comercio de Bogotá* (Bogotá, 1903); and Gonzalo París Lozano, *Guerrilleros del Tolima* (Manizales, 1937).

status to the revolutionaries, and thus pave the way for a negotiated settlement. The prolongation of the war, they argued, was causing the conflict to take on "atrocious and frightening" aspects shocking to the civilized world of the twentieth century. If civil war was the "almost normal state" of "equatorial" America, then the regularization of the rules of war was vital. By making warfare more civilized the practices spawned by "semi-barbarous traditions" could be moderated and the few seeds of civilization which had taken hold in Colombia might be preserved.[63]

Historical Conservatives were also concerned with the new dimensions of the conflict and the apparent inability of Sanclemente's government to end the war. Like peace Liberals they were convinced that only a political agreement involving some concessions to long-standing Liberal grievances would bring an end to the fighting. Furthermore, as Rafael Ortiz had warned, many Historical Conservatives lacked confidence in the government which had threatened to tax exports in gold. All these factors stimulated Historical Conservative leaders to consider the possibility of fulfilling their long-standing political ambition of gaining control of the government through extra constitutional means. During the last days of July, 1900, they formulated serious plans for a coup to replace Sanclemente's Nationalist government with a Historical Conservative government headed by Vice-president Marroquín. The mechanics of such a coup were facilitated by the fact that the old President and his minister of government, Rafael M. Palacio, had moved their warm-country residence even farther from the capital to the town of Villeta, Cundinamarca, situated some eighty-one kilometers to the west of Bogotá.

The coup began haphazardly on the morning of July 31, 1900, when General Jorge Moya Vásquez, a Historical Conservative recently appointed by Minister of War Casabianca as commander of the garrison at Soacha just south of the capital, announced his intention to march on Villeta and impose a change in government. In reality Moya marched on Bogotá, but discovering that only a portion of his officers were willing to support a coup, and finding the city in absolute calm upon his arrival, he quartered his troops and prepared to surrender his sword to Casabianca. The only other armed support for the coup was a group of Historical Conservative gentlemen and students organized by Luis Martínez Silva and José Vicente Concha. Casabianca might have controlled the meager and indecisive threat posed by the conspirators, but early in the day he declined the opportunity to arrest all of the prominent civilian leaders of the coup and later he refused to

63. The petition was signed by José María Quijano Wallis, Santiago Samper, Juan E. Manrique, and several other Liberal leaders.

use armed force to protect the government. Casabianca's attitude left Director of Police Aristides Fernández in the position of exercising a decisive influence on the fate of the coup. For a long time Fernández kept both sides in doubt concerning his inclinations while his police took up positions in the plaza de San Agustín in an impressive show of force. Fernández's ultimate decision not to oppose the coup signaled the success of the movement and formed the basis for his inclusion within Marroquín's new government.[64]

The coup of July 31 was a logical consequence of the personal ambitions, ideological commitments, and economic interests which had divided Historical Conservatives from Nationalists throughout the 1890's. Most of the participants in the coup, planned by the leaders of the Historical Conservative faction in Bogotá headed by Carlos Martínez Silva, had been signers of the famous "Motives of Dissidence" in 1896 or supporters of the reform movement in the Chamber of Representatives in 1898.[65] Backing the coup outside Bogotá were Marceliano Vélez and the bulk of the antioqueño Conservatives and the prestigious military leader Ramón González Valencia of Santander. Peace Liberal leader Aquileo Parra, informed by the Historical Conservative conspirators of their intention to secure a negotiated settlement of the war on the basis of political reforms, gave the movement his full approval and support. According to one account, Historical Conservative negotiators promised to offer the Liberals in arms an honorable peace without reprisals, convoke elections for a constituent congress, issue a decree granting Liberals sufficient participation on electoral boards to insure free elections, free all political prisoners who promised not to take up arms against the new government, and send Liberal commissioners chosen by the government and the peace Liberals to negotiate with the Liberals in arms. Marroquín reportedly refused to accede to the Liberal demand that he pledge not to include Director of Police Fernández in his future government.[66] Whatever the nature of the understanding between the Historical Conservatives backing Marroquín and the peace Liberal leadership—Marroquín subsequently denied he had entered into any secret agreements with the Liberals and even declared that he had been unaware of negotiations between Historical Conservatives and Aquileo Parra—the initial hopes that the new government would seek a political settlement to end the war were soon corrected by the course of events.[67]

64. This account of the coup is taken from Martínez Delgado, *Historia,* pp. 76-114, and Tamayo, *Revolución,* pp. 105-18. Martínez Delgado's study, cited extensively in this section, attempts to justify the coup and provides a wealth of background information, eyewitness accounts, and pertinent documents.

65. A complete list is furnished in Martínez Delgado, *Historia,* p. 76.

66. *Ibid.,* pp. 71-72.

67. José Manuel Marroquín to Aquileo Parra, Bogotá, August 27, 1900, and Aquileo

Although the Historical Conservatives appeared to dominate the new government, controlling most of the ministries and many of the military governorships, Marroquín remained very much his own man and utilized another basis of support, centered on Aristides Fernández, to counterbalance and eventually outweigh the Historical Conservative influence on his government. In his appointments of military governors of the departments, Marroquín named Historical Conservatives Marceliano Vélez and Ramón González Valencia to head Antioquia and Santander respectively, but a major crisis developed among his supporters over his decision to appoint Aristides Fernández to the powerful post of military governor of Cundinamarca. The terms of the appointment specified that in addition to his new duties as military governor, Fernández would continue as director of police.[68]

Marroquín later recalled his anger when a group of Historical Conservative supporters of the coup rebuked him for his appointment of Fernández. "I got angry: I cursed them; I informed them that if they had hoped, in elevating me, to secure in me an instrument, they had been mistaken."[69] A few weeks after the coup, in a letter urging Próspero Pinzón to accept the ministry of war, Marroquín commented on what he termed the "apparent" preponderance of Historical Conservatives in his government and candidly summarized his political strategy.

[S]ince most of those who brought about the movement of the 31st of July belonged to that group, and since they really risked their hides, I have not been able to avoid summoning them to my side; but I have done it with the intention of bringing them over to our way of thinking or discarding them little by little. The second or third of August they demanded that I free the political prisoners and thereby gave me the opportunity to show them that it is I who command. From that time on they have been submissive, silently enduring certain rigorous measures I have taken against the revolutionaries, measures that are very much against their ideas.[70]

Parra to José Manuel Marroquín, Chapinero [Cundinamarca], September 4, 1900, published in Martínez Delgado, *Historia*, pp. 182-85.

68. Decree No. 3 of 1900 (August 1, 1900), *Diario Oficial*, No. 11,310 (August 13, 1900).

69. Marroquín's informal account of the coup, probably written some years after the event, was published in *El Debate*, August 12, 1927, and is reproduced in Martínez Delgado, *Historia*, pp. 103-114. The quotation is from p. 114. A vivid description of the circumstances surrounding Marroquín's crucial decision to appoint Fernández can be found in *Datos históricos contenidos en las réplicas del Senador Groot al Senador Caro* (Bogotá, 1904), pp. 66-70.

70. J. Manuel Marroquín to Próspero Pinzón, n.p., n.d. in Martínez Delgado, *Historia*, p. 202.

As his letter to Pinzón indicates, Marroquín pursued a conscious policy of avoiding political concessions to the revolution from the beginning. Even his first public statements revealed his aversion to a political settlement and his determination to pursue a military victory if necessary. In his address to the nation upon assuming power he promised only to respect "the civil and political rights of all" and asserted that he hoped the sincerity of that promise would induce the revolutionaries to lay down their arms. If they did not, Marroquín went on, "I will find myself in the painful, extremely painful position of having to continue the war with the energy required of one who occupies a post like the one I hold defending the redeeming principles embodied in the present Constitution."[71]

On August 19 Marroquín began to implement his policy by issuing an ultimatum calling upon the revolutionaries to lay down their arms and specifying severe sanctions against those who did not take advantage of the offer within two weeks. The decree distinguished between those revolutionaries who might have had honorable intentions and had fought with some hope of victory from those who continued a hopeless fight either out of a misguided sense of military honor or because of "the lure of marauding." Those who turned themselves in before the deadline would be guaranteed safe-conduct passes; those who did not would be treated with the full rigor of the laws governing the crime of rebellion. In any department not pacified within two weeks, the government would begin to enforce the decree on war contributions passed December 1, 1899. Individuals still in revolt or considered to be sympathetic with the revolutionaries would be assigned a weekly war contribution, payable either in cash or property. Those unable or unwilling to pay would be jailed. The contribution would continue until the department was completely pacified and could be raised or lowered at the discretion of the military governor.[72]

Although Marroquín's Historical Conservative sponsors were dismayed at his political independence and his uncompromising attitude toward the Liberal revolution, his behavior was in many ways consistent with his character and background. He was born an only child into a family of the highest social distinction and was educated exclusively in Bogotá; his longest trip away from the Sabana de Bogotá was to nearby highland Boyacá. Most of his public life was devoted to furthering his ideal of Catholic education for Colombian youth. In 1865 he co-founded the Sociedad de Estudios Religiosos to combat the anticlerical ideas circulating in Colombia with the advent of Liberal hegemony. A decade later he joined others in an attempt to found

71. *Diario Oficial*, No. 11,306 (August 2, 1900).
72. Decree No. 29 of 1900 (August 19), *Diario Oficial*, No. 11,314 (August 23, 1900).

a Catholic University. Although that effort failed, the university was later established and Marroquín served as its rector for a few months in 1883. During the first administration of Núñez, Marroquín served as a member of the Concejo Académico charged with restoring religious principles to the educational system, and in 1887 he was named rector of the Colegio del Rosario, where he worked to transfrom that previously Liberal institution into a training ground for the Conservative elite.[73]

In 1892 Marroquín retired to "Yerbabuena," the hacienda on the Sabana de Bogotá near Chía which had been part of his family's patrimony for generations.[74] There he devoted himself to the pleasures of being a gentleman farmer and writing *costumbrista* novels in which he elegantly and faithfully portrayed the life he observed around him. Years later José Joaquín Casas described the impression Marroquín made on him when he chanced to meet the "country hidalgo" near "Yerbabuena" one morning in the early 1890's. Dressed as a rich hacienda owner with "a blue woolen cape, a high Panama hat of the best quality, lion skin chaps, and suede gloves," mounted on a flawlessly outfitted chestnut horse, and followed by a servant boy on a mare, Marroquín seemed to symbolize in Casas's mind "a culture of inestimable value and . . . an era glorious for Colombia." "With deep affection and passionate delight Señor Marroquín was able to experience, love, and savor his native land. . . ." Because he could not resign himself to the thought that with his death "the many excellent social and domestic virtues he had witnessed and been influenced by" might disappear without a trace, he sought to preserve the world he knew and cherished in literature.[75]

The novels written by Marroquín during this period of retirement from public life reveal as much about their author as they do about the late nineteenth-century highland Colombian society he described so carefully.[76] For example, in *Entre primos*, the romantic story of a childhood love between cousins threatened by a suitor outside the family, Marroquín ridicules the effete, myopic son of an English merchant whose absurd mimicking of foreign ways and consumption patterns, and shallow, fickle attraction to his fiancée, contrasts sharply with the true love of her solidly Colombian cousin whose courage, intelligence, and hard work make him an ideal mate. *Blas Gil* is a

73. This information is taken from José Manuel Marroquín Osorio, *Marroquín íntimo* (Bogotá, 1915), which draws heavily on Marroquín's own unpublished "Apuntes biográficos," and from Jorge Roa's insightful prologue to a collection of Marroquín's stories published in 1893 and reprinted in Martínez Delgado, *Historia*, pp. 245-51.

74. (Presbítero) José Manuel Marroquín, *En familia*, 2nd ed. (Bogotá, 1921).

75. Casas, *Semblanza*, pp. 157-59.

76. Marroquín wrote four novels during this period, *Blas Gil* (1896), *Entre primos* (1897), *Amores y leyes* (1898), and *El Moro* (1899).

devastating satire of Colombian political culture written, ironically, just a few years before Marroquín found himself thrust into the midst of the corruption and opportunism of wartime politics. As in *Entre primos*, Marroquín's deep religiousness is apparent in *Blas Gil*. The epitome of the unscrupulous politician who has chosen his career as a way of avoiding honest work and pursuing personal gain, Blas is finally rescued from his cynicism through a renewal of his Catholic faith and the pure love of a virtuous girl.

Maroquín's religiousness and love of things Colombian, interrelated threads that run through every aspect of his life and thought, would give him strength and purpose in his struggle to resist the policy of political concessions to the Liberal revolutionaries advocated by the Historical Conservative and peace Liberal sponsors of his accession to power. As the war entered a new and more desperate phase with the adoption of guerrilla tactics by the Liberal revolutionaries, Marroquín would preside over a government ever more contemptuous of the reformists' strategy for ending the conflict and determined to eradicate the threat to traditional Colombian institutions posed by the Liberal guerrillas and the philosophy of liberalism in general.

Chapter VII

The Guerrillas' War

Prolongation of the war through guerrilla tactics for an additional two and one-half years after Palonegro and the coup of July 31, 1900, had profound consequences for the economic, political and social life of the nation. Economically, guerrilla warfare not only worsened the effects of the coffee depression by disrupting production and commerce, but indirectly stimulated the massive emissions of paper money used by the government to finance its war effort. Politically, the guerrillas, increasingly independent of traditional Liberal political leaders and deaf to overtures from moderate Liberals and Conservatives to work out a negotiated settlement, contributed to the rise to power of the most intransigent, antireformist elements of the Conservative party. Finally, protracted guerrilla warfare, by undermining upper-class control of economic and political power, began to threaten the social foundations of Colombian life. As traditional leaders of all political persuasions perceived that threat they began to minimize their long-standing differences and acted to bring the conflict to a close. The end of the fighting effectively curbed the wartime challenge to the class interests of all traditionally privileged groups in Colombian society, but left unresolved the economic and political issues which had divided sectors within the Colombian upper class and helped to precipitate the war. In fact the war only intensified the economic and fiscal problems facing the country while strengthening the hold on national power of those Conservatives most opposed to reform.

Economic conditions must have greatly influenced the decision of the Liberal revolutionaries to adopt guerrilla tactics and continue the struggle after the defeat of the regular Liberal armies in the first months of the war. Unlike the Liberal revolutionaries of 1895, who returned from the battlefield to an expanding economy paced by a dynamic coffee sector, defeated Liberal officers and men in 1900 found themselves in the midst of a severe economic depression. Coffee prices had continued to fall after the start of the war, and by the middle of the year 1900 stood at seven cents per pound, a price which made coffee cultivation even in favored areas economically marginal. The effects of the coffee depression were exacerbated by the war. In

the coffee zones and in other areas agricultural production was disrupted as a consequence of the recruitment or flight of able-bodied
workers, the destruction caused by the fighting, and the depredations
of both government and revolutionary forces. Moreover, wartime
damage to transportation and communication systems and the general
climate of insecurity fostered by the war, restricted the movement of
goods, especially imports and exports, and inhibited productive investment.[1]

Suggestive of the influence of economic conditions in precipitating
and perpetuating the war is the fact that coffee regions proved to be
major theaters of military activity. While political and geographic factors greatly influenced the course of military events, it is also true that
it was in the coffee-growing regions of the department of Santander,
areas hardest hit by the coffee depression, that the war began and the
largest battle of the war was fought. In Cundinamarca, the coffee
provinces of Sumapaz and Tequendama in the southwest and La
Palma in the northwest (see the map on the following page) were the
major foci of guerrilla activity during the war.[2]

Government victories in these areas proved chimerical throughout
the war. Less than three months after momentous government victories in these areas in February and March, 1902, a frustrated Marroquín wrote Archbishop Herrera that everything had returned to the
state it was in before the government offensive. "In the provinces of
Sumapaz, Tequendama, and La Palma," he added, "the guerrillas survive and are gaining strength."[3] In their unsuccessful efforts to control
the coffee zones military commanders resorted to mass arrests of both
men and women considered Liberal sympathizers or potential guerrillas. After his defeat of a guerrilla band and sweep of the coffee-
producing area around Cumacá and Calandaima in southwestern
Cundinamarca near Viotá in 1901, General Sicard Briceño advised the
minister of war that he had captured hundreds of men and women.

> [B]oth the men and the women are accomplices and auxiliaries of
> ... bandits who they hide in their houses; as a result I am send-
> ing all of them to Bogotá believing that the men should be sent as
> recruits to the coast and the women punished as Your Excellency
> sees fit, since they are a very bad breed.

1. By August, 1901, the United States minister to Colombia estimated that the quantity of coffee awaiting shipment figured in the hundreds of thousands of bags, much of it
owned by foreigners. Charles Burdett Hart to John Hay, Bogotá, August 11, 1901,
USNA.

2. Guerrilla forces were also active in the coffee-producing regions of northern Tolima. Guerrilla activity does not seem to have been widespread in the other important
coffee region in the country, southern Antioquia, perhaps because coffee farmers in that
area were almost entirely affiliated with the Conservative party.

3. José Manuel Marroquín to Bernardo Herrera Restrepo, Bogotá, May 28, 1902,
MDT, ACH.

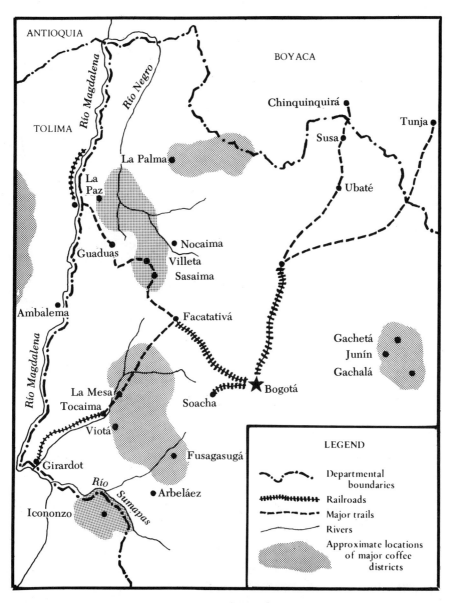

Major coffee zones of Cundinamarca

In a subsequent telegram sent the same day Briceño reiterated his advice on the men, but changed his position on the women: "I will return the 200 women to the coffee groves warning them that they will be severely punished if they aid the guerrillas."[4]

Characteristic of the guerrilla strongholds of southwestern Cundinamarca was the rich coffee *municipio* of Viotá. Controlled by Liberal forces throughout most of the war, Viotá was a haven for guerrilla bands retreating from defeats in government-dominated areas. Dubbed the "wet nurse of the Revolution" by grateful guerrilla leaders who depended on the resources of the *municipio* and the support of its people to replenish supplies and restore the fighting capability of their forces,[5] Viotá was described by contemporaries as being made up of valuable coffee plantations

> most of which belong to progressive men, some of whom owed their fortune, others their modest well-being, to years of honorable, constant, energetic, and intelligent labor; men who, it is well understood, had to be hostile to the government in power.[6]

According to Conservative intelligence reports dated June, 1901, Liberal hacienda owners from Viotá and surrounding areas had turned over their workers to the guerrilla leaders, swelling their ranks.[7]

Charged with governing the *municipio* of Viotá for the revolutionary forces was a successful coffee planter, Aurelio Masuera y Masuera. He used his organizational skills to build an effective guerrilla force and plan a rudimentary government for the *municipio*. One of his primary concerns was the organization of revenue for his government. Exempting those under arms in the revolutionary forces and those too poor to pay, Masuera y Masuera stipulated procedures for the collection of local transit and liquor taxes, donations, forced loans, expropriations, and confiscations. He also provided for maintenance of trails, called for the establishment of a permanent postal service, and ordered construction of a telegraph line through Viotá to connect El Colegio and Fusagasugá. In order to assure continued agricultural production Masuera y Masuera offered protection and guarantees to cooperative landowners and established the practice of allowing members of guerrilla forces to work the coffee plantations during lulls between battles.[8] Although only a few of the large Liberal coffee growers from Viotá followed Masuera y Masuera's example and took up arms against the government, most seem to have supported the

4. Sicard Briceño to the Minister of War, Fusagasugá [Cundinamarca], June 21, 1901. Both telegrams can be found in AMD, vol. 05764.

5. Masuera y Masuera, *Memorias*, p. 11.

6. *La Guerra en el Tolima*, p. 142.

7. Masuera y Masuera, *Memorias*, pp. 14-15.

8. *Ibid.*, pp. 16-17, 29.

revolution. In June, 1901, exasperated government officials in south-western Cundinamarca insisted that unless the government adopted a policy of concentrating the Liberal hacienda owners in Bogotá, pacification of the region would be very difficult.[9]

The most famous of the guerrilla leaders to come out of Viotá was Cesáreo Pulido, a Liberal merchant who also owned two coffee estates in the municipio at the time the war began. Born in nearby La Mesa, Cundinamarca in 1847, he acquired a limited formal education and devoted himself to agriculture and commerce. Owner of a store in La Mesa, Pulido experienced severe financial difficulties as a result of the coffee crash, but did not join the revolution until a government commission allegedly mistreated his property and relatives in Viotá.[10] Starting with only a dozen men "collected from among the workers on his hacienda and two or three friends," at times during the war he reportedly commanded hundreds of men. Denounced as a bandit leader primarily concerned with plundering the property of Conservatives in southwestern Cundinamarca and one of the few revolutionaries still operating in the interior during the last months of the war, he was finally captured and summarily executed in September, 1902.[11]

Some insight into the sociology of Liberal guerrilla forces like Pulido's can be gleaned from a list of Liberal prisoners captured in Iquirá, Tolima, in December, 1900.[12] The list includes data on the military rank, place of residence, age, and occupation of some 91 Liberal officers and 205 common soldiers. Most of the prisoners came from towns in Tolima although a sizable number were from Cundinamarca and a smattering from Boyacá, Cauca, and Antioquia. While a few listed large towns or cities as their place of residence, the vast majority were from small towns. Of the two generals captured, thirty-one-year-old José Joaquín Caicedo R. was listed as a land surveyor from Guamo, Tolima. The other, Victoriano Tirso Trujillo, was a thirty-four-year-old merchant from Villavicencio on the eastern plains of Cundinamarca. Most of the seventeen colonels were in their twenties or thirties but ranged in age from nineteen to eighty-two. Lower rank officers tended to be in their twenties with a large percentage of first and second lieutenants in their late teens. The vast majority of

9. Federico Tovar to the Minister of War, Anapoima [Cundinamarca], June 21, 1901, AMD, vol. 05764. See also Masuera y Masuera, *Memorias*, p. 11.

10. *La Guerra en el Tolima*, p. 239; Paris, *Guerrilleros*, p. 107; Arbeláez, *Episodios*, p. 19.

11. Arbeláez, *Episodios*, pp. 16-19. The quotation is from p. 19.

12. Located in what is now the department of Huila, Iquirá is situated in the mountainous coffee country some thirty-five kilometers southeast of Neiva. The list was republished in Benjamín Latorre, *Recuerdos de campaña, 1900-1902* (Bogotá, 1938), pp. 129-42.

common soldiers were in their teens and twenties with a large number, more than 11 percent of the sample, fourteen years of age or younger.[13]

Analysis of the information on the occupations of these captured Liberal revolutionaries reveals the not surprising fact that officers were of much higher social status than their men. What is striking about the occupational breakdown of the officers (see Table 7:1) is that merchants constitute fully one-third of the total. While only two officers are listed as landowners, the data may hide the fact that many merchants, as the case of Cesáreo Pulido demonstrates, were also owners of haciendas. About half of the common soldiers were listed agriculturalists, a term which presumably was applied to landowners, tenants, and sharecroppers alike. Another third of the rank and file were day laborers and most of the rest were artisans or cowboys.

On occasion the government was able to repeat the success at Iquirá, Tolima, and capture a large band of Liberal revolutionaries. Such was the fate, for example, of the more than a hundred officers and men under the command of Benito Ulloa defeated and captured near the coffee-producing *municipio* of Sasaima, Cundinamarca, in

Table 7:1. Occupations of ninety-one Liberal officers captured in Iquirá, Tolima, December, 1900

comerciantes (merchants)	30
agricultores (agriculturalists)	13
artesanos (artisans)	10
abogados (lawyers)	6
estudiantes (students)	6
ingenieros (engineers)	4
arquitectos (architects)	3
empleados (employees)	3
hacendados (landowners)	2
contabilistas (bookkeepers)	2
vaqueros (cowboys)	2
mayordomos (foremen)	2
aqrimensor (land surveyor)	1
institutor (educator)	1
dentista (dentist)	1
navegante (pilot)	1
músico (musician)	1
fotógrafo (photographer)	1
negociante (trader)	1
dependiente (dependent)	1
Total	91

13. Five were listed as fourteen years old, seven as thirteen, nine as twelve, one as eleven, and one as ten.

mid-April, 1901. In an effort to demonstrate government effectiveness in combating the guerrillas, Ulloa and his men were paraded with much fanfare through the streets of Bogotá before being imprisoned.[14] Despite their best efforts, however, government officials could not hide the fact that throughout almost three years of war guerrillas in the coffee zones of Cundinamarca and Tolima successfully resisted government control.

The tactics of the Liberals in arms conformed to the classic pattern of successful guerrilla warfare. Surrounded in their mountain enclaves by government troops greatly superior in numbers and firepower, the revolutionaries resorted to surprise attacks, ambushes, and strategic retreats. The Liberal guerrillas enjoyed the advantages of a sympathetic population and an intimate knowledge of the terrain.[15] There was ample precedent for this kind of warfare; guerrilla tactics had been utilized in Colombian civil wars since Independence, and many of the Liberal revolutionaries, having participated in previous civil conflicts, had first-hand experience with guerrilla methods. In addition, some Liberal leaders had access to formal and quite sophisticated codifications of the maxims of guerrilla warfare. Besides the previously noted guerrilla strategy drawn up by Liberals for Cundinamarca before the war at least a few Liberal officers were acquainted with Código de Maceo. Circulated by General Avelino Rosas, who had fought along with the Cuban guerrillas in the war for Cuban independence in the late 1890's, the Código de Maceo covered every aspect of guerrilla warfare ranging from the proper attitude, training, and equipment of the individual guerrilla fighter to the internal organization, military tactics, and strategy of the guerrilla group as a whole.[16]

Although Rosas argued that five hundred guerrilla bands of a hundred men each could bring down the government, Liberal guerrilla leaders were wont to unite and attack government forces and major towns in conventional style. Often these attempts ended in disaster, and even when Liberal forces did manage to take important towns, they were invariably forced to relinquish them within a matter of hours or days. The government's greatly superior resources in men and equipment, the revolutionaries' perennial lack of ammunition, the constant friction between Liberal guerrilla leaders, and the lack of

14. Circular signed José de los Santos Cuervo, Honda [Tolima], April 17, 1901, AMD [no number, April, 1901]; *El Colombiano*, April 16, 1901. Sasaima itself was one of the few coffee *municipios* in Cundinamarca dominated by Conservatives.

15. José M. Cogollos to the Minister of War, La Mesa [Cundinamarca], April 28, 1901, AMD [no number, April, 1901]; Nicolás Perdomo to Minister of War, Tocaima [Cundinamarca], April 24, 1901, AMD [no number, April, 1901].

16. Flórez Alvarez, *La campaña en Santander*, pp. 51-54. The guide derived its name from the famous Cuban independence fighter, Antonio Maceo.

discipline among their troops, all contributed to the Liberals' inability to win conventional battles and retain control of important urban centers. But government troops were no match for guerrillas in the countryside. Under pressure from government forces guerrillas would subdivide infinitely, their members reuniting days later at a previously accorded place. In extreme emergencies individual guerrillas would return to farming or even join government forces temporarily. Once government pressure in an area eased, guerrillas would regroup and commence activities anew.[17]

The success of the Liberals' guerrilla tactics forced the government to press tens of thousands of men into service and involved massive outlays of funds to provision and equip government armies. Deprived of the bulk of its normal revenues, the government met these expenses through frequent emissions of paper money. The virtual cessation of exports and the ever-increasing supply of paper money caused the exchange rate to skyrocket. After falling during the first few months of Marroquín's second administration, the rate doubled between January and May, 1901, then doubled again between May and October (see Table 6:1).

Protracted guerrilla warfare also seriously compromised the discipline and morale of the government army. Particularly in the theaters of guerrilla activity like southwestern Cundinamarca, where the fighting was difficult, the climate unhealthy, and the people hostile, attrition among government troops was great and replacement difficult. Ordered to draft more men and reorganize his decimated forces, the military head of La Mesa complained in 1901 that many of his troops were sick or recovering from yellow fever, dysentery, or smallpox and that because of the constant warfare that had afflicted the region and the hostility of most of its inhabitants towards the government, such a military reorganization was impractical. Two months later the same official informed his superiors that as a result of constant government conscription servants and food peddlers had disappeared and warned them that even the supporters of the government became alienated when they lost their servants to the government armies.[18] Desertion on a scale one officer called "disgraceful" was another problem faced by government forces operating against the guerrillas.[19] The effectiveness of government forces was also hampered by the fact that while volunteers in Conservative towns

17. Paris, *Guerrilleros*, pp. 50-52, 21, 32, 69; Masuera y Masuera, *Memorias*, pp. 31, 35; Arbeláez, *Episodios*, pp. 32-33; *La guerra en el Tolima*, pp. 192-98.

18. José M. Cogollos to the Jefe, Estado Mayor del Ejército, La Mesa [Cundinamarca], April 18, 1901, AMD [no number, April, 1901]; José M. Cogollos to the Minister of War, La Mesa [Cundinamarca], June 16, 1901, AMD, vol. 05764.

19. Sicard Briceño to the Minister of War, Tocaima [Cundinamarca], June 23, 1901, AMD, vol. 05764.

often fought bravely in defense of their own homes, they refused to pursue guerrillas outside their own districts.[20]

As the war continued and the strength of the guerrillas grew, rather than declined, charges of government military incompetence became frequent. The most common reason advanced for the failure of the military to deal effectively with the guerrillas was the corruption of the officers in the field. Many Conservatives charged that military commanders were more concerned with lining their pockets than with winning difficult victories over the guerrillas. While Marroquín often complained that the army was "sick with politics" and difficult to subordinate to civil authority, he considered that problem insignificant when compared with the spirit of "speculation and, I can rightfully say, of robbery, that holds sway in most of our army camps and garrisons and in this city." Officers of all ranks neglected their duties to dedicate themselves to the "buying and selling of mules, livestock, provisions, and merchandise of every kind." Worse, some trafficked with Liberals. Even military men were scandalized by the corruption they observed among their colleagues. In June, 1901, General Federico Tovar blamed the defeat of part of his forces operating in the coffee zone of southwestern Cundinamarca on the insubordination of an officer who disobeyed orders and delayed an attack in order to realize a profit on cattle he was butchering. Officers were interested solely in business deals, Tovar went on, and the worst abuses occurred in the expropriation of horses and mules. The best animals were shamefully stolen by higher officers and sold for personal gain while lower officers were often left afoot and the army deprived of the means to move supplies and equipment.[21]

Moderates from both political parties were alarmed at the threat to property posed by the Liberal guerrillas and the corrupt government officers charged with combating them, but what most disturbed moderates was the way in which the guerrillas' continued success strengthened the hand of the intransigent Conservatives in Marroquín's government. Capitalizing on the general frustration over the military's inability to deal effectively with the Liberals' guerrilla tactics and the growing alarm over the threat posed by the guerrillas to the security and property of Conservatives in large areas of the interior, Conservative extremists succeeded in convincing the government to adopt ever more radical measures to prosecute the war. When the guerrillas refused to surrender under the terms of his initial ultimatum

20. A. Duque to Mariano Tovar, Villeta [Cundinamarca], April 27, 1901, AMD [no number, April, 1901].
21. José Manuel Marroquín to J. F. Vélez, Bogotá, July 30, 1901, MDT, ACH. Federico Tovar to Mariano Tovar, Anapoima, June 28, 1901, AMD [no number, June, 1901]. See also the resolution of the minister of war dated August 17, 1901, and published in *El Colombiano*, August 23, 1901.

of August 19, 1900, Marroquín sent a circular to his cabinet officers and departmental governors outlining a new policy toward the revolution. The government's peace offer, the vice-president explained, had been widely interpreted "as a sign of weakness or fear." Far from responding favorably to his efforts for peace, some bands of revolutionaries had been encouraged to commit depredations including the burning of several private estates. As a result, he declared, his government would utilize the numerous and effective means at its disposal to deal with the revolutionaries in arms and their auxiliaries, and he instructed his subordinates to implement this policy in their respective areas.[22]

In the department of Cundinamarca Military Governor Aristides Fernández demonstrated the government's new resolve by assigning a forced contribution in the amount of twenty thousand pesos to the important Bogotá export-import merchant Antonio Samper Uribe. Samper Uribe had joined the revolution in April, 1900, when he attempted to raise an additional guerrilla force to operate in the coffee zone of southwestern Cundinamarca. After an initial defeat he became an aide to Aristóbulo Ibáñez, whose forces had been operating successfully in the area for months.[23] In order to force Samper Uribe to pay, Fernández took the unprecedented step of closing the important export-import house, Samper Uribe & Co., in which Samper Uribe had a major interest. Other partners in the firm were quick to protest. In a lengthy petition sent Marroquín, Guillermo Uribe, speaking on behalf of the company, cited European legal scholars and historical antecedents to bolster his argument that in "civilized nations" private property could not be confiscated. The closing of the business not only worked undue hardship on innocent employees and their families, Uribe went on, but cut off the sustenance of many Colombians living in Europe and threatened the future of the house itself, an important Colombian commercial establishment with branches in Paris and Buenos Aires.[24] A week later Marroquín resolved to instruct Fernández to lift his order closing Samper Uribe & Co. on the condition that one of the partners or someone else pledge to guarantee payment of the war contribution assigned Samper Uribe. On September 20 Samper Uribe informed Marroquín that under protest he had authorized his partners to pay the twenty thousand pesos assigned him.[25]

22. José Manuel Marroquín to his ministers and the military governors, August 29, 1900, MDT, ACH.

23. *La Guerra en el Tolima*, pp. 143-49; Masuera y Masuera, *Memorias*, p. 10. As the contemporary account in *La Guerra en el Tolima* makes clear Samper Uribe's support of the war was an exception among wealthy Liberal merchants.

24. Guillermo Uribe to José Manuel Marroquín, August 20, 1900, MDT, ACH.

25. Antonio Samper Uribe to José Manuel Marroquín, Icononzo [Tolima], September 20, 1900, MDT, ACH.

Fernández's actions against Samper Uribe were typical of his severe measures to deal with the guerrilla threat. Convinced that the rural guerrillas in Cundinamarca and Tolima were encouraged, supplied, and directed from Bogotá, Fernández established rewards for information regarding Liberal collaborators and ordered nighttime patrols of the city and surprise searches of houses. On November 11, 1900, the number of police at Fernández's disposal was increased by half, raising the total force to fifteen hundred men.[26] Using the wide discretionary powers accorded him as military governor of Cundinamarca and the tools available to him as director of police, Fernández assigned forced contributions to some suspected sympathizers and jailed others outright. Fernández strong-arm methods spared no one; details of his "reign of terror" were later vividly recalled by upper-class Liberals who lived through the period as children. "I cannot recall those violent, nauseating days without my hair standing on end, without being afraid and . . . angry," wrote one Liberal.

The walls had eyes and ears. So did the streets. Repugnant young men served as secret police. The slightest tip got results. On the basis of nothing gentlemen from the highest rungs of society were carried off to infected cells, assigned forced loans, or threatened by night patrols.[27]

The destination of most prisoners of war, alleged revolutionary sympathizers, and those arrested by Fernández's police for failure to pay forced loans was the Panóptico de Bogotá, a massive stone prison located on the outskirts of the city. Hopelessly overcrowded by the end of 1900, the dank filthy corridors and cells of the Panóptico teemed with thousands of prisoners of all social classes jailed for common as well as political crimes. Fine Liberal gentlemen found themselves competing for space in filthy cells with prisoners from the lowest social strata. Peace Liberals often learned to their discomfort that despite urgent appeals to their acquaintances among the Conservative and ecclesiastical authorities, Fernández effectively barred their release from prison. After the war one such Liberal gentleman, Adolfo León Gómez, recorded his impressions of life in prison in a book called *Secretos del panóptico* (Bogotá, 1905). Intended to document the barbarous extremes to which Fernández carried political repression, León Gómez's book also provides much insight into the nature of Colombian social relations as observed in the microcosm of the prison.

26. *Diario Oficial*, No. 11,402 (January 21, 1901).
27. Luis Eduardo Nieto Caballero, *Por qué soy liberal* (Bogotá, 1931), pp. 40-41. The repression is described and in some cases documented in Tamayo, *Revolución*, pp. 148-62.

Initially living conditions in the prison were difficult but not unbearable for upper-class Liberals incarcerated on Fernández's orders. Although subjected to many inconveniences and frequent humiliations at the hands of abusive prison guards, upper-class prisoners usually managed to avoid the severe conditions endured by their lowerclass companions. Wealthy prisoners could buy a prime spot to set up their beds because poor prisoners were eager to acquire money with which to supplement their miserable diet with food purchased from outside. Provided with adequate clothing and food by their relatives, upper-class prisoners suffered primarily from boredom. Characteristically, some entertained themselves by setting up a mock government with Eustacio de la Torre, coordinator of the Revolution of 1895, as governor of Cundinamarca. José María Pérez Sarmiento founded a hand-written newspaper, and Abel Camacho, the export-import merchant, gave classes in English and fencing.

Treatment of upper-class Liberal prisoners began to change as Fernández's influence in the government grew. After some forty Liberals, including prominent military leaders, successfully escaped on October 23, 1900, government officials retaliated by throwing many upper-class prisoners into the filthiest and coldest section of the prison, where they were forced to share unbearably crowded quarters with prisoners from the lowest social classes. With time, however, "decent people" like León Gómez, generally managed to procure a servant or two to run errands and attend to their personal needs and thus avoid contact with the ragged, half starved common people within their cell.[28]

While fastidious Liberal gentlemen like León Gómez were scandalized by the lack of conveniences, the forced contact with the masses, and the invasions of their privacy, which, "although they go unnoticed by the common people, are insufferable . . . for a gentleman,"[29] most inmates were concerned with the lack of proper sanitation, food, and shelter within the prison that threatened their very existence. Government officials routinely denied charges of intolerable prison conditions, but in May, 1900, the Junta Central de Higiene reported to the military governor of Cundinamarca that numerous cases of smallpox, as well as cases of "typhus-like diseases," had been reported in the Panóptico. Since the majority of prisoners had no resources and could not feed or clothe themselves adequately, the report went on, the possibility of an epidemic was great. The commission recommended improved sanitation, less crowding, and initiation

28. Adolfo León Gómez, *Secretos del panóptico* (Bogotá, 1905), pp. 11, 17, 20, 23-29, . 44-57, 136-37.
    29. *Ibid.*, p. 91.

of a vaccination program to reduce disease among prisoners.[30] In an effort to reduce crowding and quiet criticism of his policies, Fernández ordered the release of some three hundred prisoners in early March, 1901. His instructions to the director of the Panóptico established three guidelines for selecting prisoners for release: (1) that they be from the lowest social class, (2) that they not be accused of common crimes, and (3) that they be conscripts, not men who had volunteered for service in the Liberal army.[31]

Prisoners could also obtain their freedom by signing a witnessed statement affirming their disillusionment with the Liberal cause and pledging either to support the government or to remain neutral during the rest of the war. The content of these documents reveals something of the increasingly religious tone of the Conservative position. One illiterate from Guasca, Cundinamarca, for example, declared that contrary to what some believed he had never been a Liberal since he could not form part of a party that had demonstrated during the course of the war "the most ferocious and depraved instincts, and that is supported today by gangs of murders and thieves who are the terror of society and of all honorable men."[32] A nineteen-year-old boy from San Juan de Rioseco, Cundinamarca, signed a similar statement in the Panóptico on April 30, 1901. He declared that he had been forced into Liberal ranks and that he never had been a Liberal since his parents were devout Catholics and he was a Christian above all. Witnesses, including the subdirector of the Panóptico, confirmed the spontaneity of the declaration whose wording, whether provided by prison officials or the imprisoned youth, reveals the moral fervor of many Conservative partisans by mid-1901.

> [I] know very well that an abyss stretches between Liberalism and Catholicism, the same abyss that exists between light and darkness, between truth and error; consequently, I declare myself to be Conservative, politically speaking, and I place myself at once at the service of the Christian Republic, and I offer my person in defense of the blue and white flag, sublime and alluring symbol of the great Conservative party.[33]

30. Junta Central de Higiene to the Jefe Civil y Militar de Cundinamarca, May 3, 1900, Sanclemente, ANC, 4, ff. 903-904. Apparently no food was furnished prisoners by the institution. Some poor prisoners were fed by the Hermanas del Buen Pastor, an order of nuns. Aristides Fernández to the Minister of Government, Bogotá, October 18, 1900, Sanclemente, ANC, 4, f. 948.

31. Aristides Fernández to Leonidas Posada Gaviria, Bogotá, February 28, 1901, referred to in *El Colombiano*, March 8, 1901.

32. Signed for Santiago Prieto by José Luis Chacón in Guaduas, Cundinamarca, December 15, 1900, *El Colombiano*, January 4, 1901. The same issue contains two similar declarations. For other examples of the tone of these repudiations of the Liberal cause, see *El Colombiano*, February 12, 1901.

33. *La Opinión*, May 3, 1901. Similar declarations appear in *La Opinión* on November 20 and November 24.

The energetic measures taken by Fernández to exterminate the Liberal guerrillas and the militant Catholic ideological position adopted by the government provide concrete evidence of the limited influence of Historical Conservatives in Marroquín's government. In fact in October, 1900, Marroquín had decided to relieve Carlos Martínez Silva of his cabinet post and send him to Washington, D. C. as minister to the United States. By the end of the year José Domingo Ospina Camacho, a militant Catholic and a strong advocate of repressive measures to crush the revolution, was named minister of war. Ospina Camacho's activity within the government was soon reflected in the promulgation of two decrees that outlined a new and radical policy for dealing with the Liberal revolt. The provisions of the two decrees provide insight into the nature of the guerrilla threat confronting the government by the beginning of 1901 as well as the hardening attitude of the government toward the revolutionaries.

The first of these decrees, signed January 14, 1901, argued that since the government faced a guerrilla movement that was incapable of giving conventional battle or defeating the government and that sustained itself by plundering public and private wealth, new and drastic measures were justified to deal with the challenge. Henceforth military commanders in rebellious provinces would supply their forces from the property of those opposed to the government. Guerrilla chiefs who had not surrendered within thirty days and continued to sustain their forces through forced loans and expropriations or any other kind of despoliation would be considered "as authors of robbery perpetrated by bands of armed criminals." Buyers or auctioneers of goods expropriated or taken by the revolution would be considered "accomplices in the crime of robbery" and subject to a fine equal to the value of the goods involved and imprisonment for a period of three years. Finally, anyone who encouraged the guerrilla forces, either by sending them falsely optimistic war news or material resources would be confined to the prisons of Cartagena until the war was over.[34]

Marroquín's government took an even more serious step in the promulgation of a decree in February 1901, which provided for verbal military trials for guerrillas accused of any of a series of crimes. These ranged from such traditional crimes as assault, armed robbery, murder, and the counterfeiting of money, to more bizarre transgressions that, although one must be careful to distinguish between the language of a decree and real conditions, nevertheless may suggest the growing savagery of conditions in the countryside. Among these crimes were castration; mutilation of limbs; the wounding or abuse of any Catholic priest, person within a Catholic church, or woman, child, or defenseless person; kidnaping; rape; grave robbing; and finally,

34. *El Colombiano,* January 18, 1901.

damage to another's property which redounded to the personal benefit of the perpetrator. Sentences fixed in these summary military trials could not be appealed, and were to be executed immediately. The only exception was in the case of capital punishment, which could be appealed to the respective military governor, who was allowed forty-eight hours to rule on the case.[35]

The Conservative government and its supporters sought to justify the government's repressive measures by dramatizing and exaggerating the excesses of the Liberal revolutionaries. A typical example was a speech given by the military governor of Tolima that denounced the "cowardly taunts and mutilations" with which the rebels "adorn" their assassinations. The pro-government newspaper, *El Colombiano*, often published accounts of what it termed revolutionary crimes of "savage ferocity."[36] Liberals, on the other hand, always contended that the government lied, that the telegrams it published describing Liberal atrocities were apocryphal.[37] Real conditions in the countryside lay somewhere between these de facto Liberal denials and the exaggerations of the Conservative press and government officials. Subsequent Liberal accounts and the military telegrams of zone commanders reveal that robbery, assassination, and cruelty were common in the theaters of guerrilla activity by 1901.

One thing Liberal revolutionaries did not deny was that they sustained themselves by expropriating or taking what they needed from the Conservative supporters of the government, and pro-government papers often published accounts of these abuses. In one such account, written by a Conservative from southwestern Cundinamarca, the motives of the Liberal guerrillas are described as being more than simply political. According to him the "revolutionary hordes" under the leadership of Cesáreo Pulido had plundered the rich provinces of Tequendama and Sumapaz for a full year, "having as their favorite pursuit the destruction of Conservative property." One of their frequent targets was the hacienda of Tiberio Quintero in Bellavista. The last time, the informant went on, the guerrillas had stayed four days at Quintero's hacienda and taken everything, including livestock, barnyard fowl, clothing, kitchen utensils, tools, cacao, coffee, and hides. Then out of spite they had burned the buildings. "Since several of Pulido's companions owed Quintero money," the correspondent added, "they were very careful to pry open the locks of trunks and tear up the account books and the documents that bound them in debt."[38]

35. Decree No. 112 of 1901 (February 18), *El Colombiano*, February 22, 1901.
36. See, for example, *El Colombiano*, January 11, 1901, and March 19, 1901.
37. Typical was the report "N. N." sent to Rafael Uribe Uribe, dated Honda, February 9, 1901, Uribe, 9, ACH.
38. *El Colombiano*, January 22, 1901.

It was precisely these aspects of the continued fighting that so appalled traditional Liberal and Conservative leaders. In early 1901, despairing of the Historical Conservatives' ability to moderate the course of Marroquín's government, Marceliano Vélez noisily tendered his resignation from the military governorship of Antioquia. Vélez's vigorous statement, which was printed for public dissemination, argued that the government should morally compel the revolutionaries to lay down their arms by offering them undeniable proof of goodwill, ironclad guarantees, and political reforms. Specifically he urged the government to free all political prisoners, offer ample terms of surrender, and convoke an extraordinary convention attended by all political groups to enact political reforms.[39] Peace Liberals concurred with Vélez. On March 1, 1901, they had publicly expressed their alarm that the "indefinite prolongation" of savage guerrilla warfare would lead to "chronic anarchy" and the militarization of the republic. They beseeched the revolutionaries to come to an understanding with the government.[40]

Although these exhortations initially generated some hope for a political settlement, embryonic peace negotiations were destroyed by intransigent Liberal guerrillas and uncompromising Conservatives. Cundinamarcan guerrillas rejected Marroquín's vague promise, made through peace Liberal intermediaries, to work for electoral and political reform after peace had been established,[41] and Marroquín himself undercut further efforts by declaring that he would enter into no agreement which might be construed as granting belligerent status to the revolutionaries.[42]

As these abortive efforts to secure a settlement were taking place in Colombia, Rafael Uribe Uribe attempted to exercise his influence from New York to bring the war to an end. In mid-April, 1901, Uribe Uribe issued what he called a plea for peace which argued that given the military impossibility of winning the war, Liberals should temporarily lay down their arms.[43] Although Carlos Martínez Silva worked hard to convince Uribe Uribe to make the statement, Uribe Uribe's motives were based on his own aversion to guerrilla warfare and his inability to secure sufficient aid from Liberals in other Latin

39. The major points of the resignation letter are revealed in Vélez's clarification statement dated Medellín, April 22, and published in *La Opinión*, May 2, 1901.
40. "Por la Patria y por la Paz," March 1, 1901, Manrique, ACH.
41. Marroquín's conditions are quoted in the circular sent the Liberal revolutionary chiefs in arms by Juan E. Manrique on April 13, 1901, Manrique, ACH. A typical guerrilla response was Max Carriazo to Juan E. Manrique, Viotá, April 18, 1901, Manrique, ACH. See also the separate responses of Manuel and Ruperto Aya, Cumaná, April 19 and April 20, 1901, Manrique, ACH.
42. José Manuel Marroquín to Juan E. Manrique, Bogotá, May 1, 1901, Manrique, ACH.
43. The manifesto was dated New York, April 12, 1901. Uribe, Box 7, ACH.

American countries to launch a new invasion of Colombia.[44] Reaction to Uribe Uribe's peace manifesto was adverse. Liberals in arms denounced it and government authorities discredited it.[45] The fact that Uribe Uribe, prewar darling of the most militant within the Liberal party, failed in his attempt to convince the guerrillas to lay down their arms revealed not only the intransigence of the active revolutionary leadership but also illustrated the degree to which events were slipping beyond the control of traditional political leaders.

For Historical Conservatives and peace Liberals one positive aspect of the peace overtures of March-April, 1901, was the temporary removal of two of the most powerful Conservative extremists in Marroquín's government. As evidence of his good faith, in late March Marroquín replaced the military governor of Cundinamarca, Aristides Fernández, and the minister of War, Ospina Camacho, with Historical Conservatives José Vincente Concha and Ramón González Valencia. But despite their intentions, these Historical Conservatives proved powerless in their efforts to induce Marroquín's government to offer political concessions to the Liberals in arms and to negotiate a settlement of the war. Finally, out of desperation, sometime in August, 1901, moderate Conservatives once again began to conspire to topple the government as the only means of achieving the political reforms they believed necessary to bring the fighting to an end.

Chosen to lead the coup against Marroquín was the *antioqueño* Historical Conservative Pedro Nel Ospina, who had recently joined Marroquín's cabinet as minister of war. Ospina's motives in joining the conspiracy against Marroquín were many and complex. Close examination of his views reveals much about the concern of Conservative and Liberal moderates as they contemplated the nature of Marroquín's government and the seemingly interminable guerrilla war around them.

A long-time advocate of the policies advanced by Marceliano Vélez, Ospina personified the industrial and commercial values embraced by many Liberals and Historical Conservatives. Born in 1858 while his father, Mariano Ospina Rodríguez, occupied the presidency of the country, Pedro Nel spent most of his childhood in exile in Guatemala, where his family successfully engaged in coffee production. Having returned to Medellín in 1871, Pedro Nel fought in the civil war of 1876, serving on the staff of Marceliano Vélez. After the war he fol-

44. Uribe Uribe to Antonio José Restrepo, New York, February 28, 1901, Uribe Uribe to Cipriano Castro, New York, April 20, 1901, Uribe Uribe to J. S. Zelaya, April 28, 1901, and Uribe Uribe to Eloy Alfaro, April 28, 1901, all in Uribe, Box 14, ACH.
45. Uribe Uribe to Enrique Cortés, New York, May 25, 1901, Uribe Uribe to Carlos Martínez Silva, New York, May 30, 1901, Uribe Uribe to José I. Vargas Vila, New York, May 30, 1901, all in Uribe, ACH.

lowed his brother Tulio to Berkeley, California, where, like his brother, he received a degree in mining engineering. After traveling in the United States and Europe he returned to Medellín, where he played an active role in the administration and development of the Ospina family interests, which were based primarily in coffee, but which included other enterprises, among them mines. Known as a man of action, like his *antioqueño* countryman Rafael Uribe Uribe, Pedro Nel was famous for having carved extensive coffee plantations from the forest. After declining an offer from Núñez to serve as minister of the treasury, Pedro Nel became rector of the Medellín school of mines. Elected to congress in 1892, he generally followed the politics of Marceliano Vélez and was an outspoken critic of the National Bank. In 1894 he was named director of the ironworks at Amagá, Antioquia, where he pioneered in the manufacture of small hand-driven machines for the processing of coffee beans. Once again elected to congress in 1896, he was deprived of his seat by Caro's government, which claimed he had been elected by irregular procedures. When the war broke out in 1899, like most *antioqueño* Historical Conservatives Pedro Nel was reluctant to support the Nationalist government, but after Peralonso he organized an army and led a successful campaign against Rafael Uribe Uribe on the Atlantic coast at the end of 1900. Having contracted fever, Ospina retired from public life until called to the ministry of war by Marroquín in August, 1901.[46]

Upon taking office Ospina found himself embroiled almost immediately in a series of disagreements with other high officials of Marroquín's government, especially José Vicente Concha, whose place he had taken as head of the ministry of war and who still occupied the military governorship of Cundinamarca. Ospina believed that Concha had played into the hands of Conservative extremists by authorizing, in late July, 1901, a preemptive invasion of Venezuela against a Liberal force under the command of Uribe Uribe. That strike had ended in failure and had threatened to turn Colombia's civil war into an impossible war with Venezuela. According to Ospina, Concha's incompetence had also allowed the guerrillas to take the offensive in Cundinamarca and Tolima. Ospina claimed that military inertia largely explained the lack of production in the rich coffee zones of southwestern Cundinamarca. On two occasions he formulated plans to sweep that area clean of guerrillas, but both times his proposals were vetoed by Marroquín, who agreed with other members of his government that police from Bogotá should not be used in military campaigns in the countryside. Ospina also violently objected to Concha's

46. Laureano Gómez, *El carácter del general Ospina* (Bogotá, 1928); Emilio Robledo, *La vida del General Pedro Nel Ospina* (Bogotá, 1959).

emergency decision during the Venezuelan war scare to exact a forced loan from the banks of Bogotá.[47]

Although Ospina shared with fellow Historical Conservative Concha a belief that the war could be ended only by a political settlement, he was much more insistent than Concha in promoting that view. Ospina proposed to Marroquín that the basis of such an agreement be a new election law that embodied the principle of minority representation for Liberals. According to Ospina's plan, the election law could be enacted by passage of a simple legislative decree. Accompanied with the reform of the boundaries of electoral districts, a measure already agreed upon by the government, such an election law would be sufficient to induce the Liberal revolutionaries to lay down their arms. Finally, Ospina believed that the government's only significant source of revenue, paper money, was depreciating so rapidly that eventually it would lose all value, and he claimed that from the time he joined the government he labored to convince Marroquín that he must end the war quickly or his government would collapse.

Ospina had only scorn for what he called the preposterous revenue-producing schemes dreamed up by Marroquin's incompetent financial advisors. Reviewing the fiscal record of Marroquín's administration, Ospina scored the lack of fiscal planning and trained personnel with practical experience in finance. From time to time, Ospina conceded, the administration came up with plans to meet the crisis, but these worsened, rather than improved, the fiscal situation. One such plan, formulated by one of Marroquín's advisors, called for the government to acquire all hides in the country and export them on its own. Another, in Ospina's words, proposed that every coffee exporter who managed to get his coffee to port cede half of it to the government on the grounds that the government had provided the security that had allowed him to get that far. For practical men "like me who have developed in the struggle, handling men and surmounting difficulties" this "colonial and arbitrary empiricism" would be laughable if it did not constitute a "terrible threat to property and to the reputation of the Fatherland."[48]

Stymied in his efforts to reverse the drift of Marroquín's government, Ospina began to conspire against it. Joining forces with prominent Historical Conservatives, sympathetic peace Liberals, and a few disaffected Nationalists, he planned to dislodge Marroquín from power by bringing old President Sanclemente, still under house arrest in Villeta, to Bogotá to head a new government. High government

47. The bankers refused to comply and for a time closed their doors to business. *El Colombiano*, September 17, 1900.

48. Pedro Nel Ospina to Marceliano Vélez, Bogotá, October 3, 1901, published in Robledo, *Pedro Nel Ospina*, pp. 197-217.

officials were apparently aware of the details of the plan, for on September 21, just as the plot was put in motion, Ospina and other conspirators within the military were arrested and subsequently exiled from the country.[49]

Although the movement to bring Sanclemente to Bogotá to reassume power constituted an attempt to implement a counter coup against Marroquín, the conspirators clearly had legality on their side. Marroquín's coup of July 31, 1900, had been justified on the legal grounds that Sanclemente could not govern from outside the capital city. After the arrest of the military backers of the coup many civilian political leaders who had supported the movement seized upon this legal issue to express publicly their solidarity with the idea of Sanclemente's reassuming power. More than a dozen prominent peace Liberals petitioned Marroquín with feigned ingenuousness inquiring whether, given the gravity of the problems facing the country, Marroquín would oppose the activities of citizens who wanted to further the intentions of the president. Among the transcendental problems listed by the Liberals were the threat of invasion, the "indefinite and frightening prolongation" of the civil war, and the "extremely delicate economic and fiscal problems" whose solution was imperative if the "dismemberment of the Fatherland" was to be avoided. Sanclemente, they added, considered himself capable of uniting around his person the "great national constituencies" needed to solve and avert these problems. A similar petition, signed by sixteen Historical Conservatives, was sent to Marroquín on the same date; and two days later three Nationalist conspirators wrote an apology to Marroquín justifying their actions on grounds similar to those expressed by the Liberals and the Historical Conservatives.[50]

Coupled with the growing military threat of the Liberal guerrillas in late 1901, the attempted coup headed by Pedro Nel Ospina had the effect of placing Marroquín's government securely in the hands of the Conservative extremists. Beginning in 1902 and for the remainder of the war the immediate postwar period, formal political power in Colombia was monopolized by the most intransigent elements of the Conservative party.

Leader of the Conservative extremists and chief beneficiary of the abortive coup was Aristides Fernández. The growing influence and prestige of Fernández and the extremists as the war progressed was a

49. José Manuel Marroquín to Marceliano Vélez, Bogotá, September 29, 1901, MDT, ACH.

50. Laureano García Ortíz, *et al.* to José Manuel Marroquín, September 28, 1901; Wenceslao Pizano, *et al.* to José Manuel Marroquín, Bogotá, September 28, 1901; Antonio Roldán, Jorge Holguín, and [Enrique?] Arboleda to José Manuel Marroquín, Bogotá, September 30, 1901, MDT, ACH.

logical consequence of the prolongation and radicalization of the conflict following the adoption of guerrilla tactics by the Liberals in arms, but Fernández's remarkable rise to national power was also a result of the special nature of his relationship with Marroquín. Strikingly different in their class backgrounds, the two men seemed to complement each other in the exercise of power.

The early life of Aristides Fernández is obscure. According to one source, he was an illegitimate child born to Eriqueta Mora in Guaduas, Cundinamarca, in 1862.[51] In Guaduas Fernández attended public school, and at the age of fifteen his brother took him to Facatativá, where he was placed in the employ of a retail merchant. Little is known about the next ten years, but Fernández must have made some political connections, for in 1887 Rafael Núñez appointed him doorman of the National Academy of Music.[52] In subsequent years Fernández rose rapidly in the Nationalist bureaucracy, becoming the fee collector for Bogotá's utilities before he was named director of police, a post he held at the time of the tumultuous events surrounding Sanclemente's assumption of power on November 3, 1898. On that day, a Nationalist later wrote Sanclemente, Fernández had demonstrated "just how much he was capable of." Of all those who aided the National cause on November 3, Sanclemente's correspondent went on, Fernández was the most deserving of the president's regard.[53]

Throughout the period of Sanclemente's government, Fernández provided vital support and services to the regime. Commenting on one of Fernández's reports, his immediate superior, Minister of Government Rafael Palacio, congratulated him on his police activities in support of Sanclemente's government, but encouraged him to be more severe in his efforts to repress enemies of public order. Palacio's instructions are significant in the light of Fernández's subsequent reputation for brutality.

[I]t is necessary to continue actively the work undertaken to furnish examples and punish the enemies of order and public tranquility. At all events dispense with sensitivities that do not

51. José Manuel Pérez Sarmiento, *Reminiscencias liberales, 1897-1937* (Bogotá, 1938), p. 152. Pérez Sarmiento claims he knew Fernández's brothers and his father, Carlos Fernández, who lived in Facatativá. Fernández is the *bête noire* of this period of Colombian history, maligned by Liberal and Conservative authors alike. Although Fernández's personal papers may have been destroyed, much of the man's personality and political philosophy can be deduced from his actions, his public statements, and the strong emotions he stimulated in adversaries and supporters alike.

52. *Ibid.*, p. 153.

53. José Ignacio Barberi [?] to José Manuel Sanclemente, Sanclemente, ANC, 2, ff. 488-489.

affect your good name and can impede the energy and unity of action demanded by the present circumstances.[54]

Fernández's ability to translate armed force into political influence was again demonstrated on July 31, 1900, when his decision not to oppose the Historical Conservative coup insured the success of the conspiracy. During Marroquín's second administration, despite temporary setbacks, Fernández continued his rise to national power. As military governor of Cundinamarca he offered Marroquín a degree of political independence by furnishing the vice-president with a basis of support distinct from that of the Historical Conservatives. In Fernández, Marroquín also found an honest, hard-working administrator possessed of the energy and concern for detail needed to direct the government's ponderous civil and military bureaucracies. On the other hand, Fernández enjoyed the respectability Marroquín provided him. Laboring under the stigma of his social origins, Fernández found the close association and approval of a man of Marroquín's status helpful in legitimizing his position. But Marroquín and Fernández shared an ideological commitment which transcended the terms of short-term political convenience. Both men believed that the Liberal revolt was part of an international conspiracy which treatened not only Colombia's sovereignty, but the very basis of her traditional Catholic society.

Beginning in 1902 changes in Marroquín's ministry confirmed the predominance of Fernández and the extremists. José Vicente Concha was sent to Washington to replace Carlos Martínez Silva, who had continued his efforts to convince Marroquín to seek a political settlement of the war. With this move Marroquín removed one of the most influential Historical Conservatives from his government and isolated another from the domestic political scene. Concha was also more sympathetic than Martínez Silva had been to Marroquín's tough position on the canal treaty negotiations in progress with the United States. Named to replace Concha as minister of war was Aristides Fernández. Moderates were scandalized by Fernández's appointment and Minister of Government Guillermo Quintero Calderón, the last Historical Conservative in the cabinet, resigned in protest. Marroquín stuck to his decision, however, and later declared that his faith in Fernández's ability to revitalize the government's war effort had been completely vindicated.[55]

Fernández returned to a position of power in the government at a

54. Rafael María Palacio to Aristides Fernández, Anapoima [Cundinamarca], July 29, 1899, Sanclemente, ANC, 6, f. 626.
55. José Manuel Marroquín to Marceliano Vélez, Bogotá, March 3, 1902, in Martínez Delgado, *Historia*, pp. 197-99.

time when the guerrillas of Cundinamarca and Tolima were stronger than at any time during the war and operating with impunity at the very edge of Bogotá. Meanwhile Uribe Uribe had invaded the country from Venezuela, and was marching on the capital from the east threatening to link up with the guerrillas and take Bogotá. Faced with a demoralized and corrupt army and a war-weary Conservative populace, in the weeks following his appointment Fernández demonstrated the power of his conviction and the effectiveness of his organization talents. In a burst of activity the new minister of war issued a battery of directives designed to improve army discipline and morale, eliminate abuses, and increase efficiency.[56] Within Bogotá he drastically increased security measures and organized a citizens' militia to defend the city made up of Conservative volunteers "devoted to the government."[57]

In an effort to ease the government's fiscal burden and at the same time retaliate for Liberal expropriations, in mid-January Fernández issued a decree that provided that the value of any property expropriated by the revolution would immediately be returned to the victims by summary expropriation of an equal amount from the enemies of the government.[58] Although it is doubtful that this decree, like many previous government decrees dealing with forced loans or expropriations, was generally or uniformly enforced, Fernández did implement a measure to exact a forced contribution from alleged sympathizers with the revolution. On February 3 the United States minister to Colombia reported that the government had closed and sealed many business houses belonging to Liberals who had refused to pay their assigned contributions. The government was expected to sell the embargoed merchandise in order to cover the levy.[59] Whatever the method by which the government exacted the contribution, in early March *El Colombiano* published a long list of Liberals, including most prominent peace Liberals, that specified the amount each had been forced to contribute to the war.[60]

Partly as a result of the dynamism and confidence with which Fer-

56. See Fernández's Resolutions Nos. 4, 6, and 7 issued in the last days of January, 1902, and published in *Diario Oficial*, No. 11,622 (January 30, 1902), and No. 11,624 (February 3, 1902). Also Decree No. 220 of 1902 (February 4), and No. 372 (February 26, 1902) in the *Diario Oficial*, No. 11,628 (February 12, 1902) and No. 11,637 (March 4, 1902).

57. Decree No. 371 of 1902 (February 26), *Diario Oficial*, No. 11,636 (February 28, 1902); Decree No. 44 of 1902 (January 13), *Diario Oficial*, No. 11,621 (January 28, 1902).

58. Decree No. 48 of 1902 (January 15), *Diario Oficial*, No. 11,618 (January 22, 1902).

59. Charles Burdett Hart to John Hay, Bogotá, February 3, 1902, USNA. It appears that the decree referred to by Hart was No. 1,799 of 1901 (November 21), which was not published in the *Diario Oficial* until the end of February, *Diario Oficial*, No. 11,618 (February 22, 1902).

60. *El Colombiano*, March 4, 1902.

nández directed military affairs and the enthusiasm he generated for the Conservative cause, the government succeeded in smashing the Liberal threat to the capital in February and March, 1902. On February 23 Fernández won a critical victory over combined guerrilla forces at Soacha a few miles south of the capital. A few weeks later government armies decisively defeated Uribe Uribe as he attempted to gain the Sabana de Bogotá from the east. Following this defeat Uribe Uribe once again fled the country, but the guerrilla leaders split into groups vowing to continue the fight.

Following these victories Fernández set out to implement a policy of unrestricted repression to exterminate the remaining guerrillas in the interior. Aware that his policies would inevitably incur the opposition of moderates, Fernández embarked on a campaign designed to create a climate of opinion and build a base of support sufficient to put his plans into operation. Fernández found a firm ally in the semi-official Conservative press. During the first months of 1902 sensational accounts of the pillage and burning of haciendas and assassinations of Conservatives in the countryside frequently appeared in the pages of *El Colombiano* and *La Opinión*. In late February Fernández hit on a perfect vehicle for his purposes in a celebrated exchange of letters he had with the Cundinamarca guerrilla leader Juan Mac Allister. The exchange redefined the terms of the war and overnight catapulted Fernández into a position of uncontested power within the government.

The confrontation began when Mac Allister, in a calculated move to annoy Fernández, protest the treatment of Liberal prisoners, and establish precedent for the Liberal claim to belligerency status, informed the minister of war that he was sending four recently captured Conservative officers to a Liberal prison on the eastern plains. The Conservative officers could be spared that fate, Mac Allister proposed, if the government were willing to enter into a prisoner exchange. Fernández reacted violently. Imprisonment in the insalubrious climate of the eastern plains was tantamount to execution, he exclaimed. If the four Conservative officers were not returned safely to government lines by March 20, four Liberal officers—Emilio Angel, Celso Román, Juan de la R. Barrios, and Victor Julio Zea, imprisoned in the Panóptico, would be executed. Fernández then broadened his warning. He would take the lives and property of Liberal prisoners in retaliation for any loss of life among any of the prisoners held by the revolutionaries.[61]

The ultimatum created a furor among traditional political leaders in Bogotá, but elicited unbridled enthusiasm from Conservative ex-

61. "Prevención" dated Bogotá, February 28, 1902, published in *La Opinión*, March 1, 1902.

tremists. Throughout the first two weeks of March the newspapers of the capital were filled with telegrams from Conservative leaders from towns all over Cundinamarca congratulating Fernández on the courage of a stance which would finally bring the war to an end. The extremist Conservative youth from the distinguished Jesuit-run national secondary school, El Colegio de San Bartolomé, offered their enthusiastic support to Fernández on March 2.[62] That the elite Conservative youth at an institution of such distinguished tradition should endorse the policies of a man bent on initiating a veritable reign of terror was profoundly disturbing to Miguel Antonio Caro, who along with twelve other prominent Nationalists drafted a public letter of protest to Felip F. Paúl, a long-time Nationalist serving as Marroquín's minister of foreign relations. The Nationalists argued that what was needed was peace treaties, not a declaration of war to the death. The "fanatic" supporters of Fernández sought not the pacification of the country but its destruction, not reconciliation but revenge. The rage with which these extremists looked upon the revolutionaries in arms and the fierceness with which they attacked the property of pacific people in Bogotá, the Nationalists concluded, would engender inextinguishable hatreds and irreparable damage.[63]

Meanwhile Fernández stepped up his campaign to discredit the revolution and justify the unprecedented measures he had adopted to crush it. By his order on March 14 the residents of Bogotá were presented with a macabre exhibition in the Plaza de Bolívar of the mutilated remains of three victims of the guerrillas' machetes.[64] The next day, five days before the ultimatum expired, the Papal Nuncio in conjunction with the Archbishop of Bogotá asked Fernández to desist from carrying out this threat. On the sixteenth a huge demonstration was organized to pledge support for Fernández's iron-fisted policy. Supporters from all over the Sabana de Bogotá met at two o'clock in the afternoon in the Plaza de Bolívar to hear a series of speeches extolling the virtues of the minister of war.

Fernández was introduced as the savior of Colombia come to cut the cancer of Liberal radicalism out of the body politic. His speech was stirring and well received. A man of unctuous manner and exquisite attire,[65] he electrified the crowd, proclaiming the government's mission "the cause of God, civilization, and the aggrandizement of the fatherland." For decades the same Liberals who now invaded the country as puppets of petty foreign tyrants had persecuted the Church,

62. Fernández's gratified response appeared in *El Colombiano*, March 14, 1902.

63. Miguel Antonio Caro, *et al.* to Felipe F. Paúl, Bogotá, March 9, 1902, Manrique, ACH.

64. Masuera y Masuera, *Memorias*, p. 31; *El Colombiano*, March 14, 1902.

65. Luis Eduardo Nieto Arteta, *Por qué soy liberal* (Bogotá, 1931), p. 44.

he began. The Church, repository of redeeming traditional values, guided aspirations, inspired wise laws, encouraged peace and conciliation, and provided the immovable foundation for lasting social peace. In contrast, the work of Liberals in Colombia had been destructive in the extreme. Mercilessly attacking the Church, Liberals had encouraged the spread of dissociative ideas. Liberal propagation of the principle of "absolute leveling" had spawned unhealthy ambitions and encouraged the hatred of superiority, authority, and restrictions. Liberalism had caused the paralysis of the "nation's vital forces." From a political ideal Liberalism had become an "endemic disease . . . that corrodes and poisons the social organism." By pursuing a war they had no chance of winning, Liberals had changed the countryside from a place where the simple patriarchal values of honesty and hard work prevailed to a theater for rapine and plunder. The habit of laziness and the yearning for a life of adventure, values inevitably associated with revolution, were spreading throughout the countryside with alarming rapidity. In order to remedy evils of this magnitude, Fernández concluded, palliatives would not do. What was needed was "inexorable repression, prompt cauterizing of the wound, burning faith, resolute determination, invincible firmness." It was necessary to adopt a new direction in government, end fruitless political theorizing and innovation, and support a government based on scrupulous honesty in the handling of public funds, effective security for "the good citizen," and unflinching repression of the revolutionary spirit and the slightest attempt at revolt.[66]

Three days after his speech and two days before the expiration of his ultimatum Fernández could reply to the Papal Nuncio that since he had just received notice that the Conservative prisoners in question had been freed by the revolutionaries he would not have to carry out the terms of the ultimatum. He added that had the situation not been resolved in that way he would not have desisted except under the command of the Nuncio, whose authority he considered "omnipotent" and whose humble soldier he hoped to be.[67]

Taking advantage of the outpouring of public support at the rally in the Plaza de Bolívar and the prestige gained by Mac Allister's capitulation to his demands, Fernández began to implement the policy of "inexorable repression" he had called for in his speech. On March 20 he issued a directive from the ministry of war instructing the military governors, prefects, and mayors to begin rigorous implementation of the decree on summary military trials passed the year before. All persons in jail and those captured in the future would be immediately

66. *El Colombiano*, March 18, March 21, 1902.
67. *Ibid*, March 21, 1902.

judged. Those guilty of the gravest crimes such as rebellion would be subject to the maximum penalties specified in the Penal Code. Moreover rebels would be held jointly responsible for all common crimes committed singly during the time they participated in the revolt. The rest of the lengthy resolution furnished an exhaustive list of crimes and respective penalties not covered in the Penal Code, most of which dealt with involvement in invasions of Colombia by forces composed at least in part of foreigners. The resolution had the effect of making not only the Liberal guerrillas of the interior, but also Uribe Uribe, Benjamín Herrera, and most of the members of their armies subject to capital punishment in summary trials.[68]

During the course of the next few months Fernández's tactics of extreme repression succeeded in reducing guerrilla activity but failed to pacify the interior completely. As evidence of continuing guerrilla activity accumulated, Fernández sent out a circular to all military governors and their subordinates in which he warned against laxness in the light of government victories and promised the complete pacification of the country by Independence Day, July 20.[69] Fernández was to be disappointed . In the following weeks guerrilla activity once again revived in the coffee-growing provinces of Sumapaz, Tequendama, and La Palma, and pressure increased for a more moderate approach to the guerrillas.[70] Once again peace Liberals, their ranks swollen by Liberals who had previously declined to participate in calls for peace, began to petition Marroquín decrying the growing savagery of the conflict and urging him to make some concessions to secure the surrender of the revolutionaries.[71] Marroquín's first response to the peace Liberals, written at the end of April, was a testy, querulous document,[72] but as Fernández's inability to end the war became clearer, the vice-president became more accommodating. In reply to a new peace Liberal memorial dated May 23, Marroquín offered the revolutionaries a general amnesty and vowed to work for reform of the electoral law, although he was careful to promise no outright political concessions.[73] These provisions were embodied in a decree issued June 12 that offered amnesty and personal guarantees to any revolutionaries who turned themselves in by July 1, 1902.[74]

68. *Diario Oficial*, No. 11,648 (March 26, 1902).

69. Circular dated Bogotá, May 14, 1902, and published in *La Patria*, May 16, 1902.

70. A government decree dated June 12, discussed below in another connection, referred specifically to these three Cundinamarcan provinces as well as northern and central Tolima as the location of the principal revolutionary bands still in arms. Decree No. 933 of 1902 (June 12), *Diario Oficial*, No. 11,696 (June 21, 1902).

71. "Representación" dated Bogotá, April 14, 1902, and signed by some eighty-six peace Liberals, Uribe, Box 7, ACH.

72. Marroquín's response was published in *La Patria*, April 30, 1902.

73. Both the Liberals' petition and Marroquín's reply were published in *La Patria*, June 13, 1902.

74. Decree No. 933 of 1902 (June 12), *Diario Oficial*, No. 11,696 (June 21, 1902).

The promise of reform and the offer of general amnesty of June 12 constituted a temporary setback for the policies advocated by Fernández. Marroquín did not accept his resignation, however, and in fact the continuing influence of Fernández's position within the government could be detected in the deadline of less than three weeks allowed the revolutionaries to take advantage of the amnesty. The decree of June 12 was successful in securing the surrender of a few guerrilla leaders in Cundinamarca, but the major groups in the southwestern portion of the department were still operating when the period of grace expired.[75] On July 14 Fernández sent out a circular, which was soon made public, declaring that the amnesty offer had failed and urging his subordinates to utilize every military and legal instrument at their disposal to eliminate the revolutionaries in arms.[76]

Aware that his reputation rested on his successful pacification of the interior, behind this public appearance of uncompromising severity, Fernández used every means at his disposal, including extensions of the terms of the June 12 amnesty and payments of large sums of money, to cajole the guerrillas into surrendering. According to Masuera y Masuera, after the promulgation of the amnesty, on two occasions he was offered the sum of 30,000 in new paper pesos to surrender. Masuera y Masuera claimed he was scandalized by the suggestion of government negotiators that he use the money to set up a business after the war, but in the end he accepted the money as a kind of severance bonus to be divided among his officers and men. Finally, at the huge Viotá coffee hacienda "Liberia," on August 27, 1902, by virtue of a special extension of the terms of the amnesty on June 12, Masuera y Masuera and other officers surrendered a numerous army to the government.[77]

The surrender of the guerrillas in Viotá was both a material and psychological victory for the government. To be sure, other guerrilla leaders, especially in the northwestern corner of Cundinamarca, continued to defy government efforts to secure a total pacification of the interior.[78] In addition, as one government officer reported after surveying the situation around Viotá following the surrender of Masuera y Masuera, large numbers of revolutionaries "from the dregs of society" continued to pillage the countryside, "assaulting haciendas and committing innumerable crimes."[79] These guerrilla bands ultimately either surrendered or their members were captured and executed by government forces in the months to come.

The most celebrated of these executions was that of Cesáreo Pulido

75. *La Patria*, June 30, 1902.
76. *La Patria*, July 18, 1902.
77. Masuera y Masuera, *Memorias*, pp. 42-44, 75, 76, 80.
78. Juan C. Arbeláez to the Minister of War, September 17, 1902, AMD, vol. 05781.
79. Masuera y Masuera, *Memorias*, p. 80.

and several of his companions captured by government forces on August 6, 1902, and executed in Tolima the next month over the protests of distinguished Conservatives and ecclesiastical authorities.[80] Paramount among the public protests was one drafted by Carlos Martínez Silva upon his return to Colombia from Washington, D. C. The protest, signed by twelve prominent Historical Conservatives, was really a legal brief disputing the legal right of the government to execute anyone for political crimes. The government reacted immediately, condemning the petitioners for their rebellious attitude and Liberal sympathies. Martínez Silva and some of the other signers were jailed and then exiled to Gachalá, Cundinamarca, located over the mountains to the east of Bogotá. What most disturbed Fernández about the protesters, judging from a letter to Archbishop Herrera in which he declined to moderate his action against Martínez Silva and the other Historical Conservatives, was the fact that they called themselves Conservatives but considered the revolution justified.[81] Although Martínez Silva was allowed to return to the capital somewhat later, his imprisonment and exile broke his spirit and health and he died a few months later en route to his native Santander, where he planned to write his memoirs.

Military victories and progress toward pacification of the interior may have created the impression in Bogotá that the war was almost over, but to those people with a broader perspective it was apparent that the final drama would be played out in Panama, where by 1902 Benjamín Herrera had built a large, well-equipped, and disciplined army which had proved capable of defeating the best armies the government could send against it.[82] The Bogotá government, preoccupied with the guerrillas in the interior, had tended to discount the gravity of the situation in Panama, an attitude José Vicente Concha strove to correct after he arrived in Washington, D. C., in April, 1902. Because of the military strength of Herrera, the threat of United States intervention to protect lives and property associated with the railway, and the overriding issue of the United States' desire to expedite matters concerning the canal, Concha argued, it behooved the government to come to some agreement with the revolution to end the war. During April and May Concha repeatedly urged the government to give him instructions to enter into peace negotiations with Vargas Santos to end the war on the basis of political concessions.[83] By the end of May Concha and Vargas Santos had signed a tentative agreement that not

80. Arbeláez, *Episodios*, pp. 98-111, provides a detailed account of the trial.
81. Aristides Fernández to Archbishop Herrera, Bogotá, August 27, 1902, MDT, ACH.
82. Caballero, *Memorias*, pp. 300-1.
83. José Vincente Concha to José Manuel Marroquín, Washington, D. C., April 3 and May 15, 1902, MDT, ACH.

only promised reform of the election law and the immediate convocation of congress upon the establishment of peace to enact political, monetary and fiscal reforms, but in clauses signed only by Vargas Santos provided that the Colombian government would assume the revolution's debts abroad and guarantee that Liberal governors would be named in four of the nation's departments and two of its territories.[84] After the draft agreement was sent off to Bogotá for inspection, Liberal negotiators added further conditions. These included the declaration of a cease fire while delegates to a special convention, one-third of them Liberals, met to enact reforms, and the naming of a new ministry from a list of candidates, most of them Historical Conservatives, acceptable to the Liberal revolutionaries. These additional demands were subsequently reduced to one, the naming of an acceptable ministry.[85] Even before it learned of the additional conditions, Marroquín's government flatly rejected the terms of the agreement.

By September, 1902, Uribe Uribe was also operating on the Caribbean coast, having returned to Colombia to assume command of a small army in the department of Magdalena. Uribe Uribe appears to have rejoined the ranks partly to preserve his position of leadership and partly out of a desire to wield some influence on the final outcome of the war. Central to Uribe Uribe's concerns was the removal of Fernández from the government. Through intermediaries Uribe Uribe conveyed this primary condition to Ramón González Valencia, who promised to work for the dismissal of Fernández.[86] Herrera and his officers also indicated a willingness to make concessions for peace but refused to deal with Fernández. In a declaration signed by all officers on October 5, Fernández was singled out as a "national disgrace."[87] Bowing to this single pre-condition, in mid-October Marroquín's government announced the temporary retirement of Fernández from the ministry of war "for reasons of health."[88] A little more than a week later, after being decisively defeated in an attempt to take the Magdalena town of Ciénega, Uribe Uribe capitulated and signed the Treaty of Neerlandia.[89]

The treaty, which granted ample guarantees to the persons and property of the surrendering revolutionaries, but which offered no

84. "Projecto de Acuerdo," Washington, D. C., May 26, 1902, New York, June 3, 1902, MDT, ACH.

85. José Vicente Concha to José Manuel Marroquín, Washington, D. C., June 13, 1902 and Enrique Cortés to José Vicente Concha, Washington, D. C., June 17, 1902, MDT, ACH.

86. C. Hernández to Rafael Uribe Uribe, San Cristóbal, Venezuela, October 9, 1902, Uribe, Box 9, ACH.

87. Published in Caballero, *Memorias*, p. 323.

88. *El Colombiano*, October 14, 1902.

89. Uribe Uribe, *Documentos*, pp. 345-405.

political concessions, was a great psychological and material defeat for the revolution. More than any one man Uribe Uribe had been the author and soul of the revolt. Defeated and driven from the country on two occasions, he had returned to fight again. His unconditional surrender signaled the beginning of the end for the revolution. Although the army under his command was small, his position on the Magdalena was of great strategic importance to Herrera. Herrera controlled much of the Isthmus, but he was blocked by the threat of United States intervention should he attempt to take Panama City and Colón, the terminals of the United States-owned Panama Railroad. If Herrera were to continue the fight, he had to carry the war to the Colombian mainland, an undertaking made much more difficult with Uribe Uribe's capitulation.

On November 21, 1902, less than a month after Uribe Uribe's surrender, Herrera signed a treaty with government representatives which effectively brought the war to a close. Symbolic of the United States interests behind the scenes that influenced the conclusion of the war and within a year would insure the successful separation of Panama, the treaty was negotiated and signed aboard the United States warship *Wisconsin* and subsequently known as the Treaty of Wisconsin. By the terms of the treaty the government promised to repeal the state of siege immediately except in districts where groups were still in arms, to free political prisoners and grant amnesty to all revolutionaries accepting the terms of the treaty, and to hold free elections for congress, which would then be convoked to devote utmost attention to the following three questions: canal negotiations, political reform, and monetary reform. The revolutionaries agreed to surrender all war equipment, including two valuable warships. In exchange, by virtue of a secret clause, the government turned over 16,000 pounds sterling to cancel debts contracted by the revolution with Liberals in Central America.[90]

Several factors coalesced to induce Colombians to end the war. By mid-1902 the cost and fatigue of more than two and one-half years of struggle had dampened the enthusiasm of even the most militant Liberal partisans. Fear of United States intentions in Panama was another major influence working to bring the war to a close. Colombian leaders had worried over the possible session of Panama for decades, but as the perennial talk of a canal came close to reality and the United States began to consider alternate routes, influential Panamanians resolved that if the Bogotá government did not cooperate in securing the canal for Panama they would take matters into their own hands. This attitude was appreciated by many high Colombian officials. Once

90. Tamayo, *Revolución*, pp. 224-28.

Panama became the primary theater of the war and the United States temporarily landed marines to demonstrate its resolve to prevent fighting along the railway, Conservative and Liberal leaders alike became nervous about the possible consequences of continuing the war.[91] Liberals were able to use the threat to Panama as a face-saving way to end their revolt. The possibilities of this idea were eloquently outlined by Modesto Garcés and conveyed to Uribe Uribe in a letter from Vargas Vila in mid-October. Uribe Uribe used them to good advantage in his justification of the signing of the Treaty of Neerlandia.[92] Herrera was in an even better position to cast his surrender as an unselfish sacrifice that put the interests of the nation above those of party. Government officials could grant along these same grounds the few concessions they offered to the revolutionaries at the peace negotiations.

Perhaps even more than their concern over potential developments in Panama, upper-class leaders of all political parties were preoccupied with signs that forces unleashed by the war had gotten beyond their control and were eroding their monopoly on economic, social, and political power. Although rarely expressed outright, this growing fear can be detected in the pleas for peace drafted at different times by traditional political leaders of all persuasions. Peace Liberals, Historical Conservatives, and ultimately, Nationalists always stressed the growing "savagery" of the conflict and the threat the war posed to "civilization" in Colombia. Their language reflected their alarm over the breakdown of respect for private property and upper-class privilege which resulted from the forced loans and contributions, expropriations, and robberies practiced by both the government and the revolutionary forces as the war dragged on.

Similarly, the petitioners' often-expressed concern over the urgent need for peace to solve the grave economic and fiscal problems confronting the nation was partly an expression of upper-class consternation over the fact that while profits in traditional agricultural and commercial endeavors declined during the war the opportunities for windfall profits in speculation, smuggling, and profiteering mushroomed. Unrestrained inflation favored those willing and able to move their money rapidly and stimulated wild speculation in goods and currency.[93] One careful observer noted that the war witnessed the

91. Ciphered telegrams from Hart to the Secretary of State, received, Washington, September 25, 1902, USNA.

92. José Ignacio Vargas Vila to Rafael Uribe Uribe, Maracaibo, October 16, 1902, Uribe, Box 7, ACH.

93. Julio H. Palacio cheerfully recounted how he transformed his situation of relative personal poverty into one of considerable wealth through speculation in currency during the war. "Memorias," *El Tiempo*, March 14, 1942. For graphic accounts of speculation in foodstuffs and currency in Bogotá, see *El Colombiano*, June 4, 1901. Government decrees tried periodically to correct these abuses, apparently with little result.

creation of "colossal fortunes in exchange for pitiful bankruptcies."[94] Banks sprang up to meet the credit needs of the fluid wartime economic situation. One of them, the Bank of Commercial Credit, was founded expressly to "protect and support young men just beginning in business." It was resounding success after six months of operation, and its manager, Liberal Eduardo Rodríguez Piñeres, attributed the enterprise's good fortune, despite the obstacles of the war situation, to several innovations. These included longer banking hours, more working days, and the specialization in extending credit on an extremely short-term basis, usually for just a few days.[95] Another bank founded in 1902 attempted to attract small savers by instituting a monthly lottery with cash prizes among its depositors.[96] Although the fate of that bank is not clear, banks founded in Manizales in 1901 and Honda in early 1902 were soon pronounced enormous successes.[97] Perhaps the biggest success of the period, however, was a real estate management company founded by Historical Conservative Jorge Roa.[98] Most old banks and commercial houses were not so fortunate, and a few were forced out of business during the war.[99]

The demands of government armies and revolutionary bands for equipment and supplies created new and often risky economic opportunities. The government awarded contracts for livestock, blankets, uniforms, footwear, tents, drugs, saddles, and a variety of other supplies used by the army. The value of such contracts ranged from under a hundred thousand to over half a million pesos per month. Unless they had excellent connections and were considered solid supporters of the government, contractors could suffer long delays in receiving payment.[100] Willingness to lend the hard-pressed government money was a gamble which paid off handsomely for at least one man, Pepe Sierra, whose wartime profits catapulted him from a position of moderate wealth into the circle of high Colombian finance by

94. Fernando Garavito A., "El problema monetario y las crisis en Colombia," Speech delivered to the Sociedad Colombiana de Jurisprudencia, Bogotá, April 2, 1903, and published in several installments in the *Diario Oficial*, Nos. 11,855 to 11,860 (June 9 to June 20, 1903).

95. Eduardo Rodríguez Piñeres, *Informe del gerente y balance de las cuentas correspondientes al 2° semestre de 1901* [del Banco de Crédito Comercial] (Bogotá, 1902), pp. 4-7.

96. *La Patria*, July 30, 1902.

97. *Ibid.*, July 23, 1902; *El Colombiano*, March 7, 1902.

98. Rodríguez Piñeres, *Informe*, p. 4.

99. For an account of the difficulties of traditional banks during the war see "Un siglo de progreso y servicio bancario: Banco de Bogotá," *El Tiempo*, November 14, 1970, pp. 25-27.

100. For a typical monthly list of military contracts see the *Diario Oficial*, No. 11,425 (February 22, 1901). Friends of the government were given preference in payment in Decree No. 1,362 of 1902 (September 11), *Diario Oficial*, No. 11,736 (September 19, 1902).

the end of the war.[101] The supply needs of the revolutionary bands also provided opportunities for high profits for those willing to engage in the high-risk illegal trade. Smuggling associations sometimes stretched across party lines and included Liberal guerrilla leaders as well as Conservative officers.[102]

Members of the upper class deplored a situation in which they watched their livestock expropriated, their haciendas burned, their workers conscripted, and their businesses paralyzed while new men, willing to take risks and often utilizing unscrupulous or illegal means, profited from the war situation. Writing much later about the wartime Bogotá he experienced as a youth, Holguín Arboleda recalled the ways in which wartime profiteers and speculators, "a new breed in our social universe," squandered their easily acquired wealth purchasing expensive jewels, especially contraband emeralds, gambling in the halls which abounded on the principal streets of the capital, and hosting sumptuous meals for friends.[103] León Gómez deplored the circumstances that allowed so many individuals, both Liberal and Conservative, to leave for war in poverty only to return wealthy, thereby transforming a war fought over principles into a theater for pillage.[104] As the war dragged on charges became common that speculators, profiteers, and others with vested economic interests were encouraging and supplying the revolutionaries in order to prolong the war for their own gain. Marroquín himself expressed this view most succinctly in his New Year's address to the nation on January 1, 1902, when he blamed the perpetuation of the conflict on the "infernal spirit of sordid speculation and gain" that had come to dominate the activities of the many Colombians who had found in the chaos of war "undreamed of opportunities to trade and accumulate wealth."[105]

The opportunities created by the fluid war situation were not only economic but social and political as well. As a result of meritorious service in the revolutionary army many men of moderate wealth and limited education rose greatly in terms of social prestige and political influence. Benjamín Herrera's lackluster career, which was transformed by his brilliant campaign in Panama, provides an excellent case in point. After the war Herrera continued to be one of the

101. Bernardo Jaramillo Sierra, *Pepe Sierra: el método de un campesino millonario* (Medellín, 1947). Although confused in its account of Sierra's wartime activities, this little book is suggestive of the ways in which the great Colombian land speculator got his start.

102. París, *Guerrilleros*, p. 112, provides a revealing description of the nature of these associations.

103. Holguín Arboleda, *Mucho en serio*, p. 62.

104. León Gómez, *Secretos*, p. 161.

105. *Diario Oficial*, No. 11,610 (January 2, 1902).

paramount leaders of the Liberal party, served in high congressional and diplomatic posts, and became minister of agriculture and commerce under president José Vicente Concha. Three years before his death in 1924 he ran unsuccessfully for president of the Liberal ticket.

Although most Liberal armies and bands of guerrillas were led by men of property and some education, occasionally men of lower-class origin rose to positions of leadership and power. One band of guerrillas in the Tequendama region of southwestern Cundinamarca was reported in 1901 to be pillaging the haciendas of both Liberals and Conservatives. The leader, a man by the name of Herrera, was described in *El Colombiano* as "an Indian day laborer."[106] The career of Ramón Marín provides one of the best examples of mobility through service in the Liberal army. Born in Marmato, Antioquia, of African descent, "El Negro" Marín worked before the war as a straw boss in the gold mines of northern Tolima, where he made a reputation for successfully putting down a workers' revolt and later acquired a mine of his own. Leading guerrillas and commanding small armies of several hundred men Marín operated successfully against overwhelming odds in northern Tolima and Cundinamarca throughout the war. Probably the most famous of the Liberal guerrilla leaders, in the years immediately following the war Marín continued to have a voice in regional Liberal politics. As time passed, however, his influence waned and he died in poverty of tuberculosis in Honda in 1923.[107]

The most spectacular case of political mobility was of course that of Aristides Fernández himself. Hailed as the savior of the Conservative party and the Colombian nation by large segments of the army and the bureaucracy as well as many Conservatives of all classes on the Sabana de Bogotá, Fernández's power clearly rivaled that of Marroquín by the end of the war. From the first, traditional political leaders, especially Historical Conservatives and Liberals, had distrusted Fernández as a dangerous usurper. Fernández's actions in power confirmed their fears. Eight months after the coup of July 31, Carlos Martínez Silva was writing Uribe Uribe of their mutual interests as educated, tolerant, civilized republicans in ending the war. As long as the fighting continued, he said, the prestige of "vulgar guerrilla leaders" would hold sway in the Liberal party while the Conservatives would be dominated by the "worst Conservative, or better said, Nationalist element" that had managed to take control of Marroquín's government after July 31.[108] After Carlos Martínez Silva's imprisonment by order of Fernández in August, 1902, some of his Historical

106. *El Colombiano*, August 20, 1901.
107. París, *Guerrilleros*, pp. 109-111.
108. Carlos Martínez Silva to Rafael Uribe Uribe, Washington, April 2, 1901, Uribe, Box 7, ACH.

Conservative supporters urged an unidentified military man to stage a coup to eliminate the "social threat" posed by Fernández.[109] What Carlos Martínez Silva called the "fanatic, violent" element headed by Fernández so greatly preoccupied Uribe Uribe and Herrera that Fernández's removal from the ministry became their central condition for agreeing to participate in peace negotiations.[110]

The motivation behind the intense efforts of traditional political leaders to bring the war to an end are most candidly revealed in a letter written in mid-1902 by Liberal leader Celso Román. Speaking of the Liberal guerrillas still in arms, Román's social fears could just as easily have been aroused by the extremist elements in the Conservative army and bureaucracy.[111] Román was a member of the Liberal elite, having studied in the best Liberal schools under such luminaries as Camacho Roldán and Santiago Pérez; his letter was published in the peace Liberal paper *El Nuevo Tiempo*, a direct descendant of *La Crónica* and edited by José Camacho Carrizosa. Having fought in much of the war and suffered imprisonment during most of the rest, Celso Román said he spoke from experience as he sought to analyze the situation and convince his readers of the urgent need to end the war. As the war progressed, he argued, the most noble and valiant men were eliminated. Those who went to war to enrich themselves, on the other hand, were generally cowards and consequently less likely to be shot. The honorable people in all political parties desired peace, he continued; only those who derived economic advantage or supported themselves by the war wanted it to continue. Román then concluded his remarks with a phrase that encapsulated what he felt to be the disturbing tendencies at work during the last stages of the conflict and appealed to the class interests of traditional leaders of all parties to bring the war to an end. "It is advisable," he cautioned, "that the tempest cease in order that people and things return to occupy the position and level to which, given their background and their conduct, they are suited."[112]

---

109. Unsigned and undated, this curious, but genuine document appears in Uribe Uribe's papers marked only with a paper clip bearing the initials "E R-P." The initials would lead one to believe that the author was peace Liberal Eduardo Rodríguez Piñeres, but the content seems to indicate that the author was a Historical Conservative probably writing in September, 1902.

110. Carlos Martínez Silva to Rafael Uribe Uribe, Washington, April 2, 1901, Uribe, Box 7, ACH.

111. It will be remembered that Celso Román was one of the four prisoners threatened with retaliatory execution by Fernández in March, 1902.

112. *El Nuevo Tiempo*, June 21, 1902.

Part Three

The Winning of the Peace

Chapter VIII

The Eclipse of the Conservative Intransigents

As the more than three years of war came to an end and the struggle over the organization of the peace began, the bipartisan opponents of the Regeneration surveyed the extent of their failure to influence public policy and despaired at the weakness of their political position. The war had not brought an end to the Nationalist government's political and economic policies that most Liberals and Historical Conservatives had opposed in the press, the congress, or on the battlefield since the first years of the Regeneration. On the contrary the war had ensconced men in power from among the most authoritarian and Catholic elements of the Conservative party, the military, and the government bureaucracy. Led by Aristides Fernández these men sought to organize the peace on the basis of proscription of Liberals and dissident Conservatives from government.

But if the Liberal and Historical Conservative factions tied to the export-import economy lost the war, they were to win the peace. Just as Carlos Martínez Silva had predicted, soon after the fighting stopped the position of the extremist Conservatives began to decay. The history of the postwar period reveals the slow, painful progress made by the bipartisan critics of the Regeneration in implementing the economic, fiscal and political policies they had advocated since the early 1890's. That progress was not only difficult and slow, it was often uneven. At times advance on the political front was accompanied by reverses on the economic front or vice versa. The efforts of the prewar reformers to gain access to power and implement their political and economic program were complicated by the continued slump of the coffee economy. Although coffee prices improved somewhat over the nadir registered in 1900, they remained at low levels until the end of the first decade of the new century.

Postwar politics was also complicated by the unsettling events surrounding the United States-backed separation of Panama in 1903 and subsequent efforts by Colombians first to recover the lost department and later to regularize relations with the United States. Throughout the postwar period bipartisan export-import interests managed to use the Panama question to their political advantage. The issue of the canal and fear of United States intentions on the Isthmus had already served the political interests of moderate political factions within the two traditional parties by providing them with a face-saving way of ending a war over which they had begun to lose control. After the war the secession of Panama bolstered the political fortunes of bipartisan export-import interests by fostering a consensus among Colombian leaders that the nation must unite politically and develop itself materially if it were to avoid further dismemberment.

During the first months following the cessation of hostilities on the battlefield few could have predicted the future political success of dissident Conservatives and Liberals. Liberals, shattered by their defeat and powerless to influence government policy, engaged in furious intra-party bickering and recrimination. Peace Liberals argued that the defeat of the revolution vindicated their policy of avoiding war at any cost and blamed war Liberals, particularly Uribe Uribe, for the disastrous condition in which the party found itself after the war. War Liberals, on the other hand, claimed that peace Liberals had doomed a potentially successful revolt by their refusal to endorse the revolution in October, 1899, their lack of support during the war, and their constant efforts to temporize with the government to obtain a negotiated peace.

The end of the war found the Historical Conservatives discredited and demoralized. According to the indictment of Conservative party militants, the Historical Conservatives had encouraged the Liberal revolt and then strengthened it by their initial neutrality. Moreover, the militants argued, it was military victory, not political concessions that had finally brought the war to an end. Their policies discredited by the extremists, Historical Conservative leaders were dismayed by the results of the coup they had conceived and executed to bring Marroquín to power. Following July 31, 1900, Historical Conservatives had proved powerless in their efforts to steer Marroquín's course away from the policies advocated by the extremists. Marroquín, they observed with alarm as the war ended, appeared to be a puppet of Fernández and the intransigent Conservatives surrounding him. For Historical Conservatives, as well as Liberals and many traditional leaders of the Nationalist Conservatives, Fernández was a poorly educated social upstart, a man ignorant of economics and capable of any political excess. Fernández, they feared, was bent on establishing a dictatorship of the most ruthless, retrograde kind.

Such fears were inspired by the political course of the faction of the Conservative party supporting Fernández in the months following the signing of the peace treaties. At the intransigents' urging the government steadfastly refused to declare officially the end of the war, thus conserving the ability to govern the nation by executive decree. Fernández was hailed in the progovernment press as the "savior" of the country, the man "responsible" for the defeat of the Liberal party.[1] Poets made Fernández's intransigence his primary virtue, while pro-government political analysts declared Fernández not only "a guarantee of order, but a brake on the revolutionary element that conspires, whether under warlike, reformist, or anarchistic pretexts."[2]

In late 1902 Fernández's supporters moved to give their movement political organization and ideological expression by forming a new political party, the Catholic Party of Colombia. "Said party will be the same Conservative Party bettered, in other words, The Holy League, which, in order to maintain peace, contain liberalism, and assure the salvation of Colombia, so preoccupies the illustrious General Fernández."[3] The organizers of the party called for a new kind of leadership composed of men not related by "ties of family and god-parentage" to the Liberal adversary, men who were not deceived by the prospect of concessions to Liberals. The Catholic party would not take away the rights and guarantees of anyone, but would govern the nation "with its Party and for its Party." Liberals "will be still . . . like children who after their madness the father constrains to be quiet and diligent, working or learning the Commandments in his presence." Peace would be maintained by strong government aided by a Catholic militia, a kind of paramilitary organization to aid the government in times of crisis. The organizers envisioned a centrally directed party of perfect unity. "At election time all Catholics will vote solely for those candidates indicated by the directorship of the party." The party would have newspapers in the capital and each of the major cities of the country. All of these papers "will speak with one voice" and employ a prose style distinguished by "clarity, simplicity, pleasantness, and elegance of style." The Colombian Catholic party would coordinate its activities with Catholic parties in other nations to work "unanimously" for Catholic government everywhere.

As these plans to organize his followers progressed, Fernández proceeded to consolidate his power within Marroquín's government. Having rejoined the cabinet following the Liberals' capitulation, Fernández vastly increased his power as a result of a cabinet reorganization at the end of January, 1903. For a time he became minister of government as well as minister of war. In early February, in another shift of cabinet positions, he retained the ministry of government and

1. *La República*, October 18, 1902, and November 26, 1902.
2. *El Colombiano*, November 25, 1902, and January 20, 1903.
3. This quotation and subsequent ones are taken from an undated newspaper clipping fround in Uribe Uribe, Box 3, ACH. The article appeared in *La Constitución* (Bogotá), the official organ of the new party. The paper apparently was published during the apogee of Fernández's career. For an incisive characterization of the Catholic party and *La Constitución* as well as other Conservative factions and their respective press organs, see *El Nuevo Tiempo*, April 21, 1903.

was named acting minister of finance. At the same time, his firm supporter, José Joaquín Casas, was named acting minister of war and continued to hold his post as minister of public instruction.

A doctrinaire Conservative, a militant Catholic, and a member of Colombia's cultural elite, Casas helped to articulate the ideological position of the Fernández bloc of intransigent Conservatives. He also lent the movement much needed social prestige. Born in Colombia's eastern highlands in 1866, Casas, like Marroquín, had never traveled abroad and devoted much of his life to furthering Catholic education in Colombia. Son of the rector of a Catholic secondary school located in Zipaquirá, Cundinamarca, he studied at Bogotá's Jesuit-run Colegio de San Bartolomé and taught Latin at that institution after his graduation in 1886. During the Regeneration he organized three Catholic secondary schools on the Sabana de Bogotá. Joining Marroquín's government as the war came to an end, he proved to be among the most intransigent advocates of Liberal proscription in the postwar period. In a famous telegram he instructed government negotiators to treat Uribe Uribe as a traitor and judge him in a summary military trial (the instructions were disregarded by the Conservative general charged with conducting the negotiations at Neerlandia). A writer and poet of some distinction, Casas is best remembered as founder of the Colombian Academy of History in December, 1902, an act which was part of his many-faceted program to revitalize the cultural life of the nation in the months following the end of the war.[4]

In control of the four powerful ministries which encompassed the political, coercive, fiscal, and ideological arms of the government, Fernández and Casas found themselves at the end of January, 1903, in a unique position to dictate the terms of the organization of the peace. The tenor of the intransigents' policies was revealed in the comprehensive press decree issued by the government on January 26, 1903. In sharp contrast to the ample freedoms granted by the press law of 1898, the decree closely defined the limits of public discussion and stipulated severe sanctions in the case of transgressions. Although the decree granted the press the right to discuss public policy and the qualifications of candidates for office, it strictly limited the terms of such discussion. Crimes against society, punishable by sanctions ranging from fines to permanent suspension of the offending paper, included attacks on the Catholic religion, the military, the "dignity and prerogatives" of civil and ecclesiastical authorities, and the legal tender of the nation. It was also a crime to "assume the name of and representation of the people; oppose the legitimate organization of

4. On Casas, see the biographical sketch in Casas, *Semblanzas*, pp. 11-12; Ospina, *Diccionario*, I, 505-06; and Luis María Mora, *Croniquillas de mi ciudad* (Bogotá, 1931), p. 252.

property; incite some social classes against others," or to "offend public decency with obscene writings or scandalous reports." Moreover, any person or entity censured within the legal bounds of newspaper discussion was to be given the opportunity to respond with an article up to twice the length of the original, offensive piece. The response was to be published free of charge within a day after its submission to the editor. Finally, all articles published anonymously or under a pseudonym had to appear under original signature in the files of the newspaper's publisher.[5]

The press decree formed part of the ground rules established by Fernández and his supporters for the important departmental and congressional elections to be held in March, 1903. (Because the war had disrupted normal procedures two-thirds of the Senate seats were at stake, those for 1900 and 1902, and all of the Chamber seats. Members elected to the Chamber would serve only a special one-year period, July, 1903, to July, 1904.) In early February, Minister of Government Fernández sent a circular to all department governors outlining the government's position in the upcoming elections. Noting the fact that the government in its magnanimity had pardoned the revolutionaries and maintained their political rights, Fernández went on to suggest that these acts

> do not in any way exclude social justice, nor do they tend to stifle the sentiments of understandable indignation and universal vindictiveness. [It is the body politic, the citizens themselves] who should apply this elevated concept of justice, which is not found expressed in artificial formulas [but] resides in the national conscience and should express itself in an explosion of patriotism, denying the vote to those who ... making use of violence ... insulted the religious sentiments, heart and soul of the Colombian people.[6]

Under these conditions it was not surprising that election returns from the March 8, 1903, congressional election gave an overwhelming victory to Conservative candidates. Only two Liberals were elected to congress. Among them, however, was the influential critic of Regeneration finance, José Camacho Carrizoza, who, as will be seen, was to play a pivotal role in achieving monetary reform in the congress of 1903.

Successful in their initial efforts to organize the political aspects of the peace, Fernández and his supporters faced overwhelming prob-

5. Decree No. 84 of 1903 (January 26), *Diario Oficial,* No. 11,794 (January 31, 1903).

6. Resolucion #151, February 4, 1903, published in *El Colombiano* February 6, 1903. The decree was condemned by moderate Conservatives and Liberals. Carlos E. Restrepo penned a spirited denunciation from Medellín. See Carlos E. Restrepo et al., "Explicación," Medellín, Feb. 26, 1903, MDT, ACH.

lems in dealing with the fiscal and economic problems confronting the nation as the war came to an end. Wartime government finance had depended on special measures (such as the income from the extension of the concession granted the New Panama Canal Company), expropriation of property and forced loans, and, most important, on the printing of paper money. Government needs had led to large-scale printing of paper during the last months of the war. The poor quality of bills printed in Colombia during the war (at one point the government bought paper destined to wrap bars of chocolate for use in the lithograph), provided counterfeiters with ample opportunities.[7] Efforts by Colombian merchants and capitalists to bypass the vagaries of the paper money system led the government to reiterate the illegality of specifying any but official government currency in contracts, letters of exchange, and price lists, and to establish severe penalties, ranging from large fines to the closing of businesses, for violators. Steady depreciation of the currency forced government to continually raise salaries of government civil and military personnel. Counterfeiting and speculation in paper currency were endemic problems which demanded the constant attention of government officials. The dilemmas involved in dependence on ever greater emissions of paper money are ironically illustrated in a single October issue of the *Diario Oficial*. In addition to the decree reiterating the prohibition of "free stipulation" noted above, the same issue included another decree establishing monetary rewards for those furnishing information on counterfeiters, and a third decree fixing the rate of overtime pay for nightwork in the Litografía Nacional.[8]

As a result of continuing emissions and the activities of speculators, paper money exchange rates fluctuated wildly during the last months of the war and reached the astonishing average of 18,900 in October 1902 (see Table 6:1). During that month, the United States consul reported:

> Excited, feverish crowds, thinking of nothing but the crisis, filled the streets of Bogotá, and the borrowing became rampant on all sides, people borrowing paper money at exorbitant rates of interest to buy gold, hoping to pay the paper with a small part of the gold bought. Exchange continued to rise, reaching 25,000 percent, and even then there were speculators who bought gold at thirty days' credit, confident in the belief of a further rise....[9]

The declining value for paper money during the war and the post-

7. Holguín Arboleda, *Mucho en serio*, p. 61.
8. *Diario Oficial*, No. 11,748 (October 14, 1903).
9. U. S. Dept. of Commerce and Labor, "Financial Conditions in Colombia," in *Commercial relations of the United States with Foreign Countries during the year 1903*, 2 vols. (Washington, 1904), I, 294-95.

war period greatly reduced the amount of government revenue since many duties and taxes continued to be assessed in paper money at virtually prewar levels. Table 8:1 compares Colombian tariff duties (in Colombian paper pesos and their equivalents in U. S. gold dollars) for the period preceding the war and the immediate postwar period. The table reveals the great loss of government customs revenue because of wartime inflation. For example, a class 10 item taxed in January, 1898 at the rate of slightly less than U. S. $0.33 was being assessed at a rate of only slightly more than U. S. $0.03 in February, 1903. Revenue produced by taxes on exports was further reduced because of the fall off in production and the disruption of transport occasioned by the war, as well as by the fact that many merchants, both foreign and domestic, held back shipments in the hope of postwar abolition of export duties. This strategy was common among coffee exporters who could store their product for long periods of time without fear of serious deterioration.[10]

At the same time that it grappled with the problems of insufficient revenue, Marroquín's postwar government was burdened with extraordinary expenditures. The cost of maintaining a swollen civil bureaucracy and an army which still numbered in the tens of thousands consumed a large portion of government revenue. In December, 1902, the Conservative paper *El Colombiano* estimated the government's deficit at about 16,692,935 pesos a month, more than two-thirds of which was spent by the minister of war. According to the paper, the deficit was being covered by a daily emission of 566,431 paper pesos.[11] Efforts to reduce the size of the civil and military establishment involved political costs, and progress was limited and gradual.[12] Hopelessly behind in its payment not only of civil and military salaries but of official contracts to supply the army with food, clothing, and equipment, in November the government was forced to suspend payment of all but the most pressing obligations.[13] To make its future financial situation even more pressing, the government could look forward to the obligation of settling considerable foreign and domestic claims for damages and expropriations suffered at the hands of government forces during the course of the war.[14]

10. On January 30, 1903, in an effort to shake these exports loose, Marroquín's government abolished export taxes on all items except gold. *El Nuevo Tiempo*, February 3, 1903.

11. *El Colombiano*, December 5, 1902.

12. Government decrees in November, 1902, and January, 1903, reduced the legal limit of the army's manpower to 50,000 men, then 25,000. In December, 1902, the internal intelligence section of the ministry of war was eliminated and a unit under the jurisdiction of the National Police disbanded.

13. Decree No. 1,613 of 1902 (November 5) and Decree No. 1,650 of 1902 (November 12), *Diario Oficial*, Nos. 11,760 and 11,762 (November 7 and 13), 1902.

14. Procedures for dealing with these claims were set up in Decree No. 104 of 1903, *Diario Oficial*, No. 11,800 (February 17, 1903).

Table 8:1. Prewar and postwar Colombian customs duties (in Colombian paper pesos and equivalents in U. S. gold).

Class	January, 1898 Pesos	Dollars	February, 1903 Pesos	Dollars	March, 1903 Pesos	Dollars
1	free	free	free	free	.20	.002
2	.015	.005	.05	.0006	.45	.004
3	.037	.013	.112	.001	1.25	.012
4	.075	.027	.225	.003	2.25	.022
5	.15	.054	.45	.006	4.50	.045
6	.30	.109	.90	.012	9.00	.090
7	.45	.163	1.35	.019	13.50	.135
8	.60	.218	1.80	.025	18.00	.18
9	.75	.272	1.87	.028	22.60	.22
10	.90	.327	2.25	.032	27.00	.27
11	1.05	.381	3.15	.045	31.50	.315
12	1.20	.436	3.60	.051	36.00	.36
13	1.35	.490	4.05	.057	40.50	.40
14	1.87	.581	5.62	.08	56.25	.56
15	2.25	.818	6.75	.095	67.50	.67
16	3.75	1.363	11.25	.16	112.50	1.12

Source: Adapted from Spencer S. Dickson "Report on the Trade of Colombia (excepting the Panama District) for the Year 1903," Great Britain, Foreign Office, *Diplomatic and Consular Reports, Colombia* (London, 1904), p. 35. Equivalencies are computed at an exchange rate of 275 percent, Jan., 1898; 7000 percent, Feb., 1903; 10,000 percent, March, 1903.

Beneath the monetary and fiscal difficulties facing the government lay the basic problem of a depressed economy disrupted by the ravages of three years of civil turmoil. Coffee prices improved somewhat from the ruinous level of 7 cents a pound reached in late 1900, but remained at the moderately low level of 10 to 11 cents a pound in the years following the war. The war had disrupted production, transportation, and labor systems. Livestock herds had been depleted by marauding armies and guerrilla forces, while portions of the coffee and sugar cane crops had been allowed to rot in the fields. In many areas farm buildings had been destroyed, machinery allowed to fall into disrepair, and tools had been stolen. Contemporary and subsequent observers are unanimous in stressing the severity of the economic dislocation caused by the war, but their judgments, often influenced by political considerations, are undoubtedly often exaggerated. Some haciendas were almost totally destroyed, but others resumed production with a minimum of difficulty. In what may be a typical case, an administrator of one of Guillermo Durán's coffee haciendas in Cundinamarca wrote his employer that reports of wartime destruction of the hacienda were "exaggerated." Eighteen sacks of coffee on the hacienda at the start of the revolution had been lost, the cane press needed a part, and many hand tools were missing. Most of the tools, the administrator claimed, could be recovered (apparently they were in the hands of the hacienda's tenants). The coffee groves, the administrator went on, although covered with weeds, could be saved; only a few trees had died. The coffee harvest would begin in about a month and a half and thirty-two workers were on hand ready to begin work immediately.[15] The report is consistent with two points made by Julio H. Palacio in what may be the most balanced published appraisal of the economic impact of the war. Given the rudimentary nature of the Colombian economy at the turn of the century, Palacio asserted, actual destruction was moderate. The greatest economic loss was occasioned by the interruption of production and expansion during the period of insecurity fostered by the war situation.[16]

Damage to the communications system during the war was considerable. The end of the war found the telegraph network, constant target of Liberal guerrilla bands, in a shambles.[17] While the nation's short railroad lines suffered little damage, and river transportation, despite the fact that many boats had been sunk or disabled during the war, was functioning, the nation's vital system of mule transport was seriously disrupted. Mule trails and bridges fell into disrepair during the war, and since mules were used extensively by government armies and guerrilla forces the number available for postwar transport was probably considerably less than prewar levels because of wartime casualties. Prices for mule transport rose at a much higher rate than rail or river transport during the war and immediate postwar period. One careful contemporary study of the impact of emissions of paper currency on prices between 1898 and February, 1903, found that while railroad freight rates had increased 37 times, and river freight rates 27 times, mule freight rates had risen 56 times.[18]

One of the most serious postwar economic problems concerned the supply and manageability of labor. Throughout the war government recruitment took thousands of agricultural workers out of production. Those soldiers who escaped death or incapacitation by battle and disease had to be re-integrated into the work force following the war. The same was true of the men and women who had fled from recruitment or the depredations of marauding armies and guerrilla bands.

15. "Gustavo" to Guillermo Durán, "Montecristo," September 14, 1902, Durán, ACH.
16. Palacio, Historia, *El Tiempo*, October 3, 1943. For an intelligent discussion of the problem of the extent of economic dislocation caused during Colombian civil wars, see Delpar, "The Liberal Party," pp. 19-20.
17. República de Colombia, Dirección de Correos y Telégrafos, *Informe* (Bogotá, 1904), pp. 4-5.
18. The study found that on the average prices rose 37 times during the period, a result the depreciation of paper currency. Fernando Garavito A., "Conferencia ante la Sociedad Colombiana de Jurisprudencia," *Diario Oficial*, No. 11,859 (June 18, 1903).

Some had joined guerrilla bands, others were engaged in subsistence agriculture in the forests or farmed land on haciendas abandoned by landlords during the war. An example of the problems faced by hacienda owners as the war came to an end in Cundinamarca is this report from an administrator of one of Guillermo Durán's coffee haciendas near Junín, Cundinamarca.

> I have had to struggle a great deal with the problem of organizing the people at Junín. They have had a commission on the hacienda for about two weeks, recruiting without any considera-tion. The tenants have had to make do living in the forest and for that reason you can easily judge the situation here. Work in little spurts, full of uncertainty and spies so that they do not disor-ganize the hacienda; I'd really like to be a thousand miles away and not endure the rabble around here.[19]

Even after the signing of the peace treaties marauding bands con-tinued to disrupt life in some rural areas. A large band was caught and executed by government forces in the Viotá region in southwestern Cundinamarca at the end of December, 1902, and bands of up to thirty were reported operating about the same time near the western Cun-dinamarcan towns of Vergara and Viani.[20]

During the first months following the war, Marroquín's government was primarily concerned with keeping itself afloat financially and dealt with the enormous economic, fiscal, and monetary problems facing the nation on an ad hoc, day-to-day basis. With the cabinet reorganization of early 1903, which named Fernández acting minister of finance, however, the government attempted to formulate a com-prehensive program to deal with the crisis. Export-import interests were appalled at the choice of Fernández, a man who could claim no special knowledge of economics and whose economic and fiscal pro-grams, never solicitous of their interests in the past, were to reveal an assessment of the causes of the postwar crisis quite different from their own.

Fernández attacked his new job with his accustomed vigor. In a forcefully worded circular to the departmental governors announcing his appointment he confessed his lack of training in economics, but asserted his determination to improve the government's fiscal position and deal with the economic and monetary crisis. Fernández's plan

19. Victor Manuel Zarzón Nieto to Guillermo Durán L., "Hoyagrande," July 23, 1902. Durán, ACH. Similar problems of a Liberal coffee farmer in a predominantly Conserva-tive *municipio,* are documented in Deas, "Una finca cundinamarquesa."

20. Martín González G. to Minister of War, La Mesa [Cund.], December 31, 1902; Manuel A. Corrales, Prefect, to Minister of War, Viani, December 27, 1902; Nemencio García Ch. to General Comandante en Jefe del Ejército, Sasaima [Cund.], December 29, 1902, all in AMD, vol. 05752.

was simple and straightforward. He would balance the budget and stop new emissions by drastically decreasing government expenditures while augmenting government income. The first would be accomplished through an austerity budget and by shifting a significant portion of the national government's financial burden to the departments.[21] To increase government revenues Fernández outlined a comprehensive tariff reform. His decree of February 13 raised customs duties nine to twelve times (depending on category) the rate prevailing when he took office. (See the column marked March, 1903, in Table 8:1). The new tariff took effect on March 1, 1903, and, according to the British viceconsul in Bogotá, caused great consternation among import merchants, some of whom canceled large orders previously made in England. The tariff placed the highest ad valorem tax on what the British official termed "necessaries," items "on which the poorer people have entirely to depend for their clothing, i.e., Manchest[er] goods (cotton shirtings, trouserings, etc.). . . ."[22] According to the British viceconsul the primary objection of importers to the new tariff was not the increased rate of taxation, but the fact that by establishing duties in paper the new tariff perpetuated the vagaries of fluctuating exchange rates and left merchants unable to make sound commercial decisions on a long-range basis. These difficulties would be eliminated after the fall of Fernández by reform forces in the congress of 1903.

Fernández believed that the activities of speculators, profiteers, and counterfeiters were a major cause of the problems of depreciating paper currency, wide fluctuations in exchange rates, and the high cost and scarcity of essential goods. Throughout the war Fernández had used every means at his disposal to attack these immoral economic "parasites," and he would insist on the power to deal with them inexorably in his final confrontation with Marroquín.[23]

21. Decree No. 152 of 1903 (February 7), *Diario Oficial*, No. 11,799 (February 16, 1903).

22. Spencer S. Dickson, "Report on the Trade of Colombia (excepting the Panama District) for the Year 1903," Great Britain, Foreign Office, *Diplomatic and Consular Reports* (London, 1903), p. 30.

23. For example, in a telegraphed circular to local governmental officials dated November 1, 1902, Fernández denounced what he termed "el beduinismo agiotista," a clear reference to the activities of Syrian traders who engaged in commerce in Colombia. *La República*, November 5, 1902. Dissatisfaction with shortages and high costs culminated in anti-Syrian riots and the pillaging of stores in the river port of Honda in August, 1903. According to some reports the action was taken in connivance with government military authorities. *El Eco Nacional*, August 22, 1903. One of Uribe Uribe's correspondents made a similar charge and stated that Conservative intransigents had declared that Liberal merchants would be the next targets, a threat made plausible since "ya hemos llegado todos a ocupar n/. puestos [in the commerce of the town] y de consiguiente quedan ellos [the Syrians] anulados." General Castellanos to Rafael Uribe Uribe, Honda, August 31, 1903. Uribe, Box 8, ACH.

That confrontation, which finally led to the resignations of Fernández and Casas and the beginning of the eclipse of the intransigent Conservative bloc in national politics, was slow in developing. Marroquín sympathized with many of the ideas of Fernández and Casas. In his New Year's message to the Colombian people, he lamented the spread of "the spirit of speculation" and the unprecedented decline of "respect for the right of property" caused by the war. Marroquín urged all Colombians to forget petty politics, "dedicate themselves to the tasks to which each is called," and work "to make that morality of which we used to set an example reign in Colombia." But Marroquín sought a broader political and ideological base for his postwar government than that offered by the Conservative intransigents. He may have feared the consequences of overdependence on the intransigents or he may have detected a growing consensus among traditional leaders of all persuasions in favor of economic reforms and political moderation. At any rate in his New Year's speech Marroquín praised the political stance of the peace Liberal faction and committed his government to an effort to balance the budget, end future emissions, and begin amortization.[24]

Since the conclusion of the fighting Marroquín had attempted to steer a more moderate political course than the one advocated by Fernández and the intransigents. Analyzing the political situation in a private letter to an influential Historical Conservative in November, 1902, Marroquín emphasized the need to "expurgate" those among the supporters of his government unwilling to reform the "system that [my government] has had to follow with respect to fiscal and economic matters" and who sought to organize the peace along vindictive, exclusivist lines. But so great was the prestige of the intransigents in the months following the war that Marroquín was forced to bide his time. While it was necessary to purge the extremists, that process, Marroquín claimed, could be accomplished only gradually since the group "is composed of military men and men of action who will obstruct [progress] greatly should they become enemies." Besides their strength in the military and civil bureaucracy, the intransigents had the support of many clerics who, in Marroquín's words, viewed Fernández "as the instrument that Providence utilized to end the war."[25]

Whatever the extent of Marroquín's commitment to the intransi-

24. Marroquín also endorsed the need for more railroads, "sobre todo los que unan con el Océano nuestras comarcas centrales." The speech appears in the *Diario Oficial*, No. 11,784 (January 2, 1903).

25. José Manuel Marroquín to Eduardo Posada, Bogotá, November 10, 1902; José Manuel Marroquín to Ramón González Valencia, Bogotá, December 18, 1902, MDT, ACH.

gents' position, he eventually became alarmed over the threat they posed to his own authority. Throughout his administration, Marroquín had jealously guarded his ultimate authority to determine government policy, an attitude strikingly revealed in his confrontation with the Historical Conservatives after the coup of July 31, 1900. Although he was content to leave day-to-day administration in the hands of his cabinet ministers, he used his considerable political skill to conserve his own course of action. Marroquín's close working relationship with Fernández found a basis in the two men's common philosophical ground and the energy with which Fernández tackled the demands of administration. But Marroquín also had found Fernández's collaboration attractive because he felt assured of Fernández's personal loyalty and because Fernández deferred to Marroquín's ultimate authority.[26] But as the new year progressed Marroquín was forced to revise that opinion.

During the months following the cabinet reorganization of late January and early February, 1903, Fernández and Casas sought ever more forceful measures to deal with the political opposition and implement their fiscal program. In late February the government issued a decree written by Fernández that declared invalid the appointment of four judges to the district courts of Cundinamarca. According to the decree the men named by the tribunal of Cundinamarca to fill the local judgeships had taken up arms against the government during the war. The decree argued that the appointments were invalid since the state of seige was still in force and since by previous decree (No. 677 of 1900) the government had removed from all government posts any employee who by word or action had been hostile to the government. But the Tribunal of Cundinamarca, in a tightly argued legal brief dated March 6, held that constitutional separation of powers and de facto termination of the war invalidated the government's position. The Tribunal instructed Minister of Government Fernández to give the judges possession of their offices.[27]

The incident served to polarize the Colombian body politic. A groundswell of moderate, bipartisan opinion urged Marroquín to implement the spirit of the peace treaties, declare the war officially ended, and return the nation to normal constitutional processes. At the same time intransigent Conservatives pressured Marroquín to harden his attitude against Liberals and dissident Conservatives and argued that the extraordinary political and economic situation confronting the nation justified extending the state of seige for an indefinite period. As

26. José Manuel Marroquín to Ramón González Valencia, Bogotá, December 18, 1902, MDT, ACH.

27. The decree and the tribunal's response can be found in *El Comercio*, May 25, 1903.

the dispute continued, Marroquín appeared to side with the moderates and refused to implement the decree. In late April Fernández was granted a "leave of absence" from his posts as minister of government and acting head of the ministry of finance.[28] Two weeks later Fernández made a desperate move to regain his lost power. On May 10, together with José Joaquín Casas, Fernández submitted an ultimatum to Marroquín in the form of a joint resignation. The impassioned language of the ultimatum illustrates the depth of intransigents' postwar commitment to exclude Liberals and dissident Conservatives from government. More important, the terms of the ultimatum reveal the stakes involved in the political confrontation that would determine the immediate direction of the postwar reorganization of the country.

The ultimatum began by painting a macabre picture of Colombia following the conclusion of the "most barbarous" of the civil wars "ever to affect the American continent." "[P]ools of blood still flowed and the bones of more than one hundred thousand Colombians bleached unburied [in the fields]." But at this time when it was necessary to build dikes against the prospect of anarchy, the "eternal enemy" had begun to clamor for "who knows what liberties and guarantees" and was accumulating powder for the next conflagration. "Liberalism (and it seems to us that it is made up not only of those who call themselves liberals but anyone who professes the essential ideas of that system)," Fernández and Casas went on, was "by nature revolutionary" and needed to be repressed inexorably. Employees of the judicial branch had been the first to utter the cry of rebellion. Interpreting the constitution in a "juridical and servile" manner they had sought to limit the power of the government, as if the government were the entity which needed to be fought and shackled. The separation of powers was a necessary guarantee, but it should not be used to disrupt the government and give authority to those who had just rebelled against authority.

"It has been," the two ministers stated categorically, "and continues to be, impossible to declare public order re-established." To do so would be to promulgate a legal fiction, for in fact public order was profoundly disturbed. The press, "no longer free but rather licentious and insolent," continually provokes government and propagates "the same dissociative doctrines" that had led Colombia into the deplorable situation in which she finds herself today. The utmost energy and abnegation was necessary to extricate Colombia from this deplorable state of affairs. Power, the ministers contended, was "a burden imposed by God" and carried with it great responsibility. Colombia, tired of theories and utopias, clamored for "the supreme remedy," which consisted of the vigorous exercise of power.

28. *Diario Oficial*, No. 11,832 (April 27, 1903).

As practical steps to implement these principles, the ministers insisted that the government adopt the following measures: (1) inflexible implementation of executive decrees relating to the judiciary; (2) immediate, exemplary punishment of those individuals involved in revolutionary plots; (3) suppression of all private newspapers; (4) complete compliance with the fiscal plan adopted; (5) an end to all government contracts which do not benefit the public services; (6) adoption of all possible measures against usury, against the monopolization of foodstuffs, and in general, against any system of unjust speculation; and (7) the naming of governors who believe in these ideas and are ready to put them into practice. Should the government not accept all of these measures and proceed to implement them, the two ministers tendered their "formal and irrevocable" resignations.[29]

The conditional resignation of his two most powerful ministers placed Marroquín in a most delicate position. To accede to the conditions was to give himself over to the intransigents and lose all semblance of control over postwar politics; to deny the conditions and accept the resignations seemed to invite an intransigent Conservative coup against his government. For a time Marroquín held the resignations while he worked behind the scenes to consolidate support among moderate political, ecclesiastical, and military leaders.

Whether Fernández and Casas conceived of the ultimatum as a way to bluff their way back into positions of power or as a means for generating support for a military coup, the results of their strategy were quite the opposite. Marroquín interpreted the terms of the ultimatum as a challenge to his own authority. Moreover, moderate leaders from both traditional parties coalesced in support of the vice-president. By May 22 Marroquín felt sure enough of his position to pen a vigorous reply to the ultimatum. In his note he accepted the two ministers' resignations and characterized the powers they had sought as dictatorial.[30] Seizing the initiative, he then proceeded to name a more moderate cabinet, and on June 1 he issued the decree which declared public order reestablished and thus officially brought the war to an end.[31]

Marroquín next attempted to remove Fernández from the domestic political scene by offering him the Colombian ambassadorship to France, the choicest of diplomatic plums and a time-honored method of remunerating potentially dangerous politicians for services rendered to their party in the past. The terms of Fernández's refusal of the post were threatening. Fernández stood by his analysis of the political situation, warning that another Liberal revolt was imminent and an-

29. The complete text of the resignation appears in MDT, ACH.
30. These events are recounted with obvious satisfaction in *El Comercio* May 25 and 26, 1903.
31. Decree No. 638 of 1903 (June 1), *Diario Oficial*, No. 11,855 (June 9, 1903).

nouncing his intention to stay in Colombia to defend the institutions of the Conservative order. He went on to say that he was painfully aware of the deplorable state of the public treasury and could not be the cause of additional expenditures. Finally, he noted that it would be out of the question for him to represent a government that was in "total disagreement" with him and that had falsely accused him of attempting to establish a dictatorship.[32]

Fernández's supporters responded to Marroquín's decision by circulating a petition of support for the position advocated by Fernández and Casas in their resignation. Dated May 31, 1903, the petition stated that Fernández and Casas had "faithfully interpreted the sentiments of those of us who fought for the triumph of Conservative institutions." Signed by hundreds of militant Conservatives, the list was headed by Nicolás Perdomo, the general who had represented the government in the peace negotiations which culminated in the Treaty of Wisconsin.[33]

Marroquín was prepared for the militant Conservative reaction to his decision. The day the petition was published in the pro-Fernández press, the police who guarded the presidential palace and other public buildings were replaced by troops loyal to the government. Additional bodies of trustworthy troops were brought into the city, and units of three to four thousand men commanded by loyal officers were stationed near the capital in case of trouble. By the end of June the United States chargé d'affaires could report to Washington that "the extraordinary precautions taken by the Government renders any trouble growing out of General Fernández's resignation altogether improbable."[34]

The defeat of the Fernández bloc and the lifting of the state of seige constituted the first step in the political resurgence of the Liberal party and the moderate Conservatives. In the freer political climate that prevailed after June 1, the prewar opponents of Regeneration political and economic policies pushed their reforms in the press and, after the installation of the congress on July 20, in the legislative chambers.

The congress which convened in Bogotá on July 20, 1903, faced the awesome task of political and economic reconstruction following the longest and most destructive civil war in the nation's history. Besides dealing with specific problems growing out of the war, the congress

32. *La República*, June 10, 1903. Fernández's refusal to accept an honorable position replete with material rewards was typical of his conduct during his last years in government. Even his most severe critics, men who suffered under his repressive political and economic measures during the war, are unanimous in recognizing his personal honesty and integrity.

33. The petition and list of signers was published in *La República* June 17, 1903.

34. A. M. Beaupré to John Hay, Bogotá, June 29, 1903, USNA.

was forced to come to terms with the continuing economic malaise and the basic economic and political issues which had divided the Colombian upper class since the start of the Regeneration and had contributed so significantly to the outbreak of the war itself. Given the limited number of congressmen identified with the reform movement elected during Fernández's tenure as minister of government, it is remarkable that reform forces achieved important legislative victories during the sixty-day congressional session. The ability of reform forces to push their measures through congress can be explained in part by the climate of public opinion. Many postwar political leaders of all persuasions sought to eliminate the causes of the political contention which had helped to unleash a war of such magnitude and had threatened the basis of upper-class social control. Reform forces were also aided by the discredit brought the political policies of the intransigent Conservatives following Fernández's bid for extraordinary powers, and by the chaos of the monetary system resulting from massive wartime emissions of paper money and the activities of speculators.

On the political front the most important achievement of the reform forces was the passage of a new press law. Law No. 7 of 1903 repealed the stringent press decree issued under Fernández's auspices in January, 1903, and replaced it with the liberal press law No. 51 of 1898.[35] Another law (No. 8 of 1903), which backers felt might be important in determining the outcome of the 1904 presidential election, affirmed the right of congress to name its representatives to the Gran Concejo Electoral, the body which scrutinized electoral returns for irregularities and had the power to annul or validate disputed returns. The law repealed Decree No. 1,719 of 1902, which had conceded to the executive the power to name all members to the Gran Concejo. As will be seen, the prescience of reformist forces was borne out: the Gran Concejo did determine the outcome of one of the most bizarre, closest—and most important—elections in Colombian history. In a related matter, however, despite their best efforts, reform forces failed to pass a new electoral law that would have made Liberal representation on all electoral boards mandatory.

On the economic front, Liberal and Historical Conservative opponents of Regeneration policies won spectacular victories during the congressional session. Law No. 33 of 1903, drafted and guided through congress by the Liberal representative José Camacho Carrizosa, embodied the heart of the reformists' monetary program. The law adopted gold as the standard for fixing the value of paper money

35. The text of this and other laws passed by the congress of 1903 can be found in República de Colombia, Consejo de Estado, *Leyes colombianas expedidas en sus sesiones extraordinarias de 1903* (Bogotá, 1903).

(Art. 1), allowed for the legal circulation of foreign gold currencies in Colombia (Art. 2), absolutely banned further emissions of paper money (Art. 3), and provided the legal right to stipulate gold in contracts (Art. 4). Articles 5-9 created a Junta de Amortización, an autonomous agency composed of five members charged with periodically fixing the exchange rate of paper to gold and invested with the authority to begin amortization of paper currency. In order to accomplish this last task the Junta was granted an income in gold to be derived from revenues produced by rent of the emerald mines, the pearl fisheries, and the national forests, as well as from the product of certain port duties and the export tax on tagua. The Junta was to use its income to buy paper for gold at public auction and incinerate it. Finally, Article 10 provided that government budgets and customs taxes be fixed in gold, although they would be payable in either gold or its paper equivalent at the current rate of exchange.

Law 33 ran into stiff resistance from some Nationalists in congress. Debate on the measure was so lengthy in the Chamber that for a time it appeared that the session would end before the mandatory third debate of the bill ran its course and the final vote was taken. Finally, however, reform forces succeeded in passing a procedural motion which called the Chamber into special evening sessions to conclude debate on the bill. This tactic was successful and the measure was finally approved by the Chamber and sent to the Senate. In the upper house the bill encountered the decided opposition of Miguel Antonio Caro, a member of the study committee headed by Pedro Nel Ospina charged with evaluating the bill. Although Caro penned a powerful dissenting opinion, the majority of the committee endorsed the central features of the bill and the Senate eventually approved the measure.[36]

Law 33 constituted a great victory for the reformist forces, but it did not abolish the paper money system. That was a fiscal impossibility given the volume of paper in circulation and the financial penury of the government. Moreover, the actual income of the Junta was so small (despite the impressive list of sources of income) that the amortization would take place on a modest scale. Still, as José Camacho Carrizosa was quick to point out, Law 33 represented a great step forward because it established important principles and set a precedent for future progress. In passing the bill the Conservatives, according to Camacho Carrizosa, had recognized the "scientific principle" behind the liberal critique of Regeneration monetary policy, for

36. Much of the debate is reported in the *Anales* of the Chamber and the Senate for 1903. The reports of the study commissions of both houses are penetrating studies of the economic and monetary problems facing the nation and offer cogent analyses of the bill's ability to solve these problems. See *Anales de la Cámara de Representantes, 1903*, pp. 141-42 and *Anales del Senado, 1903*, pp. 290-96, 302-11. Caro's minority report can also be found in his *Escritos sobre cuestiones económicos* (Bogotá, 1956), pp. 93-122.

the law declared that "paper money constitutes a debt and even though it [temporarily] maintains its status as legal tender, it must be amortized." Moreover, in Camacho Carrizosa's words, the bill

designates funds for amortization, acknowledges gold as the monetary unit, allows the circulation of foreign currencies, and by decree designates them as having intrinsic value and establishes equivalences in the national monetary unit, granting in this way complete satisfaction to liberal desires and liberal propaganda in the field of economics.[37]

Years later Liberal merchant and banker Quijano Wallis could note with satisfaction that Law 33 "laid the foundations for the economic redemption of the country," and Guillermo Camacho Carrizosa could exclaim with satisfaction that his brother's bill "opened the sources of credit [and] the aid of foreign capital to our anemic enterprise."[38]

In the last days of the congressional session, in accordance with Article 10 of Law 33, congress passed a new tariff law fixing all duties in gold. In the eyes of import merchants the new tariff removed the worst feature of Fernández's March 1 tariff decree. "A great boon has been conferred on commerce by the action," the British vice-consul reported to his government following passage of the new tariff. "Importing merchants will not be altogether contented as an all around increase and a considerable one has been made," he went on, but the new tariff was a great improvement over the paper tariff decree of March 1. Under the old law, if the exchange rate fell below 10,000 "and it has been as low as 6000 in 1903," the duties "were very burdensome."

The paper currency of Colombia is so unstable that fluctuations are always occurring. Merchants, therefore, never knew how they stood. With the gold tariff this whole difficulty has now been removed. It is stable, and though high, cannot be called exorbitantly so.[39]

While these important domestic political and economic reforms were being hammered out in the Chamber, the Senate was preoccupied with consideration of a transcendental international issue: whether to ratify the treaty negotiated by Marroquín's government in 1902 granting the United States the right to build an inter-oceanic canal across the Isthmus of Panama. Strangely enough, although the

37. José Camacho Carrizosa, *Estudios económicos* (Bogotá, 1903), p. 186.

38. Quijano Wallis, *Memorias*, p. 515. The quotation from Guillermo Camacho Carrizosa appears in Ospina, *Biografía*, I, p. 428.

39. Spencer S. Dickson, "Report on the Trade of Colombia (excepting the Panama District) for the Year 1903," Great Britain, Foreign Office, *Diplomatic and Consular Reports* (London, 1904), p. 32.

reform forces, especially prominent dissident Conservatives, found themselves on the losing side of the canal treaty debate, they were ultimately able to turn the issue of the loss of Panama, which occurred soon after the Senate's rejection of the treaty, to great political advantage. Within the climate of bipartisan solidarity and national soul-searching engendered by the secession of Panama, the reformists succeeded in thoroughly discrediting the Nationalists' policies of political exclusivism and managed to elect a president committed in large part to their economic and political program.

Colombia had been forced to negotiate the canal treaty under extreme duress. The Bogotá government, preoccupied with the civil war at home and bedeviled by poor communications with its ministers in Washington, gave the canal negotiations only limited attention and hoped to delay final negotiations until the war was over. Faced with the extraordinary costs of war, Marroquín's government weakened its negotiating position in 1901 by extending the New Panama Canal Company's concession for six years beyond the original 1904 termination date. As a result Colombia could not deal with the United States with a free hand, but was forced to contend with the interests and maneuverings of the representatives of the Canal Company in the negotiations. The Colombian government's position was most seriously threatened, however, by the growth of separatist feeling in Panama during the war and the fact that during the last year of the fighting revolutionary forces controlled much of the department. Reporting on his impressions of the situation after visiting Panama in February, 1902, Miguel Abadía Méndez, en route to assume the Colombian ambassadorship in Chile, stressed the deteriorating military and political situation and concluded his assessment with these prophetic words. "The Isthmus is lost for Colombia; it is painful to say it, but it is true. Here Yankee influence predominates, and all Panamanians, with a few exceptions, are capable of selling the Canal, the Isthmus, and even their own mother."[40]

In contrast, the United States negotiated the canal treaty from a position of strength. The United States had initially favored a Nicaraguan canal route, and even in 1902 some influential politicians in the United States threatened to abandon the Panama route and build the canal in Nicaragua should Colombia fail to approve satisfactory terms for a Panamanian canal. Even those who considered threat of a Nicaraguan canal a bluff were forced to admit that the United States had the military strength and perhaps the will to insure a successful secession of Panama should the Bogotá government refuse to meet the United States' demands.

40. Miguel Abadía Méndez to [José Manuel Marroquín?], Panama, February 22, 1902, MDT, ACH.

The terms of the final treaty signed in September, 1902, by Colombian Chargé d'Affaires Tomás Herrán and United States Secretary of State John Hay reflected the disproportionate strength of the two countries' negotiating positions and placed the Colombian government in a dilemma. The treaty clearly compromised Colombia's sovereignty in Panama by granting the United States control of a strip of land across the Isthmus in perpetuity. Yet failure to approve the treaty would encourage the separatist tendencies of the majority of Panamanian political leaders who were bent on securing the United States-built canal at any cost. Moreover, rejection of the treaty would aggravate relations with the United States, the country which by 1903 had become the largest buyer of Colombian coffee exports and a primary source of the foreign capital which many Colombians sought as a panacea for Colombian political instability in the postwar period.

These last concerns were paramount in the minds of those favoring ratification of the treaty, most influential among them Rafael Reyes. Reyes early developed a concrete analysis of the economic benefits Colombia could derive from a canal treaty with the United States. In a confidential letter to loyal supporters written at the end of 1901, he revealed that he had talked with Theodore Roosevelt about the canal and had conferred with a United States congressman "who has ties with great banking concerns in the United States and I have come to hope that through these concerns we can make a favorable deal that would permit us to valorize our paper money while at the same time placing us in a position to master the frightening fiscal and economic crisis which grips the nation."[41] Reyes reiterated these ideas in a letter to Marroquín in July, 1902. At that time he insisted that Colombia must "make sure that the Canal is constructed through Panama" while getting as much in payment as possible in order to "control the frightening economic ruin in which the nation finds itself."[42] Upon his return to Colombia in May, 1903, Reyes worked for approval of the canal and served as an informal liaison between Marroquín and the United States legation in Bogotá.[43]

For men like Reyes, then, the question of infringements on Colombian sovereignty was subordinate to the issue of economic reconstruction. Such was not the case for men like Miguel Antonio Caro, who spearheaded the successful opposition to the treaty in the Senate in 1903. Caro argued that the treaty was unconstitutional, alienating as it did a piece of Colombian territory. For Caro the questions of antagonizing the United States, encouraging Panamanian separatism,

41. Rafael Reyes to M. J. Ortiz Durana and D. A. de Castro. Mexico, Dec. 13, 1901, MDT, ACH.
42. Confidential letter from Reyes to Marroquín, Mexico, July 6, 1902, MDT, ACH.
43. Favell, "Antecedents," p. 233.

and facilitating economic reconstruction were secondary to the principle of sovereignty at issue in the treaty. The majority report of the Senate's study commission, greatly influenced by Caro, proposed amendments to the treaty designed to protect Colombian sovereignty on the Isthmus and safeguard Colombia's financial interests in the canal.[44] Caro's position in the Senate debate was strengthened by the uncompromising attitude of the United States government, which informed the Colombian government that it expected the Senate to approve the treaty without modifications and in a leaked ciphered telegram threatened retaliation if the treaty were not ratified.[45]

Marroquín fully appreciated the dilemma posed by the terms of the treaty. He had never favored United States interests in the canal. Writing a Conservative military leader in Barranquilla in 1901, Marroquín stated that his own position and that of the majority of "good Conservatives" was to "leave the project to the Yankees only as a last resort, and then only if our sovereignty does not suffer."[46] Although Marroquín used the treaty to enlist the good offices of the United States in negotiating an end to the war,[47] after the conclusion of the fighting he washed his hands of it and refused to recommend the treaty to the Senate or fight for its approval.[48]

In the end, the sovereignty issue, which Caro developed with eloquence and logical force, convinced the Senate to unanimously reject ratification of the treaty. A joint committee was then set up with the Chamber to draft a policy statement to outline Colombia's position in future negotiations. The joint committee adopted the revisions to protect Colombian sovereignty proposed by the Senate committee's majority report. The policy statement also called for better financial terms for Colombia.[49]

The Senate's rejection of the Herrán-Hay treaty was a noble, but

44. Among other changes the report called for a previous understanding with the New French Canal Company regarding transfer of the concession to Colombia before consideration of the treaty, amendments ensuring Colombian sovereignty over the canal zone and the ports of Panama and Colón, and a clause stipulating the reversion to Colombia of all rights and property if the canal were not completed within fourteen years.

45. The United States chargé d'affaires believed that the threat and the announcement by Panamanian congressmen that the department would revolt in the event the treaty were not approved, would influence the Senate to approve the treaty. Beaupré to Hay, Bogotá, July 5, 1903, USNA.

46. Marroquín to Manuel María Castro U., Bogotá, Aug. 12, 1901, MDT, ACH.

47. Marroquín's government argued that only with the end of the war could congress be convened to consider the treaty. Favell, "Antecedents," p. 262.

48. Marroquín stated his position explicitly in speeches on January 1 and June 20, 1903, *Diario Oficial*, No. 11,784 (January 2, 1903) and No. 11,861 (June 22, 1903).

49. The Herrán-Hay treaty had provided that the United States pay Colombia $10 million initially and yearly installments of $250,000; the policy statement insisted on an initial payment of $20 million, yearly installments of $400,000, plus payment to Colombia by the Canal Company of $10 million. Favell, "Antecedents," p. 257.

fateful decision. Within two months Panama seceded from Colombia with the connivance of the officials of the New Panama Canal Company and the backing of the United States government. Colombian military and diplomatic efforts to recover the lost department ended in failure, thwarted by United States naval units and Washington policy makers. The loss of Panama was partly a consequence of the War of the Thousand Days, for the war had gravely weakened and complicated the Colombians' negotiating position and stimulated separatist sentiment on the Isthmus. Moreover, those involved in the secessionist movement used the war as the primary justification for their actions. Typical of the thinking of apologists of the secession was that of Phillippe Bunau-Varilla, former official of the New Panama Canal Company and first Panamanian ambassador to the United States. His first official communication to United States Secretary of State John Hay ended with this bombastic justification of the United States action.

> In spreading her protecting wings over the territory of our Republic, the American Eagle has sanctified it; it has rescued it from the barbarism of unnecessary and wasteful civil wars, to consecrate it to the destiny assigned to it by Providence—to the service of humanity and the progress of civilization.[50]

The loss of Panama stunned Colombians. Over the years several prominent Colombian officials and politicians had warned of the possible loss of the department, but the event itself, coming so soon after the rejection of the treaty, shocked even those who had long feared the separation of the department. Colombian leaders' first reaction was to solve the problem by military force. But when efforts to land Colombian troops in Panama were blocked by United States warships and even hotheads realized the futility of war with the United States, Colombians turned to diplomatic efforts to recover the department. In late November Marroquín approved plans to send a select commission of four prestigious political and military leaders to Panama and the United States in an effort to salvage something of the situation for Colombia.[51]

The commission failed to achieve its objectives[52] but a look at its composition reveals the growing political influence of bipartisan re-

50. Phillippe Bunau-Varilla to John Hay [Washington?], November 7, 1903. Bunau-Varilla Papers, Manuscript Division, United States Library of Congress.

51. An undated copy of the commission's instructions appears in MDT, ACH.

52. The commissioners originally planned to journey to Panama and entertained the idea of fomenting a pro-Colombian revolt on the Isthmus. When that plan proved unrealistic they went on to Washington, where, after weeks of diplomatic snubs and silence concerning their mission in the Washington press, they wrote a spirited denunciation of United States actions which documented Colombia's legal claims and demanded retribution.

formist forces and demonstrates the extent of the spirit of political conciliation affecting Colombian political leaders as they united to face the crisis affecting the nation. None of the commissioners had supported the vindictive policies of the intransigent Conservatives during the last months of the war and the early postwar period. All had advocated reform of Regeneration economic and political policies. Heading the commission was Rafael Reyes, associated with Conservative reformist forces since the election of 1897 and a man who, by staying away from Colombia during the war, was untainted by the excesses of partisan hatreds generated by the conflict. Jorge Holguín, a relative and close political associate of Reyes, had served in the last Regeneration governments but had advocated political and fiscal reforms and had supported the ill-fated reformist coup of September, 1901. Pedro Nel Ospina was the third commissioner, a man closely identified with the politics of the *antioqueño* Historical Conservatives and one of the leaders of the September, 1901 coup. The fourth member of the commission was Lucas Caballero, the long-time Liberal critic of Regeneration political and economic policies. A peace Liberal who had nevertheless joined the revolution, Caballero had served as Benjamín Herrera's chief of staff during the Panama campaign of 1901–1902.

While the special bipartisan commission to deal with the Panama question labored unsuccessfully to vindicate Colombia's interests, bipartisan forces favoring political reconciliation and reform pressured Marroquín to call a special constituent assembly attended by representatives of all parties to reform the nation's institutions and cope with the reconstruction of the nation prostrated by civil war and mutilated by the loss of one of its richest departments. As early as November 9, as news reaching Bogotá confirmed the secession of Panama, one hundred representatives chosen from among the three political parties, Liberals, Historical Conservatives, and Nationalists, presented Marroquín with a statement affirming their support of his government and urging him to convoke a national constituent congress "in which all the political parties of the nation are represented" to ratify any agreements reached by the Reyes commission and to seek "the immediate solution to the other national problems."[53] Reyes himself apparently endorsed this idea on the eve of his journey to the coast en route to Panama and Washington.[54] Despite this pressure, Marroquín steadfastly refused to call such a constituent assembly,

53. Daniel J. Reyes *et al.* to José Manuel Marroquín y miembros de la misión nombrada para Panamá, Bogotá, November 9, 1903, MDT, ACH.

54. José Manuel Marroquín to Ramón González Valencia, Bogotá, December 3, 1903, MDT, ACH.

insisting, as he had done throughout the war, that to call such a congress exceeded his constitutional authority.

Having failed to win Marroquín's approval for a special constituent congress, reformists focused their hopes for reform on the congressional and presidential elections of 1904. In February Liberals of all factions petitioned Marroquín to issue a directive to the proper government functionaries urging them to name representatives of all political parties to municipal and departmental electoral boards. Unfortunately, the Liberals noted, reform forces in the congress of 1903 had failed to pass an electoral law which would have made appointment of Liberals to all electoral boards mandatory, but, they urged, Marroquín could achieve the same effect through moral suasion.[55] Marroquín refused to issue the directive. His attitude revealed his basic inconformity with the reformist efforts of the Chamber in the past and boded ill for the electoral success of reformist elements in the upcoming congressional elections.

Realizing that they would probably win few seats in the next congress, reform forces concentrated on the crucial presidential election of 1904. The man chosen to lead the nation for the next six years, they reasoned, would decisively affect the success of reformist policies. During the campaign moderates and extremists proposed the names of several candidates including those of Marroquín himself, Ramón González Valencia, Pedro Nel Ospina, and Aristides Fernández. As the April election approached, however, support coalesced around the candidacies of Rafael Reyes and Joaquín F. Vélez. Each candidate represented a faction of the Conservative party and each embraced a distinct approach to the problems of the postwar period.

On the one hand, enjoying the support of many Nationalists and exclusivist Conservatives, was Joaquín F. Vélez. Seventy-two years old in 1904, Vélez was a native of Cartagena. Educated at San Bartolomé and the Colegio del Rosario in Bogotá, he had earned a doctorate in law. As a young man he held important posts under the Conservative regimes of the late 1850's and early 1860's. With the advent of Liberal political hegemony he returned to private life in Cartagena where he founded a secondary school. An early supporter of Núñez, Vélez spent most of the Regeneration abroad, where he served as Colombian representative to the Vatican and negotiated the Concordat which restored Church privileges and regularized Colombian relations with the Vatican.[56] Vélez returned to Colombia in 1901 to serve as military governor of the coastal department of Bolívar where he

55. Nicolás Esguerra, *et al.* to José Manuel Marroquín, Bogotá, February 16, 1904, MDT, ACH.

56. Ospina, *Diccionario*, III, 932-34.

instituted draconian measures to crush the Liberal revolt.[57] Vélez had supported Fernández's policy of no political concessions to the Revolution and early opposed the reformists' idea of convoking an assembly of delegates drawn from all political parties to end the war and structure the peace.[58] A doctrinaire, uncompromising Conservative of authoritarian manner he was widely recognized, even by his political opponents, as an energetic and honest administrator.[59]

Vélez was particularly alarmed at the bipartisan approach to politics long advocated by Reyes and his followers. Such an attitude was dangerous, he wrote Marroquín in May, 1902, because it tended to blur the distinctive programs of the parties and favored the growth of personalism.

> [W]ithout common ideals to guide the group of men formed by the projected union of good men from all parties, the newly formed party would choose one man as a guide. Thus would a series of personalist parties begin, parties which are the source of the vast immorality, which today we see in other countries.[60]

Rafael Reyes, whose candidacy was supported publicly by moderate Conservatives and privately by most Liberals, was a man whose life and thought contrasted sharply with that of Vélez. In his mid-50's in 1904 Reyes had received little formal education and was known as a man of action who had made his fortune in commerce and distinguished himself as a military leader. Throughout his career, he revealed a deep commitment to the goal of developing Colombia through the importation of foreign technology and expansion of the export economy. As a youth he had left his native Boyacá for southern Colombia where, along with his brothers, he made a fortune in the export-import trade during the quinine boom. Not content with that success, Reyes committed his family's fortune with almost messianic fervor to an ambitious, ill-fated project to develop the Putumayo Basin in Colombia's southeastern jungles. After exploring the area and linking it to Europe by steam navigation via the Amazon River, he brought hundreds of Colombian colonists into the Putumayo to cultivate and collect tropical products for export. Despite his determina-

57. According to Julio H. Palacio, Vélez's measures against Liberals were unprecedented in Colombia. Vélez prohibited Liberals from leaving their houses, jailed and deported Liberals suspected of complicity in the revolt, and assigned Liberals forced loans which were covered by public sale of their property if not paid. Palacio, "Historia," *El Tiempo*, March 14, 1943.

58. Joaquín F. Vélez to José Manuel Marroquín, Barranquilla, May 16, 1902, MDT, ACH.

59. Ramón González Valencia to José Manuel Marroquín, Pamplona, Santander, November 11, 1903, MDT, ACH.

60. Joaquín F. Vélez to José Manuel Marroquín, Barranquilla, May 16, 1902, MDT, ACH.

tion, after ten years of struggle, that effort ended in failure. During the civil war of 1885 Reyes played a crucial role in securing the triumph of Conservative forces on the Isthmus of Panama, and his military reputation was secured by his decisive leadership of Conservative armies in the Revolution of 1895. Although he returned to Colombia during his unsuccessful bid for the presidency in 1897, he spent most of the late 1890's in Europe where, as Colombian ambassador to France, he worked tirelessly to interest European investors in Colombia and promote Colombian exports.[61] During the War of the Thousand Days he remained abroad, steadfastly refusing to become involved in the fighting.

In 1901 Reyes was named, along with Carlos Martínez Silva, Colombian representative to the Second Pan American Conference. The conference was held in Mexico and Reyes's speeches at the meeting revealed the extent of his admiration for the material progress which was transforming the face of the Mexican nation under the aegis of the dictator Porfirio Díaz. In one speech, subsequently much criticized in the orthodox Conservative Colombian press, Reyes exclaimed:

> In times past it was the Cross or the Koran, the sword or the book that accomplished the conquests of civilization; today it is the powerful locomotive, flying over the shining rail, breathing like a volcano, that awakens peoples to progress, well-being and liberty ... and those who do not conform to that progress it crushes beneath its wheels.[62]

The quotation reveals the influence of positivisitic and Darwinian ideas on Reyes's thinking: those nations which embraced the new technology would become civilized and would progress; those nations that did not would be eliminated.

In the excerpt quoted Reyes appears ready to abandon the ideological struggle which had pitted Liberals against Conservatives in Colombia throughout the nineteenth century. Material progress supersedes that sterile debate, he seems to imply; it is technical and material advance (the locomotive), not perfect ideological and political systems (the Conservatives' Cross, the Liberals' books), that leads to progress, well-being and liberty. Reyes's positivism offered a way to transcend the old Liberal-Conservative philosophical debate and promised a new approach to the political and economic problems facing the nation. It was this positivism which served as the ideologi-

61. Eduardo Lemaitre, *Rafael Reyes. Biografía de un gran colombiano*, 3rd ed. (Bogotá, 1967), pp. 184-85. Lemaitre's biography stresses Reyes's commercial activities and developmentalist cast of mind.
62. Quoted in *La Opinión*, February 10, 1902.

cal cement for the bipartisan reformists who flocked to his presidential banner.[63]

The image of the locomotive chosen by Reyes to convey his ideas was not merely symbolic. To be sure the locomotive, the most impressive product of contemporary Western technology, conveys his notion of speed, power, irresistible force. But railroad construction itself had become the cornerstone of his plans for revitalizing Colombia, a panacea for all the nation's ills. Moreover, as he was well aware, railroad construction in Latin America at the turn of the century implied a commitment to an integral system of political economy. Railways could only be built with foreign capital, capital which could only be attracted if investors felt the "climate" for investment in a given nation was favorable and the necessary guarantees were forthcoming. Finally, the case of Porfirian Mexico and other Latin American nations demonstrated that railways were built primarily to develop the export economy and served to fix Latin America's role in an international economy as a producer of primary goods in exchange for foreign manufactures.

While Reyes's attitudes and plans for Colombia's future were most forcefully expressed in public at the Mexico Conference, his views had long been appreciated by Colombian political leaders, and had been articulated as early as his bid for the presidency in 1897. Orthodox Conservatives branded him as a materialist and blasted his belief that material progress rather than Christian morality determined the well-being of nations.[64] Conservative intransigents like Vélez feared his resolve to bring men "of good will" from all political parties into his government. On the other hand, bipartisan export-import interests hailed his political and economic plans and organized to support his candidacy. In February, 1904, Liberal merchant and banker José María Quijano Wallis organized the bipartisan Junta de Concordancia Nacional, which became a powerful source of support for the position advocated by Reyes.[65]

Given the nature of Colombian elections at the time, both sides realized that the attitude of Marroquín's government toward the can-

63. A fully developed expression of the ideological position of the bipartisan coalition supporting Reyes can be found in the pro-Reyes broadside written after he took office by José María Quijano Wallis, Luis Martínez Silva, and Lucian Herrera preserved in Manrique, ACH. The authors decried the way Colombians, "como pueblo decendiente de latinos" had devoted preferential attention to speculative thought and had engaged in interminable political discussion, "inspirados más por instinto de raza é imaginación tropical que por el espiritu práctico de los países del Norte." Colombians had neglected "los verdaderos intereses de un pueblo, como son los morales, industriales y económicos y los que informan el progreso material. . . ."

64. This was the burden of *La Opinión's* indictment of Reyes's Mexico speeches in the February 10, 1902 issue.

65. *El Nuevo Tiempo*, Feb. 3 and 8, 1904.

didates might well determine the outcome of the election. Marroquín may have originally favored Vélez, but when Vélez announced that he planned to launch an investigation into the loss of Panama, Marroquín reportedly withdrew his support for his candidacy.[66] Government indecisiveness undoubtedly contributed to the closeness of the vote. Initial returns gave a slight edge to Vélez, but the final tabulation, which included twelve electoral votes for Reyes from the isolated district of Padilla on the Guajiran Peninsula, furnished Reyes with a plurality.[67] The voting in Padilla could be shown to have transpired in a most irregular manner, however, and the legality of the Padilla returns was hotly contested by supporters of the two candidates.[68] Finally, after months of feverish behind-the-scenes negotiation, the Gran Concejo Electoral announced its decision just three days before the new president was scheduled to be inaugurated. The Gran Concejo declared the Padilla electoral votes valid and proclaimed Reyes president-elect.[69] The result probably reflected the relative strength of the political forces much more accurately than did the close electoral returns. Vélez's supporters included many government officials placed in office during the war and the heyday of the intransigent Conservatives in the immediate postwar period. Vélez also enjoyed considerable backing in the Church and military hierarchies. But Reyes also had significant Church and military support and unlike Vélez, he was popular with Conservative rank-and-file.[70] More important, Reyes enjoyed the tacit support of the majority of Liberal leaders and the decided support of export-import interests. Vélez's supporters must have recognized that the decision of Gran Concejo reflected Reyes's popular mandate. At any rate they organized no resistance to the Concejo's decision.

66. At least this is the explanation advanced by Lemaitre, *Reyes*, p. 267.

67. Other candidates receiving small numbers of electoral votes included Pedro Nel Ospina, Miguel Antonio Caro, and Aristides Fernández. Ramón González Valencia, who figured as vice-presidential candidate on both the Reyes and Vélez tickets, was elected by a wide margin.

68. Faced with conflicting instructions on how to vote, the local strongman of the district had forced electors to sign a blank ballot. He then journeyed to Barranquilla where supporters of Reyes induced him to cast the twelve votes for their candidate. See the accounts of the election and the circumstances surrounding the Padilla register in Palacio, "Historia," *El Tiempo*, August 15 and 23, 1943, and Luis Martínez Delgado, *República de Colombia, 1885-1910*, 2 vols. (Bogotá, 1970).

69. The tortuous deliberations of the Concejo can be followed in the *Diario Oficial*, Nos. 12,131 to 12,136, July 26 to August 1, 1904, and No. 12,150, August 25, 1904. A colorful description of the final drama on August 4 and an account of the popular demonstration of support for Reyes appears in the Liberal paper *El Comercio*, August 8, 1904.

70. On July 22 in an incident which recalls similar actions at other critical junctures of Colombian political life, large numbers of lower-class Reyes supporters invaded the Senate gallery shouting *vivas* to Reyes and Francisco Groot (the reformist Conservative capitalist) and *mueras* and *abajos* to Senators Vélez and Caro. Joaquín F. Vélez, "Protesta," *Anales del Senado de 1904*, p. 9.

The election of Reyes to the presidency was a seminal victory for bipartisan export-import interests and initiated a new era in Colombian politics. Following the election politics transcended the old Regeneration debate over the issue of Liberal participation in government and the merits of economic and monetary policies at odds with accepted orthodoxy among the leading nations of the West. During the Quinquenio, as Reyes's five-year government is called in Colombian history, the nation's most important political factions accepted the principle of Liberal representation in government and demonstrated a commitment to developing the nation through the expansion of the export economy. Conflict between Reyes and many of his initial supporters developed not over the appropriateness of these political and economic goals, but over the best means to achieve them. In the years following Reyes's election bipartisan export-import interests fought the final struggles to consolidate their control of politics and institute their economic policies. By 1910 that process was complete and the pieces of the new political and economic order which was to guide Colombia through more than three decades of political stability and expansion of the export sector were finally fixed in place.

Chapter IX

The Reyes Quinquenio, 1904-1909

It is in the context of Colombia's continuing economic malaise and the legacy of a savage, destructive civil war that the nature of Reyes's economic and political policies must be understood. For if Reyes pursued a policy of political reconciliation and reform, and if he sought to govern in the interest of agriculturalists, merchants, and nascent industrialists, he was to resort to authoritarian and statist means to achieve his goals. Consequently, although Reyes served to advance many of the political and economic principles long advocated by bipartisan export-import interests, he was ultimately viewed by these groups as an obstacle to the full implementation of their liberal republican political philosophy and their laissez-faire economic beliefs. Ironically, as Reyes surmounted the political and economic difficulties confronting the bipartisan export-import interests in the postwar period, his usefulness to these groups declined. By 1909 export-import interests had abandoned Reyes and organized to install a government faithful to their political and economic principles.

Among the most important of Reyes's early political initiatives were his military reforms.[1] These reforms both helped to consolidate bipartisan support for his regime and contributed to the establishment of political stability in the postwar period. Soon after taking office Reyes implemented a program of weapons collection which disarmed many of the local strongmen who conserved large quantities of arms after the war came to an end. At the same time the program virtually eliminated banditry in the rural areas.[2] Reyes also sought more effective enforcement of the principle of universal military service, a policy designed to make the ranks of the army truly bipartisan in composition. Moreover, through his procurement of a Chilean military mission, contracted at his instruction by Uribe Uribe in 1906, and the

1. Secondary literature on the Quinquenio is extremely limited. The most useful single work is Lemaitre's biography of Reyes, cited previously. Baldomero Sanín Cano's *Administración Reyes, 1904-1909* (Lausanne, 1909) is sketchy and adulatory. The recent biography of Reyes by Mario Perico Ramírez, *Reyes* (Tunja, 1974) adds little to previously published accounts.

2. Lemaitre, *Reyes*, pp. 291-92; Holguín y Caro, *Mucho en serio*, p. 63; Sanín Cano, *Administración Reyes*, p. 42. In his message to congress on July 20, 1909 acting president Jorge Holguín claimed that as a result of Reyes's arms collection of 1904, 65,505 guns and 1,138,649 bullets were returned to the national armories. *Diario Oficial*, Nos. 13,737 and 13,738 (July 21, 1909).

establishment of army and naval officer training schools in Bogotá and Cartagena in 1907, he began the professionalization of the Colombian military in an effort to make the armed forces national institutions, beholden to no political party.[3] In addition, he fulfilled a long-standing demand of the prewar reform forces by approving a sizable reduction of the standing army.[4] In another effort to economize while promoting economic development, Reyes ordered the Bogotá garrison to work on the construction of the Girardot-Bogotá railway.[5]

Another of Reyes's political innovations was to break up Colombia's traditional departments into smaller political and administrative units. A new department of Nariño was carved out of southern Cauca, southern Tolima became the department of Huila. The department of Caldas was created out of an area mainly under the former jurisdiction of Antioquia. Several new departments were also set up in the Eastern Cordillera in the old departments of Cundinamarca, Boyacá, and Santander; but unlike the new departments created in western and southern Colombia, most did not survive the Quinquenio.[6] Reyes's policy of territorial division was designed to serve several purposes. Part of the centralist tendencies of a government which also nationalized important departmental revenues, it aimed primarily at weakening regional power centers which had often revolted against central authority in the past and sought to quiet separatist rumblings (especially audible in Cauca and Antioquia) following the secession of Panama. Reyes hoped also to encourage the economic development of subregions by giving them a distinct administrative and political life and a voice in national political institutions.

Reyes's most important contribution to the future political stability of the nation, however, was his effort to institutionalize the principle of Liberal representation in government. He began by naming Liberals to important executive positions within his government. Lucas Caballero and Enrique Cortés, both closely identified with export-import interests, were named to his first cabinet, and although they would leave to occupy important diplomatic posts within a few months, he continued to call Liberals into his ministry throughout his tenure in office. In addition to cabinet posts, Liberals were frequently appointed to lesser positions in the executive branch during the Quinquenio and also served as judges and electoral officials.[7]

3. The Chilean mission, in turn influenced by German training, arrived in 1907 and remained in Colombia until 1915.

4. Maximum troop levels were fixed at five thousand men by Law 31 of 1904, *Anales del Senado de 1904*, p. 102.

5. Palacio, "Historia," *El Tiempo*, Jan. 23, 1944.

6. An exception was the later division of Santander into two departments.

7. L. E. Nieto Caballero in Abel Cruz Santos, *Economía y hacienda pública. De la república unitaria a la economía del medio siglo*, 2 vols. (Bogotá, 1966), II, 107.

Reyes also appointed Liberal leaders to prestigious diplomatic positions, a policy which, like the domestic political appointments, not only discouraged potentially dangerous opposition, but satisfied the Liberals' thirst for public posts and gave them a sense of participation in the formation and implementation of government policy. In early 1905 Uribe Uribe was designated Colombian ambassador to Brazil, Argentina, and Chile.[8] The aforementioned Enrique Cortés was named special envoy to Washington in 1905 and served as Colombian ambassador to the United States from 1906 to 1908. Carlos Arturo Torres filled the post of Colombian consul in Liverpool throughout the Quinquenio, and Juan E. Manrique served for a time as Colombian ambassador to France.

Reyes further demonstrated his commitment to Liberal participation in government by naming Benjamín Herrera to the sensitive post of commander of Colombian troops on the Venezuelan border when tensions escalated between the two countries in 1905. In February, 1906, following an abortive attempt to assassinate Reyes (which Reyes believed was instigated by intransigent Conservatives) Reyes resolved to name Herrera minister of war. Although Reyes abandoned this initiative at the insistence of a delegation of retired Conservative army officers and the pleadings of José Manuel Marroquín and Archbishop Bernardo Herrera, Benjamín Herrera continued to support the government and later in the year accepted a diplomatic mission to Venezuela.[9]

Reyes's inclusion of Liberals in his government set an important precedent, but infinitely more significant was his establishment of the principle of minority representation in the legislative bodies of the nation. Only two Liberals had won seats in the Congress of 1904, but after Reyes dissolved that body and instituted a National Constituent Assembly to ratify his executive decisions in early 1905, one-third of the seats in that new legislative body were occupied by Liberals.[10] The principle of minority representation was written into the constitution of the nation by the Assembly in the Acto Reformatorio No. 8 of April 13, 1905. Article 4 of that constitutional amendment provided that

8. Uribe Uribe spent most of his years abroad in Brazil, where he dutifully studied the Brazilian coffee industry and reported to the newly formed Society of Coffee Growers in Bogotá on Brazilian efforts to improve and stabilize world coffee prices by regulating the quantity of Brazilian coffee exports. Rafael Uribe Uribe, *Estudios sobre el café* (Bogotá, 1952).

9. Palacio, "Historia," *El Tiempo*, June 25, 1944.

10. By the terms of Reyes's Executive Decree No. 29 of February 1, 1905, two Conservatives and one Liberal were named to the National Assembly from each department. Conservatives chosen were men supportive of Reyes from several factions within the party. A list of the deputies to the National Assembly appears in *Anales de la Asamblea Nacional de 1905*, pp. 1-2.

In all popular elections held to elect members to public bodies and in the naming of Senators, the right of minority representation is acknowledged, and the law will determine the specific means to implement [this right].

To implement the reform Article 33 of Law 42 of April 28, 1905, provided that in any election of representative officials the number of functionaries to be elected be divided by three, that votes be cast for two-thirds of the functionaries to be elected, and that those candidates with the highest number of votes be declared elected until the requisite number of functionaries was met. Votes would be cast separately for principals and alternates on the same ballot. The reform thus insured minority representation, for the dominant party could elect only two-thirds of the functionaries for any representative body. Ironically, this political reform which was of transcendental importance for the future political stability of the nation and which was incorporated into the Constitutional Reform of 1910 after Reyes's fall from power, was accompanied by another constitutional amendment which boded ill for republican government in Colombia. The Acto Reformatorio No. 5 of March 30, 1905, extended Reyes's presidency, which by 1905 had developed into a full-blown dictatorship, for four years beyond the previous constitutional limit.[11]

The trade-off of political reform for grants of extraordinary executive power, so strikingly illustrated in the case of minority representation, was characteristic of the politics of the Quinquenio. Liberals proved to be especially willing to participate in such quid pro quo. For example, Uribe Uribe was a strong supporter of the fiscal plan presented by Reyes to the congress of 1904 to deal with the nation's enduring monetary problems and the government's fiscal penury. When congress balked at approving the measure, Representative Uribe Uribe urged Reyes to implement the reforms by fiat if approval was not forthcoming from congress.[12] In this respect Uribe Uribe's attitude was typical of Liberal leaders during the first years of the Quinquenio. Reflecting on the general support extended Reyes during the period, Juan E. Manrique later wrote that it was natural that the party, defeated in war, had embraced Reyes's program of *concordia nacional.* After the loss of Panama, he added, everyone was convinced of the need to reform the nation's institutions "by extraordinary means."[13]

While most Liberals initially tolerated or encouraged Reyes's as-

11. *Ibid.*, pp. 275, 151, 274.

12. Palacio, "Historia," *El Tiempo*, Oct. 3, 1943.

13. Juan Evangelista Manrique to Carlos Arturo Torres, Madrid, April 8, 1909, Manrique, ACH. A major exception to this trend was Domingo Esguerra who never approved of Reyes's policies and would form the vanguard of Liberal opposition to Reyes in the last years of the Quinquenio.

sumption of dictatorial powers to implement his political and economic reforms, some Historical Conservative leaders early became disenchanted with Reyes's violation of republican principles. Several Historical Conservatives joined the political opposition and participated in the abortive conspiracies against Reyes which punctuated the history of the Quinquenio.[14]

For export-import interests of both parties Reyes's economic policies proved no less problematical than his political initiatives. On the one hand Reyes worked to follow sound principles of fiscal administration, stabilize the monetary system, return to the gold standard, restore Colombian credit abroad, attract foreign capital, improve the nation's transportation system, and encourage export agriculture. All of these goals were heartily approved by export-import interests. But to implement his ambitious program in a period of economic stagnation, Reyes was to pursue policies at variance with some of the principles of orthodox liberal economics. Moreover, at the same time that he worked to foment the export economy, Reyes pursued a conscious policy of aid to domestic industry.

During his administration Reyes enjoyed no large fiscal benefits from an expanding coffee economy. As Figure 9:1 indicates, throughout the Quinquenio the volume of Colombian coffee exports remained virtually constant. At the same time, continuing low prices on the world market, although slightly improved over wartime lows, limited the amount of foreign exchange earned from coffee exports.

Close inspection of Figure 9:1 reveals, however, that during Reyes's tenure in office, coffee cultivation in Colombia expanded considerably. After 1911 the volume of coffee exports, which had remained fairly uniform during the years 1905-1909, rose substantially. The yearly increases after 1911 are the result of the cumulative effect on production as coffee trees planted during the Quinquenio matured and began to produce.

The expansion of coffee cultivation during the Quinquenio obeyed a series of factors that combined to produce a fundamental shift in the axis of Colombian coffee production away from the eastern cordillera (Santander, Boyacá, and Cundinamarca) to the central cordillera (Antioquia, northern Tolima, and northeastern Cauca). Although, as Figure 9:1 shows, there was a modest improvement in average price levels, the data in the figure mask the importance of regional price

14. Historical Conservatives figured among those who, after protesting Reyes's closing of the extraordinary session of congress in late 1904, were exiled to the isolated town of Oracué by Reyes's order. Luís Martínez Silva was involved in a plot against Reyes in late 1905. Details of these events were given in Lemaitre, *Reyes,* pp. 295-300, 334-35. For an extensive account of his own and other Historical Conservatives' opposition to Reyes, see Carlos E. Restrepo's *Orientación republicana,* 2 vols. (Medellín [1917?] and 1930), I, 215-82.

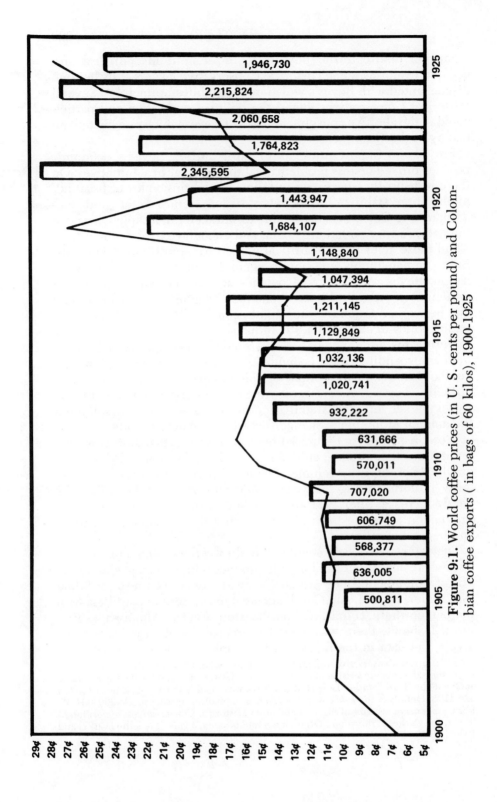

Figure 9:1. World coffee prices (in U. S. cents per pound) and Colombian coffee exports (in bags of 60 kilos), 1900-1925

differentials. As noted in Chapter II, coffee produced in the department of Santander fetched much lower prices on the world market than did the superior coffees of the other main coffee-growing regions of Colombia. Coffee price quotations reproduced from a commercial publication of Enrique Cortés and Company in London in 1904 subdivided Colombian coffees into two main categories: "green, fine coffees" from Cundinamarca, Antioquia and Cauca; and "pallid coffees" from the provinces of Cúcuta, Bucaramanga, and Ocaña in Santander. Prices for the former were quoted at levels about 50 percent higher than those for the Santander coffees.[15] Coffee growing in Santander was also hampered by the high cost of transportation and Venezuelan transit taxes. Other factors, especially the existence of suitable land and the availability of labor, favored coffee expansion in the central cordillera. Large tracts of unclaimed public domain land excellent for coffee cultivation encouraged the migration of thousands of families from central Antioquia into the coffee frontier to the south. Many of the new coffee-producing units were family-size farms which capitalized on the labor of women and children in the labor-intensive process of gathering, cleaning, and selecting the coffee beans.[16]

But if the expansion and regional shift of coffee cultivation in Colombia during the Quinquenio obeyed geographic and social forces beyond Reyes's control, his policies also worked in several ways to encourage the expansion of coffee cultivation. While the effect of such intangibles as political stability, monetary reform, and fiscal responsibility at home and abroad is hard to measure, Reyes's transportation and communications policies and his subventions to coffee exporters were a real boon to the coffee industry. Unfortunately for him, however, his government did not remain in power long enough to reap the secondary financial benefits of expanded coffee cultivation.

Deprived of expanded revenue from the coffee economy throughout his administration, Reyes turned to unorthodox, statist means to solve the fiscal problems inherited from the previous administration and finance his own ambitious projects for economic development. The tolerance with which import-export groups initially accepted his economic reforms reflected their appreciation of the magnitude of the problems he faced and their general agreement over the indispensable nature of the economic goals he pursued. Yet a review of the economic policies he developed during the period 1904-1909 not only demonstrates the initial support for his government by export-import interests, but also reveals the origins of the opposition to Reyes among

15. *El Nuevo Tiempo*, May 21, 1904.
16. The magnitude and nature of this shift are treated in Beyer, "Coffee Industry" and in Parsons's classic study, *Antioqueño Colonization*.

these same groups and clarifies the economic issues on which his opponents would mobilize to topple him from power in 1909.

Of course some of the economic policies and programs instituted by Reyes were of a noncontroversial nature and were consistently endorsed by export-import interests. For example, during his reorganization of government finance Reyes rationalized accounting and payment procedures and established the principle of approving only those expenditures for which the government had on hand sufficient funds for payment. As a result discounts on government obligations and long delays in payment were virtually eliminated. He also initiated the collection of economic statistics and established institutions for commercial and industrial training.[17]

Another of his non-controversial policies was his expeditious handling of foreign and domestic claims against the government for wartime damages, claims which during the first years of the Quinquenio constituted a significant drain on government revenues. Payment of domestic claims was made in bonds to be redeemed gradually by special funds set aside by congress. Foreign claims were settled by issuing special bonds earning 6 percent annual interest which could be used in payment of customs duties. Eight percent of the gross income from customs duties collected on the Atlantic coast and the Cúcuta customs houses was set aside to retire these bonds. Payment of foreign claims consumed a significant portion of Colombian customs revenues during the first three years of the Quinquenio, but by mid-1907 an official of Reyes's government could announce that most of the government's obligations to foreign claimants had been canceled by the customs houses of the nation.[18]

A much more critical and controversial economic problem facing Reyes upon his assumption of power was the state of continuing crisis in the nation's monetary system. Although Law 33 had legalized the stipulation of foreign gold currencies in contracts and established the dual principles of amortization of paper money and eventual return to the gold standard, by 1905 little progress had been made toward amortization, and the law had proved powerless to eliminate the problem of considerable daily fluctuation in the exchange rate.[19] By 1905 less than two-thirds of 1 percent of the more than one billion pesos in circulation in the country had been exchanged for gold and

17. Lemaitre, *Reyes*, pp. 350, 259; Palacio, "Historia," *El Tiempo*, October 3, 1943; Sanín Cano, *Administración Reyes*, p. 300.

18. José María Vesga y Avila, *Fiestas patrias* (Bogotá, 1907), p. xxvi. In 1909 Sanín Cano estimated that some 2,500,000 pesos gold had been paid out to foreign claimants and predicted that the final amount might reach 3,000,000. *Administración Reyes*, p. 38.

19. For an excellent, detailed discussion of the practical defects of the law, see Luis Eduardo Nieto Caballero's published doctoral dissertation, *El curso forzoso y su historia en Colombia* (Bogotá, 1912), pp. 32-39.

incinerated by the Junta.[20] Daily fluctuation in the value of Colombian currency inhibited domestic commercial transactions, inflated interest rates, and helped to foster the climate of economic insecurity which enveloped the nation in the early postwar period.

Reyes's bold solution to the monetary problem, a large devaluation of Colombian currency, recognized the short-range inability of the nation to amortize paper money and sought primarily to give the paper money in circulation a constant value. Because the exchange rate of Colombian paper pesos to United States gold had oscillated around the figure of 10,000 percent (i.e., 100 Colombian pesos to 1 cent U. S. gold) since late 1903 (see Table 9:1), Reyes chose to devalue the Colombian peso by a factor of 100. The devaluation thus gave legal force to a commercial fact of life and proved of singular effectiveness in eliminating many of the most vexing problems surrounding the regime of paper money in the postwar period. By reducing the quantity of paper in circulation, the administrative problems of control and quality (and thus of counterfeiting) were greatly diminished.[21] By fixing the value of Colombian paper, the devaluation eliminated the problem of reckless speculation characteristic of the postwar period even after the passage of Law 33.[22] The greatly reduced quantity and the increased value of the paper left in circulation also had a psychological effect. Paper currency became relatively scarce, the quality of the bills themselves improved as old Colombian-printed bills were exchanged for high quality foreign-printed Colombian currency, and Colombians no longer needed to carry around large wads of paper money to make even minor purchases. For all these reasons the simple, ingenious devaluation effected by Reyes in early 1905 contributed greatly to a climate of renewed confidence and security essential to the economic reconstruction of the nation.[23]

Reyes's monetary reform conserved the hard-fought victories of the opponents of paper money by maintaining the principle of free stipulation and embracing the objective of eventual amortization and return to the gold standard. A central bank, conceived as a joint venture of private and public capital, was set up by Reyes in early 1905 and

20. According to Guillermo Torres García only 62,247,095 pesos of the 1,010,463,429 pesos in circulation had been amortized by the Junta at the time of Reyes's monetary reforms of January-February, 1905. *Historia de la moneda en Colombia*, p. 298.

21. Reyes's minister of the treasury and finance declared in April, 1907, that during the first six months of Reyes's government over fifty counterfeiters had been apprehended by government officials. After the devaluation the problem was reduced to minor proportions. "Exposición," *Anales de la Asamblea Nacional de 1907*, p. 188.

22. In 1904 a major monetary and banking crisis triggered by speculation precipitated the failure of several Antioqueño banks.

23. This explanation and assessment of Reyes's devaluation closely follows Torres García's excellent treatment of the measure in his history of Colombian monetary policy cited above. See especially pp. 285-87, 292-93.

Table 9:1. Average monthly exchange rate of Colombian pesos 1903-1905

	1903	1904	1905
January	8,700	10,200	10,350
February	7,900	10,100	9,900
March	10,000	9,600	9,800
April	10,300	9,300	9,700
May	9,500	9,400	10,000
June	9,800	9,400	9,900
July	9,400	9,800	9,850
August	9,200	9,400	10,050
September	9,200	9,800	10,150
October	10,500	9,800	10,500
November	10,600	10,300	10,500
December	10,000	11,000	10,400

Source: Adapted from Torres García, *Historia de la moneda*, p. 276.
Note: Procedure for finding equivalencies in U. S. gold is explained in note to Table 2:2.

granted revenues and authority to begin amortization.[24] The bank, which ultimately generated severe criticism from doctrinaire economic liberals, is discussed in more detail below. Here it is important to note that as a result of continuing economic stagnation and Reyes's other demands on national fiscal resources, the bank never began amortization, and the definitive effort to back Colombian currency with gold occurred after the fall of Reyes.

One of Reyes's most significant economic achievements was his restoration of Colombian credit abroad. Acting under his instructions, in July, 1905, his close political associate Jorge Holguín celebrated an agreement with the Committee of Foreign Holders of Colombian Bonds in London. The terms of the agreement signed by Holguín and bondholders' representative Lord Avebury, and subsequently approved by the Colombian government and the bondholders, were generous to Colombia's creditors. In the negotiations Holguín sought not to reduce the principle and interest due on the debt, a strategy commonly adopted and successfully pursued by other Latin American nations in renegotiating their foreign debts during the same period. Rather, Reyes and Holguín recognized almost the entirety of the principle and interest due on the debt,[25] hoping in this way to re-establish Colombian credit abroad, secure an additional foreign loan, and place the nation in a favorable position to attract the foreign capital they felt

24. In its structure, powers, and purpose the bank closely resembled the one proposed by Liberal Roberto de la Torre in his prewar doctoral dissertation. See Chapter V.
25. The terms of the Holguín-Avebury agreement are conveniently summarized in Cruz Santos, *Economía y hacienda*, p. 115, and Martínez Delgado, *República de Colombia*, II, 327.

vital to the development of the nation's export agricultural and mineral economy. Evaluating the terms of the agreement he was about to conclude, Holguín wrote Reyes in April, 1905: "I believe I have understood that more than a few pounds sterling saved what is important to the nation is to maintain a very high credit rating and a full sense of national honor."[26] Holguín later recounted his emotion at seeing the name of Colombia erased from the blackboard of delinquent debtor nations at the London Stock Exchange.[27] Although politicians representative of export-import interests would later argue that the restoration of Colombian foreign credit could have been accomplished on terms more favorable to Colombia, they never criticized the end pursued by Reyes and Holguín.[28] Throughout the remainder of the Quinquenio Reyes religiously met the terms of Colombia's obligations to the nation's foreign creditors. As a result, foreign capital began once more to flow into the country, a trend most notable in the fields of railroad construction, export agriculture (particularly banana production), and mining. In 1907 Reyes's finance minister estimated that during the first three years of his government more than three million pesos gold had been invested in the country by foreigners.[29]

Railroad construction, as noted earlier in the discussion of Reyes's speeches at the Second Pan American Conference in Mexico in 1901, formed the cornerstone of his political economy. In his inaugural speech he emphasized the vital role of railroads in the resurrection of the fatherland.

> The immense, still unexploited riches enclosed in our soil invite us to find in them the independence and comfort that result from persistent, sustained work; the obstacles that the physical structure of our country presents to the development of transport for the products of industry and communication with the civilized world demand, with insistence, the establishment of the systems of locomotion and transport characteristic of the age.[30]

Among the extraordinary powers Reyes solicited unsuccessfully from the congress in 1904 was authorization to negotiate binding contracts with railroad entrepreneurs not subject to subsequent congressional

26. Jorge Holguín to Rafael Reyes, Paris, April 25, 1905, Correspondencia Oficial de Jorge Holguín, transcribed by Luis Martínez Delgado, ACH.

27. Jorge Holguín. *Desde Cerca* (Paris, 1908), Chapter X, "La Pizarra," pp. 71-75.

28. The terms of the covenant generated a famous polemic between Holguín and Liberal Santiago Pérez Triana that can be followed in Pérez Triana's books *Desde lejos* (1908) and *Desde lejos y desde cerca* (1910), and Holguín's rejoinders *Desde Cerca* (1908), and *Cosas del día* (1910). Pérez Triana, son of the leader of the Liberal party exiled by Caro in 1893, had extensive financial contacts in London and criticized Holguín's unduly generous terms.

29. "Informe," *Anales de la Asamblea Nacional de 1907*, p. 189.

30. Lemaitre, *Reyes*, p. 273.

approval. Following his assumption of dictatorial powers in late 1904, Reyes proceeded to sign several railroad contracts which accorded extremely ample subventions and concessions to railroad companies that actually completed construction of trackage.[31] Although the extent of railroad construction completed during the Quinquenio has been exaggerated by some of Reyes's apologists, he did preside over an increase of approximately 50 percent in the railroad trackage of the nation.[32]

The railroad construction completed under Reyes was often of extraordinary economic importance. As a result of his determined support, the most difficult stretch of the Giradot-Bogotá railroad was completed by an English firm, and the line was ready for inauguration by the time he left office in 1909. Completion of the line meant that for the first time the nation's capital was linked to the outside world by rail and steamship navigation. The line also served the major coffee zone of southwestern Cundinamarca. Construction of the Girardot-Bogotá line was complemented by extension of the British-owned Dorada railroad to the old tobacco port of Ambalema. The Ambalema-La Dorada line bypassed the rapids of the Magdalena River at Honda and linked shipping on the Upper and Lower Magdalena. During the Quinquenio substantial progress was made on the Cali-Buenaventura line, which would provide the Cauca Valley with an outlet to the Pacific, and which would assume great importance with the opening of the Panama Canal in 1914. Reyes's policies also contributed to the lengthening of the Antioquia railway, which advanced a total of thirty-six kilometers during the Quinquenio. The Antioqueños had built much of the line with their own resources and many resented the national government's nationalization of the line in 1905.[33] Despite his efforts Reyes was unable to proceed with plans to begin construction of a rail line to link Santander to the Magdalena, a line that because of the formidable climatological and geographic obstacles to rail construction remains unbuilt even today. Finally, with Reyes's support, the Santa Marta Railway, serving the banana region around that port city and controlled by United Fruit, engaged in considerable expansion during the Quinquenio.

Reyes's railroad policies were complemented by an ambitious attempt to regularize and improve steamship transportation on the Magdalena. During the Quinquenio he pressured most of the com-

31. Subventions ranged from 9,900 to 15,000 pesos per kilometer constructed, granted in 6 percent bonds payable with customs receipts. Lemaitre, a devoted apologist of Reyes's government, admits that under these terms "la financiación salía extremamente recargada, pero las obras mientras tanto avanzaban." *Ibid.*, p. 332.

32. This is a rough estimate derived from scattered data in Ortega Díaz, *Ferrocarriles colombianos.*

33. Accomplished by Acto Legislativo No. 7 of 1905 and Law 60 of 1905.

panies operating on the river to pool their resources in a consortium headed by a German subject, Louis Gieseken. The consortium received a government subsidy and undertook to improve the channel, upgrade equipment, and establish a fixed time schedule for service. For a time it also granted rebates to coffee exporters. It was originally hailed as a great improvement by export-import interests but ultimately they became disenchanted with the size and terms of the rebates and began to accuse the consortium of graft and faulty service.[34]

Reyes also lent his support to highway and mule trail construction. During the Quinquenio the Carretera del Norte, a road for wheeled vehicles begun under the presidency of Carlos Holguín and extending only a few kilometers north of Bogotá at the start of the Quinquenio, was rapidly pushed north to Reyes's native Santa Rosa de Viterbo in Boyacá, a distance of more than two hundred kilometers from Bogotá. Then in a symbolic gesture typical of his style, Reyes undertook an arduous trip to Boyacá in the first automobile introduced in Colombia.

Much more significant were Reyes's efforts to improve and extend mule trails. In mid-1907 he undertook a comprehensive program to build more than 780 kilometers of mule trails which, in his words, would constitute a

> powerful aid to the construction of both railroads already contracted for and those to be contracted for in the future because the trails facilitate the delivery of freight and augment the volume of freight and will thus help to attract the foreign capital necessary for the exploitation of the great mineral resources of our cordilleras.

Under the plan the central government was to lend the departments money for the construction of mule trails, and the loans were to be repaid out of a percentage of the departmental revenues administered by the Central Bank.[35] It is difficult to determine how much actual construction on these trails was completed before Reyes's fall from power, but Ospina Vásquez concludes that transportation improvements during the Quinquenio, which included centralized administration and maintenance of mule trails, the design of the railroad and trail network, as well as the system of transportation tariffs, contributed to an "increased dependency of the nation on imports" during the Quinquenio.[36] Thus it would appear that Reyes's transportation policy worked at cross purposes with another aspect of his plans to improve the nation's economy, his policy of encouraging domestic industry.

34. Palacio, "Historia," *El Tiempo,* Jan. 28 and Feb. 4, 1945.
35. "Mensaje de Clausura," July 15, 1907, *Anales de la Asamblea Nacional de 1907,* p. 395.
36. Ospina Vásquez, *Industria,* p. 325.

Reyes's administration is justly remembered for its support of domestic manufacturing, especially the textile industry. Less well known are his concerted efforts to promote Colombian agricultural exports. Both his support of domestic industry and his encouragement of export agriculture were part of an overall policy to expand Colombian exports while reducing imports. Reyes believed that the core of Colombia's economic, fiscal, and monetary problems lay in the imbalance of foreign trade plaguing the country at the beginning of the twentieth century. Through manipulation of the tariff and direct subventions he fostered the growth of textile factories and cotton cultivation. The result was to insure the survival of the nascent textile industry of Antioquia. He also granted marketing privileges and tax incentives to aid in the establishment of concerns to process petroleum and food products and manufacture acid, glass and paper. None of these latter experiments prospered. Much more successful were his extremely generous subventions to encourage the cultivation and refining of sugar. By the end of the Quinquenio one large refinery, Central Colombia, spontaneously repaid the government the amount it had received in subsidies.[37]

During his years in power Reyes acted vigorously to promote the embryonic banana export industry in Colombia. As early as 1901 the United States-based United Fruit Company acquired land and began operations in the Santa Marta region on the Caribbean coast. Under a system employed by United Fruit in other areas of the Caribbean, most of the actual production was contracted out to Colombian growers. United Fruit served as sole buyer and transported the fruit out of Colombia and marketed it in the United States and Europe. Profits in the industry were high, and after United Fruit entered the picture, banana exports from Colombia grew rapidly, rising from 263,193 bunches in 1901 to 1,397,388 bunches in 1906. This encouraging start and the knowledge that bananas were rapidly becoming an important item of world trade, led many Colombians, Reyes among them, to hope that given proper encouragement banana exports might develop into an important earner of foreign exchange for Colombia. Acting on that belief, in early 1907 Reyes submitted a bill to his congress which exempted the banana industry of any export taxes for a period of eight years. Although at least one deputy to the National Assembly objected to the measure and voiced fears of foreign control of the industry, the Assembly passed the bill as Law 9 of May 29, 1908. During his last two years in office Reyes tirelessly urged Colombians to invest in banana cultivation, made trips to inspect developments in the banana zone, and established a penal colony near Santa Marta whose inmates en-

37. Ospina Vásquez, *Industria*, pp. 335-38.

gaged in banana cultivation. In late 1908 he intervened in favor of United Fruit in a railway freight rate dispute between the company and the Department of Magdalena. Partly as a result of these efforts, under the auspices of United Fruit, Colombian banana exports continued to rise dramatically during the Quinquenio. By 1909, the year Reyes left power, Colombian banana exports stood at 3,139,307 bunches.[38]

The most spectacular of Reyes's efforts to promote export agriculture came in mid-1907 when he issued a decree (No. 832 of July 20) conceding bounties to exporters of coffee, tobacco, and plantation rubber and producers of cotton "for use within the nation or for export." The decree, which granted a bounty of one peso gold on each hundredweight of coffee exported and was to remain in effect for at least three years, met with the enthusiastic approval of coffee exporters. On July 24 scores of coffee exporters, acting through the Society of Agriculturalists, sent Reyes an effusive letter of appreciation declaring their most "intense pleasure" over the decree.[39] Coffee growers, who had suffered so much in the war and as a result of the depression in world prices, the editor of the journal of the Society declared, had finally received effective encouragement. The president of Colombia, he went on, "as a man formed in the classical and experimental school of private initiative, lends his powerful hand to the development of exports in Colombia. . . ."[40]

A little more than five months after the decree went into effect, exporters proposed to Reyes that the export bounties be transformed into direct subsidies to Magdalena steamship companies in exchange for a 40 percent reduction of freight tariffs for exporters.[41] Reyes agreed to this plan and on December 16, 1907, he issued decree No. 1520, which suspended export bounties and set aside the sum of 120,000 pesos gold annually for subventions of river steamship companies willing to reduce tariff rates for exporters and grant the government a role in determining the new rates.

38. Monsalve, *Colombia cafetera*, pp. 735-37; *Anales de la Asamblea Nacional de 1907*, pp. 284, 344-45; Ortega Díaz, *Ferrocarriles colombianos*, pp. 600-1; P. A. Pedraza, *Excurciones presidenciales* (Norwood, Mass., 1909), *passim*. In the years following the Quinquenio Colombian banana exports continued to expand rapidly. By the mid-1920's, although the value of banana exports constituted only about one twelfth of the value of coffee exports, Colombia had become the largest exporter of bananas in the world.

39. *Revista Nacional de Agricultura*, August 1, 1907, pp. 141-44. In 1906 the Society of Coffee Growers, founded in late 1904 with Reyes's blessing, broadened its membership and changed its name to the Society of Agriculturalists. Francisco Ospina Alvarez, "Informe," *Revista Nacional de Agricultura*, November 1, 1906, pp. 257-63.

40. *Revista Nacional de Agricultura*, August 1, 1907, p. 131.

41. I was unable to determine the reasons for the request. Most probably exporters believed the subventions would be easier to administer and may have calculated that savings to exporters would be even higher.

It was in executing this new decree that Reyes established the river transport consortium headed by Louis Gieseken, noted previously. But the resulting tariff reduction of river freight rates did not live up to the coffee exporters' expectations. The general rate was set at a level higher than before and the special reductions granted coffee exporters amounted to only 25 percent instead of the 40 percent proposed by the exporters. The result, as the exasperated coffee-growing president of the Society of Agriculturalists informed Reyes in a forceful memorial dated March 17, 1908, was that in exchange for renouncing the export bounties to secure cheaper river freight rates, coffee exporters had only secured higher river freight rates. Moreover, the creation of the river transport consortium meant "an end to competition and that removes all hope of obtaining favorable modification of those freight charges." To make matters worse, the Agricultural Society president continued, the steamship companies were prohibited by the terms of the contracts with the government from granting differential freight rates. Thus, "respectable groups of exporters [i.e. big ones] like the one made up of the coffee growers of this Society, have lost the advantage customarily granted in commercial dealings to those who sell or buy in large quantities."[42]

Coffee exporters wanted a freight rate reduction of 70 percent, but to this request Reyes turned a deaf ear. In March, 1908, he did grant a reduction in the ship manifest tax on coffee exports, but the savings to coffee exporters were minor, and although they refrained from criticizing the dictator directly, they remained bitter. The president of the Society of Agriculturalists later wrote, "We were defrauded."[43] Reyes may have wanted to help coffee exporters and certainly recognized the danger of alienating this powerful interest group, but by 1908 his government found itself in a precarious financial situation. Reyes had overcommitted himself in implementing his ambitious economic plans and was engaged in a frantic struggle to secure new government revenues.

The financial situation of his government by 1908 represented a serious setback for Reyes. During his first four years in power he had not only overcome the disastrous state of the government's finances inherited from Marroquín, but had managed to fund his ambitious program of economic development. Reyes's record was even more impressive since he had accomplished all this within the terms of a balanced budget. Recourse to deficit spending through continued emissions of paper money had been politically impossible as well as

42. Aristides Forero to Rafael Reyes, Bogotá, March 17, 1908. The letter is published in the *Revista de Agricultura,* April 1, 1908, pp. 339-44.

43. "Informe," November 1, 1908, *Revista Nacional de Agricultura,* December 1, 1908, p. 323.

repugnant to Reyes's own economic principles.[44] In order to accomplish his fiscal goals he implemented a series of fiscal reforms which doubled and then trebled the amount of government income. These reforms included both increases in traditional taxes and the creation of new ones, centralization of collection procedures, national administration of departmental revenues, and the establishment of fiscal monopolies on items of popular consumption.

One of the traditional taxes subjected to a general increase was the tariff. Reyes's tariff policy was designed to greatly increase government revenues through a general increase of 70 percent in customs duties, and at the same time to stimulate domestic agriculture and industry by raising duties on imported agricultural and manufactured goods generally while reducing duties on such items as machinery, industrial raw materials, and fertilizers. The Reyes tariff is usually interpreted as a great boon to domestic industry. In fact, some contemporaries viewed the tariff as the savior of Colombian agriculture, "the principal source of the progress and well being of the nation." According to this view the tariff would furnish the government with the revenue needed to construct railroads vital to Colombian agriculture, would help domestic wheat and sugar production displace foreign imports of flour and beet sugar, and, through its encouragement of the Colombian textile industry, would stimulate domestic cotton production.[45] The protection afforded by the Reyes tariff complemented the policy of direct subventions discussed above and was particularly successful in fomenting the textile and sugar industries.

Crucial to Reyes's tax initiatives was the nationalization of important departmental revenues. Such departmental revenues as taxes collected on the sale of alcoholic beverages, tobacco, and the slaughter of animals were transferred to the national government, which then returned a percentage of revenue collected to the departments. Reyes also reconstituted the system of fiscal monopolies on the sale of matches and cigarettes. Most of these taxes were placed under the stewardship of the Central Bank. The bank was also charged with supervision of the nation's monetary system, and required to make a

44. Reyes did solicit and the congress of 1904 approved, however, a special emergency emission of 100,000 pesos to enable the government to meet its most pressing obligations until government finance could be reorganized. The issue was the last outright emission of unbacked paper currency.

45. See the article by Rafael Camacho L. in *El Nuevo Tiempo*, February 14, 1905. Reyes's original tariff decrees, Nos. 15 and 46 of 1905, are discussed in Ospina Vásquez, *Industria*, p. 334. Subsequent decrees modified tariff schedules to benefit particular agricultural and manufacturing interests. For example, Decree No. 1026 of August 28, 1906, specifically reduced duties on, among other items, "la tela de hierro galvanizado, agujerada, para el beneficio del café," certain types of fertilizer, and henequen bags used for packing. The decree, of special interest to coffee growers, was reproduced in the *Revista Nacional de Agricultura*, September 15, 1906, p. 203.

large loan to the government. In return the bank was granted special privileges, including a commission in return for implementing the terms of the devaluation and replacement of deteriorated bills, sole authority to issue gold-backed paper currency for a period of thirty years, and 10 percent of the government tax revenues it collected.[46] The result of Reyes's fiscal reorganization was an unqualified financial success. Government revenues rapidly increased from about 5 million to 10 million gold pesos a year, and rose to 15 and 16 million annually by the last years of the Quinquenio.

But the political cost of the fiscal reforms was high. Although groups of Colombian agriculturalists and industrialists benefited under the Reyes tariff, import interests suffered.[47] The centralization of departmental revenues was particularly offensive to wealthy, dynamic departments which chafed under the fiscal limitations imposed by Reyes's centralism.[48] The system of fiscal monopolies, like the policy of direct subvention of industrial, agricultural, and transportation enterprises, and the grant of special privileges to the Central Bank, gave rise to allegations of graft and favoritism and denunciations of violation of laissez-faire principles.[49] By late 1908 and early 1909, anonymous handbills alleging torture of political prisoners and detailing incidences of graft and corruption in the administration were being printed in Bogotá and circulated throughout the country.[50]

Adding fuel to the growing political dissatisfaction was the fact that by 1908 the financial edifice which Reyes had so carefully constructed threatened to collapse. His government had overcommitted itself financially, and European and United States recession had dried up easy foreign credits. For months Jorge Holguín attempted to secure a

46. A thorough discussion of the formation and functions of the Central Bank can be found in Cruz Santos, *Economía y hacienda*, II, 122-27.

47. This point should not be exaggerated, however, for exporters, importers, and nascent industrialists were often the same people, as the case of Pedro Nel Ospina, coffee-grower, merchant, and founder of the first important textile plant in Antioquia, illustrates.

48. Regional animosity toward Reyes's government was also a result of other centralist policies, such as the breaking up of large departments, and the transfer to the central of executive of control over immigration, foreign investments and railroad construction.

49. Ospina Vásquez contends that although Conservatives and Liberals criticized the system of privilege, monopoly, and subsidies, they did so not primarily because of their commitment to laissez-faire principles, but because the system lent itself to abuses. There is undoubtedly some merit in this argument: as long as Reyes's policies served their interests, exporters and importers tolerated and even approved of some of his statist measures during the difficult economic years of the Quinquenio.

50. Lemaitre, *Reyes*, pp. 355-57 gives a description of the nature of these charges and admits that many of them had some basis in fact. Anti-Reyes propaganda had long circulated outside Colombia. Perhaps the most famous example is the series of virulently hostile books written by Juan Bautista Pérez y Soto that began with *INRI* (San José, Costa Rica, 1907).

new foreign loan, but tight European money markets and rumors of opposition to Reyes's government made European bankers chary. The difficult terms proposed by European bankers may also have reflected their disappointment over their earlier failure to negotiate participation in the Central Bank. From Holguín's letters it is apparent that the bankers, who, Holguín noted, formed a kind of clique and pooled information, had been very eager to participate in the bank and used the issue of foreign participation as a condition for granting a large loan to Colombia under favorable conditions.[51] Holguín finally did secure a loan of one million pounds sterling, but the terms were much more burdensome to Colombia than those of the large 1905 loan. In increasingly desperate moves to secure more revenue, Reyes nationalized even more departmental revenues, reduced the commission granted the Central Bank for revenue collection to a mere 2 percent, and at the same time sought to trim government expenditures. For the first time the government began to fall behind in its commitments. Much to the government's embarrassment, the Girardot-Bogotá railway, whose completion had been a triumph for the government and whose inauguration promised to serve as a forum for government propaganda, could not be consummated because funds to pay the subsidies for the last kilometers constructed were not available. At the end of 1908 Reyes's representatives succeeded in negotiating a contract with an English company for the exploitation of Colombian emerald mines. The agreement would have provided the government with significant new revenues, but before it could be implemented by the National Assembly the political events which led to Reyes's fall intervened.[52]

The issue which enabled Reyes's critics to organize and begin to voice their discontent was his decision in early 1909 to convene the National Assembly in extraordinary session to approve the treaties his government had negotiated with the United States and Panama settling the differences arising out of the separation of Panama. The so-called tripartite treaties had been signed by Enrique Cortés, Colombia's ambassador to the United States, in Washington on January 9, 1909. By the terms of these treaties Colombia recognized Panamanian independence and Panama agreed to remit to Colombia the first ten yearly canal zone rental payments of $250,000 each. That sum was to

51. Jorge Holguín to Ministro de Hacienda y Tesoro, Paris, December 12, 1905, and Jorge Holguín to Nemesio Camacho, Paris, April 26, 1906. Correspondencia Oficial de Jorge Holguín, transcribed by Luis Martínez Delgado, ACH. Although both Holguín and Reyes approved of such participation, the agreement was never consummated, apparently as a result of delays in communication between Reyes and Holguín.

52. The terms of the contract were much criticized as overly generous to the foreign company and rejected by the Congress of 1909. *Anales de la Cámara de Representantes de 1909*, pp. 287-96.

fully satisfy Panama's share of the Colombian national debt. At the same time Panama renounced any claim to Colombia's fifty thousand shares in the New Panama Canal Company. The United States for its part agreed to begin canal zone rental payments in 1908, instead of 1913 as required in the original canal treaty signed between the United States and Panama after the secession. In addition, the United States granted Colombia special privileges and preferential treatment in the use of the future canal.[53]

Reyes's impolitic decision to proceed with the treaty ratification despite signs that the terms of the treaty were generally unacceptable in Colombia is best understood in the context of his firm belief that the future economic development of Colombia depended on the normalization of relations with the United States. In the postwar period the United States had become the major buyer of Colombian exports and the primary market for Colombian coffee. Furthermore, Reyes recognized that the United States was the most promising source of the foreign investment that he believed was vital to Colombian economic development. Reyes had held these beliefs since before his inauguration in 1904, and even after the failure of Colombia to ratify the tripartite treaties and his own fall from power, he continued to press for ratification of a treaty resolving the Panama question with the United States. The extent to which the economic progress of Colombia and good relations with the United States were inextricably linked in his mind is admirably illustrated in the following excerpt from a letter written to Francisco J. Urrutia in 1913.

> As long as you fail to settle [the Panama] question with the United States, [Colombia] will remain as it is today, excluded from the worldwide movement toward progress and will vegetate in poverty . . . because capital and immigration do not flow into a nation that does not have lines of communication and is in the situation Colombia finds herself with respect to the United States, and for the same reason there will be lack of capital both to construct needed railroads and to exploit and give value to our natural resources.[54]

Ratification of the treaties would also benefit the short-term goals of Reyes's government. Once all parties had ratified, the first two rental installments, a sum of half a million dollars, would become payable to Colombia within a period of ninety days. The opposition must have realized that rejection of the treaties would not only discredit the

53. *Anales de la Asamblea Nacional de 1909*, pp. 43-55, 66-75, 162-67.
54. Rafael Reyes to Francisco J. Urrutia, Biarritz, January 12, 1913, Correspondencia Oficial de Jorge Holguín, transcribed by Luis Martínez Delgado, ACH.

government politically, but deny the government financial resources much needed to avoid embarrassment on just those issues of fiscal responsibility and prompt payment of commitments which Reyes had championed since his inauguration.

The question of the treaties furnished Reyes's opponents with a specific and inflammatory issue that they used to channel pent-up resentment against the dictator. Bitterness over the United States' role in the secession of Panama still ran deep, but the opposition concentrated on the issue of the separate treaty with Panama. How could a secessionist department, they asked, be treated as a sovereign nation on equal footing with Colombia and the United States? Despite censorship, the press began to criticize the treaties, and small groups of students roamed the evening streets of Bogotá chanting their opposition to ratification. On March 11 Nicolás Esguerra, a leading Liberal politician who had never actively supported Reyes, submitted a memorial to the National Assembly alleging that body's constitutional incapacity to ratify international treaties. Esguerra's memorial cleverly linked the issue of the treaties to the broader question of the legitimacy of the regime itself. Two days later, on March 13, large, unruly popular demonstrations erupted in Bogotá. On the same day, in an effort to control the situation, Reyes designated power to Jorge Holguín. Within hours Holguín withdrew the treaties from consideration by the National Assembly and declared a state of seige in the capital. Although Reyes reassumed power the next day, his prestige and control of Colombian politics had been shattered.

In the three months he remained in the presidency, Reyes was forced to preside over the dismantling of part of the fiscal and administrative structure he had labored so hard to create. As a result of the passage of Law 8 of 1909 departments regained their traditional revenues and reacquired the right to collect local taxes and determine their own expenditures. Antioquia regained exclusive ownership and control of its railroad (Law 7 of 1909). In June Reyes presided over a congressional election that gave a majority to a new party, the Republican Union. The new party was bipartisan in composition, led by Liberals and Historical Conservatives not closely identified with Reyes during the last years of the Quinquenio, and committed to a program of strict republicanism, bipartisan participation in government, and laissez-faire economics.[55]

After the June elections, Reyes left Bogotá on a presidential inspection trip of the kind he frequently engaged in during the last years of

55. According to Lemaitre, Reyes himself cast his vote for the Republican Union, a move which would not have been inconsistent with his long-standing commitment to bipartisanship and his support for export-oriented economic development.

his regime. Unknown to all but a few, he had left his undated resignation in the hands of Designate Holguín. Arriving in Santa Marta, Reyes toured the prospering banana zone he had helped to create. Then, on the evening of June 13 he unexpectedly failed to appear at a glittering reception organized in his honor and attended by local dignitaries and officials of the United Fruit Company. Finally, word arrived that he would not attend the reception: he had secretly boarded a United Fruit banana boat bound for England. It was a fitting departure for the president who had done so much to attract foreign capital and expand export agriculture in Colombia.[56]

56. *El Conservador* (Barranquilla), June 16, 1909. Some of the flavor of Reyes official excursions and his relations with United Fruit officials in the Santa Marta banana zone emerges from Pedraza's profusely illustrated *Excurciones presidenciales*, cited earlier.

Chapter X

The Outline of the New Order

Within a few short years after Reyes's fall from power, bipartisan export-import interests cemented into place the economic and political elements of the new order they had labored so intensely to install since the 1890's. The new order diverged radically from the political and economic characteristics of nineteenth-century Colombia. The unstable politics of the previous century, the politics of fundamental ideological contention and partisan exclusiveness, of chronic civil war and ephemeral constitutions, was succeeded after 1910 by a new era of remarkable political stability. Colombian politics during the teens and twenties and even in the thirties and early forties, while not free of party conflict, partisan polemics, and a significant degree of rural violence and unrest, was nevertheless qualitatively different from the political chaos of the previous century. Public order was maintained and upper-class exercise of civil liberties generally respected. Elections were held in relative calm and freedom, their results accepted. Presidents (with the exception of one who resigned in 1921) served out their full terms. In 1930 control of the national executive changed hands peacefully as Liberals elected their first president in almost half a century. Many of the governments after 1910 were bipartisan in composition, and the principle of minority representation assured meaningful representation to both traditional parties in the legislative bodies of the nation.

The political dimensions of the new order were complemented, and in large part explained, by economic changes accompanying the consolidation of the coffee-export economy. The unsuccessful and short-lived export booms of the nineteenth century gave way to a coffee boom of unprecedented proportions and duration. Although the foundations of the new economic order had been laid during the coffee boom of the 1890's and reinforced by the economic policies followed during the Quinquenio, the towering economic structure of the new order emerged only after 1910. Despite occasional dislocations caused by world war and overproduction, and the more severe disruption brought on by the Great Depression, world coffee prices remained at generally high levels in the decades following 1910. Colombian coffee exports expanded enormously during the same period rising to one million bags by 1913, two million by 1921, and five million by 1944.

(Price and production data to 1925 are illustrated in Figure 9:1.) By the mid-1920's Colombia had become the major producer of mild coffee in the world and second only to Brazil in total coffee production.

The prolonged and steady expansion of the coffee economy effected a transformation of Colombian politics. In the first place, the coffee boom consolidated the political hegemony of bipartisan export-import interests. By 1910 a basic ideological and programmatic consensus had developed between dominant elites in both parties. That consensus was reflected in the final solutions to the economic and political problems inherited from the past and found legal expression in the constitutional reforms of 1910.

But the expanding coffee economy worked in other, less obvious ways to modify the structure of politics inherited from the nineteenth century. As a result both of certain characteristics of coffee export economies in general, and the unique sociological structure of the Colombian coffee economy in particular, coffee expansion created significant new economic opportunities for ambitious Colombians, attenuated the disruptive force of clientelist politics discussed in Chapter I, and greatly contributed to the political legitimacy and stability of the new order.

Fast-moving political events marked the final transition to the new order. After the fall of Reyes three different men held the office of chief executive within a short period of fourteen months while two separate congresses convened to consider and enact political and economic reforms. In stark but vigorous strokes these reformers sketched the outline of the new order, and if circumstance forced upon them a certain economy of expression, their successors could afford to fill in body and detail.

Reyes's voluntary exile on June 13, 1909, left Jorge Holguín in charge of the government until the new congress convened in July and elected a successor to serve out the remainder of Reyes's original six-year term, due to expire on August 7, 1910. The man elected by the congress was Ramón González Valencia, the Historical Conservative, coffee-growing general from Santander who had taken office as vice-president along with Reyes in 1904.[1]

According to his biographer, González Valencia should be remembered as the "Agriculturalists' President" for two reasons. First, "because he spent his life as a farmer"; and second, because he "created the Agricultural Society, founded the agricultural journal, and laid the foundation of the College of Agriculture with the creation of the School of Agriculture. . . ."[2] Although this account, in its enthusiasm

1. González Valencia had been relieved of that position when Reyes abolished that office in favor of a designate in 1905.

2. Guillermo Solano Benítez, *El bayardo colombiano, Ramón González Valencia* (Puente Nacional, 1953), pp. 6-7, 170-73.

to exalt its subject, slightly distorts the historical record, there can be no doubt of González Valencia's identification with agricultural and export-import interests. Still, although he did authorize a subvention for the Society of Agriculturalists and did organize a school for formal agricultural training, his administration made only limited headway in solving the economic and monetary problems still facing the nation. Severe fiscal restraints imposed both by the on-going commitments of the preceding administration and the continuing slump in coffee prices during González Valencia's year in power, limited the scope and efficacy of the programs formulated by both the administration and the reform-minded congress.

The manner in which the good intentions of the new administration were stymied by the fiscal realities facing the government is poignantly illustrated by the position taken on the issue of amortization by González Valencia's first minister of finance, Joaquín Samper. As the son of the great critic of Regeneration finance, Samper confessed to congress his desire to begin serious amortization, but, he went on, after surveying the disastrous state of government finance he had concluded that nothing could be undertaken at the present juncture. He urged the amortization forces in the Senate led by José Francisco Groot not to pass legislation which would deprive the government of crucial revenue. At that, Groot took the Senate floor, and addressing the minister of finance directly, evoked the memory of Miguel Samper. The elder Samper, Groot exclaimed, had believed that the worst calamity for the republic was the existence of the regime of paper money. Perhaps the minister of finance should study his father's writings. "That respected public figure would turn over in his grave if, at the suggestion of the minister of finance, his most worthy son, this issue were to be left without solution at this time."[3]

The question of the means to begin effective amortization preoccupied the senators and deputies throughout the session. Finally, thanks to the determination of Uribe Uribe, the Senate version of an amortization bill passed the Chamber on the last day of the session. Uribe Uribe successfully opposed efforts by the minister of finance Dávila Flores to close the session. Uribe Uribe argued that to leave unapproved the legislation upon which the congress had labored so diligently would be to "defraud the hopes of the Colombian people to see themselves one day free of the plague of paper money, principal cause of their misery." The day after congress approved the legislation González Valencia changed his cabinet installing several members of the congress who had supported Uribe Uribe and voted in favor of the monetary legislation.[4]

3. *Anales del Senado de 1909*, pp. 141-51.
4. "Ultima sesión de la Cámara" in Rafael Uribe Uribe, *Labor parlamentaria del General Rafael Uribe Uribe en el congreso de 1909* (Bogotá, 1909), pp. 197-99.

The amortization bill, Law 69 of December 20, 1909, established a junta to convert paper money and granted it various sources of revenue. Most significant among these were all earnings from the emerald mines of Muzo and Consquez and redirected income from a 2 percent increase in the tariff schedule which at Uribe Uribe's urging had been enacted earlier in the session to fund a campaign against the locusts which plagued Colombian agriculture. In recognition of the government's current fiscal plight, only half of the earnings of the two emerald mines was to be applied to amortization during 1910, the first year of the junta's operation. The Law also empowered future congresses to appropriate additional funds to the conversion fund. As events were to show, Law 69 provided the machinery and procedures which would begin the definite process of conversion to a gold-based currency.[5]

As the terms of the amortization law indicate, the congress also rescinded the contract signed by the Reyes government with an English firm to exploit the emerald mines. Likewise the Central Bank, which Deputy José Vicente Concha denounced as an "octopus" that embodied the corrupt, monopolistic, and arbitrary nature of the Reyes regime, was stripped by congress of its official status and privileges.[6] The congress also acted to restore the administrative and fiscal autonomy enjoyed by the departments prior to Reyes's reforms. In a related move, most of the new administrative units created during the Quinquenio were reintegrated into the departments to which they formerly pertained.

Both the administration and the congress of 1909 devoted special attention to the promotion of the export economy, but here again the fiscal penury of the nation limited the scope of the measures they could realistically enact. For example, the minister of finance proposed an ambitious program to set up an agrarian mortgage bank, capitalized by a large foreign loan and charged with making low-interest loans for agricultural expansion and improvement. Although the goal of the proposal was heartily endorsed by a congressional committee composed of Pedro Nel Ospina, Tomás Samper, and Lucas Caballero, men noted for their support of agricultural interests, the committee members concluded that the proposal was unrealistic given the fiscal position of the government and the priority they assigned to efforts to begin amortization of paper money.[7]

But the congress did approve other, less costly, measures to promote Colombian exports. The bills passed to organize a school of agriculture, fund a campaign to eliminate locusts, and provide a subsidy to

5. *Anales de la Cámara de Representantes de 1909*, pp. 911-12, 892-94.
6. *Ibid.*, pp. 469-71.
7. *Ibid.*, pp. 825-27.

the Agricultural Society have already been mentioned.[8] Another law approved a contract with a German company to develop banana production and build a railroad in the Gulf of Urabá region on the Caribbean coast.[9] Finally, a bill to eliminate the export tax on precious metals, with a list of sponsors which reads like a roster of reformist forces in the Chamber of 1909, was passed as Law 19 of 1909. José Medina C., who reported the bill out of committee, probably summed up the sentiments of the measure's twenty-nine sponsors when he wrote:

> [Measures which establish export taxes on precious metals], and in general all measures that tax any kind of exports, have effects that we could call contrary to the progress of the nation; experience and good economic sense clearly demonstrate that in a nation like ours, impoverished and lying in ruins as a result of various kinds of mistakes, but blessed with the exceptional resources of its soil, the wise and practical thing to do is to stimulate industries which exploit these resources. When such a stimulus has been attempted, export bounties, not export taxes, have been established.[10]

While fiscal considerations reduced the scope of efforts to promote exports and impeded definitive solutions to the nation's monetary problems in the congress of 1909, reformist forces were under no such restraint in dealing with the political institutions inherited from the Regeneration and Quinquenio. The first law passed by the congress of 1909 re-established the liberal press law (No. 51) of 1898. The only changes made by the new law involved reduction of sanctions stipulated for infractions of the 1898 law.[11] In order to deal with the issue of constitutional reform, on February 25, 1910, González Valencia decreed the convocation of a new National Assembly invested with the power "to introduce into the present constitution the reforms which public opinion has long demanded."[12] Elected by the municipios in April, 1910, the National Assembly convened in Bogotá on May 25. The Assembly was dominated by reformist forces and delegates included such long-time Liberal and Historical Conservative advocates of political and economic reform as Guillermo Quintero Calderón, Rafael Uribe Uribe, Pedro Nel Ospina, and Benjamín Herrera. After long deliberation the National Assembly passed a series of

8. Passed as Law 46 of November 10, 1902, the subsidy amounted to 2,300 pesos annually. *Anales del Senado de 1909*, p. 690.

9. Law 66 of December 4, 1909. *Ibid.*, pp. 889-93.

10. *Anales de la Cámara de Representantes de 1909*, pp. 125, 386, 390.

11. Cacua Prada, *Legislación*, pp. 81-82.

12. Decree No. 126 of February 25, 1910, *Anales de la Asamblea Nacional de 1910*, pp. 1-2.

constitutional reforms designated as the Legislative Act No. 3 of October 31, 1910. The reforms dealt not only with political issues that had preoccupied reformist forces during the Regeneration and the Quinquenio, but also addressed the institution of paper money, which the delegates considered to be of such transcendental importance as to merit attention in the fundamental law of the land. The most important political reforms limited executive power (especially Articles 25-34); augmented the administrative, legislative, and fiscal powers of the departments (especially Articles 50, 51, and 54); and guaranteed minority party representation (Article 45). Article 7 was of a nature uncommon in political constitutions; in a single sentence it "absolutely prohibited" new emissions of unbacked paper currency.[13] The Assembly complemented its political reform by enacting new legislation to govern elections. Law 80 of November 10, 1910, sought to curb electoral abuses and established, through the procedure known as the "incomplete vote," the right of the minority party to one-third representation in the legislative bodies of the nation.[14] With these decisive measures, in a few short months in 1910, reformers enacted all major aspects of the reform program articulated in the 1890's against the politics of the Regeneration. At the same time, the new laws established the legal basis for the liberal political and economic policies that would characterize the new order.[15]

Although one of the provisions of the Constitutional Reform of 1910 called for the direct popular election of the president of the nation, the National Assembly, perhaps because reformist forces feared that a popular election might endanger their recently acquired control of national politics, made an exception for the presidential term beginning on August 7, 1910. That presidential term would be filled by a man elected by the National Assembly itself.[16] Chosen as president by the Assembly was forty-three-year-old Carlos E. Restrepo.

An *antioqueño* Conservative long associated with the politics of Marceliano Vélez and Pedro Nel Ospina, and closely identified with the liberal critique of the policies of the Regeneration, Restrepo had

13. *Ibid.*, pp. 666-70.

14. *Ibid.*, pp. 706-07.

15. As an expression of their gratitude and approval of the policies successfully pursued by González Valencia, and their hopes for a continuation of these policies under the succeeding administration, twenty-five members of the Bogotá Liberal elite, "all associated with industry, commerce, and banking," offered an exclusive banquet in honor of the outgoing president at the Gun Club on the evening of August 6, 1910. The other honored guest was president-elect Carlos E. Restrepo, who was to be inaugurated the following day. The toast to the two presidents was given by Abel Camacho, president of the Bogotá Chamber of Commerce. Solano Benítez, *El bayardo colombiano*, pp. 191-93.

16. The Assembly also decided that it would function as the legitimate congress of the nation until a congress elected under the provisions of the Constitutional reform of 1910 and the new election law inaugurated its sessions on July 20, 1911.

emerged in the last years of the Quinquenio as one of Reyes's primary political opponents. He had served in the departmental bureaucracy of Antioquia during the last years of the Regeneration and after the war broke out he fought as an officer under the command of Pedro Nel Ospina. In 1903 he was elected to congress, but refused to serve as a gesture of protest against the electoral fraud and political exclusiveness which had denied Liberals and reformist Conservatives adequate representation. After the separation of Panama Restrepo organized a bipartisan Junta de Conciliación in Antioquia which drew up a series of proposals for constitutional reform based on the following principles: administrative decentralization, separation of governmental powers, religious tolerance, abolition of paper money through strict economies, proportional representation for political parties, and improvement of public instruction. Although some of the Junta's principles were implemented under Reyes's administration, Restrepo early became disenchanted with Reyes's authoritarian and statist measures and engaged in a series of efforts to discredit and embarrass the dictator.[17]

After the fall of Reyes, Restrepo was instrumental in founding a new party, the Republican Union, to champion the ideals of bipartisan republican government, religious tolerance, and laissez-faire economics.[18] Many other Historical Conservatives associated themselves with the new party, as did that faction of the Liberal party led by Benjamín Herrera and Enrique Olaya Herrera. The Republican Union held a majority in the National Assembly convoked by González Valencia in 1910 and through its control of the Assembly set up the special procedures for the presidential election of 1910 that gave the election to the party's candidate, Carlos E. Restrepo.

True to the principles of the new party and like Ramón González Valencia before him, Restrepo named a bipartisan cabinet. According to political observer Julio H. Palacio the political identification of the new ministers was as follows: acting minister of government, Bernardo Escovar (Historical Conservative); minister of foreign affairs, Enrique Olaya Herrera (Liberal identified with Benjamín Herrera); minister of finance, Tomás O. Eastman (peace Liberal); minister of war, Mariano Ospina Vásquez (Historical and *velista* Conservative); minister of public works, Celso Rodríguez (Liberal identified with Benjamín Herrera); minister of the treasury, Gregorio Martínez Aycardi (Conservative who had supported Reyes). The only two po-

17. Restrepo, *Orientación Republicana*, I, 176-77, 215-58. In this first volume Restrepo provides a wealth of evidence to document his ties with and sympathy toward Historical Conservative and moderate Liberal politics in the 1890's, the war years, and during the Quinquenio. See, for example, his comments on the "Motives of Dissidence," *ibid.*, pp. 104-5.

18. *Ibid.*, pp. 378-82.

litical factions excluded from the coalition government were the intransigent Nationalists and that part of the Liberal party under the leadership of Uribe Uribe.[19]

Restrepo's administration was blessed with the fiscal boom generated by the resurgence of world coffee prices. Coffee prices during his tenure in office, 1910-1914, averaged almost 50 percent more than the levels maintained during the Quinquenio (see Figure 9:1). After 1911 the price rise was matched by a 50 percent increase in the volume of coffee exports as plantings undertaken during the Quinquenio matured. As a result Colombian coffee exports began to produce unprecedented quantities of foreign exchange. The value of coffee exports, which had fluctuated between five and six million pesos between 1905 and 1910, suddenly shot up to almost nine and a half million in 1911 and almost 17 million in 1912 (see Table 10.1). The impact of the resurgent coffee industry on the economy of the nation was neatly summarized by Restrepo's minister of finance in 1912. "The economic situation improves daily, and it can be asserted that once the present coffee harvest is completed, that is, by the middle of the year, the entire nation will begin to experience real well-being."[20]

The greatly improved economic situation, which was soon reflected in the volume of revenue available to government, enabled export-import interests to implement important features of their economic program. On the question of tariff reform export-import interests reduced rates generally, but accommodated the emerging textile manufacturers of Antioquia. A special survey commissioned by the congress of 1909 had recommended a tariff designed to favor agricultural, livestock, and mining interests and had called for a reduction of duties on cloth consumed by the common people. Yet the same study had

19. Uribe Uribe voted against Restrepo in the special presidential election of 1910. In part he was forced into a position of formal opposition to the Republican Union because of his close identification with Reyes even during the last years of the dictatorship. The reluctance of Uribe Uribe to disassociate himself from Reyes obeyed both ideological and personal interests. As early as 1904 in a celebrated lecture Uribe Uribe had proclaimed himself a "state socialist," by which he meant that he was an advocate of state intervention in the economy to promote economic development (especially agriculture) and a believer in a moderate brand of paternalistic social welfare. "Socialismo de Estado" in Rafael Uribe Uribe, *El pensamiento social de Uribe Uribe* (Bogotá, 1960), pp. 6-23. But Uribe Uribe, always plagued by severe personal financial worries, was also deeply grateful for the remunerative diplomatic sinecures extended him by Reyes. This side of the question emerges poignantly in the private correspondence recently selected and published by Rafael Gómez Picón, *Rafael Uribe Uribe en la intimidad* (Bogotá, n.d.), especially, pp. 165-66. With the resurgence of the export economy, Uribe Uribe, like other would-be statists, modified his views and moved toward a more doctrinaire laissez-faire economic stand. See the platform of his "Bloque Liberal" for 1912-13 in *Pensamiento social*. Uribe Uribe never fully abandoned his concern for social welfare, however, and he is rightly viewed as the harbinger of that dimension of Liberal ideology which would become pronounced in the 1930's.

20. *Informe del Ministro de Hacienda* (Bogotá, 1912), p. x.

also favored low rates on items used in national manufacturing enterprises already established, or to be established in the future. Both of these recommendations were implemented in the tariff reform of 1913, which lowered tariff rates in most categories while protecting special interests including textiles.[21] The increase in revenue available to the government also enabled Restrepo to preside over a feat which none of his predecessors, no matter how committed to the goal, had been able to accomplish. Beginning in 1914, under the provisions of Law 69 of 1909, gold-based currency began to circulate once more in Colombia after almost thirty years of experience with a monetary system based on unbacked paper currency. Restrepo also began the practice of paying public employees in pounds sterling, a measure which prompted an approving contemporary to jest in a public speech that Restrepo had not only brought Colombia "the liberty of the free" (*libres*) but "the liberty of the pound" (*libras*).[22]

Table 10:1. Volume and value of Colombian coffee exports, 1900-1925

Year	Exports (sacks of 60 kilos)	Value (Col. pesos)
1900-4	——	——
1905	500,811	5,036,240
1906	636,005	6,131,760
1907	568,377	5,338,273
1908	606,749	5,549,064
1909	707,020	6,346,952
1910	570,011	5,517,408
1911	631,666	9,475,448
1912	932,222	16,777,908
1913	1,020,741	18,369,768
1914	1,032,136	16,098,185
1915	1,129,849	18,278,631
1916	1,211,145	15,996,031
1917	1,047,394	17,651,569
1918	1,148,840	20,675,023
1919	1,684,107	54,291,638
1920	1,443,947	36,328,333
1921	2,345,595	41,945,052
1922	1,764,823	36,291,812
1923	2,060,658	45,088,906
1924	2,215,824	68,793,353
1925	1,946,730	66,524,056

Source: Beyer, "Coffee Industry," Table I, pp. 335-38.

21. Ospina Vásquez, *Industria y protección*, pp. 381-85.
22. Restrepo, *Orientación republicana*, II, 130. Restrepo attributed his success primarily to government economies made possible by his orthodox liberal philosophy of limited government, *Ibid.*, 128-46.

Restrepo also presided over the satisfactory resolution, at least so far as Colombia was concerned, of the Panama issue. On April 6, 1914, the Urrutia-Thomson treaty was signed in Bogotá and quickly ratified in unamended form by the Colombian congress. The treaty included a statement of the United States' "sincere regret" for anything that had occurred to mar the long friendship between the two nations and granted Colombia special privileges in the use of the canal. Moreover, by the terms of the treaty the United States agreed to pay Colombia a sum of twenty-five million dollars. Although the United States was willing to ratify only an amended version of the treaty (and that several years later), the calm with which the Urrutia-Thomson treaty was discussed and ratified in Colombia signified a general improvement in relations between the two countries and established the basis for the final settlement and indemnification in 1922.[23]

Thus by the end of Restrepo's administration, the conscious political efforts of reformist forces, aided by a resurgent coffee economy, had settled in the interest of export-import groups virtually all the outstanding political and economic problems inherited from the Regeneration, the war years, and the Quinquenio. The new-found ideological and political hegemony of bipartisan export-import interests was reflected in the personnel and policies of the executive and legislative branches of government beginning in 1909, demonstrated by the terms of the Constitutional Reform of 1910 and accompanying legislation, and found its most typical expression in the efforts to return to a gold-based circulating currency, a feat well under way by 1914.

It is true that, like other third parties in Colombian history, the Republican Union was not an enduring success; a bipartisan coalition of elites, it lacked the grass roots support of the traditional parties. But after the dissolution of the Republican Union, the founders of the party would reassume leadership roles in the traditional parties; and along with the newspaper *El Tiempo,* founded in 1911 to promote the party's political and economic ideals, they would continue to exercise a powerful influence over Colombian politics. One measure of the continuity of the party's ideals and the enduring influence of its founders was the election on the Liberal ticket of Enrique Olaya Herrera to the presidency in 1930. Olaya named a bipartisan cabinet with Carlos E. Restrepo as his minister of government. The fidelity of Olaya's electoral platform to the Republican ideals of 1910 is striking.

23. Ratification of the treaty by the United States congress was delayed until April 20, 1921, and achieved only after elimination of the "sincere regret" clause and a slight reduction of Colombia rights in the use of the canal. Colombia agreed to these terms and the ratified treaties were exchanged on March 1, 1922. E. Taylor Parks, *Colombia and the United States, 1765-1934* (Durham, N. C., 1935), pp. 440-57.

Even after the start of the crisis of world capitalism and the international division of labor which it entailed, that platform declared that "agriculture is the axis and foundation of our economic life" and fully endorsed the concept of the "open door for foreign capital." Like the program of the Republican Union before it, the platform also stressed the ideas of sectional autonomy, religious peace, and budget economies.[24]

But in the changed political environment of the new order even those politicians not connected with the Republican Union tacitly accepted the liberal political and economic ideals of the new party, although they refused to abandon their identification with the traditional parties. Thus, although the Republican Union's presidential candidate, Liberal Nicolás Esguerra, lost the election of 1914, the winning candidate, former Historical Conservative José Vicente Concha, was elected with the support of that section of the Liberal party led by Uribe Uribe. Concha named a bipartisan cabinet and the policies of his government did not diverge significantly from the political and economic initiatives begun by his immediate predecessors.[25] Even in 1918, when a three-way presidential race resulted in the election by plurality of old-time Nationalist Marco Fidel Suárez, the once doctrinaire supporter of the Regeneration governed with a bipartisan cabinet and initiated a policy he dubbed "the Polar Star," a policy of forging ever closer relations with the United States through the promotion of large-scale foreign investment.[26] The policy of promotion of the export economy through close relations with the United States and massive foreign investment in public works reached its apogee during the administrations of Pedro Nel Ospina (1922-26) and Miguel Abadía Méndez (1926-30), men whose early careers, especially that of the former, had closely identified them with the reformist forces opposed to the Regeneration.[27]

The enduring stability of the new order is only partly explained, however, in terms of the reformers' acquisition of power, their passage of institutional reforms, and their successful implementation of their liberal economic and political policies. For the expansion of the coffee economy not only worked to consolidate the ideological and political hegemony of export-import groups; it also acted in ways, largely independent of the policies pursued by reformist groups, to modify the dynamics of politics and promote the legitimacy and stability of the

24. The only new departures were moderate statements endorsing policies to promote greater social justice. *Orientación republicana*, II, 421-26.

25. It should be noted, however, that with the severe dislocation of Colombian foreign trade accompanying the outbreak of World War I, Concha was temporarily forced to suspend the conversion of paper to gold currency.

26. Cruz Santos, *Economía y hacienda*, II, 160.

27. J. Fred Rippy, *The Capitalists and Colombia* (Durham, N. C., 1931), pp. 152-76.

new order. This was true because of the special characteristics of the coffee economy as it developed in Colombia.

First of all, as already noted in Chapter IX, the regional focus of coffee expansion in twentieth-century Colombia assured the bipartisan nature of interest groups related to the coffee industry. Nineteenth-century production was concentrated in the hands of Liberals in the departments of Santander and Cundinamarca. But as the bulk of production shifted to the central cordillera, where migrants from the predominantly Conservative department of Antioquia founded thousands of new farms, Conservative coffee growers became much more numerous and important and their influence rivaled that of their Liberal counterparts by the 1920's.[28]

The bipartisan and national character of coffee-interest groups was also strengthened as Conservative (and Liberal) elites not formerly involved in the coffee economy invested in coffee farms in both the eastern and central cordilleras during the boom years after 1910. The case of Jorge Holguín is illustrative. In 1896 Holguín was the butt of Uribe Uribe's sarcastic congressional polemic contrasting the virtues of coffee farmers with the vices of owners of cattle ranches and cold country estates. By the mid-1920's, however, Holguín had invested heavily in coffee and owned seven large coffee farms, containing just under a million and a half producing trees, in the Cundinamarcan municipios of Tibacuy, Nilo, and Viotá.[29]

Secondly, the stability of politics and the political legitimacy of the export-import groups in control of Colombian politics after 1910 was greatly enhanced as a result of the fact that the Colombian export economy developed in a manner largely free of foreign penetration and control. Coffee cultivation was labor intensive and neither offered considerable economies of scale nor depended on a sophisticated technology and large-scale outlays of capital. Consequently, while ownership of mines and plantations gravitated into foreign hands in many other Latin American export economies, ownership of coffee farms in Colombia remained largely in domestic hands. It is true that many foreign import agents established commercial houses dealing in the coffee trade in Colombia, and that international transport, insurance, and marketing were primarily (although not exclusively) in foreign hands. But significant foreign ownership of coffee farms themselves was never widespread.[30]

The implications for domestic politics and economic development

28. McGreevey has published the data which trace this shift in *An Economic History*, Table 22, p. 196.

29. *Colombia Cafetera*, pp. 419, 423.

30. Beyer discusses foreign interests in the Colombian coffee economy in his chapter on marketing, "Coffee Industry," pp. 219-32.

of domestic control of the dynamic sector of the national economy can hardly be overestimated. Earnings from the lucrative export economy remained largely in Colombian hands and thus furnished domestic capital for development of infrastructure and manufacturing enterprises. Several students of Colombian economic history have stressed the link between the coffee economy and the development of manufacturing (particularly the textile industry) in Antioquia.[31] An expanding coffee sector, owned primarily by Colombians, had important political ramifications as well. Opportunities for economic and social mobility outside politics attenuated the disruptive influence of clientelism, a point fully understood by contemporaries.[32] No less significant was the fact that the absence of foreign control of the coffee economy limited the force and appeal of economic nationalists bent on organizing leftist political movements outside the structure of the two traditional parties.[33]

The impact of these economic and political tendencies was greatly magnified by a third characteristic of the coffee economy as it developed in Colombia. Colombian coffee production was not confined to large economic units where land, labor, and capital were concentrated in the hands of a small group. Unlike coffee production in Brazil, a great deal of Colombian coffee was produced on small and medium-sized family farms. A series of factors, including the relative availability of capital and labor, and the fact that coffee competitive on the world market could be produced on small plots with a rudimentary technology, all contributed to the distinct structure of the Colombian coffee economy. Although a detailed comparative study of the evolution of the Colombian and Brazilian coffee economies would be necessary to confirm this interpretation, it appears that in Brazil the existence of large accumulations of capital (generated by that country's previous export booms) and the availability of foreign migrant labor (first the forced migration of African slaves, later the voluntary migration of southern Europeans) worked to create an artificial scarcity of land and favored the emergence of the large coffee plantation as the typical unit of production. In Colombia, on the other hand, the

31. Most explicit is McGreevey, *An Economic History,* Chapter VIII.

32. Endorsing a previous editorial which had appeared in *La Razón* (Honda), *El Conservador* of Barranquilla traced *empleomanía* to economic depression and big government. Growth in the private sector would solve the problem. A large, productive hacienda, for example, employed an "administrador, tenedor de libros o contabilista, cajero, escribiente, herrero, carpintero y sobrestantes." *El Conservador,* November 3, 1909. See also the discussion of a report of the minister of finance in *El Liberal,* December 14, 1911.

33. The contrast with the twentieth-century political history of nations like Mexico, Cuba, Chile, and Venezuela is clear. In all these countries foreign penetration and control of the export economy fostered the growth of economic nationalism and leftist political parties.

existence of large quantities of unclaimed land on the slopes of (particularly) the central cordillera, the relative scarcity of large accumulations of capital, and the country's inability to attract foreign immigrants favored the emergence of small farms on the coffee frontier in the central cordillera, the area destined to become the heart of the Colombian coffee economy in the twentieth century. In those areas of Colombia where capital and labor were relatively more abundant, and hence land became artificially scarce, large units or production were much more typical, as the case of southwestern Cundinamarca illustrates.

Whatever the precise reasons for the growth of small and medium-sized coffee farms in Colombia, there is no doubt that by the 1920's units of small size, concentrated in the central cordillera, comprised the great bulk of the coffee farms of the nation. The first official coffee census, taken in 1932, listed some 150,000 coffee farms, most of which were under 10 hectares (1 hectare equals 2.471 acres).[34] A comparison of the number of coffee farms in the major coffee growing *municipios* of Cundinamarca and Antioquia reveals the contrast in size of production units in these two areas. In statistics published in 1927 Monsalve listed only 30 coffee producing units in the *municipio* of Viotá, Cundinamarca. By way of contrast, Fredonia, the major coffee-producing *municipio* of Antioquia contained 1079 coffee farms, and the first-rank coffee producing *municipio* of Caldas (a department formed in 1905 out of southern Antioquia), Santa Rosa de Cabal, had 653 coffee producing units. But small and medium-sized coffee farms were fairly common in other regions of Colombia as well. In Norte de Santander the two most important coffee producing *municipios*, Convención and Carmen, were listed by Monsalve as having 414 and 603 coffee farms respectively. Even in Cundinamarca there were some small-farm coffee *municipios*: the *municipio* of Sasaima was listed as having approximately 1000 coffee farms; La Peña, some 350.[35]

William Paul McGreevey has most thoroughly probed the impact of the large proportion of family-size coffee farms on the economic development of Colombia. Following the lines of analysis developed by Fernando Ortiz in his classic comparison of the influence of tobacco and sugar on Cuban society,[36] McGreevey develops a Colombian counterpoint contrasting the negative implications for economic development of the foreign-dominated, highly concentrated tobacco enclave economy of the third quarter of the nineteenth century, with the positive developmentalist implications of the domestically owned, small-farm coffee economy of the first decades of the twentieth century.

34. McGreevey, *An Economic History*, p. 196.
35. *Colombia Cafetera*, pp. 426, 271, 359, 502, 426.
36. *Cuban Counterpoint: Tobacco and Sugar* (New York, 1947).

Tobacco produced for export from Colombia in the nineteenth century was grown on large estates concentrated in a small enclave on the upper Magdalena River. Tobacco production in this area generated a dual social order typical of plantation economies: a small class of owners which appropriated most of the economic surplus and a large impoverished and dependent labor force kept near the subsistence level. Earnings from the tobacco economy were sent directly overseas or were largely dissipated in luxury consumption of articles produced abroad. Although the tobacco export economy contributed to the establishment of steam navigation on the Magdalena River, this improvement in transportation, by lowering the cost of foreign imports, hurt domestic artisan industry.

In contrast, the economic benefits of coffee production were widely, although thinly, spread. The coffee economy created thousands of small, independent property owners who shared in the earnings of the export economy and created a market for goods and services—everything from small machines for hulling coffee, to textiles and education—which could be, and were, provided locally. Coffee encouraged the construction of railways that penetrated the hinterland, reducing the cost of foreign consumer goods, but according to McGreevey, reducing even more the cost of raw materials and machinery, a factor of considerable importance since the textile industry of Medellín initially depended on the importation of almost all components needed to manufacture textiles.[37]

The influence of the small-farm coffee economy, so impressive in its implications for Colombian economic and social development, was no less important in the sphere of politics. The way the increasing economic opportunities afforded ambitious Colombians by an expanding coffee economy reduced the importance of clientelist arrangements and political avenues to economic and social mobility has already been stressed. Equally important is the fact that a large proportion of the Colombian body politic identified with the political economy of the export-import interests in control of the government after 1910. As small property owners vitally concerned with the promotion of coffee export agriculture, coffee smallholders fully endorsed the liberal political ideology, social conservatism, and pro-export economic policies of the new order. The fact that national policy did not always favor the interests of small coffee growers—it more likely worked (as did the policies pursued by the Colombian Federation of

37. McGreevey, *An Economic History,* Chap. IX. McGreevey's contrast between the developmental implications of these two Colombian export economies may be overdrawn, but his argument is extremely suggestive and similar lines of analysis have been profitably applied to the study of comparative export-oriented development in other Latin American countries by, among others, Celso Furtado, *Economic Development of Latin America* (Cambridge, 1970).

Coffee Growers formed in 1927) to favor the interests of large coffee producers—does not diminish the importance of this statement. Such unique characteristics of twentieth-century Colombian politics as the continued vitality of the traditional parties, the limited success and moderate goals of social reformers, and the continuing strength of the Catholic Church are all related in part to the special structure of the Colombian coffee economy. Only as the legitimacy and stability-inducing nature of small-farm coffee expansion began to break down (as lands suitable for coffee expansion were used up, the size and economic viability of small units diminished, and trends in the international and domestic economy favoring industrialization and urban migration created new interest groups) did the structure of the new order and the stability of Colombian politics begin to be threatened.

But the breakdown of the new order is the subject for another study and a consideration far removed from the minds of the bipartisan export-import interests in control of Colombian politics in 1910. After decades of struggle they had institutionalized a new order in Colombia in conformity with their economic and ideological interests. At the dawn of the new era they probably shared the optimism about the future voiced by Uribe Uribe in a survey of the coffee economy written for the journal of the Society of Agriculturalists in October, 1910.

In that article Uribe Uribe presented his Colombian readers with new statistics on the world coffee economy and offered a detailed analysis of the progressive increase in world coffee consumption during the previous decade, an increase which amounted to 45 percent in the United States, Colombia's primary coffee market and far and away the leading consumer of coffee in the world. After reminding his readers of the correctness of his earlier reports which had predicted the current excellent price of fifteen cents per pound, Uribe Uribe concluded his article with a new prediction and a call to action:

> It is possible that the good prices that I predicted for 1910 and 1911 will not be as alluring by 1914 when the production of plantings now undertaken will come in. Nevertheless, prices will be good.
>
> *Colombians:*
>
> IT IS STILL TIME TO PLANT COFFEE
>
> RAFAEL URIBE URIBE
>
> Bogotá, October, 1910.[38]

38. *Revista Nacional de Agricultura*, November 30, 1910, p. 147.

Bibliography of sources cited

Unpublished materials

Manuscript materials

Archivo del Congreso, Bogotá

Archivo Historico Luis Martínez Delgado, 5 vols. of transcribed letters, Academia Colombiana de Historia, Bogotá [MDT, ACH]

Bunau-Varilla Papers, Manuscript Division, United States Library of Congress, Washington, D. C.

Correspondencia del Presidente Manuel A. Sanclemente, 26 vols., Archivo Nacional de Colombia, Bogotá [Sanclemente, ANC]

Correspondencia Oficial de Jorge Holguín, documents transcribed by Luis Martínez Delgado, Academia Colombiana de Historia, Bogotá

Documentos relacionados con la Guerra de los Mil Días, 170 vols., Archivo del Ministerio de Defensa, Bogotá [AMD]

Durán Family Papers, 1 box, Academia Colombiana de Historia, Bogotá [Durán, ACH]

Notary Archive, Fusagasugá, Cundinamarca

Personal Papers of Carlos Calderón, 1 box, Academia Colombiana de Historia, Bogotá [Calderón, ACH]

Personal Papers of Juan E. Manrique, 2 boxes, Academia Colombiana de Historia, Bogotá [Manrique, ACH]

Personal Papers of Aquileo Parra, 3 boxes, Academia Colombiana de Historia, Bogotá [Parra, ACH]

Personal Papers of Rafael Uribe Uribe, 32 boxes, Academia Colombiana de Historia, Bogotá [Uribe, ACH]

United States, Department of State, Diplomatic Despatches from United States Ministers to Colombia, microfilm, United States National Archives, Washington, D. C. [USNA]

Theses

Beyer, Robert Carlyle. "The Colombian Coffee Industry: Origins and Major Trends, 1740-1940." Ph.D. diss., University of Minnesota, 1947.

Child, Martha Cleveland. "Politics, Revolution and Reform: The Liberal Challenge to the Colombian Status Quo: Rafael Uribe Uribe (1859-1914)." Master's thesis, Vanderbilt University, 1969.

Davis, Robert Henry. "Acosta, Caro, and Lleras. Three Essayists and Their Views of New Granada's National Problems, 1832-1853." Ph.D. diss.,

Vanderbilt University, 1969.

Delpar, Helen V. "The Liberal Party of Colombia, 1863-1903." Ph.D. diss., Columbia University, 1967.

Favell, Thomas R. "The Antecedents of Panama's Separation from Colombia: A Study in Colombian Politics." Ph.D. diss., Tufts-Fletcher, 1950.

Hoffman, Theodore H. "A History of Railway Concessions and Railway Development Policy in Colombia." Ph.D. diss., American University, 1947.

Safford, Frank R. "Commerce and Enterprise in Central Colombia, 1821-1870." Ph.D. diss., Columbia University, 1965.

Published Materials

Articles

Bergquist, Charles W. "On Paradigms and the Pursuit of the Practical," *Latin American Research Review*, XIII: 2 (February, 1978), 247-51.

Bushnell, David. "Two Stages in Colombian Tariff Policy: The Radical Era and the Return to Protection (1861-1885)." *Inter-American Economic Affairs*, IX:4 (Spring, 1956), 3-23.

Bustamante, Darío. "Efectos económicos del papel moneda durante la Regeneración." Mimeograph, Universidad Nacional de Colombia, Centro de Investigaciones para el Desarrollo. Bogotá, 1970.

Deas, Malcom. "Una finca cundinamarquesa entre 1870 y 1910." Mimeograph, Universidad Nacional de Colombia, Centro de Investigaciones para el Desarrollo. Bogotá, 1974.

Delpar, Helen V. "Aspects of Liberal Factionalism in Colombia, 1875-1885." *Hispanic American Historical Review*, LI:2 (May, 1971), 250-74.

Harrison, John P. "The Evolution of the Colombian Tobacco Trade to 1875." *Hispanic American Historical Review*, XXXII:2 (May, 1952), 163-74.

Helguera, J. Leon. "The Problem of Liberalism versus Conservatism in Colombia: 1849-85" in Frederick B. Pike, ed., *Latin American History: Select Problems* (New York, 1969), pp. 223-58.

Higuita, V. J. de D. "Estudio histórico-analítico de la población colombiana en 170 años." *Anales de Economía y Estadística*, III:2, Supplement (April, 1940), 1-113.

Kaufman, Robert R. "The Patron-Client Concept in Macro-Politics: Prospects and Problems." *Comparative Studies in Society and History*, XVI:3 (June, 1974), 285-308.

Kling, Merle. "Toward a Theory of Power and Political Instability in Latin America." *Western Political Quarterly*, IX:7 (March, 1956), 21-35.

Powell, John Duncan. "Peasant Society and Clientelist Politics." *American Political Science Review*, LXIV:2 (June, 1970), 411-25.

Ramsey, Russell W. "Critical Bibliography on La Violencia in Colombia." *Latin American Research Review*, VIII:1 (Spring, 1973), 3-44.

"Régimen alimenticio de los jornaleros de la sabana de Bogotá." *Anales de la Academia Nacional de Medicina*, I (1893), 104-39.

Torres Restrepo, Camilo. "La violencia y los cambios socioculturales en las áreas rurales colombianas." *Memoria del Primer Congreso Nacional de Sociología*, 8, 9 y 10 de Marzo de 1963, pp. 95-152.

Umaña, Alberto. "Problemas estadísticos en el análisis del período liberal, 1845-1885," Mimeograph, Seminario sobre Historia de Colombia, Bogotá, julio, 1975.

Uribe Uribe, Heraclio. "El General Uribe." *Pan*, No. 11 (December, 1936), pp. 50, 52.

Books

Arbeláez, Tulio. *Episodios de la guerra de 1899-1903: compañas del General Cesáreo Pulido*. 2nd ed. Bogotá, 1936.

Arboleda Cortés, Henrique. *Palonegro*. Bucaramanga, 1953.

Berrío Cruz, Lopera. *Colombia agraria*. Manizales, 1920.

Blair Gutiérrez, Bernardo. *Don Marco Fidel Suárez, su vida y su obra*. Medellín, 1955.

Bushnell, David. *The Santander Regime in Gran Colombia*. Newark, Delaware, 1954.

Caballero, Lucas. *Bancarrota nacional*. Bogotá, 1899.

———. *Memorias de la guerra de los mil días*. Bogotá, 1939.

Cacua Prada, Antonio, comp. *Legislación sobre prensa en Colombia*. Bogotá, 1966.

Calderón, Carlos. *La cuestión monetaria en Colombia*. Madrid, 1905.

Camacho Carrizosa, José. *Estudios económicos*. Bogotá, 1903.

Camacho Roldán, Salvador. *Memorias*. Bogotá, 1923.

Caro, Miguel Antonio. *Escritos sobre cuestiones económicos*. Bogotá, 1956.

Caro, Victor E., and Antonio Gómez Restrepo, eds. *Obras completas de don Miguel Antonio Caro*. 8 vols. Bogotá, 1918-45.

Casas, José Joaquín. *Semblanzas (Diego Fallón y José Manuel Marroquín)*. Bogotá, 1936.

Collver, O. Andrew. *Birth Rates in Latin America*. Berkeley, 1965.

[Cortés, Enrique.] *La lección del pasado: ensayo sobre la verdadera misión del partido liberal*. Bogotá, 1877.

Cruz Santos, Abel. *Economía y hacienda pública. De la república unitaria a la economía del medio siglo*. 2 vols. Bogotá, 1966.

De la Torre, Roberto. *Estudio sobre nuestra circulación monetaria*. Bogotá, 1899.

Durán, Justo L. *La revolución del 99*. Cúcuta, 1920.

Eder, Phanor James. *Colombia*. 5th ed. London, 1921.

Flórez Alvarez, Leonidas. *Campaña en Santander, 1899-1900*. [Bogotá], n.d.

Franco Holguín, Jorge. *Evolución de las instituciones financieras en Colombia*. Mexico, 1966.

Furtado, Celso. *Economic Development of Latin America*. Cambridge, 1970.

Galvis Salazar, Fernando. *Rafael Uribe Uribe*. Medellín, 1962.

Garavito A., Fernando. *Influencia perniciosa de las guerras civiles en el progreso de Colombia*. Bogotá, 1897.

266

García Prada, Carlos, ed. *José Asunción Silva; Prosas y versos*. Madrid, 1960.

Gastelbondo, J. Roberto. *El procedimiento para denunciar minas y terrenos baldíos y compilación de leyes, decretos y relaciones de los mismos ramos*. Bogotá, 1893.

Gibson, William Marion. *The Constitutions of Colombia*. Durham, N. C., 1948.

Gómez, Laureano. *El carácter del general Ospina*. Bogotá, 1928.

Gómez Picón, Rafael. *Rafael Uribe Uribe en la intimidad*. Bogotá, n.d.

Greiff, Luis de. *Semblanzas y comentarios*. Bogotá, 1942.

Grillo, Max. *Emociones de la Guerra*. Bogotá, 1934.

Groot, Francisco. *Datos históricos contenidos en las réplicas del Senador Groot al Senador Caro*. Bogotá, 1904.

La Guerra en el Tolima, 1899-1902; apuntes y relaciones de la campaña recopilados por El Comercio de Bogotá. Bogotá, 1905.

Guerra, José Joaquín. *Estudio sobre los concordatos celebrados entre Su Santidad León XIII y el Gobierno de Colombia en los años 1887 y 1892*. Bogotá, 1895.

Guillén Martínez, Fernando. *Raíz y futuro de la revolución*. Bogotá, 1963.

Holguín, Jorge. *La bestia negra*. Bogotá, 1892.

———. *Cosas del día*. Bogotá, 1910.

———. *Desde cerca*. Paris, 1908.

Holguín Arboleda, Jorge. *Mucho en serio y algo en broma*. Bogotá, 1959.

Jaramillo Sierra, Bernardo. *Pepe Sierra: el método de un campesino millonario*. Medellín, 1947.

Jaramillo Uribe, Jaime. *El pensamiento colombiano en el siglo XIX*. Bogotá, 1964.

Latorre, Benjamín. *Recuerdos de campaña, 1900-1902*. Bogotá, 1938.

Lemaitre, Eduardo. *Rafael Reyes. Biografía de un gran colombiano*. 3rd ed. Bogotá, 1967.

León Gómez, Adolfo. *Secretos del panóptico*. Bogotá, 1905.

Liévano Aguirre, Indalecio. *Rafael Núñez*. Lima [1944].

McGreevey, William Paul. *An Economic History of Colombia, 1845-1930*. Cambridge, Eng., 1971.

Marroquín, José Manuel. *Amores y leyes*. Bogotá, 1898.

———. *Blas Gil*. Bogotá, 1896.

———. *El Moro*. Bogotá, 1899.

———. *En familia*. 2nd ed. Bogotá, 1921.

———. *Entre primos*. Bogotá, 1897.

Marroquín, Lorenzo. *Las cosas en su punto. Ojeada sobre la situación de la iglesia en Colombia*. Bogotá, 1898.

———. *Pax*. Bogotá, 1907.

Marroquín Osorio, José Manuel. *Don José Manuel Marroquín íntimo*. Bogotá, 1915.

Martínez Delgado, Luis. *A propósito de Carlos Martínez Silva*. Bogotá, 1926.

———. *Historia de un cambio de gobierno*. Bogotá, 1958.

———. *República de Colombia, 1885-1910*. 2 vols. Bogotá, 1970.

———, ed. *Revistas políticas publicadas en el Repertorio Colombiano*. 2 vols. Bogotá, 1934.

Masuera y Masuera, Aurelio. *Memorias de un revolucionario*. Bogotá 1938.
Monsalve, Diego. *Colombia cafetera*. Barcelona, 1927.
Nieto Arteta, Luis Eduardo. *Economía y cultura en la historia de Colombia*. Bogotá, 1942.
Nieto Caballero, Luis Eduardo. *El curso forzoso y su historia en Colombia*. Bogotá, 1912.
———. *Por qué soy liberal*. Bogotá, 1931.
Núñez, Rafael. *La reforma política*. 2nd ed. Bogotá, 1886.
Olarte Camacho, Vicente. *Guía para denunciar y pedir en adjudicación tierras baldías por cualquier título*. Bogotá, 1895.
Ortega Díaz, Alfredo. *Ferrocarriles colombianos*. Bogotá, 1920.
Ortiz, Fernando. *Cuban Counterpoint: Tobacco and Sugar*. New York, 1947.
Ortiz, Sergio Elías. *Santiago Pérez Triana*. Bogotá, 1971.
Osorio Lizarazo, J. A. *Biografía del café*. Bogotá, 1945.
Ospina, Joaquín, comp. *Diccionario biográfico y bibliográfico de Colombia*. 3 vols. Bogotá, 1927-39.
Ospina Rodríquez, Mariano. *Cultivo del café: nociones elementales al alcance de todos los labradores*. Medellín, 1880.
Ospina Vásquez, Luis. *Industria y protección en Colombia, 1810-1930*. Medellín, 1955.
Otero Múñoz, Gustavo, and Luis Martínez Delgado, eds. *Obras completas del doctor Carlos Martínez Silva*. 9 vols. Bogotá, 1934-38.
Palacio, Julio H. *Historia de mi vida*. Bogotá, 1942.
París Lozano, Gonzalo. *Guerrilleros del Tolima*. Manizales, 1937.
Parks, E. Taylor. *Colombia and the United States*. Durham, N. C., 1931.
Parra, Aquileo. *Memorias*. Bogotá, 1912.
Parsons, James J. *Antioqueño Colonization in Western Colombia*. Berkeley, 1949.
Patiño, Manuel José. *Guía práctica de la capital; directorio especial del comercio*. Bogotá, 1902.
Payne, James L. *Patterns of Conflict in Colombia*. New Haven, 1968.
Pedraza, P. A. *Excurciones presidenciales*. Norwood, Mass., 1909.
Peñuela, Cayo Leonidas. *El Doctor y General Próspero Pinzón*. Bogotá, 1941.
Pérez Sarmiento, José Manuel. *Reminiscencias liberales, 1897-1937*. Bogotá, 1938.
Pérez Triana, Santiago. *Desde lejos*. London, 1908.
———. *Desde lejos y desde cerca*. London, 1909.
Perico Ramírez, Mario. *Reyes*. Tunja, 1974.
Pombo, Jorge and Carlos Obregón, comps. *Directorio general de Bogotá*. Bogotá, 1893.
Porras, Belisario. *Memorias de las campañas del istmo, 1900*. Panamá, 1920.
Quijano Wallis, José María. *Memorias*. Rome, 1919.
Rangel, Domingo Alberto. *Los andinos en el poder*. Caracas, 1964.
Restrepo, Carlos E. *Orientación republicana*. 2 vols. Medellín [1917?] and 1930.
Restrepo H., Julián. *El tratado noveno de la codificación cundinamarquesa*. Bogotá, 1900.

Restrepo, Ricardo. *Defensa del coronel Rafael Uribe Uribe*. Medellín, n.d.

Rippy, J. Fred. *The Capitalists and Colombia*. Durham, N. C., 1931.

Rivadeneira Vargas, Antonio José. *Don Santiago Pérez: Biografía de un carácter*. Bogotá, 1966.

Rivas, Medardo, *et al. Cuadros de costumbres*. Bogotá, 1925.

———. *Los trabajadores de tierra caliente*. Bogotá, 1946.

Robledo, Emilio. *La vida del General Pedro Nel Ospina*. Bogotá, 1959.

Rodríguez, Gustavo Humberto. *Benjamín Herrera en la guerra y la paz*. Bogotá, 1973.

Rodríguez Piñeres, Eduardo. *Diez años de política liberal, 1892-1902*. Bogotá, 1945.

———. *Informe del gerente y balance de las cuentas correspondientes al 2o semestre de 1901 [del Banco de Crédito Comercial]*. Bogotá, 1902.

———, *et al. Don Santiago Pérez y su tiempo*. Bogotá, 1952.

Sáenz Pinzón, Nicolás. *Memoria sobre el cultivo del cafeto*. Bogotá, 1888.

Safford, Frank. *The Ideal of the Practical*. Austin, 1976.

Samper Brush, José María and Luis Samper Sordo, eds. *Escritos político-económicos de Miguel Samper*. 4 vols. Bogotá, 1925-27.

Sánchez Camacho, Jorge. *Marco Fidel Suárez, biografía*. Bucaramanga, 1955.

Sanín Cano, Baldomero. *Administración Reyes, 1904-1909*. Lausanne, 1909.

Santa, Eduardo. *Rafael Uribe Uribe*. 2nd ed. Bogotá, 1968.

Sierra, Luis F. *El tabaco en la economía colombiana del siglo XIX*. Bogotá, 1971.

Solano Benítez, Guillermo. *El bayardo colombiano, Ramón González Valencia*. Puente Nacional, 1953.

Tamayo, Joaquín. *La revolución de 1899*. Bogotá, 1938.

Torres García, Guillermo. *Historia de la moneda en Colombia*. Bogotá, 1945.

———. *Miguel Antonio Caro, su personalidad política*. Madrid, 1956.

Uribe Uribe, Rafael. *De cómo el liberalismo político colombiano no es pecado*. Bogotá, 1912.

———. *Discursos parlamentarios*. Bogotá, 1897.

———. *El pensamiento social de Uribe Uribe*. Bogotá, 1960.

———. *Estudios sobre el café*. Bogotá, 1952.

———. *Labor parlamentaria del General Rafael Uribe Uribe en el congreso de 1909*. Bogotá, 1909.

———. *Querella*. Bogotá, 1904.

Urrutia, Miguel, and Mario Arrubla, eds. *Compendio de estadísticas históricas de Colombia*. Bogotá, 1970.

Vargas Santos, Gabriel. *La razón de mi dicho*. Bogotá, 1904.

Vesga y Avila, José María. *La guerra de los tres años*. Bogotá, 1914.

Public documents

Bureau of the American Republics. *Bulletin*. Washington, D. C.

Colombia. Asamblea Nacional. *Anales*.

Colombia. Cámara de Representantes. *Anales*.

Colombia. Consejo de Estado. *Leyes colombianas expedidas en sus sessiones extraordinarias de 1903*.

Colombia. Departamento de Cundinamarca. *Gaceta de Cundinamarca.* Bogotá.

Colombia. *Diario oficial.* Bogotá.

Colombia. Dirección General de Correos y Telegrafos. *Informes.*

Colombia. Ministerio de Hacienda. *Informes.*

Colombia. Senado. *Anales.*

Great Britain. Foreign Office. *Diplomatic and Consular Reports.* Annual Series. London.

Great Britain. Foreign Office. *Diplomatic and Consular Reports.* Miscellaneous Series. London.

United States. Department of Commerce and Labor. *Commercial Relations of the United States with Foreign Countries during the Year 1903.* 2 vols.

Newspapers and magazines

El Agricultor (Bogotá)
El Autonomista (Bogotá)
Bogotá (Bogotá)
Boletín Militar (Bogotá)
El Colombiano (Bogotá)
El Comercio (Bogotá)
El Conservador (Barranquilla)
El Conservador (Bogotá)
El Constitucional (Bogotá)
El Correo Nacional (Bogotá)
La Crónica (Bogotá)
El Diario (Bogotá)
El Guasca (Bogotá)
El Heraldo (Bogotá)
El Nacionalista (Bogotá)
El Nuevo Tiempo (Bogotá)
La Opinión (Bogotá)
El País (Bogotá)
La República (Bogotá)
Revista Nacional de Agricultura (Bogotá)
El Tiempo (Bogotá)

Index

272

274